Chevrolet Nova & Geo Prizm Automotive Repair Manual

by Jon LaCourse and John H Haynes
Member of the Guild of Motoring Writers

Models covered:
All Chevrolet Nova and Geo Prizm models
1985 through 1990

ABCDE
FGHIJ
KLMNO
PQRS

Haynes Publishing Group
Sparkford Nr Yeovil
Somerset BA22 7JJ England

Haynes Publications, Inc
861 Lawrence Drive
Newbury Park
California 91320 USA

Acknowledgements

We are grateful for the help and cooperation of the Chevrolet Motor Division of General Motors Corporation for assistance with technical information and the vehicle photo, and the Champion Spark Plug Company, who supplied the illustrations of various spark plug conditions. Technical writers who contributed to this project include Mike Stubblefield and Ken Freund.

© **Haynes Publishing Group 1990**

A book in the **Haynes Automotive Repair Manual Series**

Printed by J.H. Haynes & Co., Ltd. Sparkford Nr. Yeovil, Somerset BA22 7JJ, England

ISBN 1 85010 642 8

Library of Congress Catalog Card Number 90-81410

While every attempt is made to ensure that the information in this manual is correct, no liability can be accepted by the authors or publishers for loss, damage or injury caused by any errors in, or omissions from, the information given.

Contents

1990 Geo Prizm four-door hatchback

About this manual

Its purpose

The purpose of this manual is to help you get the best value from your vehicle. It can do so in several ways. It can help you decide what work must be done, even if you choose to have it done by a dealer service department or a repair shop; it provides information and procedures for routine maintenance and servicing; and it offers diagnostic and repair procedures to follow when trouble occurs.

We hope you use the manual to tackle the work yourself. For many simpler jobs, doing it yourself may be quicker than arranging an appointment to get the vehicle into a shop and making the trips to leave it and pick it up. More importantly, a lot of money can be saved by avoiding the expense the shop must pass on to you to cover its labor and overhead costs. An added benefit is the sense of satisfaction and accomplishment that you feel after doing the job yourself.

Using the manual

The manual is divided into Chapters. Each Chapter is divided into numbered Sections, which are headed in bold type between horizontal lines. Each Section consists of consecutively numbered paragraphs.

At the beginning of each numbered section you will be referred to any illustrations which apply to the procedures in that section. The reference numbers used in illustration captions pinpoint the pertinent Section and the Step within that section. That is, illustration 3.2 means the illustration refers to Section 3 and Step (or paragraph) 2 within that Section.

Procedures, once described in the text, are not normally repeated. When it's necessary to refer to another Chapter, the reference will be given as Chapter and Section number. Cross references given without use of the word "Chapter" apply to Sections and/or paragraphs in the same Chapter. For example, "see Section 8" means in the same Chapter.

References to the left or right side of the vehicle assume you are sitting in the driver's seat, facing forward.

Even though we have prepared this manual with extreme care, neither the publisher nor the author can accept responsibility for any errors in, or omissions from, the information given.

NOTE

A **Note** provides information necessary to properly complete a procedure or information which will make the procedure easier to understand.

CAUTION

A **Caution** provides a special procedure or special steps which must be taken while completing the procedure where the **Caution** is found. Not heeding a **Caution** can result in damage to the assembly being worked on.

WARNING

A **Warning** provides a special procedure or special steps which must be taken while completing the procedure where the **Warning** is found. Not heeding a **Warning** can result in personal injury.

Introduction to the Chevrolet Nova and Geo Prizm

These vehicles are available in two and four-door hatchback and sedan body styles.

The transversely-mounted inline four-cylinder engines used in these models are equipped with either a carburetor or fuel injection. The engine drives the front wheels through a five-speed manual or four-speed automatic transaxle via independent driveaxles.

Independent suspension, featuring coil springs and struts, is used at all four wheels. The rack and pinion steering unit is mounted behind the engine.

The brakes on most models are disc at the front and drums at the rear, with power assist standard. Some models are equipped with front and rear disc brakes.

Vehicle identification numbers

Modifications are a continuing and unpublicized process in vehicle manufacturing. Since spare parts lists are compiled on a numerical basis, the individual vehicle numbers are essential to correctly identify the component required.

Vehicle Identification Number (VIN)

This very important identification number is stamped on a plate attached to the left side of the dashboard, just inside the windshield on the driver's side of the vehicle **(see illustration)**. The VIN also appears on the Vehicle Certificate of Title and Registration. It contains information such as where and when the vehicle was manufactured, the model year and the body style.

Vehicle Certification Plate

The Vehicle Certification Plate (VC label) is attached to the left front door pillar. The plate contains the name of the manufacturer, the month

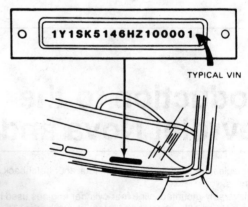

TYPICAL VIN

The Vehicle Identification Number (VIN) is visible from outside the vehicle through the driver's side of the windshield

and year of production, the Gross Vehicle Weight Rating (GVWR) and the certification statement.

left (driver's) end **(see illustration)**.

Transaxle ID number

The transaxle ID number is located on top of the transaxle housing **(see illustrations)**.

Engine serial number

The engine serial number is stamped into the front of the block at the

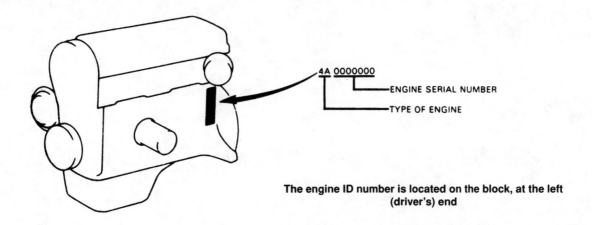

The engine ID number is located on the block, at the left (driver's) end

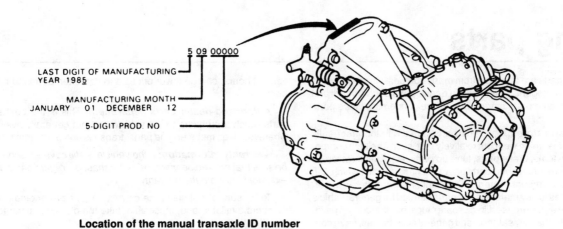

Location of the manual transaxle ID number

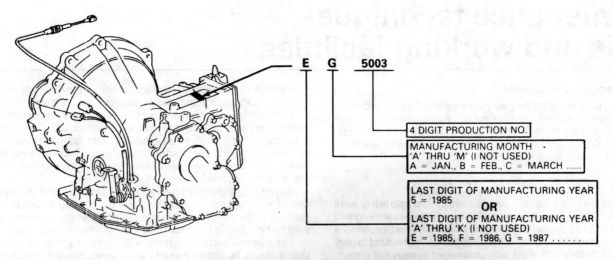

Location of the automatic transaxle ID number

Buying parts

Replacement parts are available from many sources, which generally fall into one of two categories – authorized dealer parts departments and independent retail auto parts stores. Our advice concerning these parts is as follows:

Retail auto parts stores: Good auto parts stores will stock frequently needed components which wear out relatively fast, such as clutch components, exhaust systems, brake parts, tune-up parts, etc. These stores often supply new or reconditioned parts on an exchange basis, which can save a considerable amount of money. Discount auto parts stores are often very good places to buy materials and parts needed for general vehicle maintenance such as oil, grease, filters, spark plugs, belts, touch-up paint, bulbs, etc. They also usually sell tools and general accessories, have con-

venient hours, charge lower prices and can often be found not far from home.

Authorized dealer parts department: This is the best source for parts which are unique to the vehicle and not generally available elsewhere (such as major engine parts, transmission parts, trim pieces, etc.).

Warranty information: If the vehicle is still covered under warranty, be sure that any replacement parts purchased – regardless of the source – do not invalidate the warranty!

To be sure of obtaining the correct parts, have engine and chassis numbers available and, if possible, take the old parts along for positive identification.

Maintenance techniques, tools and working facilities

Maintenance techniques

There are a number of techniques involved in maintenance and repair that will be referred to throughout this manual. Application of these techniques will enable the home mechanic to be more efficient, better organized and capable of performing the various tasks properly, which will ensure that the repair job is thorough and complete.

Fasteners

Fasteners are nuts, bolts, studs and screws used to hold two or more parts together. There are a few things to keep in mind when working with fasteners. Almost all of them use a locking device of some type, either a lockwasher, locknut, locking tab or thread adhesive. All threaded fasteners should be clean and straight, with undamaged threads and undamaged corners on the hex head where the wrench fits. Develop the habit of replacing all damaged nuts and bolts with new ones. Special locknuts

with nylon or fiber inserts can only be used once. If they are removed, they lose their locking ability and must be replaced with new ones.

Rusted nuts and bolts should be treated with a penetrating fluid to ease removal and prevent breakage. Some mechanics use turpentine in a spout-type oil can, which works quite well. After applying the rust penetrant, let it work for a few minutes before trying to loosen the nut or bolt. Badly rusted fasteners may have to be chiseled or sawed off or removed with a special nut breaker, available at tool stores.

If a bolt or stud breaks off in an assembly, it can be drilled and removed with a special tool commonly available for this purpose. Most automotive machine shops can perform this task, as well as other repair procedures, such as the repair of threaded holes that have been stripped out.

Flat washers and lockwashers, when removed from an assembly, should always be replaced exactly as removed. Replace any damaged washers with new ones. Never use a lockwasher on any soft metal surface (such as aluminum), thin sheet metal or plastic.

Fastener sizes

For a number of reasons, automobile manufacturers are making wider and wider use of metric fasteners. Therefore, it is important to be able to tell the difference between standard (sometimes called U.S. or SAE) and metric hardware, since they cannot be interchanged.

All bolts, whether standard or metric, are sized according to diameter, thread pitch and length. For example, a standard 1/2 – 13 x 1 bolt is 1/2 inch in diameter, has 13 threads per inch and is 1 inch long. An M12 – 1.75 x 25 metric bolt is 12 mm in diameter, has a thread pitch of 1.75 mm (the distance between threads) and is 25 mm long. The two bolts are nearly identical, and easily confused, but they are not interchangeable.

In addition to the differences in diameter, thread pitch and length, metric and standard bolts can also be distinguished by examining the bolt heads. To begin with, the distance across the flats on a standard bolt head is measured in inches, while the same dimension on a metric bolt is sized in millimeters (the same is true for nuts). As a result, a standard wrench should not be used on a metric bolt and a metric wrench should not be used on a standard bolt. Also, most standard bolts have slashes radiating out from the center of the head to denote the grade or strength of the bolt, which is an indication of the amount of torque that can be applied to it. The greater the number of slashes, the greater the strength of the bolt. Grades 0 through 5 are commonly used on automobiles. Metric bolts have a property class (grade) number, rather than a slash, molded into their heads to indicate bolt strength. In this case, the higher the number, the stronger the bolt. Property class numbers 8.8, 9.8 and 10.9 are commonly used on automobiles.

Strength markings can also be used to distinguish standard hex nuts from metric hex nuts. Many standard nuts have dots stamped into one side, while metric nuts are marked with a number. The greater the number of dots, or the higher the number, the greater the strength of the nut.

Metric studs are also marked on their ends according to property class (grade). Larger studs are numbered (the same as metric bolts), while smaller studs carry a geometric code to denote grade.

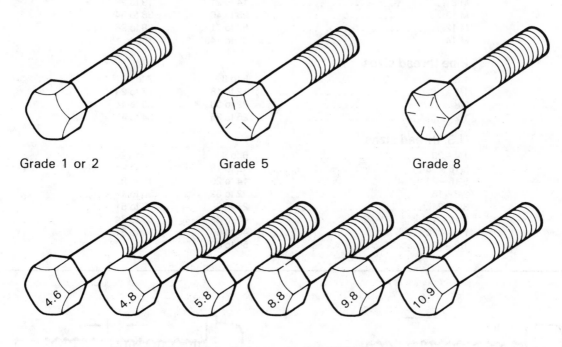

Bolt strength markings (top – standard/SAE/USS; bottom – metric)

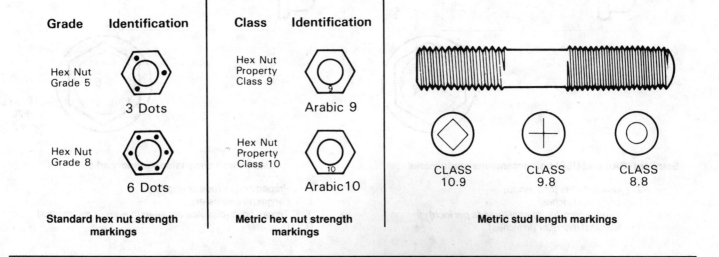

Standard hex nut strength markings

Metric hex nut strength markings

Metric stud length markings

It should be noted that many fasteners, especially Grades 0 through 2, have no distinguishing marks on them. When such is the case, the only way to determine whether it is standard or metric is to measure the thread pitch or compare it to a known fastener of the same size.

Standard fasteners are often referred to as SAE, as opposed to metric. However, it should be noted that SAE technically refers to a non-metric *fine thread* fastener only. Coarse thread non-metric fasteners are referred to as USS sizes.

Since fasteners of the same size (both standard and metric) may have different strength ratings, be sure to reinstall any bolts, studs or nuts removed from your vehicle in their original locations. Also, when replacing a fastener with a new one, make sure that the new one has a strength rating equal to or greater than the original.

Tightening sequences and procedures

Most threaded fasteners should be tightened to a specific torque value (torque is the twisting force applied to a threaded component such as a nut or bolt). Overtightening the fastener can weaken it and cause it to break, while undertightening can cause it to eventually come loose. Bolts, screws and studs, depending on the material they are made of and their thread diameters, have specific torque values, many of which are noted in the Specifications at the beginning of each Chapter. Be sure to follow the torque recommendations closely. For fasteners not assigned a specific torque, a general torque value chart is presented here as a guide. These torque values are for dry (unlubricated) fasteners threaded into steel or cast iron (not aluminum). As was previously mentioned, the size and grade of a fastener determine the amount of torque that can safely be

Metric thread sizes	Ft-lbs	Nm
M-6	6 to 9	9 to 12
M-8	14 to 21	19 to 28
M-10	28 to 40	38 to 54
M-12	50 to 71	68 to 96
M-14	80 to 140	109 to 154

Pipe thread sizes		
1/8	5 to 8	7 to 10
1/4	12 to 18	17 to 24
3/8	22 to 33	30 to 44
1/2	25 to 35	34 to 47

U.S. thread sizes		
1/4 – 20	6 to 9	9 to 12
5/16 – 18	12 to 18	17 to 24
5/16 – 24	14 to 20	19 to 27
3/8 – 16	22 to 32	30 to 43
3/8 – 24	27 to 38	37 to 51
7/16 – 14	40 to 55	55 to 74
7/16 – 20	40 to 60	55 to 81
1/2 – 13	55 to 80	75 to 108

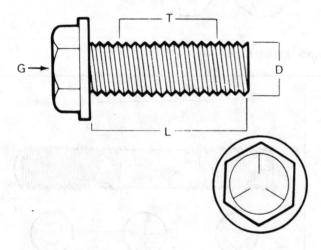

Standard (SAE and USS) bolt dimensions/grade marks

- G   Grade marks (bolt length)
- L   Length (in inches)
- T   Thread pitch (number of threads per inch)
- D   Nominal diameter (in inches)

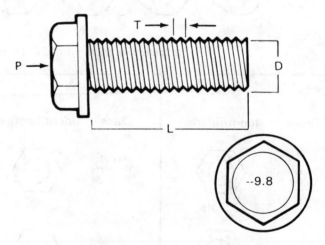

Metric bolt dimensions/grade marks

- P   Property class (bolt strength)
- L   Length (in millimeters)
- T   Thread pitch (distance between threads in millimeters)
- D   Diameter

applied to it. The figures listed here are approximate for Grade 2 and Grade 3 fasteners. Higher grades can tolerate higher torque values.

Fasteners laid out in a pattern, such as cylinder head bolts, oil pan bolts, differential cover bolts, etc., must be loosened or tightened in sequence to avoid warping the component. This sequence will normally be shown in the appropriate Chapter. If a specific pattern is not given, the following procedures can be used to prevent warping.

Initially, the bolts or nuts should be assembled finger-tight only. Next, they should be tightened one full turn each, in a criss-cross or diagonal pattern. After each one has been tightened one full turn, return to the first one and tighten them all one-half turn, following the same pattern. Finally, tighten each of them one-quarter turn at a time until each fastener has been tightened to the proper torque. To loosen and remove the fasteners, the procedure would be reversed.

Component disassembly

Component disassembly should be done with care and purpose to help ensure that the parts go back together properly. Always keep track of the sequence in which parts are removed. Make note of special characteristics or marks on parts that can be installed more than one way, such as a grooved thrust washer on a shaft. It is a good idea to lay the disassembled parts out on a clean surface in the order that they were removed. It may also be helpful to make sketches or take instant photos of components before removal.

When removing fasteners from a component, keep track of their locations. Sometimes threading a bolt back in a part, or putting the washers and nut back on a stud, can prevent mix-ups later. If nuts and bolts cannot be returned to their original locations, they should be kept in a compartmented box or a series of small boxes. A cupcake or muffin tin is ideal for this purpose, since each cavity can hold the bolts and nuts from a particular area (i.e. oil pan bolts, valve cover bolts, engine mount bolts, etc.). A pan of this type is especially helpful when working on assemblies with very small parts, such as the carburetor, alternator, valve train or interior dash and trim pieces. The cavities can be marked with paint or tape to identify the contents.

Whenever wiring looms, harnesses or connectors are separated, it is a good idea to identify the two halves with numbered pieces of masking tape so they can be easily reconnected.

Gasket sealing surfaces

Throughout any vehicle, gaskets are used to seal the mating surfaces between two parts and keep lubricants, fluids, vacuum or pressure contained in an assembly.

Many times these gaskets are coated with a liquid or paste-type gasket sealing compound before assembly. Age, heat and pressure can sometimes cause the two parts to stick together so tightly that they are very difficult to separate. Often, the assembly can be loosened by striking it with a soft-face hammer near the mating surfaces. A regular hammer can be used if a block of wood is placed between the hammer and the part. Do not hammer on cast parts or parts that could be easily damaged. With any particularly stubborn part, always recheck to make sure that every fastener has been removed.

Avoid using a screwdriver or bar to pry apart an assembly, as they can easily mar the gasket sealing surfaces of the parts, which must remain smooth. If prying is absolutely necessary, use an old broom handle, but keep in mind that extra clean up will be necessary if the wood splinters.

After the parts are separated, the old gasket must be carefully scraped off and the gasket surfaces cleaned. Stubborn gasket material can be soaked with rust penetrant or treated with a special chemical to soften it so it can be easily scraped off. A scraper can be fashioned from a piece of copper tubing by flattening and sharpening one end. Copper is recommended because it is usually softer than the surfaces to be scraped, which reduces the chance of gouging the part. Some gaskets can be removed with a wire brush, but regardless of the method used, the mating surfaces must be left clean and smooth. If for some reason the gasket surface is gouged, then a gasket sealer thick enough to fill scratches will have to be used during reassembly of the components. For most applications, a non-drying (or semi-drying) gasket sealer should be used.

Hose removal tips

Warning: *If the vehicle is equipped with air conditioning, do not disconnect any of the A/C hoses without first having the system depressurized by a dealer service department or a service station.*

Hose removal precautions closely parallel gasket removal precautions. Avoid scratching or gouging the surface that the hose mates against or the connection may leak. This is especially true for radiator hoses. Because of various chemical reactions, the rubber in hoses can bond itself to the metal spigot that the hose fits over. To remove a hose, first loosen the hose clamps that secure it to the spigot. Then, with slip-joint pliers, grab the hose at the clamp and rotate it around the spigot. Work it back and forth until it is completely free, then pull it off. Silicone or other lubricants will ease removal if they can be applied between the hose and the outside of the spigot. Apply the same lubricant to the inside of the hose and the outside of the spigot to simplify installation.

As a last resort (and if the hose is to be replaced with a new one anyway), the rubber can be slit with a knife and the hose peeled from the spigot. If this must be done, be careful that the metal connection is not damaged.

If a hose clamp is broken or damaged, do not reuse it. Wire-type clamps usually weaken with age, so it is a good idea to replace them with screw-type clamps whenever a hose is removed.

Tools

A selection of good tools is a basic requirement for anyone who plans to maintain and repair his or her own vehicle. For the owner who has few tools, the initial investment might seem high, but when compared to the spiraling costs of professional auto maintenance and repair, it is a wise one.

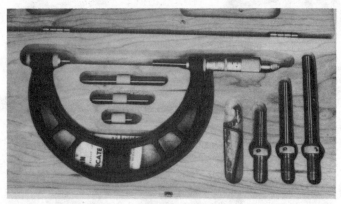

Micrometer set

Dial indicator set

Dial caliper

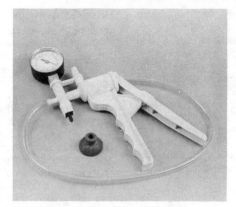

Hand-operated vacuum pump

Timing light

Compression gauge with spark plug hole adapter

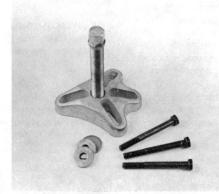

Damper/steering wheel puller

General purpose puller

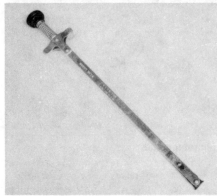

Hydraulic lifter removal tool

Valve spring compressor

Valve spring compressor

Ridge reamer

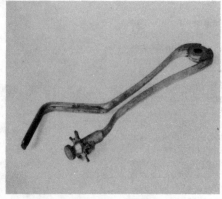

Piston ring groove cleaning tool

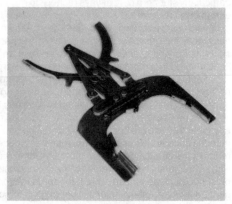

Ring removal/installation tool

Ring compressor

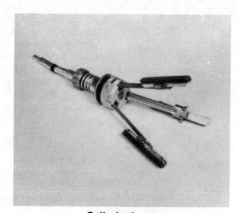

Cylinder hone

Brake hold-down spring tool

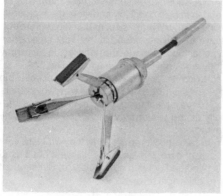

Brake cylinder hone

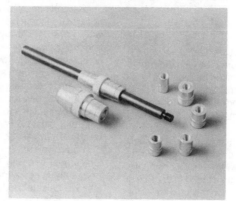

Clutch plate alignment tool

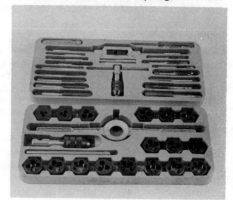

Tap and die set

To help the owner decide which tools are needed to perform the tasks detailed in this manual, the following tool lists are offered: *Maintenance and minor repair, Repair/overhaul* and *Special.*

The newcomer to practical mechanics should start off with the maintenance and minor repair tool kit, which is adequate for the simpler jobs performed on a vehicle. Then, as confidence and experience grow, the owner can tackle more difficult tasks, buying additional tools as they are needed. Eventually the basic kit will be expanded into the repair and overhaul tool set. Over a period of time, the experienced do-it-yourselfer will assemble a tool set complete enough for most repair and overhaul procedures and will add tools from the special category when it is felt that the expense is justified by the frequency of use.

Maintenance and minor repair tool kit

The tools in this list should be considered the minimum required for performance of routine maintenance, servicing and minor repair work. We recommend the purchase of combination wrenches (box-end and open-end combined in one wrench). While more expensive than open end wrenches, they offer the advantages of both types of wrench.

Combination wrench set (1/4-inch to 1 inch or 6 mm to 19 mm)
Adjustable wrench, 8 inch
Spark plug wrench with rubber insert
Spark plug gap adjusting tool
Feeler gauge set
Brake bleeder wrench
Standard screwdriver (5/16-inch x 6 inch)
Phillips screwdriver (No. 2 x 6 inch)
Combination pliers – 6 inch
Hacksaw and assortment of blades
Tire pressure gauge
Grease gun
Oil can
Fine emery cloth
Wire brush

Battery post and cable cleaning tool
Oil filter wrench
Funnel (medium size)
Safety goggles
Jackstands(2)
Drain pan

Note: *If basic tune-ups are going to be part of routine maintenance, it will be necessary to purchase a good quality stroboscopic timing light and combination tachometer/dwell meter. Although they are included in the list of special tools, it is mentioned here because they are absolutely necessary for tuning most vehicles properly.*

Repair and overhaul tool set

These tools are essential for anyone who plans to perform major repairs and are in addition to those in the maintenance and minor repair tool kit. Included is a comprehensive set of sockets which, though expensive, are invaluable because of their versatility, especially when various extensions and drives are available. We recommend the 1/2-inch drive over the 3/8-inch drive. Although the larger drive is bulky and more expensive, it has the capacity of accepting a very wide range of large sockets. Ideally, however, the mechanic should have a 3/8-inch drive set and a 1/2-inch drive set.

Socket set(s)
Reversible ratchet
Extension – 10 inch
Universal joint
Torque wrench (same size drive as sockets)
Ball peen hammer – 8 ounce
Soft-face hammer (plastic/rubber)
Standard screwdriver (1/4-inch x 6 inch)
Standard screwdriver (stubby – 5/16-inch)
Phillips screwdriver (No. 3 x 8 inch)
Phillips screwdriver (stubby – No. 2)

Pliers – vise grip
Pliers – lineman's
Pliers – needle nose
Pliers – snap-ring (internal and external)
Cold chisel – 1/2-inch
Scribe
Scraper (made from flattened copper tubing)
Centerpunch
Pin punches (1/16, 1/8, 3/16-inch)
Steel rule/straightedge – 12 inch
Allen wrench set (1/8 to 3/8-inch or 4 mm to 10 mm)
A selection of files
Wire brush (large)
Jackstands (second set)
Jack (scissor or hydraulic type)

Note: *Another tool which is often useful is an electric drill with a chuck capacity of 3/8-inch and a set of good quality drill bits.*

Special tools

The tools in this list include those which are not used regularly, are expensive to buy, or which need to be used in accordance with their manufacturer's instructions. Unless these tools will be used frequently, it is not very economical to purchase many of them. A consideration would be to split the cost and use between yourself and a friend or friends. In addition, most of these tools can be obtained from a tool rental shop on a temporary basis.

This list primarily contains only those tools and instruments widely available to the public, and not those special tools produced by the vehicle manufacturer for distribution to dealer service departments. Occasionally, references to the manufacturer's special tools are included in the text of this manual. Generally, an alternative method of doing the job without the special tool is offered. However, sometimes there is no alternative to their use. Where this is the case, and the tool cannot be purchased or borrowed, the work should be turned over to the dealer service department or an automotive repair shop.

Valve spring compressor
Piston ring groove cleaning tool
Piston ring compressor
Piston ring installation tool
Cylinder compression gauge
Cylinder ridge reamer
Cylinder surfacing hone
Cylinder bore gauge
Micrometers and/or dial calipers
Hydraulic lifter removal tool
Balljoint separator
Universal-type puller
Impact screwdriver
Dial indicator set
Stroboscopic timing light (inductive pick-up)
Hand operated vacuum/pressure pump
Tachometer/dwell meter
Universal electrical multimeter
Cable hoist
Brake spring removal and installation tools
Floor jack

Buying tools

For the do-it-yourselfer who is just starting to get involved in vehicle maintenance and repair, there are a number of options available when purchasing tools. If maintenance and minor repair is the extent of the work to be done, the purchase of individual tools is satisfactory. If, on the other hand, extensive work is planned, it would be a good idea to purchase a modest tool set from one of the large retail chain stores. A set can usually be bought at a substantial savings over the individual tool prices, and they often come with a tool box. As additional tools are needed, add–on sets, individual tools and a larger tool box can be purchased to expand the tool selection. Building a tool set gradually allows the cost of the tools to be spread over a longer period of time and gives the mechanic the freedom to choose only those tools that will actually be used.

Tool stores will often be the only source of some of the special tools that are needed, but regardless of where tools are bought, try to avoid cheap ones, especially when buying screwdrivers and sockets, because they won't last very long. The expense involved in replacing cheap tools will eventually be greater than the initial cost of quality tools.

Care and maintenance of tools

Good tools are expensive, so it makes sense to treat them with respect. Keep them clean and in usable condition and store them properly when not in use. Always wipe off any dirt, grease or metal chips before putting them away. Never leave tools lying around in the work area. Upon completion of a job, always check closely under the hood for tools that may have been left there so they won't get lost during a test drive.

Some tools, such as screwdrivers, pliers, wrenches and sockets, can be hung on a panel mounted on the garage or workshop wall, while others should be kept in a tool box or tray. Measuring instruments, gauges, meters, etc. must be carefully stored where they cannot be damaged by weather or impact from other tools.

When tools are used with care and stored properly, they will last a very long time. Even with the best of care, though, tools will wear out if used frequently. When a tool is damaged or worn out, replace it. Subsequent jobs will be safer and more enjoyable if you do.

Working facilities

Not to be overlooked when discussing tools is the workshop. If anything more than routine maintenance is to be carried out, some sort of suitable work area is essential.

It is understood, and appreciated, that many home mechanics do not have a good workshop or garage available, and end up removing an engine or doing major repairs outside. It is recommended, however, that the overhaul or repair be completed under the cover of a roof.

A clean, flat workbench or table of comfortable working height is an absolute necessity. The workbench should be equipped with a vise that has a jaw opening of at least four inches.

As mentioned previously, some clean, dry storage space is also required for tools, as well as the lubricants, fluids, cleaning solvents, etc. which soon become necessary.

Sometimes waste oil and fluids, drained from the engine or cooling system during normal maintenance or repairs, present a disposal problem. To avoid pouring them on the ground or into a sewage system, pour the used fluids into large containers, seal them with caps and take them to an authorized disposal site or recycling center. Plastic jugs, such as old antifreeze containers, are ideal for this purpose.

Always keep a supply of old newspapers and clean rags available. Old towels are excellent for mopping up spills. Many mechanics use rolls of paper towels for most work because they are readily available and disposable. To help keep the area under the vehicle clean, a large cardboard box can be cut open and flattened to protect the garage or shop floor.

Whenever working over a painted surface, such as when leaning over a fender to service something under the hood, always cover it with an old blanket or bedspread to protect the finish. Vinyl covered pads, made especially for this purpose, are available at auto parts stores.

Booster battery (jump) starting

Observe these precautions when using a booster battery to start a vehicle:

   a) Before connecting the booster battery, make sure the ignition switch is in the Off position.

   b) Turn off the lights, heater and other electrical loads.

   c) Your eyes should be shielded. Safety goggles are a good idea.

   d) Make sure the booster battery is the same voltage as the dead one in the vehicle.

   e) The two vehicles MUST NOT TOUCH each other!

   f) Make sure the transmission is in Neutral (manual) or Park (automatic).

   g) If the booster battery is not a maintenance-free type, remove the vent caps and lay a cloth over the vent holes.

Connect the red jumper cable to the positive (+) terminals of each battery.

Connect one end of the black jumper cable to the negative (–) terminal of the booster battery. The other end of this cable should be connected to a good ground on the vehicle to be started, such as a bolt or bracket on the engine block **(see illustration)**. Make sure the cable will not come into contact with the fan, drivebelts or other moving parts of the engine.

Start the engine using the booster battery, then, with the engine running at idle speed, disconnect the jumper cables in the reverse order of connection.

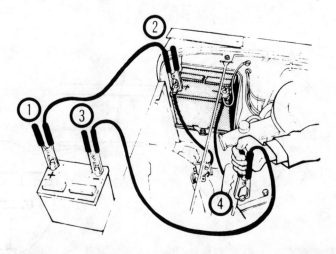

Make the booster battery cable connections in the numerical order shown (note that the negative cable of the booster battery is NOT attached to the negative terminal of the dead battery)

Jacking and towing

Jacking

Warning: *The jack supplied with the vehicle should only be used for raising the vehicle when changing a tire or placing jackstands under the frame. Never work under the vehicle or start the engine while the jack is being used as the only means of support.*

The vehicle must be on a level surface with the wheels blocked and the transaxle in Park (automatic) or Reverse (manual). Apply the parking brake if the front of the vehicle must be raised. Make sure no one is in the vehicle as it's being raised with the jack.

Remove the jack, lug nut wrench and spare tire (if needed) from the vehicle. If a tire is being replaced, use the lug wrench to remove the wheel cover. **Warning:** *Wheel covers may have sharp edges – be very careful not to cut yourself.* Loosen the lug nuts one-half turn, but leave them in place until the tire is raised off the ground.

Position the jack under the vehicle at the indicated jacking point. There's a front and rear jacking point on each side of the vehicle (**see illustration**).

Turn the jack handle clockwise until the tire clears the ground. Remove the lug nuts, pull the tire off and replace it with the spare. Replace the lug nuts with the beveled edges facing in and tighten them snugly. Don't attempt to tighten them completely until the vehicle is lowered or it could slip off the jack.

Turn the jack handle counterclockwise to lower the vehicle. Remove the jack and tighten the lug nuts in a criss-cross pattern. If possible, tighten the nuts with a torque wrench (see Chapter 1 for the torque figures). If you don't have access to a torque wrench, have the nuts checked by a service station or repair shop as soon as possible.

Stow the tire, jack and wrench and unblock the wheels.

Towing

Vehicles with a manual transaxle

As a general rule, the vehicle should be towed with the front (drive) wheels off the ground. Be sure to release the parking brake. If the vehicle is being towed with the front wheels on the ground, place the transaxle in Neutral. Also, the ignition key must be in the ACC position, since the steering lock mechanism isn't strong enough to hold the front wheels straight while towing.

Vehicles with an automatic transaxle

Caution: *Never tow an automatic transaxle-equipped vehicle with the front wheels on the ground. If the vehicle must be towed from the rear, place the front wheels on a towing dolly.*

Vehicles equipped with an automatic transaxle can only be towed with the front wheels off the ground. DO NOT tow the vehicle with the front wheels on the ground or the transaxle can be seriously damaged. The parking brake must be released during towing.

All vehicles

Equipment specifically designed for towing should be used. It should be attached to the main structural members of the vehicle, not the bumpers or brackets.

Safety is a major consideration when towing and all applicable state and local laws must be obeyed. A safety chain must be used at all times. Remember that power steering and brakes won't work with the engine off.

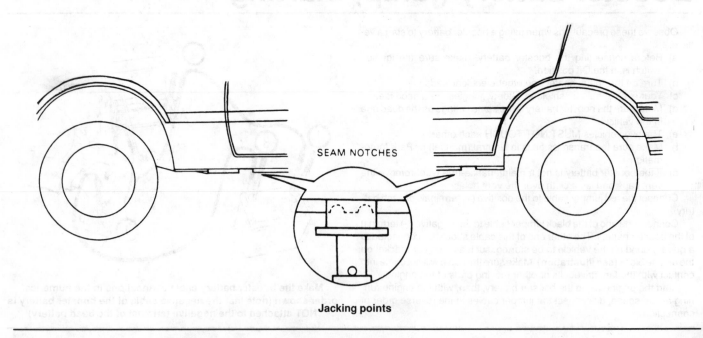

SEAM NOTCHES

Jacking points

Automotive chemicals and lubricants

A number of automotive chemicals and lubricants are available for use during vehicle maintenance and repair. They include a wide variety of products ranging from cleaning solvents and degreasers to lubricants and protective sprays for rubber, plastic and vinyl.

Cleaners

Carburetor cleaner and choke cleaner is a strong solvent for gum, varnish and carbon. Most carburetor cleaners leave a dry-type lubricant film which will not harden or gum up. Because of this film it is not recommended for use on electrical components.

Brake system cleaner is used to remove grease and brake fluid from the brake system, where clean surfaces are absolutely necessary. It leaves no residue and often eliminates brake squeal caused by contaminants.

Electrical cleaner removes oxidation, corrosion and carbon deposits from electrical contacts, restoring full current flow. It can also be used to clean spark plugs, carburetor jets, voltage regulators and other parts where an oil-free surface is desired.

Demoisturants remove water and moisture from electrical components such as alternators, voltage regulators, electrical connectors and fuse blocks. They are non-conductive, non-corrosive and non-flammable.

Degreasers are heavy-duty solvents used to remove grease from the outside of the engine and from chassis components. They can be sprayed or brushed on and, depending on the type, are rinsed off either with water or solvent.

Lubricants

Motor oil is the lubricant formulated for use in engines. It normally contains a wide variety of additives to prevent corrosion and reduce foaming and wear. Motor oil comes in various weights (viscosity ratings) from 5 to 80. The recommended weight of the oil depends on the season, temperature and the demands on the engine. Light oil is used in cold climates and under light load conditions. Heavy oil is used in hot climates and where high loads are encountered. Multi-viscosity oils are designed to have characteristics of both light and heavy oils and are available in a number of weights from 5W-20 to 20W-50.

Gear oil is designed to be used in differentials, manual transmissions and other areas where high-temperature lubrication is required.

Chassis and wheel bearing grease is a heavy grease used where increased loads and friction are encountered, such as for wheel bearings, balljoints, tie-rod ends and universal joints.

High-temperature wheel bearing grease is designed to withstand the extreme temperatures encountered by wheel bearings in disc brake equipped vehicles. It usually contains molybdenum disulfide (moly), which is a dry-type lubricant.

White grease is a heavy grease for metal-to-metal applications where water is a problem. White grease stays soft under both low and high temperatures (usually from −100 to +190-degrees F), and will not wash off or dilute in the presence of water.

Assembly lube is a special extreme pressure lubricant, usually containing moly, used to lubricate high-load parts (such as main and rod bearings and cam lobes) for initial start-up of a new engine. The assembly lube lubricates the parts without being squeezed out or washed away until the engine oiling system begins to function.

Silicone lubricants are used to protect rubber, plastic, vinyl and nylon parts.

Graphite lubricants are used where oils cannot be used due to contamination problems, such as in locks. The dry graphite will lubricate metal parts while remaining uncontaminated by dirt, water, oil or acids. It is electrically conductive and will not foul electrical contacts in locks such as the ignition switch.

Moly penetrants loosen and lubricate frozen, rusted and corroded fasteners and prevent future rusting or freezing.

Heat-sink grease is a special electrically non-conductive grease that is used for mounting electronic ignition modules where it is essential that heat is transferred away from the module.

Sealants

RTV sealant is one of the most widely used gasket compounds. Made from silicone, RTV is air curing, it seals, bonds, waterproofs, fills surface irregularities, remains flexible, doesn't shrink, is relatively easy to remove, and is used as a supplementary sealer with almost all low and medium temperature gaskets.

Anaerobic sealant is much like RTV in that it can be used either to seal gaskets or to form gaskets by itself. It remains flexible, is solvent resistant and fills surface imperfections. The difference between an anaerobic sealant and an RTV-type sealant is in the curing. RTV cures when exposed to air, while an anaerobic sealant cures only in the absence of air. This means that an anaerobic sealant cures only after the assembly of parts, sealing them together.

Thread and pipe sealant is used for sealing hydraulic and pneumatic fittings and vacuum lines. It is usually made from a teflon compound, and comes in a spray, a paint-on liquid and as a wrap-around tape.

Chemicals

Anti−seize compound prevents seizing, galling, cold welding, rust and corrosion in fasteners. High-temperature anti-seize, usually made with copper and graphite lubricants, is used for exhaust system and exhaust manifold bolts.

Anaerobic locking compounds are used to keep fasteners from vibrating or working loose and cure only after installation, in the absence of air. Medium strength locking compound is used for small nuts, bolts and screws that may be removed later. High-strength locking compound is for large nuts, bolts and studs which aren't removed on a regular basis.

Oil additives range from viscosity index improvers to chemical treatments that claim to reduce internal engine friction. It should be noted that most oil manufacturers caution against using additives with their oils.

Gas additives perform several functions, depending on their chemical makeup. They usually contain solvents that help dissolve gum and varnish that build up on carburetor, fuel injection and intake parts. They also serve to break down carbon deposits that form on the inside surfaces of the combustion chambers. Some additives contain upper cylinder lubricants for valves and piston rings, and others contain chemicals to remove condensation from the gas tank.

Miscellaneous

Brake fluid is specially formulated hydraulic fluid that can withstand the heat and pressure encountered in brake systems. Care must be taken so this fluid does not come in contact with painted surfaces or plastics. An opened container should always be resealed to prevent contamination by water or dirt.

Weatherstrip adhesive is used to bond weatherstripping around doors, windows and trunk lids. It is sometimes used to attach trim pieces.

Undercoating is a petroleum-based, tar-like substance that is designed to protect metal surfaces on the underside of the vehicle from corrosion. It also acts as a sound-deadening agent by insulating the bottom of the vehicle.

Waxes and polishes are used to help protect painted and plated surfaces from the weather. Different types of paint may require the use of different types of wax and polish. Some polishes utilize a chemical or abrasive cleaner to help remove the top layer of oxidized (dull) paint on older vehicles. In recent years many non-wax polishes that contain a wide variety of chemicals such as polymers and silicones have been introduced. These non-wax polishes are usually easier to apply and last longer than conventional waxes and polishes.

Safety first!

Regardless of how enthusiastic you may be about getting on with the job at hand, take the time to ensure that your safety is not jeopardized. A moment's lack of attention can result in an accident, as can failure to observe certain simple safety precautions. The possibility of an accident will always exist, and the following points should not be considered a comprehensive list of all dangers. Rather, they are intended to make you aware of the risks and to encourage a safety conscious approach to all work you carry out on your vehicle.

Essential DOs and DON'Ts

DON'T rely on a jack when working under the vehicle. Always use approved jackstands to support the weight of the vehicle and place them under the recommended lift or support points.

DON'T attempt to loosen extremely tight fasteners (i.e. wheel lug nuts) while the vehicle is on a jack – it may fall.

DON'T start the engine without first making sure that the transmission is in Neutral (or Park where applicable) and the parking brake is set.

DON'T remove the radiator cap from a hot cooling system – let it cool or cover it with a cloth and release the pressure gradually.

DON'T attempt to drain the engine oil until you are sure it has cooled to the point that it will not burn you.

DON'T touch any part of the engine or exhaust system until it has cooled sufficiently to avoid burns.

DON'T siphon toxic liquids such as gasoline, antifreeze and brake fluid by mouth, or allow them to remain on your skin.

DON'T inhale brake lining dust – it is potentially hazardous (see Asbestos below)

DON'T allow spilled oil or grease to remain on the floor – wipe it up before someone slips on it.

DON'T use loose fitting wrenches or other tools which may slip and cause injury.

DON'T push on wrenches when loosening or tightening nuts or bolts. Always try to pull the wrench toward you. If the situation calls for pushing the wrench away, push with an open hand to avoid scraped knuckles if the wrench should slip.

DON'T attempt to lift a heavy component alone – get someone to help you.

DON'T rush or take unsafe shortcuts to finish a job.

DON'T allow children or animals in or around the vehicle while you are working on it.

DO wear eye protection when using power tools such as a drill, sander, bench grinder, etc. and when working under a vehicle.

DO keep loose clothing and long hair well out of the way of moving parts.

DO make sure that any hoist used has a safe working load rating adequate for the job.

DO get someone to check on you periodically when working alone on a vehicle.

DO carry out work in a logical sequence and make sure that everything is correctly assembled and tightened.

DO keep chemicals and fluids tightly capped and out of the reach of children and pets.

DO remember that your vehicle's safety affects that of yourself and others. If in doubt on any point, get professional advice.

Asbestos

Certain friction, insulating, sealing, and other products – such as brake linings, brake bands, clutch linings, torque converters, gaskets, etc. – contain asbestos. *Extreme care must be taken to avoid inhalation of dust from such products since it is hazardous to health.* If in doubt, assume that they *do* contain asbestos.

Fire

Remember at all times that gasoline is highly flammable. Never smoke or have any kind of open flame around when working on a vehicle. But the risk does not end there. A spark caused by an electrical short circuit, by two metal surfaces contacting each other, or even by static electricity built up in your body under certain conditions, can ignite gasoline vapors, which in a confined space are highly explosive. Do not, under any circumstances, use gasoline for cleaning parts. Use an approved safety solvent.

Always disconnect the battery ground (–) cable *at the battery* before working on any part of the fuel system or electrical system. Never risk spilling fuel on a hot engine or exhaust component.

It is strongly recommended that a fire extinguisher suitable for use on fuel and electrical fires be kept handy in the garage or workshop at all times. Never try to extinguish a fuel or electrical fire with water.

Fumes

Certain fumes are highly toxic and can quickly cause unconsciousness and even death if inhaled to any extent. Gasoline vapor falls into this category, as do the vapors from some cleaning solvents. Any draining or pouring of such volatile fluids should be done in a well ventilated area.

When using cleaning fluids and solvents, read the instructions on the container carefully. Never use materials from unmarked containers.

Never run the engine in an enclosed space, such as a garage. Exhaust fumes contain carbon monoxide, which is extremely poisonous. If you need to run the engine, always do so in the open air, or at least have the rear of the vehicle outside the work area.

If you are fortunate enough to have the use of an inspection pit, never drain or pour gasoline and never run the engine while the vehicle is over the pit. The fumes, being heavier than air, will concentrate in the pit with possibly lethal results.

The battery

Never create a spark or allow a bare light bulb near a battery. They normally give off a certain amount of hydrogen gas, which is highly explosive.

Always disconnect the battery ground (–) cable *at the battery* before working on the fuel or electrical systems.

If possible, loosen the filler caps or cover when charging the battery from an external source (this does not apply to sealed or maintenancefree batteries). Do not charge at an excessive rate or the battery may burst.

Take care when adding water to a non maintenance–free battery and when carrying a battery. The electrolyte, even when diluted, is very corrosive and should not be allowed to contact clothing or skin.

Always wear eye protection when cleaning the battery to prevent the caustic deposits from entering your eyes.

Household current

When using an electric power tool, inspection light, etc., which operates on household current, always make sure that the tool is correctly connected to its plug and that, where necessary, it is properly grounded. Do not use such items in damp conditions and, again, do not create a spark or apply excessive heat in the vicinity of fuel or fuel vapor.

Secondary ignition system voltage

A severe electric shock can result from touching certain parts of the ignition system (such as the spark plug wires) when the engine is running or being cranked, particularly if components are damp or the insulation is defective. In the case of an electronic ignition system, the secondary system voltage is much higher and could prove fatal.

Conversion factors

Length (distance)

Inches (in)	X	25.4	= Millimetres (mm)	X 0.0394	= Inches (in)
Feet (ft)	X	0.305	= Metres (m)	X 3.281	= Feet (ft)
Miles	X	1.609	= Kilometres (km)	X 0.621	= Miles

Volume (capacity)

Cubic inches (cu in; in³)	X	16.387	= Cubic centimetres (cc; cm³)	X 0.061	= Cubic inches (cu in; in³)
Imperial pints (Imp pt)	X	0.568	= Litres (l)	X 1.76	= Imperial pints (Imp pt)
Imperial quarts (Imp qt)	X	1.137	= Litres (l)	X 0.88	= Imperial quarts (Imp qt)
Imperial quarts (Imp qt)	X	1.201	= US quarts (US qt)	X 0.833	= Imperial quarts (Imp qt)
US quarts (US qt)	X	0.946	= Litres (l)	X 1.057	= US quarts (US qt)
Imperial gallons (Imp gal)	X	4.546	= Litres (l)	X 0.22	= Imperial gallons (Imp gal)
Imperial gallons (Imp gal)	X	1.201	= US gallons (US gal)	X 0.833	= Imperial gallons (Imp gal)
US gallons (US gal)	X	3.785	= Litres (l)	X 0.264	= US gallons (US gal)

Mass (weight)

Ounces (oz)	X	28.35	= Grams (g)	X 0.035	= Ounces (oz)
Pounds (lb)	X	0.454	= Kilograms (kg)	X 2.205	= Pounds (lb)

Force

Ounces-force (ozf; oz)	X	0.278	= Newtons (N)	X 3.6	= Ounces-force (ozf; oz)
Pounds-force (lbf; lb)	X	4.448	= Newtons (N)	X 0.225	= Pounds-force (lbf; lb)
Newtons (N)	X	0.1	= Kilograms-force (kgf; kg)	X 9.81	= Newtons (N)

Pressure

Pounds-force per square inch (psi; lbf/in²; lb/in²)	X	0.070	= Kilograms-force per square centimetre (kgf/cm²; kg/cm²)	X 14.223	= Pounds-force per square inch (psi; lbf/in²; lb/in²)
Pounds-force per square inch (psi; lbf/in²; lb/in²)	X	0.068	= Atmospheres (atm)	X 14.696	= Pounds-force per square inch (psi; lbf/in²; lb/in²)
Pounds-force per square inch (psi; lbf/in²; lb/in²)	X	0.069	= Bars	X 14.5	= Pounds-force per square inch (psi; lbf/in²; lb/in²)
Pounds-force per square inch (psi; lbf/in²; lb/in²)	X	6.895	= Kilopascals (kPa)	X 0.145	= Pounds-force per square inch (psi; lbf/in²; lb/in²)
Kilopascals (kPa)	X	0.01	= Kilograms-force per square centimetre (kgf/cm²; kg/cm²)	X 98.1	= Kilopascals (kPa)

Torque (moment of force)

Pounds-force inches (lbf in; lb in)	X	1.152	= Kilograms-force centimetre (kgf cm; kg cm)	X 0.868	= Pounds-force inches (lbf in; lb in)
Pounds-force inches (lbf in; lb in)	X	0.113	= Newton metres (Nm)	X 8.85	= Pounds-force inches (lbf in; lb in)
Pounds-force inches (lbf in; lb in)	X	0.083	= Pounds-force feet (lbf ft; lb ft)	X 12	= Pounds-force inches (lbf in; lb in)
Pounds-force feet (lbf ft; lb ft)	X	0.138	= Kilograms-force metres (kgf m; kg m)	X 7.233	= Pounds-force feet (lbf ft; lb ft)
Pounds-force feet (lbf ft; lb ft)	X	1.356	= Newton metres (Nm)	X 0.738	= Pounds-force feet (lbf ft; lb ft)
Newton metres (Nm)	X	0.102	= Kilograms-force metres (kgf m; kg m)	X 9.804	= Newton metres (Nm)

Power

Horsepower (hp)	X	745.7	= Watts (W)	X 0.0013	= Horsepower (hp)

Velocity (speed)

Miles per hour (miles/hr; mph)	X	1.609	= Kilometres per hour (km/hr; kph)	X 0.621	= Miles per hour (miles/hr; mph)

Fuel consumption*

Miles per gallon, Imperial (mpg)	X	0.354	= Kilometres per litre (km/l)	X 2.825	= Miles per gallon, Imperial (mpg)
Miles per gallon, US (mpg)	X	0.425	= Kilometres per litre (km/l)	X 2.352	= Miles per gallon, US (mpg)

Temperature

Degrees Fahrenheit = (°C x 1.8) + 32   Degrees Celsius (Degrees Centigrade; °C) = (°F - 32) x 0.56

*It is common practice to convert from miles per gallon (mpg) to litres/100 kilometres (l/100km),
where mpg (Imperial) x l/100 km = 282 and mpg (US) x l/100 km = 235

Troubleshooting

Contents

This section provides an easy reference guide to the more common problems which may occur during the operation of your vehicle. These problems and possible causes are grouped under various components or systems; i.e. Engine, Cooling System, etc., and also refer to the Chapter and/or Section which deals with the problem.

Remember that successful troubleshooting is not a mysterious black art practiced only by professional mechanics. It's simply the result of a bit of knowledge combined with an intelligent, systematic approach to the problem. Always work by a process of elimination, starting with the simplest solution and working through to the most complex – and never overlook the obvious. Anyone can forget to fill the gas tank or leave the lights on overnight, so don't assume that you are above such oversights.

Finally, always get clear in your mind why a problem has occurred and take steps to ensure that it doesn't happen again. If the electrical system fails because of a poor connection, check all other connections in the system to make sure that they don't fail as well. If a particular fuse continues to blow, find out why – don't just go on replacing fuses. Remember, failure of a small component can often be indicative of potential failure or incorrect functioning of a more important component or system.

Engine

1   Engine will not rotate when attempting to start

1   Battery terminal connections loose or corroded. Check the cable terminals at the battery. Tighten the cable or remove corrosion as necessary.
2   Battery discharged or faulty. If the cable connections are clean and tight on the battery posts, turn the key to the On position and switch on the headlights and/or windshield wipers. If they fail to function, the battery is discharged.
3   Automatic transaxle not completely engaged in Park or Neutral or clutch pedal not completely depressed.
4   Broken, loose or disconnected wiring in the starting circuit. Inspect all wiring and connectors at the battery, starter solenoid and ignition switch.
5   Starter motor pinion jammed in flywheel ring gear. If manual transaxle, place transaxle in gear and rock the vehicle to manually turn the engine. Remove starter and inspect pinion and flywheel at earliest convenience (Chapter 5).
6   Starter solenoid faulty (Chapter 5).
7   Starter motor faulty (Chapter 5).
8   Ignition switch faulty (Chapter 12).

2   Engine rotates but will not start

1   Fuel tank empty.
2   Fault in the carburetor or fuel injection system (Chapter 4).
3   Battery discharged (engine rotates slowly). Check the operation of electrical components as described in the previous Section.
4   Battery terminal connections loose or corroded (see previous Section).
5   Fuel pump faulty (Chapter 4).
6   Excessive moisture on, or damage to, ignition components (see Chapter 5).
7   Worn, faulty or incorrectly gapped spark plugs (Chapter 1).
8   Broken, loose or disconnected wiring in the starting circuit (see previous Section).
9   Distributor loose, causing ignition timing to change. Turn the distributor as necessary to start the engine, then set the ignition timing as soon as possible (Chapter 1).
10   Broken, loose or disconnected wires at the ignition coil or faulty coil (Chapter 5).

3   Starter motor operates without rotating engine

1   Starter pinion sticking. Remove the starter (Chapter 5) and inspect.
2   Starter pinion or flywheel teeth worn or broken. Remove the flywheel/driveplate access cover and inspect.

4   Engine hard to start when cold

1   Battery discharged or low. Check as described in Section 1.
2   Fault in the fuel or electrical systems (Chapters 4 and 5).
3   Carburetor in need of overhaul (Chapter 4).
4   Distributor rotor carbon tracked and/or damaged (Chapters 1 and 5).
5   Choke control stuck or inoperative (carbureted models) (Chapters 1 and 4).

5   Engine hard to start when hot

1   Air filter clogged (Chapter 1).
2   Fault in the fuel or electrical systems (Chapters 4 and 5).
3   Fuel not reaching the carburetor (carburetor-equipped models) (see Section 2).

6   Starter motor noisy or excessively rough in engagement

1   Pinion or flywheel gear teeth worn or broken. Remove the cover at the rear of the engine (if so equipped) and inspect.
2   Starter motor mounting bolts loose or missing.

7   Engine starts but stops immediately

1   Loose or faulty electrical connections at distributor, coil or alternator.
2   Fault in the fuel or electrical systems (Chapters 4 and 5).
3   Insufficient fuel reaching the carburetor (carburetor-equipped models). Check the fuel pump (Chapter 4).
4   Vacuum leak at the gasket surfaces of the intake manifold, or carburetor/throttle body. Make sure all mounting bolts/nuts are tightened securely and all vacuum hoses connected to the carburetor and manifold are positioned properly and in good condition.

8   Engine lopes while idling or idles erratically

1   Vacuum leakage. Check the mounting bolts/nuts at the carburetor/throttle body and intake manifold for tightness. Make sure all vacuum hoses are connected and in good condition. Use a stethoscope or a length of fuel hose held against your ear to listen for vacuum leaks while the engine is running. A hissing sound will be heard. A soapy water solution will also detect leaks.
2   Fault in the fuel or electrical systems (Chapters 4 and 5).
3   Leaking EGR valve or plugged PCV valve (see Chapters 1 and 6).
4   Air filter clogged (Chapter 1).
5   Fuel pump not delivering sufficient fuel to the carburetor (carbureted models) (see Chapter 4).
6   Carburetor out of adjustment (Chapter 4).
7   Leaking head gasket. Perform a compression check (Chapter 2).
8   Camshaft lobes worn (Chapter 2).

9   Engine misses at idle speed

1   Spark plugs worn or not gapped properly (Chapter 1).
2   Fault in the fuel or electrical systems (Chapters 4 and 5).
3   Faulty spark plug wires (Chapter 1).

10   Engine misses throughout driving speed range

1   Fuel filter clogged and/or impurities in the fuel system (Chapter 1).
2   Faulty or incorrectly gapped spark plugs (Chapter 1).
3   Fault in the fuel or electrical systems (Chapters 4 and 5).
4   Incorrect ignition timing (Chapter 1).
5   Check for cracked distributor cap, disconnected distributor wires and damaged distributor components (Chapter 1).
6   Defective spark plug wires (Chapter 1).
7   Faulty emissions system components (Chapter 6).
8   Low or uneven cylinder compression pressures. Remove the spark plugs and test the compression with a gauge (Chapter 2).
9   Weak or faulty ignition system (Chapter 5).
10 Vacuum leaks at the carburetor/throttle body, intake manifold or vacuum hoses (see Section 8).

11   Engine stalls

1   Idle speed incorrect. Refer to the VECI label and Chapter 1.
2   Fuel filter clogged and/or water and impurities in the fuel system (Chapter 1).
3   Distributor components damp or damaged (Chapter 5).
4   Fault in the fuel system or sensors (Chapters 4 and 6).
5   Faulty emissions system components (Chapter 6).
6   Faulty or incorrectly gapped spark plugs (Chapter 1). Also check the spark plug wires (Chapter 1).
7   Vacuum leak at the carburetor/throttle body, intake manifold or vacuum hoses. Check as described in Section 8.

12   Engine lacks power

1   Incorrect ignition timing (Chapter 1).
2   Fault in the fuel or electrical systems (Chapters 4 and 5).
3   Excessive play in the distributor shaft. At the same time, check for a damaged rotor, faulty distributor cap, wires, etc. (Chapters 1 and 5).
4   Faulty or incorrectly gapped spark plugs (Chapter 1).
5   Carburetor not adjusted properly or excessively worn (carbureted models) (Chapter 4).
6   Faulty coil (Chapter 5).
7   Brakes binding (Chapter 1).
8   Automatic transaxle fluid level incorrect (Chapter 1).
9   Clutch slipping (Chapter 8).
10 Fuel filter clogged and/or impurities in the fuel system (Chapter 1).
11 Emissions control system not functioning properly (Chapter 6).
12 Use of substandard fuel. Fill the tank with the proper octane fuel.
13 Low or uneven cylinder compression pressures. Test with a compression tester, which will detect leaking valves and/or a blown head gasket (Chapter 2).

13   Engine backfires

1   Emissions system not functioning properly (Chapter 6).
2   Fault in the fuel or electrical systems (Chapters 4 and 5).

3   Ignition timing incorrect (Chapter 1).
4   Faulty secondary ignition system (cracked spark plug insulator, faulty plug wires, distributor cap and/or rotor) (Chapters 1 and 5).
5   Carburetor or fuel injection system in need of adjustment or worn excessively (Chapter 4).
6   Vacuum leak at the carburetor/throttle body, intake manifold or vacuum hoses. Check as described in Section 8.
7   Valves sticking (Chapter 2).

14   Pinging or knocking engine sounds during acceleration or uphill

1   Incorrect grade of fuel. Fill the tank with fuel of the proper octane rating.
2   Fault in the fuel or electrical systems (Chapters 4 and 5).
3   Ignition timing incorrect (Chapter 1).
4   Carburetor in need of adjustment (carbureted models) (Chapter 4).
5   Improper spark plugs. Check the plug type against the VECI label located in the engine compartment. Also check the plugs and wires for damage (Chapter 1).
6   Worn or damaged distributor components (Chapter 5).
7   Faulty emissions system (Chapter 6).
8   Vacuum leak. Check as described in Section 9.

15   Engine diesels (continues to run) after switching off

1   Idle speed too high. Refer to Chapter 1.
2   Fault in the fuel or electrical systems (Chapters 4 and 5).
3   Ignition timing incorrectly adjusted (Chapter 1).
4   Thermo-controlled air cleaner heat valve not operating properly (Chapters 1 and 6).
5   Excessive engine operating temperature. Probable causes of this are a malfunctioning thermostat, clogged radiator, faulty water pump (see Chapter 3).

Engine electrical system

16   Battery will not hold a charge

1   Alternator drivebelt defective or not adjusted properly (Chapter 1).
2   Electrolyte level low or battery discharged (Chapter 1).
3   Battery terminals loose or corroded (Chapter 1).
4   Alternator not charging properly (Chapter 5).
5   Loose, broken or faulty wiring in the charging circuit (Chapter 5).
6   Short in the vehicle wiring causing a continual drain on battery (refer to Chapter 12 and the Wiring Diagrams).
7   Battery defective internally.

17   Ignition light fails to go out

1   Fault in the alternator or charging circuit (Chapter 5).
2   Alternator drivebelt defective or not properly adjusted (Chapter 1).

18   Ignition light fails to come on when key is turned on

1   Instrument cluster warning light bulb defective (Chapter 12).
2   Alternator faulty (Chapter 5).
3   Fault in the instrument cluster printed circuit, dashboard wiring or bulb holder (Chapter 12).

Fuel system

19 Excessive fuel consumption

1 Dirty or clogged air filter element (Chapter 1).
2 Incorrectly set ignition timing (Chapter 1).
3 Choke sticking or improperly adjusted (carbureted models) (see Chapter 1).
4 Emissions system not functioning properly (Chapter 6).
5 Fault in the fuel or electrical systems (Chapters 4 and 5).
6 Carburetor or fuel injection system internal parts excessively worn or damaged (Chapter 4).
7 Low tire pressure or incorrect tire size (Chapter 1).

20 Fuel leakage and/or fuel odor

1 Leak in a fuel feed or vent line (Chapter 4).
2 Tank overfilled. Fill only to automatic shut-off.
3 Evaporative emissions system canister clogged (Chapter 6).
4 Vapor leaks from system lines (Chapter 4).
5 Carburetor or fuel injection system internal parts excessively worn or out of adjustment (Chapter 4).

Cooling system

21 Overheating

1 Insufficient coolant in the system (Chapter 1).
2 Water pump drivebelt defective or not adjusted properly (Chapter 1).
3 Radiator core blocked or radiator grille dirty and restricted (see Chapter 3).
4 Thermostat faulty (Chapter 3).
5 Fan blades broken or cracked (Chapter 3).
6 Radiator cap not maintaining proper pressure. Have the cap pressure tested by gas station or repair shop.
7 Ignition timing incorrect (Chapter 1).

22 Overcooling

Thermostat faulty (Chapter 3).

23 External coolant leakage

1 Deteriorated or damaged hoses or loose clamps. Replace hoses and/or tighten the clamps at the hose connections (Chapter 1).
2 Water pump seals defective. If this is the case, water will drip from the weep hole in the water pump body (Chapter 3).
3 Leakage from radiator core or header tank. This will require the radiator to be professionally repaired (see Chapter 3 for removal procedures).
4 Engine drain plug leaking (Chapter 1) or water jacket core plugs leaking (see Chapter 2).

24 Internal coolant leakage

Note: *Internal coolant leaks can usually be detected by examining the oil. Check the dipstick and inside of the cylinder head cover for water deposits and an oil consistency like that of a milkshake.*

1 Leaking cylinder head gasket. Have the cooling system pressure tested.
2 Cracked cylinder bore or cylinder head. Dismantle the engine and inspect (Chapter 2).

25 Coolant loss

1 Too much coolant in the system (Chapter 1).
2 Coolant boiling away due to overheating (see Section 15).
3 External or internal leakage (see Sections 23 and 24).
4 Faulty radiator cap. Have the cap pressure tested.

26 Poor coolant circulation

1 Inoperative water pump. A quick test is to pinch the top radiator hose closed with your hand while the engine is idling, then let it loose. You should feel the surge of coolant if the pump is working properly (see Chapter 1).
2 Restriction in the cooling system. Drain, flush and refill the system (Chapter 1). If necessary, remove the radiator (Chapter 3) and have it reverse flushed.
3 Water pump drivebelt defective or not adjusted properly (Chapter 1).
4 Thermostat sticking (Chapter 3).

Clutch

27 Fails to release (pedal pressed to the floor – shift lever does not move freely in and out of Reverse)

1 Leak in the clutch hydraulic system. Check the master cylinder, slave cylinder and lines (Chapter 8).
2 Clutch plate warped or damaged (Chapter 8).
3 Worn or dry clutch release shaft bushing (Chapter 8).

28 Clutch slips (engine speed increases with no increase in vehicle speed)

1 Linkage out of adjustment (Chapter 8).
2 Clutch plate oil soaked or lining worn. Remove clutch (Chapter 8) and inspect.
3 Clutch plate not seated. It may take 30 or 40 normal starts for a new one to seat.

29 Grabbing (chattering) as clutch is engaged

1 Oil on clutch plate lining. Remove (Chapter 8) and inspect. Correct any leakage source.
2 Worn or loose engine or transaxle mounts. These units move slightly when the clutch is released. Inspect the mounts and bolts (Chapter 2).
3 Worn splines on clutch plate hub. Remove the clutch components (Chapter 8) and inspect.
4 Warped pressure plate or flywheel. Remove the clutch components and inspect.

30 Squeal or rumble with clutch fully disengaged (pedal depressed)

1 Worn, defective or broken release bearing (Chapter 8).
2 Worn or broken pressure plate springs (or diaphragm fingers) (Chapter 8).

31   Clutch pedal stays on floor when disengaged

Linkage or release bearing binding. Inspect the linkage or remove the clutch components as necessary.

Manual transaxle

32   Noisy in Neutral with engine running

1   Input shaft bearing worn.
2   Damaged main drive gear bearing.
3   Worn countershaft bearings.
4   Worn or damaged countershaft end play shims.

33   Noisy in all gears

1   Any of the above causes, and/or:
2   Insufficient lubricant (see the checking procedures in Chapter 1).

34   Noisy in one particular gear

1   Worn, damaged or chipped gear teeth for that particular gear.
2   Worn or damaged synchronizer for that particular gear.

35   Slips out of high gear

1   Transaxle loose on clutch housing (Chapter 7).
2   Shift rods interfering with the engine mounts or clutch lever (see Chapter 7).
3   Shift rods not working freely (Chapter 7).
4   Dirt between the transaxle case and engine or misalignment of the transaxle (Chapter 7).
5   Worn or improperly adjusted linkage (Chapter 7).

36   Difficulty in engaging gears

1   Clutch not releasing completely (see clutch adjustment in Chapter 1).
2   Loose, damaged or out-of-adjustment shift linkage. Make a thorough inspection, replacing parts as necessary (Chapter 7).

37   Oil leakage

1   Excessive amount of lubricant in the transaxle (see Chapter 1 for correct checking procedures). Drain lubricant as required.
2   Driveaxle oil seal or speedometer oil seal in need of replacement (Chapter 7).

Automatic transaxle

Note: *Due to the complexity of the automatic transaxle, it's difficult for the home mechanic to properly diagnose and service this component. For problems other than the following, the vehicle should be taken to a dealer service department or a transmission shop.*

38   General shift mechanism problems

1   Chapter 7 deals with checking and adjusting the shift linkage on automatic transaxles. Common problems which may be attributed to poorly adjusted linkage are:
    Engine starting in gears other than Park or Neutral.
    Indicator on shifter pointing to a gear other than the one
        actually being selected.
    Vehicle moves when in Park.
2   Refer to Chapter 7 to adjust the linkage.

39   Transaxle will not downshift with accelerator pedal pressed to the floor

Chapter 7 deals with adjusting the throttle cable to enable the transaxle to downshift properly.

40   Transaxle slips, shifts rough, is noisy or has no drive in forward or reverse gears

1   There are many probable causes for the above problems, but the home mechanic should be concerned with only one possibility – fluid level.
2   Before taking the vehicle to a repair shop, check the level and condition of the fluid as described in Chapter 1. Correct fluid level as necessary or change the fluid and filter if needed. If the problem persists, have a professional diagnose the probable cause.

41   Fluid leakage

1   Automatic transaxle fluid is a deep red color. Fluid leaks should not be confused with engine oil, which can easily be blown by air flow to the transaxle.
2   To pinpoint a leak, first remove all built-up dirt and grime from around the transaxle. Degreasing agents and/or steam cleaning will achieve this. With the underside clean, drive the vehicle at low speeds so air flow will not blow the leak far from its source. Raise the vehicle and determine where the leak is coming from. Common areas of leakage are:
    a) Pan: Tighten the mounting bolts and/or replace the pan gasket as necessary (see Chapter 7).
    b) Filler pipe: Replace the rubber seal where the pipe enters the transaxle case.
    c) Transaxle oil lines: Tighten the connectors where the lines enter the transaxle case and/or replace the lines.
    d) Vent pipe: Transaxle overfilled and/or water in fluid (see checking procedures, Chapter 1).
    e) Speedometer connector: Replace the O-ring where the speedometer cable enters the transaxle case (Chapter 7).

Driveaxles

42   Clicking noise in turns

Worn or damaged outer joint. Check for cut or damaged seals. Repair as necessary (Chapter 8).

43   Knock or clunk when accelerating after coasting

Worn or damaged inner joint. Check for cut or damaged seals. Repair as necessary (Chapter 8).

44 Shudder or vibration during acceleration

1 Excessive joint angle. Have checked and correct as necessary (Chapter 8).
2 Worn or damaged CV joints. Repair or replace as necessary (see Chapter 8).
3 Sticking CV joint assembly. Correct or replace as necessary (see Chapter 8).

Rear axle

45 Noise

1 Road noise. No corrective procedures available.
2 Tire noise. Inspect tires and check tire pressures (Chapter 1).
3 Rear wheel bearings loose, worn or damaged (Chapter 1).

Brakes

Note: *Before assuming that a brake problem exists, make sure that the tires are in good condition and inflated properly (see Chapter 1), that the front end alignment is correct and that the vehicle is not loaded with weight in an unequal manner.*

46 Vehicle pulls to one side during braking

1 Defective, damaged or oil contaminated disc brake pads on one side. Inspect as described in Chapter 9.
2 Excessive wear of brake pad material or disc on one side. Inspect and correct as necessary.
3 Loose or disconnected front suspension components. Inspect and tighten all bolts to the specified torque (Chapter 10).
4 Defective caliper assembly. Remove the caliper and inspect for a stuck piston or other damage (Chapter 9).

47 Noise (high-pitched squeal with the brakes applied)

Disc brake pads worn out. The noise comes from the wear sensor rubbing against the disc (does not apply to all vehicles) or the actual pad backing plate itself if the material is completely worn away. Replace the pads with new ones immediately (Chapter 9). If the pad material has worn completely away, the brake discs should be inspected for damage as described in Chapter 9.

48 Excessive brake pedal travel

1 Partial brake system failure. Inspect the entire system (Chapter 9) and correct as required.
2 Insufficient fluid in the master cylinder. Check (Chapter 1), add fluid and bleed the system if necessary (Chapter 9).
3 Rear brakes not adjusting properly. Make a series of starts and stops while the vehicle is in Reverse. If this does not correct the situation, remove the drums and inspect the self-adjusters (Chapter 9).

49 Brake pedal feels spongy when depressed

1 Air in the hydraulic lines. Bleed the brake system (Chapter 9).

2 Faulty flexible hoses. Inspect all system hoses and lines. Replace parts as necessary.
3 Master cylinder mounting bolts/nuts loose.
4 Master cylinder defective (Chapter 9).

50 Excessive effort required to stop vehicle

1 Power brake booster not operating properly (Chapter 9).
2 Excessively worn linings or pads. Inspect and replace if necessary (Chapter 9).
3 One or more caliper pistons or wheel cylinders seized or sticking. Inspect and rebuild as required (Chapter 9).
4 Brake linings or pads contaminated with oil or grease. Inspect and replace as required (Chapter 9).
5 New pads or shoes installed and not yet seated. It will take a while for the new material to seat against the drum (or rotor).

51 Pedal travels to the floor with little resistance

Little or no fluid in the master cylinder reservoir caused by leaking wheel cylinder(s), leaking caliper piston(s), loose, damaged or disconnected brake lines. Inspect the entire system and correct as necessary.

52 Brake pedal pulsates during brake application

1 Caliper improperly installed. Remove and inspect (Chapter 9).
2 Disc or drum defective. Remove (Chapter 9) and check for excessive lateral runout and parallelism. Have the disc or drum resurfaced or replace it with a new one.

Suspension and steering systems

53 Vehicle pulls to one side

1 Tire pressures uneven (Chapter 1).
2 Defective tire (Chapter 1).
3 Excessive wear in suspension or steering components (Chapter 10).
4 Front end in need of alignment.
5 Front brakes dragging. Inspect the brakes as described in Chapter 9.

54 Shimmy, shake or vibration

1 Tire or wheel out-of-balance or out-of-round. Have professionally balanced.
2 Loose, worn or out-of-adjustment rear wheel bearings (Chapter 1).
3 Shock absorbers and/or suspension components worn or damaged (Chapter 10).

55 Excessive pitching and/or rolling around corners or during braking

1 Defective shock absorbers. Replace as a set (Chapter 10).
2 Broken or weak springs and/or suspension components. Inspect as described in Chapter 10.

56 Excessively stiff steering

1 Lack of fluid in power steering fluid reservoir (Chapter 1).
2 Incorrect tire pressures (Chapter 1).
3 Front end out of alignment.

57   Excessive play in steering

1   Excessive wear in suspension or steering components (Chapter 10).
2   Steering gearbox damaged (Chapter 10).

58   Lack of power assistance

1   Steering pump drivebelt faulty or not adjusted properly (Chapter 1).
2   Fluid level low (Chapter 1).
3   Hoses or lines restricted. Inspect and replace parts as necessary.
4   Air in power steering system. Bleed the system (Chapter 10).

59   Excessive tire wear (not specific to one area)

1   Incorrect tire pressures (Chapter 1).
2   Tires out-of-balance. Have professionally balanced.
3   Wheels damaged. Inspect and replace as necessary.
4   Suspension or steering components excessively worn (Chapter 10).

60   Excessive tire wear on outside edge

1   Inflation pressures incorrect (Chapter 1).
2   Excessive speed in turns.
3   Front end alignment incorrect (excessive toe-in). Have professionally aligned.
4   Suspension arm bent or twisted (Chapter 10).

61   Excessive tire wear on inside edge

1   Inflation pressures incorrect (Chapter 1).
2   Front end alignment incorrect. Have professionally aligned.
3   Loose or damaged steering components (Chapter 10).

62   Tire tread worn in one place

1   Tires out-of-balance.
2   Damaged or buckled wheel. Inspect and replace if necessary.
3   Defective tire (Chapter 1).

Chapter 1 Tune-up and routine maintenance

Contents

Specifications

Recommended lubricants and fluids

Engine oil
  Type .... API grade SG or SG/CD multigrade and fuel efficient oil
  Viscosity .... See accompanying chart
Fuel .... Unleaded gasoline, 87 octane or higher
Automatic transaxle fluid .... Dexron II ATF
Automatic transaxle differential lubricant .... Dexron II ATF
Manual transaxle lubricant .... API GL-5 SAE 75W90 or 80W90 gear oil
Brake fluid .... DOT 3 brake fluid
Clutch fluid .... DOT 3 brake fluid
Power steering system fluid .... Dexron II ATF

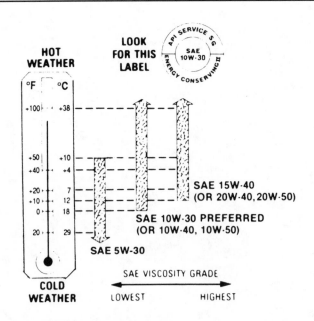

For best fuel economy and cold starting, select the lowest SAE viscosity grade oil for the expected temperature range

Ignition system

Spark plug type and gap .... Refer to the *Vehicle Emission Control Information label* in the engine compartment
Spark plug wire resistance .... Less than 25000 ohms
Ignition timing .... Refer to the *Vehicle Emission Control Information label* in the engine compartment
Firing order 1-3-4-2
Cylinder numbers (drivebelt end-to-transaxle end) 1-2-3-4

Cooling system capacity

Nova .... 6.3 Qts
Prizm .... 5.6 Qts

Accessory drivebelt tension *(with Burroughs BTG-20 95506-00020, GM J 23600-B or Nippondenso BT373F tension gauge) – used belt*

Power steering pump
  1988 DOHC engine .... 115 ± 20 lbs.
  All others .... 80 ± 20 lbs.

Alternator
    1988 DOHC engine .... 115 ± 20 lbs.
    All others .... 130 ± 20 lbs.
Air conditioning compressor
    Nova .... 80 ± 20 lbs.
    Prizm .... 100 ± 20 lbs.

Clutch pedal

Freeplay
    1985 and 1986 .... 1/2 to 29/32 in (13 to 23 mm)
    1987-on .... 3/16 to 19/32 in (5 to 15 mm)
Height
    Nova .... 5-5/32 to 6-3/64 in (144 to 154 mm)
    Prizm .... 5.71 to 6.10 in (145 to 155 mm)

Brakes

Brake pad/shoe lining thickness (minimum) .... 3/64 in (1 mm)
Parking brake adjustment
    Prizm GSI .... 5 to 8 clicks
    All others .... 4 to 7 clicks

Valve clearances*

Intake valve .... 0.008 in (0.20 mm)
Exhaust valve
    SOHC engines .... 0.012 in (0.30 mm)
    DOHC engines .... 0.010 in (0.25 mm)

* Note: *The SOHC engine must be at normal operating temperature when the valve clearances are checked/adjusted – the DOHC engine must be COLD.*

Balljoint allowable movement .... 0 in (0 mm)

Torque specifications   Ft-lbs

Automatic transaxle
    Pan bolts 4
    Filter bolts 7
    Drain plug 36
Manual transaxle drain and fill plugs 29
Fuel filter banjo bolts (fuel-injected engines only) 21
Spark plugs 13
Wheel lug nuts 76

1 Introduction

This Chapter is designed to help home mechanics maintain their vehicles with the goals of maximum performance, economy, safety and reliability in mind.

Included is a master maintenance schedule, followed by procedures dealing specifically with each item on the schedule. Visual checks, adjustments, component replacement and other helpful items are included. Refer to the accompanying illustrations of the engine compartment and the underside of the vehicle for the locations of various components.

Adhering to the mileage/time maintenance schedule and following the step-by-step procedures, which is simply a preventive maintenance program, will result in maximum reliability and vehicle service life. Keep in mind that it is a comprehensive program – maintaining some items but not others at the specified intervals will not produce the same results.

As you service the vehicle, you will discover that many of the procedures can – and should – be grouped together because of the nature of the particular procedure you're performing or because of the close proximity of two otherwise unrelated components to one another.

For example, if the vehicle is raised for chassis lubrication, you should inspect the exhaust, suspension, steering and fuel systems while you're under the vehicle. When you're rotating the tires, it makes good sense to check the brakes, since the wheels are already removed. Finally, let's suppose you have to borrow or rent a torque wrench. Even if you only need it to tighten the spark plugs, you might as well check the torque of as many critical fasteners as time allows.

The first step in this maintenance program is to prepare yourself before the actual work begins. Read through all the procedures you're planning to do, then gather up all the parts and tools needed. If it looks like you might run into problems during a particular job, seek advice from a mechanic or an experienced do-it-yourselfer.

Engine compartment components (1985 through 1988 model 4A-LC engine shown, others similar)

1	Oil filler cap	5	Distributor	9	Automatic transaxle dipstick	13	Alternator drivebelt
2	Spark plug	6	Fuse block	10	Radiator cap	14	Windshield washer fluid reservoir
3	Brake fluid reservoir	7	Battery	11	Engine oil dipstick	15	Power steering fluid reservoir
4	Air cleaner assembly	8	Coolant reservoir	12	Engine oil filter		

Typical engine compartment under side components

1 Steering arm boot
2 Crossmember bolt
3 Automatic transaxle
  differential drain plug

4 Automatic transaxle
  differential fill plug
5 Exhaust pipe

6 Engine oil drain plug
7 Automatic transaxle
  drain plug

8 Driveaxle boot
9 Brake hose
10 Brake caliper

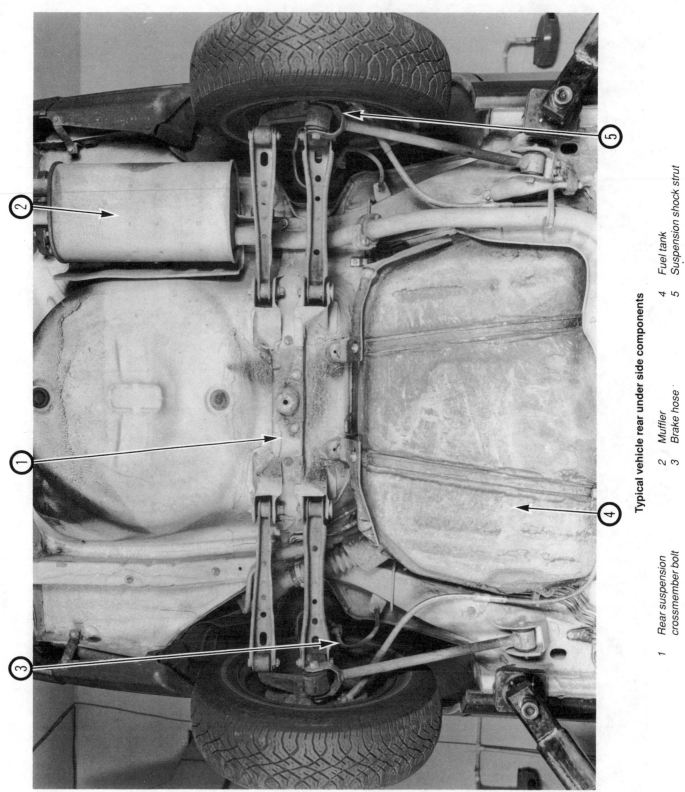

Typical vehicle rear under side components

1   Rear suspension
    crossmember bolt
2   Muffler
3   Brake hose
4   Fuel tank
5   Suspension shock strut

2 Chevrolet Nova and Geo Prizm Maintenance Schedule

The following maintenance intervals are based on the assumption that the vehicle owner will be doing the maintenance or service work, as opposed to having a dealer service department do the work. Although the time/mileage intervals are loosely based on factory recommendations, most have been shortened to ensure, for example, that such items as filters, lubricants and fluids are checked/changed at intervals that promote maximum engine/driveline service life. Also, subject to the preference of the individual owner interested in keeping his or her vehicle in peak condition at all times, and with the vehicle's ultimate resale in mind, many of the maintenance procedures may be performed more often than recommended in the following schedule. We encourage such owner initiative.

When the vehicle is new it should be serviced initially by a factory authorized dealer service department to protect the factory warranty. In many cases the initial maintenance check is done at no cost to the owner (check with your dealer service department for more information).

Every 250 miles or weekly, whichever comes first

Check the engine oil level (Section 4)
Check the engine coolant level (Section 4)
Check the windshield washer fluid level (Section 4)
Check the brake fluid level (Section 4)
Check the tires and tire pressures (Section 5)

Every 3500 miles or 3 months, whichever comes first

All items listed above, plus :
Check the power steering fluid level (Section 6)
Check the automatic transaxle fluid level (Section 7)
Change the engine oil and oil filter (Section 8)

Every 7500 miles or 6 months, whichever comes first

Inspect/replace the windshield wiper blades (Section 9)
Check/adjust the clutch pedal freeplay and fluid level (Section 10)
Check and service the battery (Section 11)
Check/adjust the engine drivebelts (Section 12)
Inspect/replace all underhood hoses (Section 13)
Check the cooling system (Section 14)
Rotate the tires (Section 15)
Inspect the brakes (Section 16)
Check/adjust the engine idle speed (Section 30)***

Every 15,000 miles or 12 months, whichever comes first

All items listed above, plus :
Check/replace the air filter (Section 17)
Replace the fuel filter (Section 18)
Inspect the fuel system (Section 19)
Inspect the steering and suspension components (Section 20)*
Check the driveaxle boots (Section 21)*

Inspect the exhaust system (Section 22)
Check the manual transaxle lubricant level (Section 23)
Check/adjust the valve clearances (Section 24)

Every 30,000 miles or 24 months, whichever comes first

Check/replace the spark plugs (Section 25)
Inspect/replace the spark plug wires, distributor cap and rotor (Section 26)*
Check the carburetor choke (Section 27)
Check the thermostatically controlled air cleaner (Section 28)
Replace the drivebelts for the water pump and alternator (Section 12)
Drain, flush and refill the cooling system (Section 29)
Check/adjust the engine idle speed (Section 30)
If the vehicle is equipped with an automatic transaxle, change the fluid and filter (Section 31)**
If the vehicle is equipped with a manual transaxle, drain it and refill with new lubricant (Section 32)
Check the throttle positioner system (Section 33)

Every 50,000 miles or 40 months, whichever comes first

Inspect the evaporative emissions control system and replace the canister (Section 34)
Check/adjust the ignition timing (Chapter 5)
Check/replace the PCV valve (Section 35)
Replace the oxygen sensor (Section 36)

Every 60,000 miles or 48 months, whichever comes first

Install a new timing belt (Chapter 2, Part A)
Replace the fuel tank cap gasket (Section 37)

This item is affected by "severe" operating conditions as described below. If the vehicle in question is operated under "severe" conditions, perform all maintenance indicated with an asterisk (*) at 7500 mile/6 month intervals.
Consider the conditions "severe" if most driving is done . . .
In dusty areas
When towing a trailer
At low speeds or with extended periods of engine idling
When outside temperatures remain below freezing and most trips are less than four miles

** *If most driving is done under one or more of the following conditions, change the automatic transaxle fluid every 15,000 miles:*
In heavy city traffic where the outside temperature regularly reaches 90-degrees F (32-degrees C) or higher
In hilly or mountainous terrain
Frequent trailer pulling

*** *Perform at this mileage one time only*

3   Tune-up general information

The term tune-up is used in this manual to represent a combination of individual operations rather than one specific procedure.

If, from the time the vehicle is new, the routine maintenance schedule is followed closely and frequent checks are made of fluid levels and high wear items, as suggested throughout this manual, the engine will be kept in relatively good running condition and the need for additional work will be minimized.

More likely than not, however, there will be times when the engine is running poorly due to lack of regular maintenance. This is even more likely if a used vehicle, which has not received regular and frequent maintenance checks, is purchased. In such cases, an engine tune-up will be needed outside of the regular routine maintenance intervals.

The first step in any tune-up or diagnostic procedure to help correct a poor running engine is a cylinder compression check (see Chapter 2). This check will help determine the condition of internal engine components and should be used as a guide for tune-up and repair procedures. For instance, if a compression check indicates serious internal engine wear, a conventional tune-up will not improve the performance of the engine and would be a waste of time and money. Because of its importance, the compression check should be done by someone with the right equipment and the knowledge to use it properly.

The following procedures are those most often needed to bring a generally poor running engine back into a proper state of tune.

Minor tune-up

Check all engine related fluids (Section 4)
Check the air filter (Section 17)
Clean, inspect and test the battery (Section 11)
Check and adjust the drivebelts (Section 12)
Check all underhood hoses (Section 13)
Check the cooling system (Section 14)
Replace the spark plugs (Section 25)
Inspect the spark plug wires, distributor cap and rotor (Section 26)
Check and adjust the idle speed (Section 30)
Check the PCV valve (Section 36)

Major tune-up

All items listed under Minor tune-up, plus . . .
Check the EGR system (Chapter 6)
Check the ignition system (Chapter 5)
Check the charging system (Chapter 5)
Check the fuel system (Chapter 4)
Replace the air filter (Section 17)
Replace the distributor cap and rotor (Section 26)
Replace the spark plug wires (Section 26)

4   Fluid level checks

Note: *The following fluid level checks should be done on a 250 mile or weekly basis. Additional fluid level checks can be found in specific maintenance procedures which follow. Regardless of intervals, be alert for fluid leaks under the vehicle which would indicate a leak to be fixed immediately.*

Warning: *The electric cooling fan can activate at any time, even when the ignition is in the Off position. Disconnect the fan motor or negative battery cable when working in the vicinity of the fan.*

1   Fluids are an essential part of the lubrication, cooling, brake and windshield washer systems. Because the fluids gradually become depleted and/or contaminated during normal operation of the vehicle, they must be periodically replenished. See Recommended lubricants and fluids at the beginning of this Chapter before adding fluid to any of the following components. **Note:** *The vehicle must be on level ground when fluid levels are checked.*

Engine oil

Refer to illustrations 4.2, 4.4 and 4.6

2   The engine oil level is checked with a dipstick located at the drivebelt end of the engine **(see illustration)**. It extends through a tube and into the oil pan at the bottom of the engine.

3   The oil level should be checked before the vehicle has been started, or about 15 minutes after the engine has been shut off. If the oil is checked immediately after driving the vehicle, some of the oil will remain in the upper part of the engine, resulting in an inaccurate reading on the dipstick.

4.2   The engine oil dipstick is at the drivebelt end of the engine

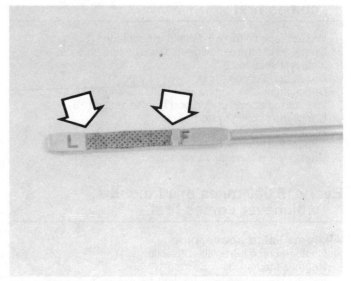

4.4   The oil level should be between the L and F marks (arrows) – if it isn't, add enough oil to bring the level up to or near the full (F) mark (it takes one quart to raise the level from the L to the F mark)

4.6 Turn the oil filler cap counterclockwise to remove it – always make sure the area around the opening is clean before unscrewing the cap (to prevent dirt from contaminating the engine)

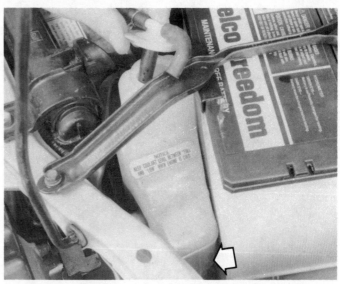

4.8 Make sure the coolant level in the reservoir is above the Low mark (arrow) – if it's below the mark, add more antifreeze/water mixture

4   Pull the dipstick out and wipe all the oil off the end with a clean rag or paper towel. Insert the clean dipstick all the way back into the tube, then pull it out again. Note the oil at the end of the dipstick. Add oil as necessary to keep the level between the L mark and the F mark on the dipstick **(see illustration)**.

5   Don't overfill the engine by adding too much oil, since it may result in oil fouled spark plugs, oil leaks or oil seal failures.

6   Oil is added to the engine after removing the cap from the camshaft cover **(see illustration)**. An oil can spout or funnel may help to reduce spills.

7   Checking the oil level is an important preventive maintenance step. A consistently low oil level indicates oil leakage through damaged seals, defective gaskets or past worn rings or valve guides. If the oil looks milky in color or has water droplets in it, the cylinder head gasket may be blown or the head or block may be cracked. The engine should be checked immediately. The condition of the oil should also be noted. Whenever you check the oil level, slide your thumb and index finger up the dipstick before wiping off the oil. If you see small dirt or metal particles clinging to the dipstick, the oil should be changed (see Section 8).

Engine coolant

Refer to illustration 4.8

Warning: *Do not allow antifreeze to come in contact with your skin or painted surfaces of the vehicle. Flush contaminated areas immediately with plenty of water. Don't store new coolant or leave old coolant lying around where it's accessible to children or pets – they're attracted by its sweet taste. Ingestion of even a small amount of coolant can be fatal! Wipe up garage floor and drip pan coolant spills immediately. Keep antifreeze containers covered and repair leaks in your cooling system as soon as they are noted.*

8   All vehicles covered by this manual are equipped with a pressurized coolant recovery system. A white plastic coolant reservoir located near the battery in the engine compartment is connected by a hose to the radiator filler neck **(see illustration)**. If the engine overheats, coolant escapes through a valve in the radiator cap and travels through the hose into the reservoir. As the engine cools, the coolant is automatically drawn back into the cooling system to maintain the correct level.

9   The coolant level in the reservoir should be checked regularly. **Warning:** *Do not remove the radiator cap to check the coolant level when the*

engine is warm. The level in the reservoir varies with the temperature of the engine. When the engine is cold, the coolant level should be at or slightly above the LOW mark on the reservoir **(see illustration 4.8).** Once the engine has warmed up, the level should be above the LOW mark but below the top of the reservoir. If it isn't, allow the engine to cool, then remove the cap from the reservoir and add a 50/50 mixture of ethylene glycol-based antifreeze and water.

10   Drive the vehicle and recheck the coolant level. If only a small amount of coolant is required to bring the system up to the proper level, water can be used. However, repeated additions of water will dilute the antifreeze and water solution. In order to maintain the proper ratio of antifreeze and water, always top up the coolant level with the correct mixture. A clean empty plastic milk jug or bleach bottle makes an excellent container for mixing coolant. Do not use rust inhibitors or additives.

11   If the coolant level drops consistently, there may be a leak in the system. Inspect the radiator, hoses, filler cap, drain plugs and water pump (see Section 14). If no leaks are noted, have the radiator cap pressure tested by a service station.

12   If you have to remove the radiator cap, wait until the engine has cooled, then wrap a thick cloth around the cap and turn it to the first stop. If coolant or steam escapes, let the engine cool down longer, then remove the cap.

13   Check the condition of the coolant as well. It should be relatively clear. If it's brown or rust colored, the system should be drained, flushed and refilled. Even if the coolant appears to be normal, the corrosion inhibitors wear out, so it must be replaced at the specified intervals.

Windshield washer fluid

Refer to illustration 4.14

14   Fluid for the windshield washer system is located in a plastic reservoir in the engine compartment **(see illustration)**.

15   In milder climates, plain water can be used in the reservoir, but it should be kept no more than 2/3 full to allow for expansion if the water freezes. In colder climates, use windshield washer system antifreeze, available at any auto parts store, to lower the freezing point of the fluid. Mix the antifreeze with water in accordance with the manufacturer's directions on the container. **Caution:** *Don't use cooling system antifreeze – it will damage the vehicle's paint.*

16   To help prevent icing in cold weather, warm the windshield with the defroster before using the washer.

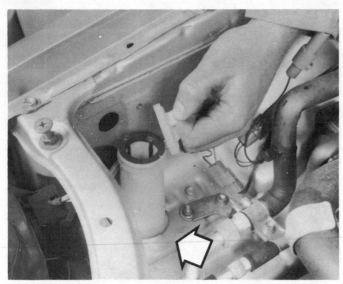

4.14   The windshield washer reservoir (arrow) is located in the right front corner of the engine compartment – be careful not to confuse it with the coolant reservoir

4.17   On conventional batteries, remove the cell caps to check the water level in the battery – if the level is low, add distilled water only

Battery electrolyte

Refer to illustration 4.17

17   All vehicles with which this manual is concerned are equipped with a battery which is permanently sealed (except for vent holes) and has no filler caps. Water doesn't have to be added to these batteries at any time. If an aftermarket maintenance-type battery is installed, the caps on top of the battery should be removed periodically to check for a low water level **(see illustration)**. This check is most critical during the warm summer months.

Brake and clutch fluid

Refer to illustrations 4.19a and 4.19b

18   The brake master cylinder is mounted on the front of the power booster unit in the engine compartment. The clutch cylinder on manual transaxle models is located adjacent to the brake master cylinder.

19   The fluid inside the reservoirs is readily visible. The level of the brake master cylinder reservoir should be between the MIN and MAX marks on the reservoir **(see illustration)**. The fluid level in the clutch reservoir should be not less than 0.2 in (5 mm) below the maximum level line **(see illustration)**. If a low level is indicated in either reservoir, be sure to wipe the top of the reservoir cover with a clean rag to prevent contamination of the system before removing the cover.

20   When adding fluid, pour it carefully into the reservoir to avoid spilling it onto surrounding painted surfaces. Be sure the specified fluid is used, since mixing different types of brake fluid can cause damage to the system. See Recommended lubricants and fluids at the front of this Chapter or your owner's manual. **Warning:** *Brake fluid can harm your eyes and damage painted surfaces, so use extreme caution when handling or pouring it. Do not use brake fluid that has been standing open or is more than one year old. Brake fluid absorbs moisture from the air. Excess moisture can cause a dangerous loss of braking effectiveness.*

4.19a   The brake fluid level should be kept between the Max and Min marks (arrows) – pry the cap off to add fluid

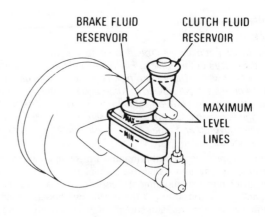

4.19b   The clutch fluid should not be lower than 5 mm below the Max line

21   At this time the fluid and master cylinder can be inspected for contamination. The system should be drained, refilled and bled if deposits or dirt particles are seen in the fluid (see Chapter 9 for brakes and Chapter 8 for clutch).

22   After filling the reservoir to the proper level, make sure the cover is on tight to prevent fluid leakage.

23   The brake fluid level in the master cylinder will drop slightly as the pads and the brake shoes at each wheel wear down during normal operation. If either master cylinder requires repeated additions to keep it at the proper level, it's an indication of leakage in the system, which should be corrected immediately. Check all fluid lines and connections (see Section 16 for more information).

24   If, upon checking the master cylinder fluid level, you discover the reservoir empty or nearly empty, the hydraulic system should be inspected for leaks and the system should be bled (see Chapters 8 and 9).

5   Tire and tire pressure checks

Refer to illustrations 5.2, 5.3, 5.4a, 5.4b and 5.8

1   Periodic inspection of the tires may spare you the inconvenience of being stranded with a flat tire. It can also provide you with vital information regarding possible problems in the steering and suspension systems before major damage occurs.

2   The original tires on this vehicle are equipped with 1/2-inch side bands that will appear when tread depth reaches 1/16-inch, but they don't appear until the tires are worn out. Tread wear can be monitored with a simple, inexpensive device known as a tread depth indicator **(see illustration)**.

3   Note any abnormal tread wear **(see illustration)**. Tread pattern irregularities such as cupping, flat spots and more wear on one side than the

other are indications of front end alignment and/or balance problems. If any of these conditions are noted, take the vehicle to a tire shop or service station to correct the problem.

4   Look closely for cuts, punctures and embedded nails or tacks. Sometimes a tire will hold air pressure for a short time or leak down very slowly after a nail has embedded itself in the tread. If a slow leak persists, check

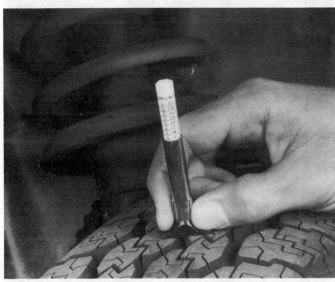

5.2   A tire tread depth indicator should be used to monitor tire wear – they're available at auto parts stores and service stations and cost very little

Condition	Probable cause	Corrective action	Condition	Probable cause	Corrective action
Shoulder wear	• Underinflation (both sides wear) • Incorrect wheel camber (one side wear) • Hard cornering • Lack of rotation	• Measure and adjust pressure. • Repair or replace axle and suspension parts. • Reduce speed. • Rotate tires.	Feathered edge Toe wear	• Incorrect toe	• Adjust toe-in.
Center wear	• Overinflation • Lack of rotation	• Measure and adjust pressure. • Rotate tires.	Uneven wear	• Incorrect camber or caster • Malfunctioning suspension • Unbalanced wheel • Out-of-round brake drum • Lack of rotation	• Repair or replace axle and suspension parts. • Repair or replace suspension parts. • Balance or replace. • Turn or replace. • Rotate tires.

5.3   This chart will help you determine the condition of the tires, the probable cause(s) of abnormal wear and the corrective action necessary

5.4a   If a tire loses air on a steady basis, check the valve core first to make sure it's snug (special inexpensive wrenches are commonly available at auto parts stores and service stations)

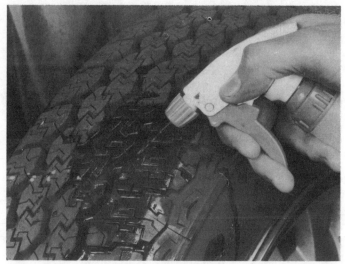

5.4b   If the valve core is tight, raise the corner of the vehicle with the low tire and spray a soapy water solution onto the tread as the tire is turned slowly – leaks will cause small bubbles to appear

the valve stem core to make sure it's tight **(see illustration)**. Examine the tread for an object that may have embedded itself in the tire or for a "plug" that may have begun to leak (radial tire punctures are sometimes repaired with a plug that's installed in a puncture). If a puncture is suspected, it can be easily verified by spraying a solution of soapy water onto the suspected area **(see illustration)**. The soapy solution will bubble if there's a leak. Unless the puncture is unusually large, a tire shop or service station can usually repair the tire.

5   Carefully inspect the inner sidewall of each tire for evidence of brake fluid. If you see any, inspect the brakes immediately.

6   Correct air pressure adds miles to the lifespan of the tires, improves mileage and enhances overall ride quality. Tire pressure cannot be accurately estimated by looking at a tire, especially if it's a radial. A tire pressure gauge is essential. Keep an accurate gauge in the vehicle. The pressure gauges attached to the nozzles of air hoses at gas stations are often inaccurate.

7   Always check tire pressure when the tires are cold. Cold, in this case, means the vehicle has not been driven over a mile in the three hours preceding a tire pressure check. A pressure rise of four to eight pounds is not uncommon once the tires are warm.

8   Unscrew the valve cap protruding from the wheel or hubcap and push the gauge firmly onto the valve stem **(see illustration)**. Note the reading on the gauge and compare the figure to the recommended tire pressure shown on the label attached to the inside of the glove compartment door. Be sure to reinstall the valve cap to keep dirt and moisture out of the valve stem mechanism. Check all four tires and, if necessary, add enough air to bring them up to the recommended pressure.

9   Don't forget to keep the spare tire inflated to the specified pressure (refer to your owner's manual or the tire sidewall).

---

6   Power steering fluid level check

Refer to illustrations 6.2 and 6.6

Warning: *The electric cooling fan can activate at any time. Disconnect the fan motor or negative battery cable when working in the vicinity of the fan.*

1   Unlike manual steering, the power steering system relies on fluid which may, over a period of time, require replenishing.

2   The fluid reservoir for the power steering pump is located at the drivebelt side of the engine near the firewall **(see illustration)**.

5.8   To extend the life of the tires, check the air pressure at least once a week with an accurate gauge (don't forget the spare!)

6.2   The power steering reservoir (shown here with the air cleaner removed), is located near the firewall

6.6 The power steering fluid level should be kept between the Hot and Cold marks (arrows) on the dipstick

3   For the check, the front wheels should be pointed straight ahead and the engine should be off.
4   Use a clean rag to wipe off the reservoir cap and the area around the cap. This will help prevent any foreign matter from entering the reservoir during the check.
5   Remove the cap and note the dipstick attached to it.
6   Wipe off the fluid with a clean rag, reinsert the dipstick, then withdraw it and read the fluid level. The level should be between the HOT and COLD marks **(see illustration)**. Never allow the fluid level to drop below the COLD mark.
7   If additional fluid is required, pour the specified type directly into the reservoir, using a funnel to prevent spills.
8   If the reservoir requires frequent fluid additions, all power steering hoses, hose connections and the power steering pump and rack should be carefully checked for leaks.

7   Automatic transaxle fluid level check

Refer to illustrations 7.4 and 7.6
Warning: *The electric cooling fan can activate at any time. Disconnect the fan motor or negative battery cable when working in the vicinity of the fan.*
1   The level of the automatic transaxle fluid should be carefully maintained. Low fluid level can lead to slipping or loss of drive, while overfilling can cause foaming, loss of fluid and transaxle damage.
2   The transaxle fluid level should be checked when the engine is at normal operating temperature. **Caution:** *If the vehicle has just been driven for a long time at high speed or in city traffic in hot weather, or if it has been pulling a trailer, an accurate fluid level reading cannot be obtained. Allow the fluid to cool for about 30 minutes.*
3   Park on level ground, apply the parking brake and start the engine. While the engine is idling, depress the brake pedal and move the selector lever through all the gear ranges, beginning and ending in Park.
4   With the engine still idling, remove the dipstick **(see illustration)**.
5   Wipe the fluid off the dipstick with a clean rag and reinsert it until the cap seats.
6   Pull the dipstick out again. The fluid level should be in the HOT range **(see illustration)**. If the level is at the low side of the range, add the specified automatic transmission fluid through the dipstick tube with a funnel.
7   Add the fluid a little at a time and keep checking the level until it's correct.
8   The condition of the fluid should also be checked along with the level. If the fluid at the end of the dipstick is black or a dark reddish-brown color, or if it smells burned, the fluid should be changed (see Section 31). If you're in doubt about the condition of the fluid, purchase some new fluid and compare the two for color and odor.

8   Engine oil and filter change

Refer to illustrations 8.3, 8.9, 8.14 and 8.18
1   Frequent oil changes are the most important preventive maintenance procedures that can be done by the home mechanic. As engine oil ages, it becomes diluted and contaminated, which leads to premature engine wear.
2   Although some sources recommend oil filter changes every other oil change, a new filter should be installed every time the oil is changed.

7.4 The automatic transaxle dipstick is located adjacent to the battery

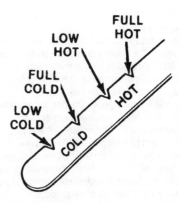

7.6 Check the fluid with the transaxle at normal operating temperature – the level should be kept in the Hot range (between the two notches)

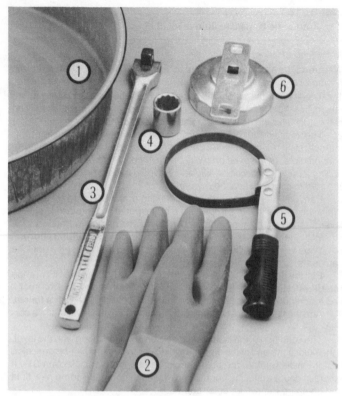

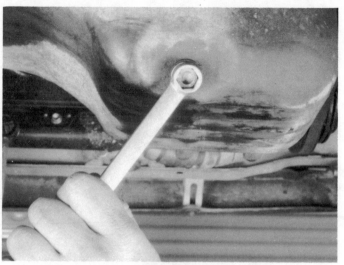

8.9 **To avoid rounding off the hex on the drain plug, use the proper size box-end wrench or a six-point socket**

8.3 **These tools are required when changing the engine oil and filter**

1 *Drain pan – It should be fairly shallow in depth, but wide to prevent spills*
2 *Rubber gloves – When removing the drain plug and filter, you will get oil on your hands (the gloves will prevent burns)*
3 *Breaker bar – Sometimes the oil drain plug is tight and a long breaker bar is needed to loosen it*
4 *Socket – To be used with the breaker bar or a ratchet (must be the correct size to fit the drain plug – 6-point preferred)*
5 *Filter wrench – This is a metal band-type wrench, which requires clearance around the filter to be effective*
6 *Filter wrench – This type fits on the bottom of the filter and can be turned with a ratchet or breaker bar (different size wrenches are available for different types of filters)*

8.14 **The oil filter is usually on very tight and will require a special wrench for removal – DO NOT use the wrench to tighten the filter**

3   Gather together all necessary tools and materials before beginning this procedure (**see illustration**).
4   You should have plenty of clean rags and newspapers handy to mop up any spills. Access to the underside of the vehicle is greatly improved if the vehicle can be lifted on a hoist, driven onto ramps or supported by jackstands. **Warning:** *Do not work under a vehicle which is supported only by a bumper, hydraulic or scissors-type jack.*
5   If this is your first oil change, get under the vehicle and familiarize yourself with the locations of the oil drain plug and the oil filter. The engine and exhaust components will be warm during the actual work, so note how they are situated to avoid touching them when working under the vehicle.
6   Warm the engine to normal operating temperature. If the new oil or any tools are needed, use this warm-up time to gather everything necessary for the job. Refer to Recommended lubricants and fluids at the beginning of this Chapter for the type of oil required.
7   With the engine oil warm (warm engine oil will drain better and more built-up sludge will be removed with it), raise and support the vehicle. Make sure it's safely supported!
8   Move all necessary tools, rags and newspapers under the vehicle. Set the drain pan under the drain plug. Keep in mind that the oil will initially flow from the pan with some force; position the pan accordingly.

9   Being careful not to touch any of the hot exhaust components, use a wrench to remove the drain plug near the bottom of the oil pan (**see illustration**). Depending on how hot the oil is, you may want to wear gloves while unscrewing the plug the final few turns.
10   Allow the old oil to drain into the pan. It may be necessary to move the pan as the oil flow slows to a trickle.
11   After all the oil has drained, wipe off the drain plug with a clean rag. Small metal particles may cling to the plug and would immediately contaminate the new oil.
12   Clean the area around the drain plug opening and reinstall the plug. Tighten it securely with the wrench. If a torque wrench is available, use it to tighten the plug.
13   Move the drain pan into position under the oil filter.
14   Use the filter wrench to loosen the oil filter (**see illustration**). Chain or metal band filter wrenches may distort the filter canister, but it doesn't matter since the filter will be discarded anyway.
15   Completely unscrew the old filter. Be careful; it's full of oil. Empty the oil inside the filter into the drain pan.
16   Compare the old filter with the new one to make sure they're the same type.

22   Pour the fresh oil through the filler opening into the engine. A funnel should be used to prevent spills.
23   Pour four quarts of fresh oil into the engine. Wait a few minutes to allow the oil to drain into the pan, then check the level on the oil dipstick (see Section 4 if necessary). If the oil level is above the L mark, start the engine and allow the new oil to circulate.
24   Run the engine for only about a minute and then shut it off. Immediately look under the vehicle and check for leaks at the oil pan drain plug and around the oil filter. If either is leaking, tighten with a bit more force.
25   With the new oil circulated and the filter now completely full, recheck the level on the dipstick and add more oil as necessary.
26   During the first few trips after an oil change, make it a point to check frequently for leaks and proper oil level.
27   The old oil drained from the engine cannot be reused in its present state and should be disposed of. Oil reclamation centers, auto repair shops and gas stations will normally accept the oil, which can be refined and used again. After the oil has cooled it can be drained into a container (capped plastic jugs, topped bottles, milk cartons, etc.) for transport to a disposal site.

8.18   Lubricate the gasket with clean oil before installing the filter on the engine

17   Use a clean rag to remove all oil, dirt and sludge from the area where the oil filter mounts to the engine.
18   Apply a light coat of clean oil to the rubber gasket on the new oil filter **(see illustration)**.
19   Attach the new filter to the engine, following the tightening directions printed on the filter canister or packing box. Most filter manufacturers recommend against using a wrench due to the possibility of overtightening the filter and damaging the seal.
20   Remove all tools, rags, etc. from under the vehicle, being careful not to spill the oil in the drain pan, then lower the vehicle.
21   Move to the engine compartment and locate the oil filler cap.

9   Windshield wiper blade inspection and replacement

Refer to illustrations 9.5, 9.6a, 9.6b and 9.7

1   The windshield wiper and blade assembly should be inspected periodically for damage, loose components and cracked or worn blade elements.
2   Road film can build up on the wiper blades and affect their efficiency, so they should be washed regularly with a mild detergent solution.
3   The action of the wiping mechanism can loosen bolts, nuts and fasteners, so they should be checked and tightened, as necessary, at the same time the wiper blades are checked.
4   If the wiper blade elements are cracked, worn or warped, or no longer clean adequately, they should be replaced with new ones.
5   Lift the arm assembly away from the glass for clearance and detach the blade assembly from the arm **(see illustration)**.
6   Pull the top end of the rubber blade element down until the rubber blade is free of the end slot and you can see the replacement hole **(see illustrations)**. Remove the rubber blade from the frame and discard it.

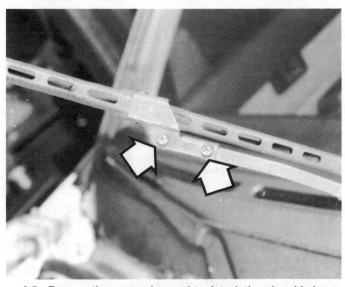

9.5   Remove the screws (arrows) to detach the wiper blade from the arm

9.6a   To remove the old wiper blade element, pull the top end of the element down until you can see the replacement hole in the frame . . .

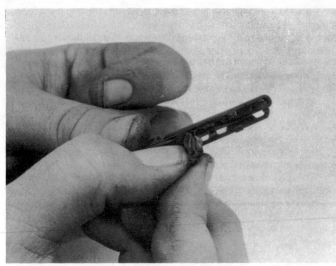

9.6b   . . . then pull the element tab out of the hole (note the
relationship to the frame) and slide the element out of the frame

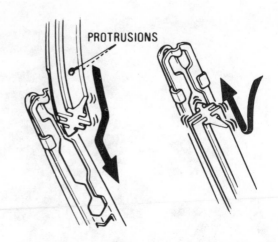

9.7   To install a new element, insert the end of the blade with the
small protrusions into the replacement hole and work the rubber
along the slot in the blade frame – once all the rubber is in the
frame slot, allow it to expand and fill in the end

7   To install a new rubber wiper element, insert the end with the small
protrusions **(see illustration)** into the replacement hole and work the rubber along the slot in the blade frame.
8   Once the rubber is in the frame slot, allow it to expand and fill in the
end.

10   Clutch pedal height and freeplay check and adjustment

Refer to illustration 10.1
1   Measure the clutch pedal height **(see illustration)** and compare the
measurement to that listed in this Chapter's specifications.
2   If the pedal height is incorrect, remove the lower dash panel and air
duct for access.

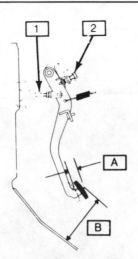

10.1   Clutch pedal adjustment details

A   *Pedal freeplay*
B   *Pedal height*
1   *Pedal freeplay adjustment point*
2   *Pedal height adjustment point*

3   Loosen the locknut and turn the adjustment bolt until the height is correct.
4   Tighten the locknut and recheck the pedal height.
5   Push down on the clutch pedal and use a small steel ruler to measure
the distance that it moves freely before the clutch resistance is felt. The
freeplay should be within the limits listed in this Chapter's specifications. If
it isn't, it must be adjusted.
6   Loosen the locknut and turn the pushrod until the freeplay is correct.
7   Tighten the locknut and recheck the freeplay. Repeat the adjustment
if necessary.
8   Reinstall the air duct and dash panel.

11   Battery check and maintenance

Refer to illustrations 11.1, 11.6, 11.7a, 11.7b and 11.7c
Warning: *Certain precautions must be followed when checking and servicing the battery. Hydrogen gas, which is highly flammable, is always present in the battery cells, so keep lighted tobacco and all other open flames
and sparks away from the battery. The electrolyte inside the battery is actually dilute sulfuric acid, which will cause injury if splashed on your skin or
in your eyes. It will also ruin clothes and painted surfaces. When removing
the battery cables, always detach the negative cable first and connect it
last!*

1   Battery maintenance is an important procedure which will help ensure
that you aren't stranded because of a dead battery. Several tools are required for this procedure **(see illustration)**.
2   When checking/servicing the battery, always turn the engine and all
accessories off.
3   A sealed (sometimes called maintenance-free), battery is standard
equipment on these vehicles. The cell caps cannot be removed, no electrolyte checks are required and water cannot be added to the cells. However, if a standard aftermarket battery has been installed, the following
maintenance procedure can be used.
4   Remove the caps and check the electrolyte level in each of the battery
cells (see Section 4). It must be above the plates. There's usually a split-
ring indicator in each cell to indicate the correct level. If the level is low, add
distilled water only, then reinstall the cell caps. **Caution:** *Overfilling the
cells may cause electrolyte to spill over during periods of heavy charging,
causing corrosion and damage to nearby components.*

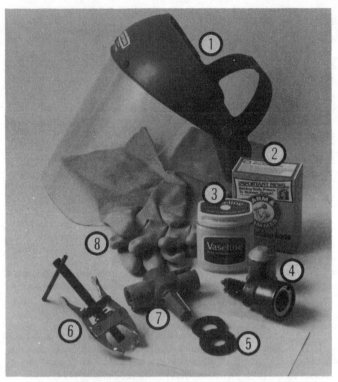

11.1 Tools and materials required for battery maintenance

1 **Face shield/safety goggles** – When removing corrosion with a brush, the acidic particles can easily fly up into your eyes
2 **Baking soda** – A solution of baking soda and water can be used to neutralize corrosion
3 **Petroleum jelly** – A layer of this on the battery posts will help prevent corrosion
4 **Battery post/cable cleaner** – This wire brush cleaning tool will remove all traces of corrosion from the battery posts and cable clamps
5 **Treated felt washers** – Placing one of these on each post, directly under the cable clamps, will help prevent corrosion
6 **Puller** – Sometimes the cable clamps are very difficult to pull off the posts, even after the nut/bolt has been completely loosened. This tool pulls the clamp straight up and off the post without damage.
7 **Battery post/cable cleaner** – Here is another cleaning tool which is a slightly different version of number 4 above, but it does the same thing
8 **Rubber gloves** – Another safety item to consider when servicing the battery; remember that's acid inside the battery!

11.6 Use a wrench to check the tightness of the battery cable bolts; when removing corroded bolts, special battery pliers may be needed

11.7a Battery terminal corrosion usually appears as light, fluffy powder

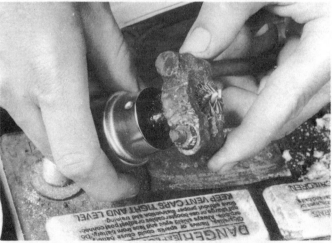

11.7b When cleaning the cable clamps, all corrosion must be removed (the inside of the clamp is tapered to match the taper on the post, so don't remove too much material)

5 The external condition of the battery should be checked periodically. Look for damage such as a cracked case.
6 Check the tightness of the battery cable bolts **(see illustration)** to ensure good electrical connections. Inspect the entire length of each cable, looking for cracked or abraded insulation and frayed conductors.
7 If corrosion (visible as white, fluffy deposits) **(see illustration)** is evident, remove the cables from the terminals, clean them with a battery brush and reinstall them **(see illustrations)**. Corrosion can be kept to a minimum by applying a layer of petroleum jelly or grease to the terminals.
8 Make sure the battery carrier is in good condition and the holddown clamp is tight. If the battery is removed (see Chapter 5 for the removal and installation procedure), make sure that no parts remain in the bottom of the carrier when it's reinstalled. When reinstalling the hold-down clamp, don't overtighten the nuts.

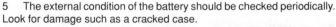

11.7c　Regardless of the type of tool used to clean the battery posts, a clean, shiny surface should be the result

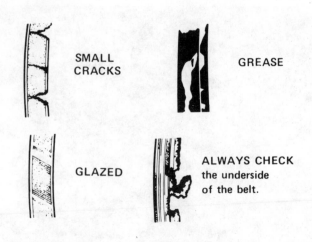

12.3　Here are some of the more common problems associated with drivebelts (check the belts very carefully to prevent an untimely breakdown)

9　Corrosion on the carrier, battery case and surrounding areas can be removed with a solution of water and baking soda. Apply the mixture with a small brush, let it work, then rinse it off with plenty of clean water.
10　Any metal parts of the vehicle damaged by corrosion should be coated with a zinc-based primer, then painted.
11　Additional information on the battery, charging and jump starting can be found in the front of this manual and in Chapter 5.
12　Always replace the battery with a like kind and size.

12　Drivebelt check, adjustment and replacement

Refer to illustrations 12.3, 12.5, 12.6a, 12.6b and 12.7
Warning: *The electric cooling fan can activate at any time. Disconnect the fan motor or negative battery cable when working in the vicinity of the fan.*

Check

1　The alternator, power steering and air conditioning compressor drivebelts, also referred to simply as "fan" belts, are located at the right (passenger's) side of the engine compartment. The condition and proper adjustment of the drivebelts is critical to the operation of the engine. Since they stretch and deteriorate as they get older, they must be inspected periodically.

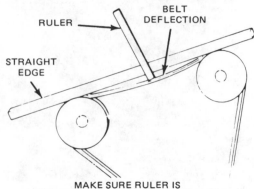

12.5　Measuring drivebelt deflection with a straightedge and ruler

2　The number of belts used on a particular vehicle depends on the accessories installed. One belt transmits power from the crankshaft to the alternator and water pump. If the vehicle is equipped with air conditioning or power steering, these are driven by separate belts.
3　With the engine off, open the hood and locate the drivebelts on the right side of the engine. With a flashlight, check each belt for separation of the adhesive rubber on both sides of the core, core separation from the belt side, a severed core, separation of the ribs from the adhesive rubber, cracking or separation of the ribs, and torn or worn ribs or cracks in the inner ridges of the ribs (**see illustration**). Also check for fraying and glazing, which gives the belt a shiny appearance. Both sides of the belt should be inspected, which means you will have to twist the belt to check the underside. Use your fingers to feel the belt where you can't see it. If any of the above conditions are evident, replace the belt (go to Step 8).
4　To check the tension of each belt in accordance with factory specifications, install a belt tension gauge on the belt (Nippondenso BTG-20, Borroughs BT-33-73F, GM J-23600-B or equivalent). Measure the tension in accordance with the manufacturer's instructions and compare your measurement to the drivebelt tension listed in this Chapter's specifications for a used belt. **Note:** *A "used" belt is defined as any belt which has been operated more than five minutes on the engine; run a new belt for at least five minutes and readjust it.*
5　If you don't have either of the special tools, and cannot borrow one, the following rule of thumb method is recommended: Push firmly on the belt with your thumb at a distance halfway between the pulleys and note how far the belt can be moved (deflected). Measure the deflection with a ruler (**see illustration**). The belt should deflect 1/4-inch if the distance from pulley center to pulley center is between 7 and 11-inches; the belt should deflect 1/2-inch if the distance from pulley center to pulley center is between 12 and 16-inches.

Adjustment

6　If the alternator or power steering pump belt must be adjusted, loosen the adjustment bolt (**see illustrations**) that secures the alternator or power steering pump to the slotted bracket and pivot the alternator or power steering pump (away from the engine block to tighten the belt, toward the block to loosen the belt). It's helpful to lever the alternator or power steering pump with a large pry bar when adjusting the belt because the pry bar enables you to precisely position the component until the adjuster bolt is tightened. Be very careful not to damage the aluminum housing of the alternator or power steering pump. Recheck the belt tension using one of the above methods. Repeat this Step until the alternator or power steering pump drivebelt tension is correct.

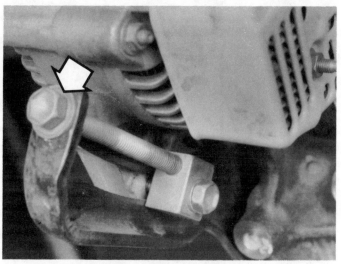

12.6a Typical alternator belt adjuster (arrow)

12.6b Typical power steering belt adjuster (arrow)

7   If the air conditioner compressor drivebelt must be adjusted, locate the idler pulley on the front right corner of the block, just above the compressor **(see illustration)**. Loosen the center bolt and turn the idler pulley adjuster bolt. Measure the belt tension in accordance with one of the above methods. Repeat this step until the air conditioning compressor drivebelt is adjusted. Tighten the center bolt.

Replacement

8   To replace a belt, follow the above procedures for drivebelt adjustment but slip the belt off the crankshaft pulley and remove it. If you're replacing the power steering belt or air conditioning compressor belt, you'll have to remove the alternator belt belt first because of the way they're arranged on the pulleys. Because of this and because belts tend to wear out more or less together, it's a good idea to replace both belts at the same time. Mark each belt and its appropriate pulley groove so the replacement belts can be installed in the proper positions.
9   Take the old belts to the parts store in order to make a direct comparison for length, width and design.
10   After replacing a new-style V-ribbed drivebelt, make sure that it fits properly in the ribbed grooves in the pulleys. It's essential that the belt be properly centered.
11   Adjust the belt(s) as described above.

12.7 Typical air conditioning compressor belt adjuster (arrow)

13   Underhood hose check and replacement

Caution: *Replacement of air conditioning hoses should be left to a dealer service department or air conditioning shop that has the equipment to depressurize the system safely. Never remove air conditioning components or hoses until the system has been depressurized.*

General

1   High temperatures in the engine compartment can cause the deterioration of the rubber and plastic hoses used for engine, accessory and emission systems operation. Periodic inspection should be made for cracks, loose clamps, material hardening and leaks.
2   Information specific to the cooling system hoses can be found in Section 14.
3   Some, but not all, hoses are secured to the fittings with clamps. Where clamps are used, check to be sure they haven't lost their tension, allowing the hose to leak. If clamps aren't used, make sure the hose has not expanded and/or hardened where it slips over the fitting, allowing it to leak.

Vacuum hoses

4   It's quite common for vacuum hoses, especially those in the emissions system, to be color coded or identified by colored stripes molded into them. Various systems require hoses with different wall thicknesses, collapse resistance and temperature resistance. When replacing hoses, be sure the new ones are made of the same material.
5   Often the only effective way to check a hose is to remove it completely from the vehicle. If more than one hose is removed, be sure to label the hoses and fittings to ensure correct installation.
6   When checking vacuum hoses, be sure to include any plastic T-fittings in the check. Inspect the fittings for cracks and the hose where it fits over the fitting for distortion, which could cause leakage.
7   A small piece of vacuum hose (1/4-inch inside diameter) can be used as a stethoscope to detect vacuum leaks. Hold one end of the hose to your ear and probe around vacuum hoses and fittings, listening for the "hissing" sound characteristic of a vacuum leak. **Warning:** *When probing with the vacuum hose stethoscope, be very careful not to come into contact with moving engine components such as the drivebelts, cooling fan, etc.*

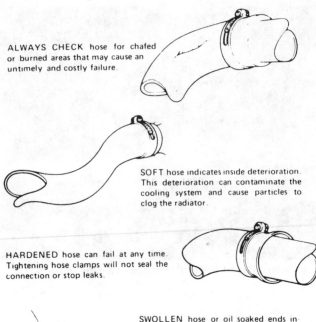

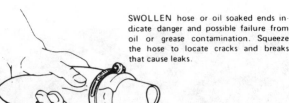

ALWAYS CHECK hose for chafed or burned areas that may cause an untimely and costly failure.

SOFT hose indicates inside deterioration. This deterioration can contaminate the cooling system and cause particles to clog the radiator.

HARDENED hose can fail at any time. Tightening hose clamps will not seal the connection or stop leaks.

SWOLLEN hose or oil soaked ends indicate danger and possible failure from oil or grease contamination. Squeeze the hose to locate cracks and breaks that cause leaks.

14.4   Hoses, like drivebelts, have a habit of failing at the worst possible time – to prevent the inconvenience of a blown radiator or heater hose, inspect them carefully as shown here

Fuel hose

Warning: *There are certain precautions which must be taken when inspecting or servicing fuel system components. Work in a well ventilated area and do not allow open flames (cigarettes, appliance pilot lights, etc.) or bare light bulbs near the work area. Mop up any spills immediately and do not store fuel soaked rags where they could ignite.*

8   Check all rubber fuel lines for deterioration and chafing. Check especially for cracks in areas where the hose bends and just before fittings, such as where a hose attaches to the fuel filter.
9   High quality fuel line, usually identified by the word Fluroelastomer printed on the hose, should be used for fuel line replacement. Never, under any circumstances, use unreinforced vacuum line, clear plastic tubing or water hose for fuel lines.
10   Spring-type clamps are commonly used on fuel lines. These clamps often lose their tension over a period of time, and can be "sprung" during removal. Replace all spring-type clamps with screw clamps whenever a hose is replaced.

Metal lines

11   Sections of metal line are often used for fuel line between the fuel pump and carburetor or fuel injectors. Check carefully to be sure the line has not been bent or crimped and that cracks have not started in the line.
12   If a section of metal fuel line must be replaced, only seamless steel tubing should be used, since copper and aluminum tubing don't have the strength necessary to withstand normal engine vibration.
13   Check the metal brake lines where they enter the master cylinder and brake proportioning unit (if used) for cracks in the lines or loose fittings. Any sign of brake fluid leakage calls for an immediate thorough inspection of the brake system.

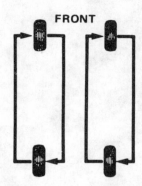

FRONT

15.2   The recommended tire rotation pattern for these vehicles

14   Cooling system check

Refer to illustration 14.4

1   Many major engine failures can be attributed to a faulty cooling system. If the vehicle is equipped with an automatic transaxle, the cooling system also cools the transmission fluid and thus plays an important role in prolonging transmission life.
2   The cooling system should be checked with the engine cold. Do this before the vehicle is driven for the day or after the engine has been shut off for at least three hours.
3   Remove the radiator cap by turning it to the left until it reaches a stop. If you hear a hissing sound (indicating there is still pressure in the system), wait until it stops. Now press down on the cap with the palm of your hand and continue turning to the left until the cap can be removed. Thoroughly clean the cap, inside and out, with clean water. Also clean the filler neck on the radiator. All traces of corrosion should be removed. The coolant inside the radiator should be relatively transparent. If it's rust colored, the system should be drained and refilled (see Section 29). If the coolant level isn't up to the top, add additional antifreeze/coolant mixture (see Section 4).
4   Carefully check the large upper and lower radiator hoses along with the smaller diameter heater hoses which run from the engine to the firewall. Inspect each hose along its entire length, replacing any hose which is cracked, swollen or shows signs of deterioration. Cracks may become more apparent if the hose is squeezed **(see illustration)**. Regardless of condition, it's a good idea to replace hoses with new ones every two years.
5   Make sure that all hose connections are tight. A leak in the cooling system will usually show up as white or rust colored deposits on the areas adjoining the leak. If wire-type clamps are used at the ends of the hoses, it may be a good idea to replace them with more secure screw-type clamps.
6   Use a garden hose or a soft brush to remove bugs, leaves, etc. from the front of the radiator or air conditioning condenser. Be careful not to damage the delicate cooling fins or cut yourself on them.
7   Every other inspection, or at the first indication of cooling system problems, have the cap and system pressure tested. If you don't have a pressure tester, most gas stations and repair shops will do this for a minimal charge.

15   Tire rotation

Refer to illustration 15.2

1   The tires should be rotated at the specified intervals and whenever uneven wear is noticed. Since the vehicle will be raised and the tires removed anyway, check the brakes (see Section 16) at this time.
2   Radial tires must be rotated in a specific pattern **(see illustration)**.
3   Refer to the information in Jacking and Towing at the front of this manual for the proper procedures to follow when raising the vehicle and changing a tire. If the brakes are to be checked, do not apply the parking brake as stated. Make sure the tires are blocked to prevent the vehicle from rolling.

16.5   You'll find inspection holes in each caliper – placing a steel rule across the hole should enable you to determine the thickness of the remaining pad material for both the inner and outer pads (arrows)

16.12   The rear brake shoe lining thickness is measured from the outer surface of the lining to the metal shoe (arrows)

4   Preferably, the entire vehicle should be raised at the same time. This can be done on a hoist or by jacking up each corner and then lowering the vehicle onto jackstands placed under the frame rails. Always use four jackstands and make sure the vehicle is firmly supported.

5   After rotation, check and adjust the tire pressures as necessary and be sure to check the lug nut tightness.

6   For further information on the wheels and tires, refer to Chapter 10.

16   Brake check

Note: *For detailed illustrations of the brake system, refer to Chapter 9.*

1   In addition to the specified intervals, the brakes should be inspected every time the wheels are removed or whenever a defect is suspected. Any of the following symptoms could indicate a potential brake system defect: The vehicle pulls to one side when the brake pedal is depressed; the brakes make squealing or dragging noises when applied; brake travel is excessive; the pedal pulsates; brake fluid leaks, usually onto the inside of the tire or wheel.

2   Loosen the wheel lug nuts.

3   Raise the vehicle and place it securely on jackstands.

4   Remove the wheels (see Jacking and towing at the front of this book, or your owner's manual, if necessary).

Disc brakes (front or rear)

Refer to illustration 16.5

5   There are two pads – an outer and an inner – in each caliper. The pads are visible through small inspection holes in each caliper **(see illustration)**.

6   Check the pad thickness by looking at each end of the caliper and through the inspection hole in the caliper body. If the lining material is less than the specified thickness, replace the pads. **Note:** *Keep in mind that the lining material is riveted or bonded to a metal backing plate and the metal portion is not included in this measurement.*

7   If it is difficult to determine the exact thickness of the remaining pad material by the above method, or if you are at all concerned about the condition of the pads, remove the caliper(s), then remove the pads from the calipers for further inspection (refer to Chapter 9).

8   Once the pads are removed from the calipers, clean them with brake cleaner and remeasure them with a small steel pocket ruler or a vernier caliper.

9   Check the disc. Look for score marks, deep scratches and burned spots. If these conditions exist, the hub/disc assembly will have to be removed (see Chapter 9).

10   Before installing the wheels, check all brake lines and hoses for damage, wear, deformation, cracks, corrosion, leakage, bends and twists, particularly in the vicinity of the rubber hoses at the calipers. Check the clamps for tightness and the connections for leakage. Make sure that all hoses and lines are clear of sharp edges, moving parts and the exhaust system. If any of the above conditions are noted, repair, reroute or replace the lines and/or fittings as necessary (refer to Chapter 9).

Rear drum brakes

Refer to illustrations 16.12 and 16.14

11   Refer to Chapter 9 and remove the rear brake drums. **Warning:** *Brake dust produced by lining wear and deposited on brake components may contain asbestos, which is hazardous to your health. DO NOT blow it out with compressed air and DO NOT inhale it! DO NOT use gasoline or solvents to remove the dust. Brake system cleaner should be used to flush the dust into a drain pan. After the brake components are wiped clean with a damp rag, dispose of the contaminated rag(s) and solvent in a covered and labelled container. Try to use non-asbestos replacement parts whenever possible.*

12   Note the thickness of the lining material on the rear brake shoes **(see illustration)** and look for signs of contamination by brake fluid and grease. If the lining material is within 1/16-inch of the recessed rivets or metal shoes, replace the brake shoes with new ones. The shoes should also be replaced if they are cracked, glazed (shiny lining surfaces) or contaminated with brake fluid or grease. See Chapter 9 for the replacement procedure.

13   Check the shoe return and hold-down springs and the adjusting mechanism to make sure they're installed correctly and in good condition. Deteriorated or distorted springs, if not replaced, could allow the linings to drag and wear prematurely.

14   Check the wheel cylinders for leakage by carefully peeling back the rubber boots **(see illustration)**. If brake fluid is noted behind the boots, the wheel cylinders must be replaced (see Chapter 9).

16.14   Peel the wheel cylinder boot back carefully and check for leaking fluid, indicating the cylinder must be replaced or rebuilt

17.2   On carburetor-equipped engines, the top of the filter housing is removed by releasing the clips on the sides and unscrewing the wing nut in the center

15   Check the drums for cracks, score marks, deep scratches and hard spots, which will appear as small discolored areas. If imperfections cannot be removed with emery cloth, the drums must be resurfaced by an automotive machine shop (see Chapter 9 for more detailed information).
16   Refer to Chapter 9 and install the brake drums.
17   Install the wheels and tighten the wheel lug nuts finger tight.
18   Remove the jackstands and lower the vehicle.
19   Tighten the wheel lug nuts to the torque listed in this Chapter's specifications.

Parking brake

20   A simple method of checking the parking brake is to park the vehicle on a steep hill with the parking brake set and the transmission in Neutral. If the parking brake cannot prevent the vehicle from rolling, it is in need of adjustment (see Chapter 9).

---

17   Air filter replacement

Refer to illustrations 17.2 and 17.5
Warning: The electric cooling fan can activate at any time. Disconnect the fan motor or negative battery cable when working in the vicinity of the fan.
1   At the specified intervals, the air filter should be replaced with a new one. The engine air cleaner also supplies filtered air to the PCV system.
2   On carburetor-equipped engines, the filter is located on top of the carburetor and is replaced by unscrewing the wing nut, detaching the clips from the top of the filter housing and lifting off the cover (**see illustration**).
3   On fuel-injected models the air cleaner housing is mounted on the left inner fender near the shock tower. Remove the screws and lift the lid off.
4   While the top cover is off, be careful not to drop anything down into the air cleaner housing.
5   Lift the air filter element out of the housing (**see illustration**) and wipe out the inside of the air cleaner housing with a clean rag.
6   Place the new filter in the air cleaner housing. Make sure it seats properly in the bottom of the housing.
7   Install the top plate and any hoses which were disconnected. Don't overtighten the wing nut or screws.

---

18   Fuel filter replacement

Warning: Gasoline is extremely flammable, so extra precautions must be taken when working on any part of the fuel system. Do not smoke or allow

17.5   Lift out the air filter element and wipe out the inside of the air cleaner housing with a clean rag

open flames or bare light bulbs in or near the work area. Also, don't work in a garage if a natural gas-type appliance with a pilot light is present.

Carburetor-equipped engines

Refer to illustrations 18.1 and 18.2
1   The fuel filter is located on the left inner fender, below the brake master cylinder (**see illustration**).
2   For easier access, pull the filter out of the spring clip so both fittings can be reached (**see illustration**).
3   Release the hose clamps at the filter fittings and slide them back up the hoses.
4   Disconnect the hoses and remove the filter. Now would be a good time to replace the hoses if they're deteriorated.
5   Push the hoses onto the new filter and position the clamps approximately 1/4-inch back from the ends.
6   Push the filter back into the spring clip. Check to make sure it's held securely and the hoses aren't kinked.
7   Start the engine and check for fuel leaks at the filter.

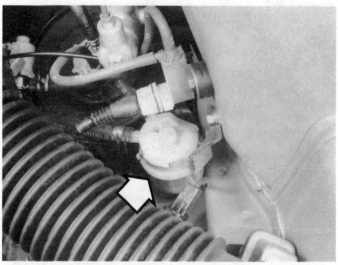

18.1 The fuel filter is mounted on the left inner fender, below the brake master cylinder (arrow)

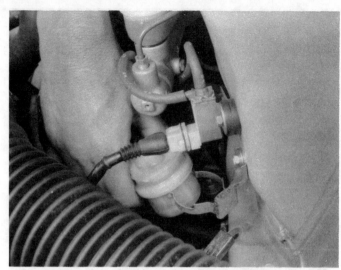

18.2 Unsnap the fuel filter from the clip and pull it out for better access to the hoses

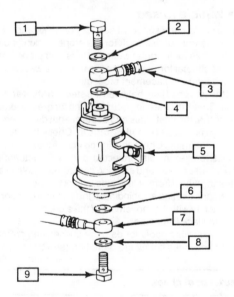

18.8 Fuel filter mounting details (fuel-injected models)

1	Banjo fitting bolt	6	Crush washer
2	Crush washer	7	Fuel line
3	Fuel line	8	Crush washer
4	Crush washer	9	Banjo fitting bolt
5	Filter		

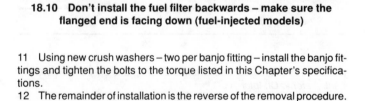

18.10 Don't install the fuel filter backwards – make sure the flanged end is facing down (fuel-injected models)

11 Using new crush washers – two per banjo fitting – install the banjo fittings and tighten the bolts to the torque listed in this Chapter's specifications.
12 The remainder of installation is the reverse of the removal procedure.
13 Start the engine and check for fuel leaks at the filter.

19 Fuel system check

Warning: *Certain precautions should be observed when inspecting or servicing the fuel system components. Work in a well ventilated area and do not allow open flames (cigarettes, appliance pilot lights, etc.) near the work area. Mop up spills immediately and do not store fuel soaked rags where they could ignite. It is a good idea to keep a dry chemical (Class B) fire extinguisher near the work area any time the fuel system is being serviced.*

1 If you smell gasoline while driving or after the vehicle has been sitting in the sun, inspect the fuel system immediately.
2 Remove the gas filler cap and inspect if for damage and corrosion. The gasket should have an unbroken sealing imprint.

Fuel-injected engines

Refer to illustrations 18.8 and 18.10
Warning: *Before removing the fuel filter, the fuel system pressure must be relieved – refer to Chapter 4 for the procedure. Wear eye protection.*

8 Loosen the banjo fitting bolts **(see illustration)** on both ends of the fuel filter (use a back-up wrench on the fitting at the filter). Disconnect both ends.
9 Remove the bracket bolts from the inner fender and remove the filter assembly from the support bracket.
10 Install the new filter assembly and tighten the bracket bolts securely. Make sure the filter is installed with the outlet facing up **(see ilustration)**.

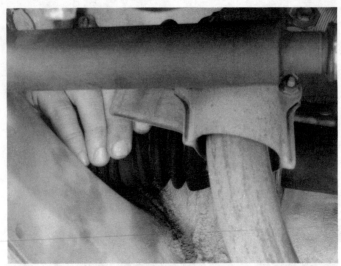

20.6   Push on the steering gear boot to check for cracks and lubricant leaks

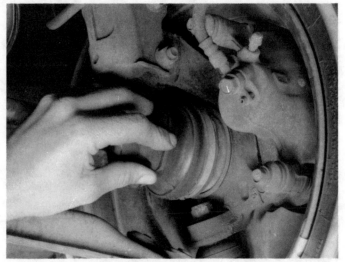

21.2   Flex the driveaxle boots by hand to check for cracks and leaking grease

3   Inspect the fuel feed and return lines for cracks. Check the metal fuel line connections to make sure they are tight.

4   Since some components of the fuel system – the fuel tank and part of the fuel feed and return lines, for example – are underneath the vehicle, they can be inspected more easily with the vehicle raised on a hoist. If that's not possible, raise the vehicle and secure it on jackstands.

5   With the vehicle raised and safely supported, inspect the gas tank and filler neck for punctures, cracks and other damage. The connection between the filler neck and the tank is particularly critical. Sometimes a rubber filler neck will leak because of loose clamps or deteriorated rubber. These are problems a home mechanic can usually rectify. **Warning:** *Do not, under any circumstances, try to repair a fuel tank (except rubber components). A welding torch or any open flame can easily cause fuel vapors inside the tank to explode.*

6   Carefully check all rubber hoses and metal lines leading away from the fuel tank. Check for loose connections, deteriorated hoses, crimped lines and other damage. Carefully inspect the lines from the tank to the engine. Repair or replace damaged sections as necessary.

20   Steering and suspension check

Refer to illustration 20.6
Note: *For detailed illustrations of the steering and suspension components, refer to Chapter 10.*

With the wheels on the ground

1   With the vehicle stopped and the front wheels pointed straight ahead, rock the steering wheel gently back-and-forth. If free play is excessive, a front wheel bearing, main shaft yoke, intermediate shaft yoke, lower arm balljoint or steering system joint is worn or the steering gear is out of adjustment or broken. Refer to Chapter 10 for the appropriate repair procedure.

2   Other symptoms, such as excessive vehicle body movement over rough roads, swaying (leaning) around corners and binding as the steering wheel is turned, may indicate faulty steering and/or suspension components.

3   Check the shock absorbers by quickly pushing down and releasing the vehicle several times at each corner. If the vehicle does not come back to a level position within one or two bounces, the shocks/struts are worn and must be replaced. When bouncing the vehicle up-and-down, listen for squeaks and noises from the suspension components. Additional information on suspension components can be found in Chapter 10.

With the vehicle raised

4   Raise the vehicle and support it securely on jackstands. See Jacking and towing at the front of this book for the proper jacking points.

5   Check the tires for irregular wear patterns and proper inflation. See Section 5 in this chapter for information regarding tire wear and Chapter 10 for the wheel bearing replacement procedures.

6   Inspect the universal joint between the steering shaft and the steering gear housing. Check the steering gear housing for grease leakage or oozing. Make sure that the dust seals and boots are not damaged and that the boot clamps are not loose **(see illustration)**. Check the steering linkage for looseness or damage. Check the tie-rod ends for excessive play. Look for loose bolts, broken or disconnected parts and deteriorated rubber bushings on all suspension and steering components. While an assistant turns the steering wheel from side to side, check the steering components for free movement, chafing and binding. If the steering components do not seem to be reacting with the movement of the steering wheel, try to determine where the slack is located.

7   Inspect the balljoint boots for damage and leaking grease. Replace the boots with new ones if they are damaged (see Chapter 10).

21   Driveaxle boot check

Refer to illustration 21.2

1   The driveaxle boots are very important because they prevent dirt, water and foreign material from entering and damaging the constant velocity (CV) joints. Oil and grease can cause the boot material to deteriorate prematurely, so it's a good idea to wash the boots with soap and water.

2   Inspect the boots for tears and cracks as well as loose clamps **(see illustration)**. If there is any evidence of cracks or leaking lubricant, they must be replaced as described in Chapter 8.

22   Exhaust system check

Refer to illustration 22.2

1   With the engine cold (at least three hours after the vehicle has been driven), check the complete exhaust system from its starting point at the engine to the end of the tailpipe. This should be done on a hoist where unrestricted access is available.

2   Check the pipes and connections for evidence of leaks, severe corrosion or damage. Make sure that all brackets and hangers are in good condition and tight **(see illustration)**.

3   At the same time, inspect the underside of the body for holes, corrosion, open seams, etc. which may allow exhaust gases to enter the passenger compartment. Seal all body openings with silicone or body putty.

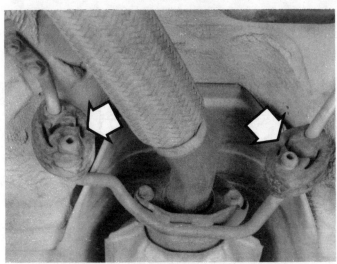

22.2 Check the rubber exhaust system hangers (arrows) for cracks and deterioration – replace any that are in poor condition

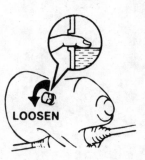

23.1 Location of the manual transaxle check/fill plug – use your finger as a dipstick, as shown, to check the lubricant level

LOOSEN

MANUAL TRANSAXLE

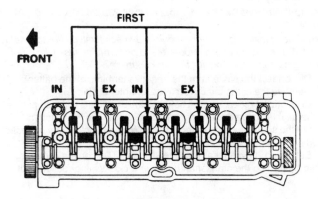

24.5 Adjust these valves first on SOHC engines

24.6 Measure the clearance with a feeler gauge

2   If the transaxle needs more lubricant (if the level is not up to the hole), use a gear oil syringe to add more. Stop filling the transaxle when the lubricant begins to run out the hole.
3   Install the plug and tighten it securely. Drive the vehicle a short distance, then check for leaks.

24   Valve clearance check and adjustment

Warning: *The electric cooling fan can activate at any time. Disconnect the fan motor or negative battery cable when working in the vicinity of the fan.*

SOHC engines

Refer to illustrations 24.5, 24.6, 24.7 and 24.11
1   The valve clearances are checked and adjusted with the engine at normal operating temperature.
2   Remove the air cleaner assembly (see Chapter 4).
3   Remove the camshaft cover (see Chapter 2, Part A).
4   Place the number one piston at Top Dead Center (TDC) on the compression stroke (see Chapter 2, Part A). The number one cylinder rocker arms (closest to the timing belt end of the engine) should be loose (able to move up-and-down slightly) and the camshaft lobes should be facing away from the rocker arms.
5   With the crankshaft in this position the valves labeled "First" can be checked and adjusted **(see illustration)**.
6   First, check and adjust the clearance of both intake valves. Loosen the locknut, turn the adjusting screw counterclockwise and insert the appropriate size feeler gauge between the intake valve stem and the adjusting screw **(see illustration)**. Carefully tighten the adjusting screw until you

4   Rattles and other noises can often be traced to the exhaust system, especially the mounts and hangers. Try to move the pipes, muffler and catalytic converter. If the components can come in contact with the body or suspension parts, secure the exhaust system with new mounts.
5   Check the running condition of the engine by inspecting inside the end of the tailpipe. The exhaust deposits here are an indication of engine condition. If the pipe is wet with oil or coated with white deposits, the engine is in need of service, including a compression test, a thorough fuel system inspection and adjustment.

23   Manual transaxle lubricant level check

Refer to illustration 23.1
1   The manual transaxle does not have a dipstick. To check the lubrication level, raise the vehicle and support it securely on jackstands. On the radiator side of the transaxle housing, you will see a plug **(see illustration)**. Remove it. If the lubricant level is correct, it should be up to the lower edge of the hole. Use your finger as a dipstick to check the level.

24.7   Hold the adjusting screw with a screwdriver and tighten the locknut with a wrench

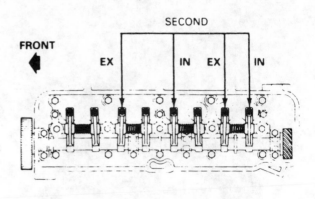

24.11   Adjust these valves next on SOHC engines

can feel a slight drag on the feeler gauge as you withdraw it from between the stem and adjusting screw.

7   Hold the adjusting screw with a screwdriver (to keep it from turning) and tighten the locknut **(see illustration)**. Recheck the clearance to make sure it hasn't changed.

8   Now adjust both exhaust valves. Loosen the locknut on the exhaust valve adjusting screw. Turn the adjusting screw counterclockwise and insert the appropriate size feeler gauge between the valve stem and the adjusting screw. Carefully tighten the adjusting screw until you can feel a slight drag on the feeler gauge as you withdraw it from between the stem and adjusting screw.

9   Hold the adjusting screw with a screwdriver (to keep it from turning) and tighten the locknut. Recheck the clearance to make sure it hasn't changed.

10   Rotate the crankshaft one full revolution (360-degrees) until the number four piston is at TDC on the compression stroke. The number four cylinder rocker arms (closest to the transaxle end of the engine) should be loose with the camshaft lobes facing away from the rocker arms.

11   Adjust the valves labelled "Second" as described in Steps 6 through 9 **(see illustration)**.
12   Install the camshaft cover and air cleaner assembly.

DOHC engines
Refer to illustrations 24.17a, 24.17b, 24.18, 24.20a, 24.20b, 24.20c, 24.21 and 24.22
Note: *The following procedure requires a special valve lifter tool set (J 37141-A or equivalent). It's impossible to perform this task without one. The engine should be cold for this procedure.*
13   Disconnect the cable from the negative terminal of the battery.
14   Remove the camshaft covers (see Chapter 2, Part A).
15   Blow out the recessed area between the camshafts with compressed air, if available, to remove any debris that might fall into the cylinders, then remove the spark plugs (see Section 25). **Warning:** *Wear eye protection when using compressed air.*
16   Set the no. 1 cylinder at Top Dead Center (TDC) on the compression stroke by turning the crankshaft pulley in a clockwise direction until the

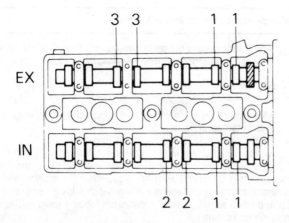

24.17a   When the no. 1 piston is at TDC on the compression stroke, the valve clearance for the no. 1 and no. 3 exhaust valves and the no. 1 and no. 2 intake valves can be checked/adjusted (DOHC engines)

24.17b   Measure the clearance for each valve with a feeler gauge of the specified thickness – if the clearance is correct, you should feel a slight drag on the gauge as you pull it out

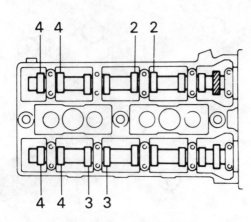

4 4   2 2

4 4 3 3

24.18   When the no. 4 piston is at TDC on the compression stroke, the valve clearance for the no. 2 and no. 4 exhaust valves and the no. 3 and no. 4 intake valves can be checked/adjusted (DOHC engines)

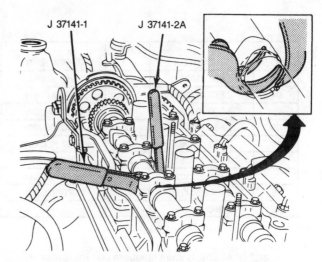

J 37141-1   J 37141-2A

24.20a   Compress the valve spring with tool J37141-1, . . .

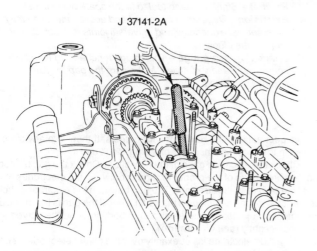

J 37141-2A

24.20b   . . . hold the spring down with J37141-2A and remove J37141-1

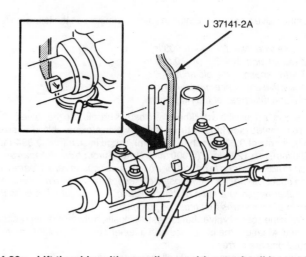

J 37141-2A

24.20c   Lift the shim with a small screwdriver and pull it out with a magnet

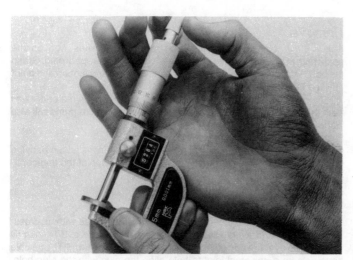

24.21   Measure the shim thickness with a micrometer

groove in the pulley is aligned with the "0" on the stationary pointer (see Chapter 2, Part A). To verify the no. 1 piston is on the compression stroke, make sure the valve lifters for the no. 1 cylinder are loose and the valve lifters for the no. 4 cylinder are tight. If they aren't, turn the crankshaft one more complete revolution.

17   Measure the clearances of the indicated valves with a feeler gauge of the specified thickness (see illustrations). Record the measurements which are out of specification. They will be used later to determine the required replacement shims.

18   Turn the crankshaft pulley one more complete revolution (360-degrees) and align the timing marks as described in Step 16 above. The no. 4 piston is now at TDC. Measure the clearances for the remaining valves (see illustration).

19   After all the valve clearances have been measured, turn the crankshaft pulley clockwise until the camshaft lobe above the first valve which you intend to adjust is pointing up, away from the shim.

20   Position the notch in the valve lifter toward the spark plug. Then compress the valve spring with the special tools (see illustrations). Remove the adjusting shim with a small screwdriver and magnet (see illustration).

21   Measure the thickness of the shim with a micrometer (see illustration). To calculate the correct thickness of a replacement shim that will

mm (in.)

SHIM NO.	THICKNESS	SHIM NO.	THICKNESS
02	2.500 (0.0984)	20	2.950 (0.1161)
04	2.550 (0.1004)	22	3.000 (0.1181)
06	2.600 (0.1024)	24	3.050 (0.1201)
08	2.650 (0.1043)	26	3.100 (0.1220)
10	2.700 (0.1063)	28	3.150 (0.1240)
12	2.750 (0.1083)	30	3.200 (0.1260)
14	2.800 (0.1102)	32	3.250 (0.1280)
16	2.850 (0.1122)	34	3.300 (0.1299)
18	2.900 (0.1142)		

24.22   Available shim numbers and thicknesses

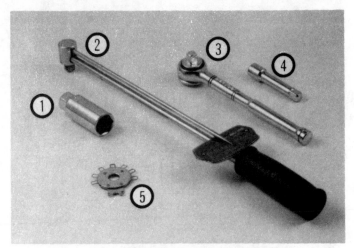

25.1   Tools required for changing spark plugs

1   **Spark plug socket** – This will have special padding inside to protect the spark plug's porcelain insulator
2   **Torque wrench** – Although not mandatory, using this tool is the best way to ensure the plugs are tightened properly
3   **Ratchet** – Standard hand tool to fit the spark plug socket
4   **Extension** – Depending on model and accessories, you may need special extensions and universal joints to reach one or more of the plugs
5   **Spark plug gap gauge** – This gauge for checking the gap comes in a variety of styles. Make sure the gap for your engine is included.

place the valve clearance within the specified limits, use the following formula:

Intake side: $N = T + (A - 0.008\ in)$
Exhaust side: $N = T + (A - 0.010\ in)$
T = thickness of the old shim
A = valve clearance measured
N = the thickness of the new shim

22   Select a shim with a thickness as close as possible to the valve clearance calculated (see illustration). Shims, which are available in 17 sizes in increments of 0.0020-inch (0.050 mm), range in size from 0.984-inch (2.500 mm) to 0.1299-inch (3.300 mm). **Note:** *Through careful analysis of the shim sizes needed to bring all the out of specification valve clearances within specification, it's often possible to simply move a shim to another valve lifter requiring a shim of that particular size, thereby reducing the number of new shims that must be purchased.*
23   With the special valve lifter tools still in position, install the new adjusting shim. Measure the clearance with a feeler gauge to make sure your calculations are correct.
24   Repeat this procedure until all the valve clearances are correct.
25   Installation of the remaining components is the reverse of removal.

25   Spark plug replacement

Refer to illustrations 25.1, 25.4a, 25.4b, 25.6 and 25.10

1   Spark plug replacement requires a spark plug socket which fits onto a ratchet wrench. This socket is lined with a rubber grommet to protect the porcelain insulator of the spark plug and to hold the plug while you insert it into the spark plug hole. You will also need a wire-type feeler gauge to check and adjust the spark plug gap and a torque wrench to tighten the new plugs to the specified torque (see illustration).
2   When replacing the plugs, purchase the new plugs in advance, adjust them to the proper gap and then replace each plug one at a time. **Note:** *When buying new spark plugs, it's essential that you obtain the correct plugs for your specific vehicle. This information can be found in this Chapter's specifications, on the Vehicle Emissions Control Information (VECI) label located on the underside of the hood or in the owner's manual. If these sources specify different plugs, purchase the spark plug type specified on the VECI label because that information is provided specifically for your engine.*

3   Inspect each of the new plugs for defects. If there are any signs of cracks in the porcelain insulator of a plug, don't use it.
4   Check the electrode gaps of the new plugs. Check the gap by inserting the wire gauge of the proper thickness between the electrodes at the tip of the plug (see illustration). The gap between the electrodes should be identical to that specified on the VECI label. If the gap is incorrect, use the notched adjuster on the feeler gauge body to bend the curved side electrode slightly (see illustration).
5   If the side electrode is not exactly over the center electrode, use the notched adjuster to align them. **Caution:** *If the gap of a new plug must be adjusted, bend only the base of the ground electrode, do not touch the center tip.*

Removal

6   To prevent the possibility of mixing up spark plug wires, work on one spark plug at a time. Remove the wire and boot from one spark plug. Grasp the boot – not the cable – as shown, give it a half twisting motion and pull it off (see illustration).
7   If compressed air is available, blow any dirt or foreign material away from the spark plug area before proceeding (a bicycle tire pump will also work).
8   Remove the spark plug.
9   Compare each old spark plug with those shown in the accompanying color photos to determine the overall running condition of the engine.

Installation

10   It's often difficult to insert spark plugs into their holes without cross-threading them. To avoid this possibility, fit a short piece of 3/16-inch ID rubber hose over the end of the spark plug (see illustration). The flexible hose acts as a universal joint to help align the plug with the plug hole. Should the plug begin to cross-thread, the hose will slip on the spark plug, preventing thread damage. Tighten the plug securely.

25.4a Spark plug manufacturers recommend using a wire-type gauge when checking the gap – if the wire does not slide between the electrodes with a slight drag, adjustment is required

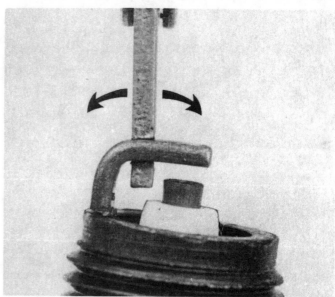

25.4b To change the gap, bend the side electrode only, as indicated by the arrows, and be very careful not to crack or chip the porcelain insulator surrounding the center electrode

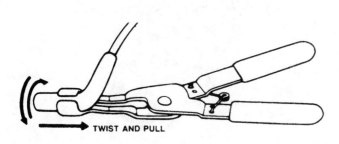

TWIST AND PULL

25.6 When removing the spark plug wires, grasp the boot and use a twisting/pulling motion

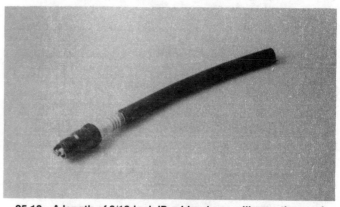

25.10 A length of 3/16-inch ID rubber hose will save time and prevent damaged threads when installing the spark plugs

11   Attach the plug wire to the new spark plug, again using a twisting motion on the boot until it is firmly seated on the end of the spark plug.

12   Follow the above procedure for the remaining spark plugs, replacing them one at a time to prevent mixing up the spark plug wires.

---

26   Spark plug wire, distributor cap and rotor check and replacement

---

Refer to illustrations 26.11a, 26.11b and 26.12

1   The spark plug wires should be checked whenever new spark plugs are installed.

2   Begin this procedure by making a visual check of the spark plug wires while the engine is running. In a darkened garage (make sure there is ventilation) start the engine and observe each plug wire. Be careful not to come into contact with any moving engine parts. If there is a break in the wire, you will see arcing or a small spark at the damaged area. If arcing is noticed, make a note to obtain new wires, then allow the engine to cool and check the distributor cap and rotor.

3   The spark plug wires should be inspected one at a time to prevent mixing up the order, which is essential for proper engine operation. Each original plug wire should be numbered to help identify its location. If the number is illegible, a piece of tape can be marked with the correct number and wrapped around the plug wire.

4   Disconnect the plug wire from the spark plug. A removal tool can be used for this purpose or you can grasp the rubber boot, twist the boot half a turn and pull the boot free. Do not pull on the wire itself.

5   Check inside the boot for corrosion, which will look like a white crusty powder.

6   Push the wire and boot back onto the end of the spark plug. It should fit tightly onto the end of the plug. If it doesn't, remove the wire and use pliers to carefully crimp the metal connector inside the wire boot until the fit is snug.

7   Using a clean rag, wipe the entire length of the wire to remove built-up dirt and grease. Once the wire is clean, check for burns, cracks and other damage. Do not bend the wire sharply, because the conductor within the wire might break.

8   Disconnect the wire from the distributor. Again, pull only on the rubber boot. Check for corrosion and a tight fit. Press the wire back into the distributor.

26.11a Remove the screws (arrows) and lift the distributor cap off (4A-LC engine shown, others similar)

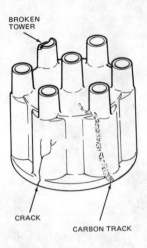

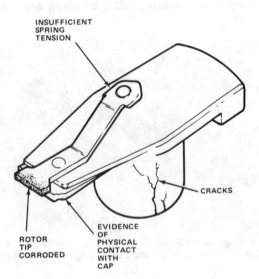

26.12   The ignition rotor should be checked for wear and corrosion as indicated here (if in doubt about its condition, install a new one)

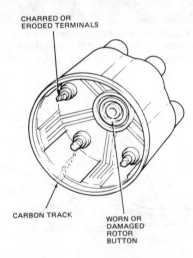

26.11b   Shown here are some of the common defects to look for when inspecting the distributor cap (if in doubt about its condition, install a new one)

13   It is common practice to install a new cap and rotor whenever new spark plug wires are installed, but if you wish to continue using the old cap, clean the terminals first.

14   When installing a new cap, remove the wires from the old cap one at a time and attach them to the new cap in the exact same location – do not simultaneously remove all the wires from the old cap or firing order mix-ups may occur.

9   Inspect the remaining spark plug wires, making sure that each one is securely fastened at the distributor and spark plug when the check is complete.

10   If new spark plug wires are required, purchase a set for your specific engine model. Pre-cut wire sets with the boots already installed are available. Remove and replace the wires one at a time to avoid mix-ups in the firing order.

11   Detach the distributor cap by removing the screws **(see illustration)**. Look inside it for cracks, carbon tracks and worn, burned or loose contacts **(see illustration)**.

12   Pull the rotor off the distributor shaft and examine it for cracks and carbon tracks **(see illustration)**. Replace the cap and rotor if any damage or defects are noted.

27   Carburetor choke check

Refer to illustration 27.3

Warning: *The electric cooling fan can activate at any time. Disconnect the fan motor or negative battery cable when working in the vicinity of the fan.*

1   The choke operates only when the engine is cold, so this check should be performed before the engine has been started for the day.

2   Take off the top plate of the air cleaner assembly. It's held in place by a wing nut at the top and clips on the side. If any vacuum hoses must be dis-

CARBON DEPOSITS

Symptoms: Dry sooty deposits indicate a rich mixture or weak ignition. Causes misfiring, hard starting and hesitation.

Recommendation: Check for a clogged air cleaner, high float level, sticky choke and worn ignition points. Use a spark plug with a longer core nose for greater anti-fouling protection.

OIL DEPOSITS

Symptoms: Oily coating caused by poor oil control. Oil is leaking past worn valve guides or piston rings into the combustion chamber. Causes hard starting, misfiring and hesition.

Recommendation: Correct the mechanical condition with necessary repairs and install new plugs.

TOO HOT

Symptoms: Blistered, white insulator, eroded electrode and absence of deposits. Results in shortened plug life.

Recommendation: Check for the correct plug heat range, over-advanced ignition timing, lean fuel mixture, intake manifold vacuum leaks and sticking valves. Check the coolant level and make sure the radiator is not clogged.

PREIGNITION

Symptoms: Melted electrodes. Insulators are white, but may be dirty due to misfiring or flying debris in the combustion chamber. Can lead to engine damage.

Recommendation: Check for the correct plug heat range, over-advanced ignition timing, lean fuel mixture, clogged cooling system and lack of lubrication.

HIGH SPEED GLAZING

Symptoms: Insulator has yellowish, glazed appearance. Indicates that combustion chamber temperatures have risen suddenly during hard acceleration. Normal deposits melt to form a conductive coating. Causes misfiring at high speeds.

Recommendation: Install new plugs. Consider using a colder plug if driving habits warrant.

GAP BRIDGING

Symptoms: Combustion deposits lodge between the electrodes. Heavy deposits accumulate and bridge the electrode gap. The plug ceases to fire, resulting in a dead cylinder.

Recommendation: Locate the faulty plug and remove the deposits from between the electrodes.

NORMAL

Symptoms: Brown to grayish-tan color and slight electrode wear. Correct heat range for engine and operating conditions.

Recommendation: When new spark plugs are installed, replace with plugs of the same heat range.

ASH DEPOSITS

Symptoms: Light brown deposits encrusted on the side or center electrodes or both. Derived from oil and/or fuel additives. Excessive amounts may mask the spark, causing misfiring and hesitation during acceleration.

Recommendation: If excessive deposits accumulate over a short time or low mileage, install new valve guide seals to prevent seepage of oil into the combustion chambers. Also try changing gasoline brands.

WORN

Symptoms: Rounded electrodes with a small amount of deposits on the firing end. Normal color. Causes hard starting in damp or cold weather and poor fuel economy.

Recommendation: Replace with new plugs of the same heat range.

DETONATION

Symptoms: Insulators may be cracked or chipped. Improper gap setting techniques can also result in a fractured insulator tip. Can lead to piston damage.

Recommendation: Make sure the fuel anti-knock values meet engine requirements. Use care when setting the gaps on new plugs. Avoid lugging the engine.

SPLASHED DEPOSITS

Symptoms: After long periods of misfiring, deposits can loosen when normal combustion temperature is restored by an overdue tune-up. At high speeds, deposits flake off the piston and are thrown against the hot insulator, causing misfiring.

Recommendation: Replace the plugs with new ones or clean and reinstall the originals.

MECHANICAL DAMAGE

Symptoms: May be caused by a foreign object in the combustion chamber or the piston striking an incorrect reach (too long) plug. Causes a dead cylinder and could result in piston damage.

Recommendation: Remove the foreign object from the engine and/or install the correct reach plug.

27.3   The choke plate is located in the carburetor throat

28.3   The air control valve is located in the air cleaner housing snorkel (arrow)

connected, make sure you tag the hoses for reinstallation in their original positions. Place the top plate and wing nut aside, out of the way of moving engine components.

3   Look at the center of the air cleaner housing. You will notice a flat plate at the carburetor opening **(see illustration)**.

4   Press the accelerator pedal to the floor. The plate should close completely. Start the engine while you watch the plate at the carburetor. Don't position your face near the carburetor, as the engine could backfire, causing serious burns. When the engine starts, the choke plate should open slightly.

5   Allow the engine to continue running at an idle speed. As the engine warms up to operating temperature, the plate should slowly open, allowing more air to enter through the top of the carburetor.

6   After a few minutes, the choke plate should be fully open to the vertical position. Blip the throttle to make sure the fast idle cam disengages.

7   You'll notice that the engine speed corresponds with the plate opening. With the plate nearly closed, the engine should run at a fast idle speed. As the plate opens and the throttle is moved to disengage the fast idle cam, the engine speed will decrease.

8   Refer to Chapter 4 for specific information on adjusting and servicing the choke components.

---

28   Thermostatically controlled air cleaner check (carburetor-equipped models only)

Refer to illustration 28.3
Warning: *The electric cooling fan can activate at any time. Disconnect the fan motor or negative battery cable when working in the vicinity of the fan.*

1   Carburetor-equipped engines have a thermostatically controlled air cleaner which draws air from different locations, depending on engine temperature.

2   This is a visual check, requiring use of a small mirror.

3   When the engine is cold, locate the air control valve inside the air cleaner assembly. It's inside the snorkel of the air cleaner housing **(see illustration)**.

4   There is a flexible air duct attached to the end of the snorkel, disconnect it at the snorkel. This will enable you to look through the end of the snorkel and see the air control valve inside.

5   Start the engine and look through the snorkel at the valve, which should move up to block off the air cleaner snorkel. With the valve closed, air cannot enter through the end of the snorkel, but instead enters the air cleaner through the flexible duct attached to the exhaust manifold and the heat stove passage.

6   As the engine warms up to operating temperature, the valve should move down to allow air to be drawn through the snorkel end. Depending on outside temperature, this may take 10-to-15 minutes. To speed up this check you can reconnect the snorkel air duct, drive the vehicle, then check to see if the valve is completely open.

7   If the thermostatically controlled air cleaner isn't operating properly, see Chapter 6 for more information.

---

29   Cooling system servicing (draining, flushing and refilling)

Warning: *Antifreeze is a corrosive and poisonous solution, so be careful not to spill any of the coolant mixture on the vehicle's paint or your skin. If this happens, rinse immediately with plenty of clean water. Consult local authorities regarding proper disposal procedures for antifreeze before draining the cooling system. In many areas, reclamation centers have been established to collect used oil and coolant mixtures. The electric cooling fan can activate at any time, even when the ignition is in the Off position. Disconnect the fan motor or negative battery cable when working in the vicinity of the fan.*

1   Periodically, the cooling system should be drained, flushed and refilled to replenish the antifreeze mixture and prevent formation of rust and corrosion, which can impair the performance of the cooling system and cause engine damage. When the cooling system is serviced, all hoses and the radiator cap should be checked and replaced if necessary.

Draining
Refer to illustrations 29.4 and 29.5

2   Apply the parking brake and block the wheels. If the vehicle has just been driven, wait several hours to allow the engine to cool down before beginning this procedure.

3   Once the engine is completely cool, remove the radiator cap.

4   Remove the splash panel located beneath the radiator (if equipped). Then move a large container under the radiator drain to catch the coolant. Attach a 3/8-inch inner diameter hose to the drain fitting to direct the cool-

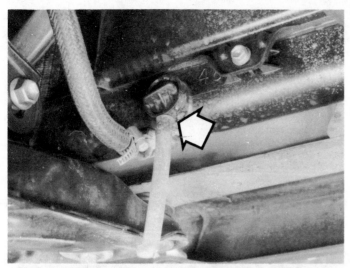

29.4 The radiator drain (arrow) is mounted in the bottom tank

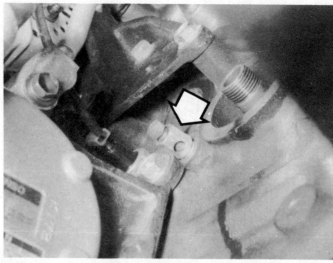

29.5 The block drain plug (arrow) is located next to the oil filter (filter removed for clarity)

ant into the container (some models are already equipped with a hose), then open the drain fitting **(see illustration)**.
5   After the coolant stops flowing out of the radiator, move the container under the engine block drain plug **(see illustration)**. Loosen the plug and allow the coolant in the block to drain.
6   While the coolant is draining, check the condition of the radiator hoses, heater hoses and clamps (refer to Section 14 if necessary).
7   Replace any damaged clamps or hoses (refer to Chapter 3 for detailed replacement procedures).

Flushing

8   Once the system is completely drained, flush the radiator with fresh water from a garden hose until water runs clear at the drain. The flushing action of the water will remove sediments from the radiator but will not remove rust and scale from the engine and cooling tube surfaces.
9   These deposits can be removed by the chemical action of a cleaner. Follow the procedure outlined in the manufacturer's instructions. If the radiator is severely corroded, damaged or leaking, it should be removed (see Chapter 3) and taken to a radiator repair shop.
10   Remove the overflow hose from the coolant recovery reservoir. Drain the reservoir and flush it with clean water, then reconnect the hose.

Refilling

11   Close and tighten the radiator drain. Install and tighten the block drain plug.
12   Place the heater temperature control in the maximum heat position.
13   Slowly add new coolant (a 50/50 mixture of water and antifreeze) to the radiator until it's full. Add coolant to the reservoir up to the lower mark.
14   Leave the radiator cap off and run the engine in a well-ventilated area until the thermostat opens (coolant will begin flowing through the radiator and the upper radiator hose will become hot).
15   Turn the engine off and let it cool. Add more coolant mixture to bring the level back up to the lip on the radiator filler neck.
16   Squeeze the upper radiator hose to expel air, then add more coolant mixture if necessary. Replace the radiator cap.
17   Start the engine, allow it to reach normal operating temperature and check for leaks.

30   Idle speed check and adjustment

Refer to illustrations 30.8a and 30.8b
1   Engine idle speed is the speed at which the engine operates when no

accelerator pedal pressure is applied, as when stopped at a traffic light. This speed is critical to the performance of the engine itself, as well as many engine subsystems.
2   Set the parking brake firmly and block the wheels to prevent the vehicle from rolling. Put the transaxle in Neutral.
3   Connect a hand held tachometer.
4   Start the engine and allow it to reach normal operating temperature.
5   Check, and adjust if necessary, the ignition timing (see Section 35).
6   Allow the engine to idle for two minutes.
7   Check the engine idle speed on the tachometer and compare it to the Vehicle Emission Control Information label in the engine compartment.
8   If the idle speed is too low or too high, turn the idle speed adjusting screw **(see illustrations)** until the specified idle speed is obtained.

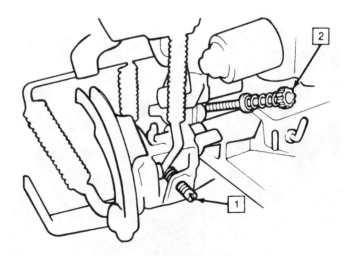

30.8a   On carburetor-equipped models, the idle speed adjusting screw is located on the rear (firewall) side of the carburetor

1   Fast idle adjusting screw
2   Idle speed adjusting screw

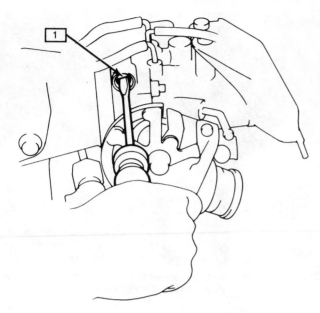

30.8b   On fuel-injected models, the idle speed adjusting screw is located on the throttle body

1   Idle speed adjusting screw

31   Automatic transaxle fluid and filter change

Refer to illustrations 31.7a, 31.7b, 31.8, 31.9, 31.11 and 31.13

1   At the specified time intervals, the automatic transaxle fluid should be drained and replaced.

2   Before beginning work, purchase the specified transmission fluid (see Recommended lubricants and fluids at the front of this Chapter).

3   Other tools necessary for this job include jackstands to support the vehicle in a raised position, a drain pan capable of holding at least two gallons, newspapers and clean rags.

4   The fluid should be drained immediately after the vehicle has been driven. Hot fluid is more effective than cold fluid at removing built up sediment. **Warning:** *Fluid temperature can exceed 350 degrees in a hot transaxle. Wear protective gloves.*

5   After the vehicle has been driven to warm up the fluid, raise it and place it on jackstands for access to the transaxle drain plug. Remove any splash pans that are in the way.

6   Move the necessary equipment under the vehicle, being careful not to touch any of the hot exhaust components.

7   Place the drain pan under the drain plugs in the transaxle housing and pan. Remove the drain plugs one at a time **(see illustrations)**. Be sure the drain pan is in position, as fluid will come out with some force. Once the fluid is drained, reinstall the drain plugs securely.

8   Remove the transaxle pan bolts **(see illustration)**, carefully pry the pan loose with a screwdriver and remove it.

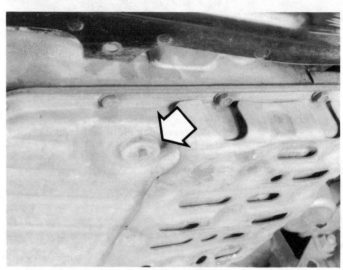

31.7a   The automatic transaxle drain plug is on the bottom of the pan (arrow)

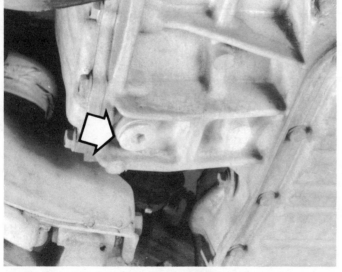

31.7b   On vehicles with an automatic transaxle, the drain plug for the differential lubricant is located in the bottom of the housing near the pan (arrow)

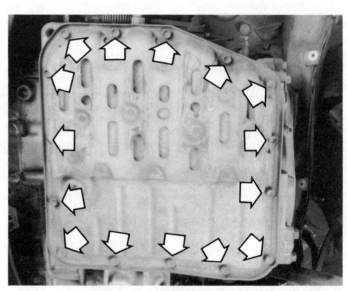

31.8   Remove the transaxle pan bolts (arrows)

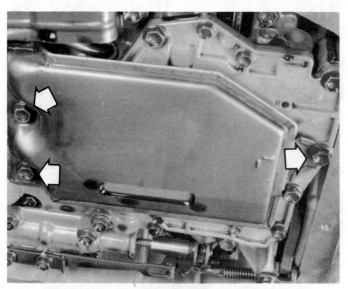

31.9   Remove the filter retaining bolts (arrows)

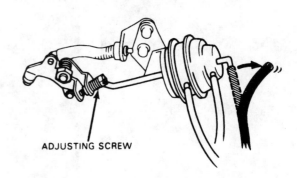

31.11   Be sure to clean and reinstall the magnets in their
original locations

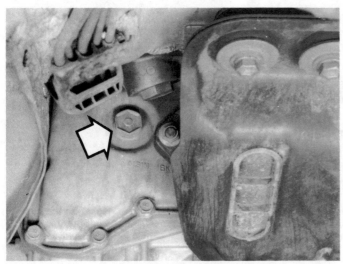

31.13   On vehicles with an automatic transaxle, the filler plug for
the differential lubricant is located on the radiator side of the
housing (arrow)

9   Remove the filter retaining bolts and detach the filter from the transaxle **(see illustration)**. Be careful when lowering the filter as it contains
residual fluid.
10   Place the new filter in position and install the bolts. Tighten the bolts to
the torque listed in this Chapter's specifications.
11   Carefully clean the gasket surfaces of the fluid pan, removing all
traces of old gasket material. Wash the pan in clean solvent and dry it with
compressed air. Be sure to clean and reinstall the magnets **(see illustration)**.
12   Install a new gasket, place the fluid pan in position and install the
bolts. Tighten the bolts to the specified torque.
13   Add the specified amount and type of fluid to the differential **(see illustration)**. Reinstall any splash pans and lower the vehicle.
14   With the engine off, add new fluid to the transaxle through the dipstick
tube (see Recommended lubricants and fluids for the recommended fluid
type and capacity). Use a funnel to prevent spills. It is best to add a little
fluid at a time, continually checking the level with the dipstick (see Section
7). Allow the fluid time to drain into the pan.

ADJUSTING SCREW

33.4   Disconnect the vacuum hose from diaphragm A . . .

15   Start the engine and shift the selector into all positions from Park
through Low, then shift into Park and apply the parking brake.
16   With the engine idling, check the fluid level. Add fluid up to the HOT
level on the dipstick.

32   Manual transaxle lubricant change

1   Remove the drain plug from the bottom of the transaxle and allow all
lubricant to drain.
2   Reinstall the drain plug. Tighten it to the specified torque.
3   Add new lubricant until it begins to run out of the filler hole (see Section 23). See Recommended lubricants and fluids for the specified lubricant type.

33   Throttle positioner adjustment check (carburetor-equipped
models only)

Refer to illustrations 33.4 and 33.7
1   Run the engine until normal operating temperature is reached.
2   Remove the air cleaner assembly and plug the vacuum hoses leading
to the engine.
3   Connect a tachometer to the engine according to the manufacturer's
directions.
4   Disconnect the vacuum hose from diaphragm A **(see illustration)**.

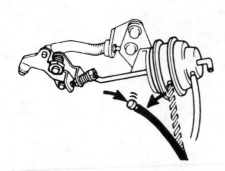

33.7   . . . and diaphragm B – the engine speed should be as
specified in the text

34.2   The evaporative emissions (charcoal) canister is located
below the brake master cylinder – check the hoses for cracks and
other damage

35.1   The PCV valve fits into a rubber
grommet in the camshaft cover (SOHC
engine shown)

36.2   The oxygen sensor (viewed from
below) is mounted on the exhaust
manifold with two bolts (arrows)

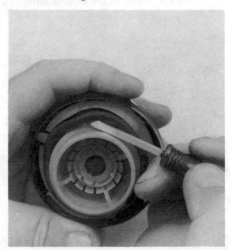

37.2   If the rubber gasket on the fuel
filler cap is damaged or deteriorated,
remove it with a small screwdriver and
install a new one

5   The idle speed should now be 800 rpm (manual transaxle) or 900 rpm (automatic transaxle). Turn the adjusting screw, if necessary to obtain the correct speed. **Note:** *Make adjustments when the cooling fan is off.*
6   Reconnect the vacuum hose to diaphragm A.
7   Disconnect the vacuum hose from diaphragm B **(see illustration)** and plug the hose.
8   The idle speed should now be: 1985 models – 1300 rpm plus or minus 200 rpm (manual transaxle) or 1400 rpm plus or minus 200 rpm (automatic transaxle). 1986 and later models – 1400 rpm plus or minus 200 rpm (manual transaxle) or 1500 rpm plus or minus 200 rpm (automatic transaxle). Turn the adjusting screw, if necessary to obtain the correct speed.
9   Reconnect the vacuum hose and check that the engine returns to idle speed in two to six seconds.
10   Install the air cleaner assembly and ensure that all hoses are properly reconnected.

34   Evaporative emissions control system check and canister replacement

Refer to illustration 34.2
1   The function of the evaporative emissions control system is to draw fuel vapors from the gas tank and fuel system, store them in a charcoal canister and route them to the intake manifold during normal engine operation.
2   The most common symptom of a fault in the evaporative emissions system is a strong fuel odor in the engine compartment. If a fuel odor is detected, inspect the charcoal canister, located in the engine compartment below the master cylinder **(see illustration)**. Check the canister and all hoses for damage and deterioration.
3   At the specified intervals, the charcoal canister must be replaced with a new one. Disconnect the hoses, release the spring clip and lift the canister from the engine compartment. Installation is the reverse of removal.
4   The evaporative emissions control system is explained in more detail in Chapter 6.

35   Positive Crankcase Ventilation (PCV) valve check and replacement

Refer to illustration 35.1
1   The PCV valve is located in the camshaft cover **(see illustration)**.
2   Disconnect the hose, pull the PCV valve from the cover, then reconnect the hose.

3   With the engine idling at normal operating temperature, place your finger over the valve opening. If there's no vacuum at the valve, check for a plugged hose or valve. Replace any plugged or deteriorated hoses.

4   Turn off the engine. Remove the PCV valve from the hose. Blow through the valve from the camshaft cover end. If air will not pass through the valve in this direction, replace it with a new one.

5   When purchasing a replacement PCV valve, make sure it's for your particular vehicle and engine size. Compare the old valve with the new one to make sure they're the same.

36 Oxygen sensor replacement

Refer to illustration 36.2

Warning: *The electric cooling fan can activate at any time. Disconnect the fan motor or negative battery cable when working in the vicinity of the fan.*

1   The oxygen sensor is located in the exhaust manifold. Starting at the oxygen sensor, follow the wire back to the connector. Unplug the oxygen sensor wire at the connector.

2   Unscrew the oxygen sensor bolts **(see illustration)** and remove the sensor.

3   Install the new oxygen sensor into the exhaust manifold. Tighten the sensor bolts securely.

4   Plug in the electrical connector.

37 Fuel tank cap gasket replacement

Refer to illustration 37.2

1   Obtain a new gasket.

2   Remove the tank cap and carefully pry the old gasket out of the recess **(see illustration)**. Avoid damaging the sealing surface inside the cap.

3   Work the new gasket into the cap recess.

4   Install the cap, then remove it and look for an impression all the way around the gasket – this indicates the gasket is sealing completely.

Chapter 2 Part A   Engines

Contents

Specifications

General

Engine type
  4A-LC . . . . SOHC, two valves per cylinder
  4A-GE, 4A-FE . . . . DOHC, four valves per cylinder
Cylinder numbers (drivebelt end-to-transaxle end) 1-2-3-4
Firing order 1-3-4-2

Timing belt

Idler pulley spring free length
  4A-LC engine . . . . 1.512 in (38.4 mm)
  4A-GE engine . . . . 1.713 in (43.5 mm)
  4A-FE engine . . . . 1.512 in (38.4 mm)

Timing belt deflection (with a pressure of 4.4 lbs)
    4A-LC engine .... 1/4 to 9/32 in (6 to 7 mm)
    4A-GE engine .... 3/16 in (4 mm)
    4A-FE engine .... 13/64 to 1/4 in (5 to 6 mm)

Camshaft and valve train

Camshaft endplay
    4A-LC engine
        Standard .... 0.0031 to 0.0071 in (0.08 to 0.18 mm)
        Service limit .... 0.0098 in (0.25 mm)
    4A-GE engine
        Standard .... 0.0031 to 0.0075 in (0.08 to 0.19 mm)
        Service limit .... 0.0118 in (0.30 mm)
    4A-FE engine (service limit) .... 0.0043 in (0.11 mm)
Camshaft journal diameter
    4A-LC engine .... 1.1015 to 1.1022 in (27.979 to 27.995 mm)
    4A-GE engine .... 1.0610 to 1.0616 in (26.949 to 26.965 mm)
    4A-FE engine (minimum)
        No. 1 exhaust journal .... 0.9822 in (24.95 mm)
        All other journals .... 0.9035 in (22.95 mm)
Camshaft bearing oil clearance
    4A-LC engine
        Standard .... 0.0015 to 0.0029 in (0.037 to 0.073 mm)
        Service limit .... 0.0039 in (0.10 mm)
    4A-GE engine
        Standard .... 0.0014 to 0.0028 in (0.035 to 0.072 mm)
        Service limit .... 0.0039 in (0.10 mm)
    4A-FE engine (standard) .... 0.0014 to 0.0028 in (0.035 to 0.072 mm)
Camshaft lobe height
    4A-LC engine (service limit) .... 1.5409 in (39.14 mm)
    4A-GE engine
        Standard .... 1.3998 to 1.4002 in (35.555 to 35.565 mm)
        Service limit .... 1.3841 in (35.155 mm)
    4A-FE engine (service limit)
        Intake camshaft .... 1.370 in (38.41 mm)
        Exhaust camshaft .... 1.359 in (34.51 mm)
Camshaft gear spring free length (4A-FE engine only) .... 0.673 to 0.689 in (17.1 to 17.5 mm)
Camshaft gear backlash (4A-FE engine only) .... 0.0008 to 0.0079 in (0.020 to 0.200 mm)
Valve lifters (DOHC engines only)
    Lifter diameter (service limit) .... 1.1014 to 1.1018 in (27.975 to 27.985 mm)
    Lifter bore diameter (service limit) .... 1.1024 to 1.1032 in (28.000 to 28.021 mm)
    Lifter-to-bore (oil) clearance
        Standard .... 0.0005 to 0.0018 in (0.015 to 0.046 mm)
        Service limit .... 0.0039 in (0.10 mm)
Rocker arm-to-shaft oil clearance (service limit)
    (4A-LC engine only) .... 0.0024 in (0.06 mm)

Torque specifications   Ft-lbs

Camshaft bearing cap bolts
    4A-LC engine 9
    4A-GE engine 9
    4A-FE engine 9.6
Camshaft cover nuts/bolts
    4A-LC engine 18
    4A-GE engine 15
    4A-FE engine 15
Camshaft idler pulley bolts 27
Camshaft sprocket bolt
    4A-LC engine 34
    4A-GE engine 34
    4A-FE engine 43
Crankshaft pulley-to-crankshaft bolt
    4A-LC engine 87
    4A-GE engine 101
    4A-FE engine 87

Torque specifications (continued)

	Ft-lbs
Cylinder head bolts	
4A-LC engine	43
4A-FE engine	44
4A-GE engine	
Step one	22
Step two	Rotate an additional 90-degrees (1/4-turn)
Step three	Rotate an additional 90-degrees (1/4-turn)
Exhaust manifold nuts/bolts	18
Flywheel/driveplate bolts	
4A-LC engine	58
4A-GE engine	58
4A-FE engine	
Manual transaxle	58
Automatic transaxle	47
Intake manifold nuts/bolts	
4A-LC engine	18
4A-GE engine	20
4A-FE engine	14
Oil pan-to-block bolts	
4A-LC engine	4
4A-GE engine	4
4A-FE engine	7.5
Oil pump-to-block bolts	
4A-LC engine	18
4A-GE engine	16
4A-FE engine	16
Oil pick-up (strainer) nuts/bolts	7
Rocker arm shaft pedestal bolts (4A-LC engine only)	18
Rear oil seal retainer bolts	7

1   General information

Refer to illustrations 1.5a and 1.5b

This Part of Chapter 2 is devoted to in-vehicle repair procedures for the engine. All information concerning engine removal and installation and engine block and cylinder head overhaul can be found in Part B of this Chapter.

The following repair procedures are based on the assumption the engine is installed in the vehicle. If the engine has been removed from the vehicle and mounted on a stand, many of the steps outlined in this Part of Chapter 2 will not apply.

The Specifications included in this Part of Chapter 2 apply only to the procedures contained in this Part. Part B of Chapter 2 contains the Specifications necessary for cylinder head and engine block rebuilding.

Three different four-cylinder engines were installed in the Chevy Nova/Geo Prizm during the years covered by this manual. The single overhead camshaft (SOHC), two-valve-per-cylinder engine used in the Nova is designated the 4A-LC.

Two different dual overhead camshaft (DOHC), four valve per cylinder engines are covered by this manual. One version has dual camshaft timing belt sprockets – this engine is designated 4A-GE (VIN code 5) **(see illustration)**. The other engine has a single camshaft timing belt sprocket – this engine is designated 4A-FE (VIN code 6) **(see illustration)**. **Note:** *DOHC is used in the text to indicate when a procedure applies to both the 4A-GE and 4A-FE engines.*

2   Repair operations possible with the engine in the vehicle

Many major repair operations can be accomplished without removing the engine from the vehicle.

Clean the engine compartment and the exterior of the engine with some type of degreaser before any work is done. It will make the job easier and help keep dirt out of the internal areas of the engine.

Depending on the components involved, it may be helpful to remove the hood to improve access to the engine as repairs are performed (refer to Chapter 11 if necessary). Cover the fenders to prevent damage to the paint. Special pads are available, but an old bedspread or blanket will also work.

If vacuum, exhaust, oil or coolant leaks develop, indicating a need for gasket or seal replacement, the repairs can generally be made with the engine in the vehicle. The intake and exhaust manifold gaskets, oil pan gasket, crankshaft oil seals and cylinder head gasket are all accessible with the engine in place.

Exterior engine components, such as the intake and exhaust manifolds, the oil pan, the oil pump, the water pump, the starter motor, the alternator, the distributor and the fuel system components can be removed for repair with the engine in place.

Since the cylinder head can be removed without pulling the engine, camshaft and valve component servicing can also be accomplished with the engine in the vehicle. Replacement of the timing belt and sprockets is also possible with the engine in the vehicle.

In extreme cases caused by a lack of necessary equipment, repair or replacement of piston rings, pistons, connecting rods and rod bearings is possible with the engine in the vehicle. However, this practice isn't recommended because of the cleaning and preparation work that must be done to the components involved.

3   Top Dead Center (TDC) for number one piston – locating

Refer to illustrations 3.8 and 3.11
Note: *The following procedure is based on the assumption the distributor is correctly installed. If you're trying to locate TDC to install the distributor*

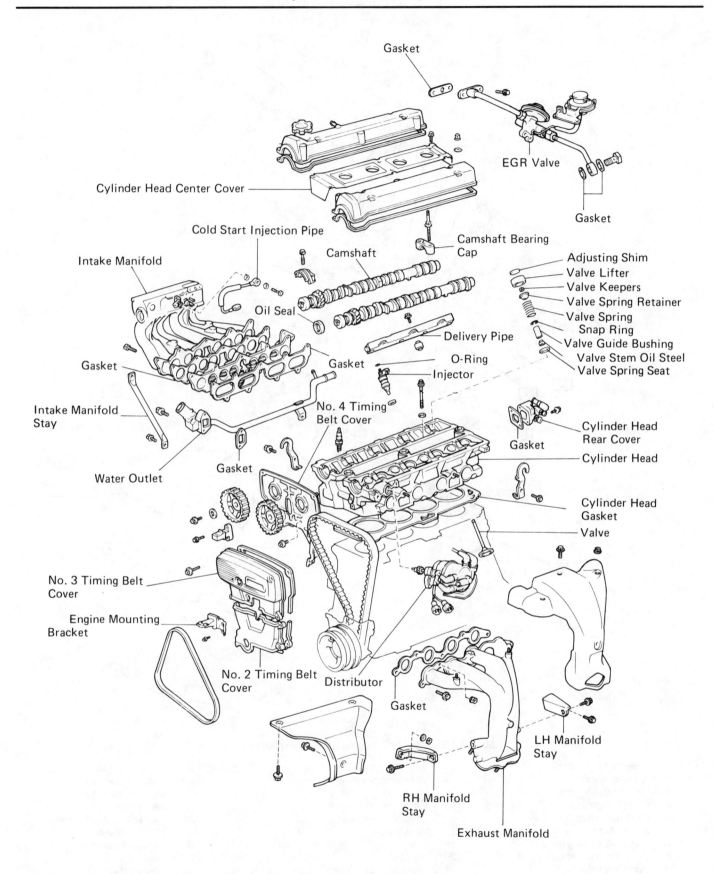

Gasket

EGR Valve

Cylinder Head Center Cover

Gasket

Cold Start Injection Pipe

Camshaft Bearing Cap

Adjusting Shim
Valve Lifter
Valve Keepers
Valve Spring Retainer
Valve Spring
Snap Ring
Valve Guide Bushing
Valve Stem Oil Steel
Valve Spring Seat

Intake Manifold

Camshaft

Oil Seal

Delivery Pipe

Gasket

Gasket

O-Ring

Injector

Intake Manifold Stay

No. 4 Timing Belt Cover

Cylinder Head Rear Cover

Gasket

Cylinder Head

Water Outlet

Gasket

Cylinder Head Gasket

Valve

No. 3 Timing Belt Cover

Engine Mounting Bracket

No. 2 Timing Belt Cover

Distributor

Gasket

LH Manifold Stay

RH Manifold Stay

Exhaust Manifold

1.5a 4A-GE upper engine components – exploded view

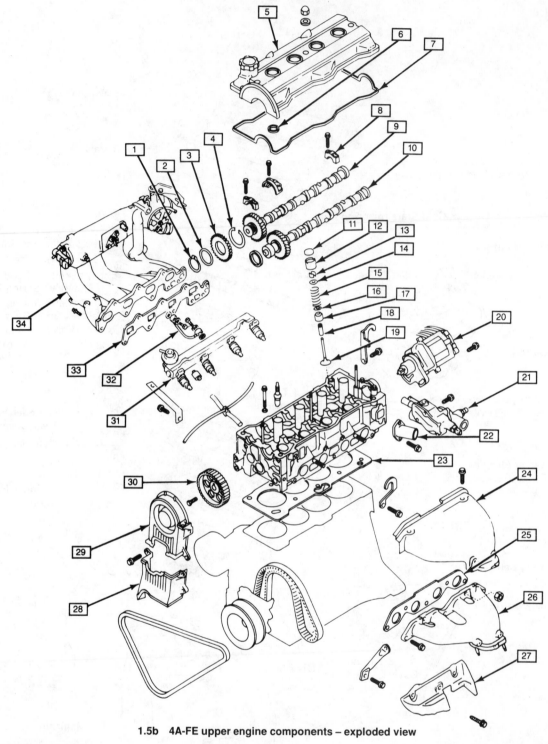

1.5b   4A-FE upper engine components – exploded view

1	Camshaft snap-ring	13	Valve keepers	25	Exhaust manifold gasket
2	Wave washer	14	Valve spring retainer	26	Exhaust manifold
3	Camshaft sub-gear	15	Valve spring	27	Exhaust manifold lower
4	Camshaft gear spring	16	Valve spring seat		heat shield
5	Camshaft cover	17	Valve stem oil seal	28	Center timing belt cover
6	Spark plug tube gasket	18	Valve guide	29	Upper timing belt cover
7	Camshaft cover gasket	19	Valve	30	Camshaft sprocket
8	Camshaft bearing cap	20	Distributor	31	Fuel rail
9	Camshaft (intake)	21	Coolant inlet housing	32	Cold-start injector
10	Camshaft (exhaust)	22	Coolant outlet housing	33	Intake manifold gasket
11	Adjusting shim	23	Head gasket	34	Intake manifold
12	Valve lifter	24	Exhaust manifold upper heat shield		

3.8 The notch in the crankshaft pulley must be aligned with the zero on the timing cover (arrows)

3.11 On 4A-GE engines, to verify the number one piston is at TDC on the compression stroke, remove the oil filler cap and look for a small dimple in the camshaft – the dimple should be aligned with the straight edge at the base of the filler neck

correctly, piston position must be determined by feeling for compression at the number one spark plug hole, then aligning the ignition timing marks as described in step 8.

1   Top Dead Center (TDC) is the highest point in the cylinder that each piston reaches as it travels up-and-down when the crankshaft turns. Each piston reaches TDC on the compression stroke and again on the exhaust stroke, but TDC generally refers to piston position on the compression stroke.

2   Positioning the piston(s) at TDC is an essential part of many procedures such as camshaft and timing belt/sprocket removal and distributor removal.

3   Before beginning this procedure, be sure to place the transaxle in Neutral and apply the parking brake or block the rear wheels. Also, disable the ignition system by detaching the coil wire from the center terminal of the distributor cap and grounding it on the block with a jumper wire. Remove the spark plugs (see Chapter 1).

4   In order to bring any piston to TDC, the crankshaft must be turned using one of the methods outlined below. When looking at the drivebelt end of the engine, normal crankshaft rotation is clockwise.

   a) The preferred method is to turn the crankshaft with a socket and ratchet attached to the bolt threaded into the front of the crankshaft.
   b) A remote starter switch, which may save some time, can also be used. Follow the instructions included with the switch. Once the piston is close to TDC, use a socket and ratchet as described in the previous paragraph.
   c) If an assistant is available to turn the ignition switch to the Start position in short bursts, you can get the piston close to TDC without a remote starter switch. Make sure your assistant is out of the vehicle, away from the ignition switch, then use a socket and ratchet as described in Paragraph a) to complete the procedure.

5   Detach the cap from the distributor and set it aside (see Chapter 1, if necessary).

6   Note the position of the terminal for the number one spark plug wire on the distributor cap. If the terminal isn't marked, follow the plug wire from the number one cylinder spark plug to the cap.

7   Use a felt-tip pen or chalk to make a mark on the distributor body directly under the location of the terminal when the cap is installed. **Note:** *The location of the wires on the outside of the cap doesn't correspond with*

the inside terminals – use the position of the inside terminals for rotor alignment.

8   Turn the crankshaft (see Paragraph 3 above) until the notch in the crankshaft pulley is aligned with the 0 on the timing plate (located at the front of the engine) **(see illustration)**.

9   Look at the distributor rotor – it should be pointing directly at the mark you made on the distributor body.

10   If the rotor is 180-degrees off, the number one piston is at TDC on the exhaust stroke.

11   If the number one piston is at TDC on the exhaust stroke, turn the crankshaft one complete turn (360-degrees) clockwise. The rotor should now be pointing at the mark on the distributor. When the rotor is pointing at the number one spark plug wire terminal in the distributor cap and the ignition timing marks are aligned, the number one piston is at TDC on the compression stroke. **Note:** *If it's impossible to align the ignition timing marks when the rotor is pointing at the mark on the distributor body, the distributor may be installed wrong, the timing belt may have jumped the teeth on the sprockets or may have been installed incorrectly. On 4A-GE engines, it is possible to verify TDC by removing the oil filler cap* **(see illustration)**.

12   After the number one piston has been positioned at TDC on the compression stroke, TDC for any of the remaining pistons can be located by turning the crankshaft and following the firing order. Mark the remaining spark plug wire terminal locations on the distributor body just like you did for the number one terminal, then number the marks to correspond with the cylinder numbers. As you turn the crankshaft, the rotor will also turn. When it's pointing directly at one of the marks on the distributor, the piston for that particular cylinder is at TDC on the compression stroke.

---

4   Camshaft cover(s) – removal and installation

Refer to illustrations 4.3, 4.7, 4.8a, 4.8b, 4.10a, 4.10b, 4.11a and 4.11b

1   Disconnect the negative cable from the battery.

2   On 4A-LC engines, remove the air cleaner assembly.

3   Detach the PCV valve and breather hose from the camshaft cover **(see illustration)**.

4   On a DOHC engines, remove the spark plug wires from the spark plugs.

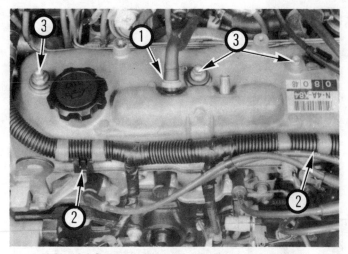

4.3   4A-LC camshaft cover and related components

1   PCV valve   3   Mounting nuts
2   Wire harness clips

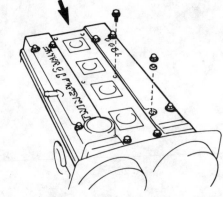

4.7   On 4A-GE engines, remove the center cover (arrow) first

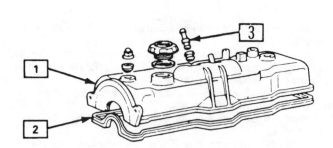

4.8a   4A-LC camshaft cover and related components – exploded view

1   Camshaft cover   3   PCV valve
2   Gasket

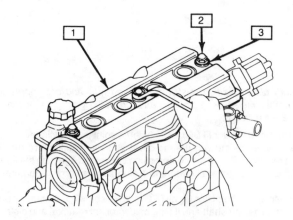

4.8b   4A-FE camshaft cover and related components

1   Camshaft cover   3   Seal
2   Mounting nut

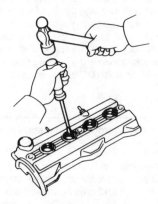

4.10a   Drive out the old spark plug tube seals (4A-FE engine only)

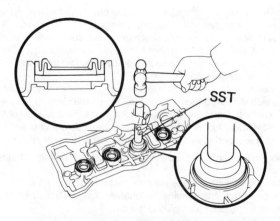

4.10b   Install the seals with a special service tool or a seal driver (4A-FE engine only)

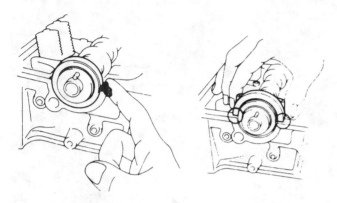

4.11a   On 4A-GE engines, apply sealant to the seal corners as shown

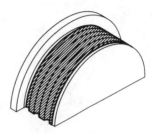

4.11b   On 4A-FE engines, coat the shaded area of the half-circle plug with sealant before installation

5   Label, detach and move aside any wiring harness that is in the way.
6   On 4A-LC engines, remove the upper timing belt cover, unclip the throttle cable from the cover and tie it aside.
7   On 4A-GE engines, remove the throttle cable (see Chapter 4) and the center cover and gasket **(see illustration)**.
8   Remove the mounting nuts/bolts and sealing washers, then detach the cover(s) and gasket from the head **(see illustrations)**. If the cover is stuck to the head, bump the end with a block of wood and a hammer to jar it loose. If that doesn't work, try to slip a flexible putty knife between the head and cover to break the seal. **Caution:** *Don't pry at the cover-to-head joint or damage to the sealing surfaces may occur, leading to oil leaks after the cover is reinstalled.*
9   The mating surfaces of the cylinder head and cover must be clean when the cover is installed. Use a gasket scraper to remove all traces of sealant and old gasket material, then clean the mating surfaces with lacquer thinner or acetone. If there's residue or oil on the mating surfaces when the cover is installed, oil leaks may develop.
10   On 4A-FE engines, drive the old spark plug tube seals out and install new ones **(see illustrations)**.
11   If you're working on a DOHC engine, apply a thin, uniform layer of sealant (GM 1052751 or equivalent) to the gasket mating surfaces and seal joints **(see illustrations)**.

12   Position a new gasket and seals (if used) on the cylinder head, then install the camshaft cover, sealing washers and nuts.
13   Tighten the nuts/bolts to the torque listed in this Chapter's specifications in three equal steps.
14   Reinstall the remaining parts, run the engine and check for oil leaks.

5   Intake manifold – removal and installation

Refer to illustrations 5.4, 5.5, 5.6, 5.7a, 5.7b, 5.7c, 5.7d and 5.8
Note: *On 4A-LC engines, the intake and exhaust manifolds share a common gasket. Therefore, you have to remove the exhaust manifold (see Section 6) to change the gasket.*
1   Disconnect the negative cable from the battery.
2   Drain the cooling system (see Chapter 1).
3   Remove the air cleaner, carburetor or throttle body, fuel injectors and fuel rail (if equipped) (see Chapter 4).
4   Remove lift the heat shield (if equipped) from the manifold **(see illustration)**.
5   Label and detach all wire harnesses, control cables, tubes, hoses and switches still connected to the intake manifold **(see illustration)**.

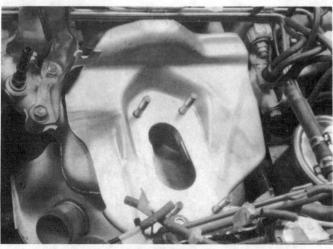

5.4   Remove the heat shield (4A-LC engine shown, others similar)

5.5   On 4A-LC engines, detach the vacuum switch (arrow) so the manifold mounting nut can be removed

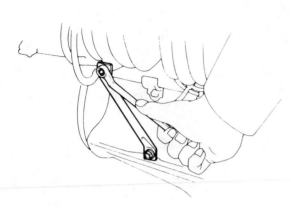

5.6   Remove all braces (note their locations to simplify installation)

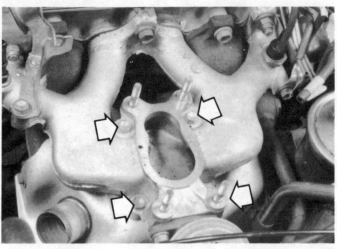

5.7a   On 4A-LC engines, remove the intake-to-exhaust manifold bolts (arrows)

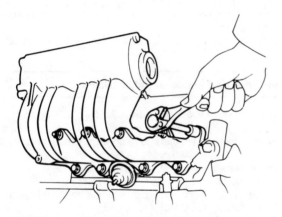

5.7b   Intake manifold mounting details (4A-GE engine)

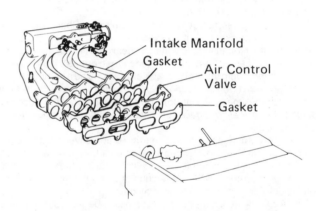

5.7c   On 4A-GE engines, remove the air control valve with the manifold

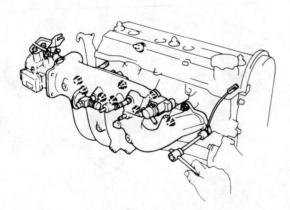

5.7d   Intake manifold mounting details (4A-FE engine)

5.8   Be very careful when scraping the gasket mating surfaces – the aluminum gouges very easily

6 Unbolt any braces still in place **(see illustration)**.

7 Remove the nuts/bolts, then detach the manifold from the engine **(see illustrations)**. If the manifold is stuck to the engine, tap it with a rubber mallet or place a block of wood on the manifold and tap it with a hammer. On 4A-LC engines, remove the exhaust manifold (see Section 6).

8 Use a scraper to remove all traces of old gasket material and sealant from the manifold and cylinder head **(see illustration)**, then clean the mating surfaces with lacquer thinner or acetone. If the gasket was leaking, have the manifold checked for warpage at an automotive machine shop and resurfaced if necessary.

9 Install a new gasket on the engine, then position the manifold on the head and install the nuts/bolts.

10 Tighten the nuts/bolts in three equal steps to the torque listed in this Chapter's specifications. Work from the center out towards the ends to avoid warping the manifold.

11 Install the remaining parts in the reverse order of removal.

12 Before starting the engine, check the throttle linkage for smooth operation.

13 Run the engine and check for coolant and vacuum leaks.

14 Road test the vehicle and check for proper operation of all accessories.

6 Exhaust manifold – removal and installation

Refer to illustrations 6.3a, 6.3b, 6.5, 6.6, 6.7a, 6.7b and 6.7c

Warning: *The engine must be completely cool before beginning this procedure.*

Note: *On 4A-LC engines, the intake and exhaust manifolds share the same gasket. To replace the gasket, the intake manifold must be removed first (see Section 5).*

1 Disconnect the negative cable from the battery.

2 Unplug the oxygen sensor wire harness. If you're replacing the manifold, transfer the sensor to the new manifold (see Chapter 6).

3 Remove the heat shield(s) from the manifold **(see illustrations)**.

4 Apply penetrating oil to the exhaust manifold mounting nuts/bolts and the exhaust pipe-to-manifold nuts.

5 Disconnect the exhaust pipe from the exhaust manifold **(see illustration)**.

6 Remove any manifold-to-block braces **(see illustration)**.

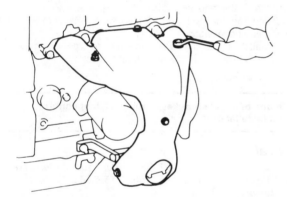

6.3a Remove the outer heat shield (4A-GE engine shown)

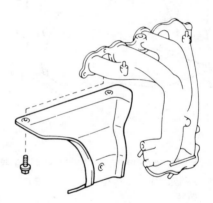

6.3b Unbolt the inner heat shield, if equipped

6.5 Apply penetrating oil, then remove the exhaust manifold-to-pipe mounting nuts

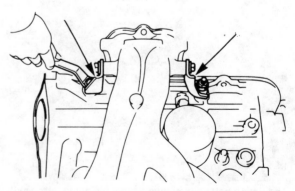

6.6 Remove the exhaust manifold braces (arrows) (4A-GE engine shown)

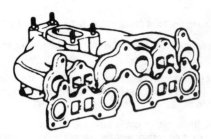

6.7a   4A-LC engine intake/exhaust manifold and gasket

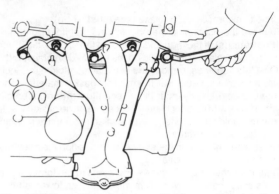

6.7b   4A-GE engine exhaust manifold mounting details

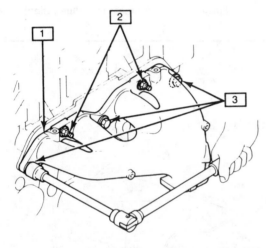

6.7c   4A-FE engine exhaust manifold mounting details

1	Exhaust manifold	3	Bolts
2	Nuts		

7   Remove the nuts/bolts and detach the manifold and gasket **(see illustrations)**.

8   Use a scraper to remove all traces of old gasket material and carbon deposits from the manifold and cylinder head mating surfaces. Be careful not to gouge the delicate aluminum surfaces on the cylinder head. If the gasket was leaking, have the manifold checked for warpage at an automotive machine shop and resurfaced if necessary.

9   Position a new gasket over the cylinder head studs. Install the manifold and thread the mounting nuts/bolts into place.

10   Working from the center out, tighten the nuts/bolts to the specified torque in three equal steps.

11   Reinstall the remaining parts in the reverse order of removal.

12   Run the engine and check for exhaust leaks.

7   Timing belt and sprockets – removal, inspection and installation

Removal

Refer to illustrations 7.1, 7.10a, 7.10b, 7.10c, 7.10d, 7.10e, 7.11a, 7.11b, 7.12a, 7.12b, 7.13a, 7.13b, 7.14a, 7.14b, 7.15, 7.16a, 7.16b, 7.16c, 7.16d, 7.17, 7.18a and 7.18b

7.1   The timing belt covers have removable plugs (arrows) that allow you to check the belt match marks without removing the covers (4A-LC engine shown)

7.10a   4A-LC engine timing belt cover bolt locations (arrows)

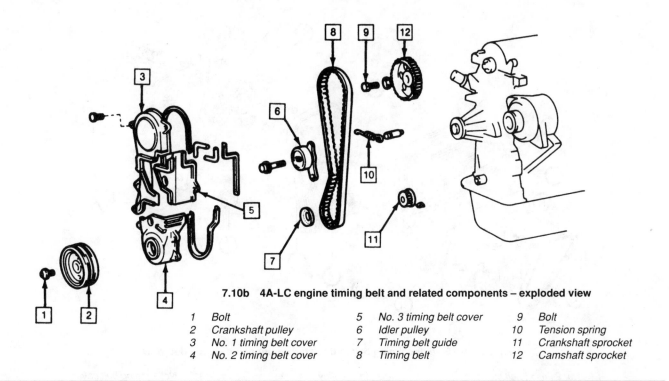

7.10b   4A-LC engine timing belt and related components – exploded view

1	Bolt	5	No. 3 timing belt cover	9	Bolt
2	Crankshaft pulley	6	Idler pulley	10	Tension spring
3	No. 1 timing belt cover	7	Timing belt guide	11	Crankshaft sprocket
4	No. 2 timing belt cover	8	Timing belt	12	Camshaft sprocket

1   The timing belt match marks may be checked without removing the covers **(see illustration)**.

2   Disconnect the negative cable from the battery.

3   Block the rear wheels and set the parking brake. Loosen the lug nuts on the right front wheel and raise the front of the vehicle. Support the front of the vehicle securely on jackstands.

4   Remove the right front wheel and right lower splash pan.

5   Loosen the water pump pulley bolts (see Chapter 3).

6   Remove the drivebelts (see Chapter 1).

7   Unbolt the cruise control actuator (if equipped) and set it aside. On models with 4A-FE engines, remove the windshield washer reservoir.

8   Support the engine and remove the engine mount (see Section 18). **Note:** *If you intend to remove the oil pan in addition to the timing belt, support the engine with a hoist from above (see Chapter 2B – engine removal).*

9   Remove the water pump pulley bolts and pulley. **Note:** *It may be necessary to remove the transaxle mount bolts (see Chapter 7) and raise the engine slightly to obtain clearance for pulley removal.*

10   Remove the upper (no. 1) timing belt cover and gaskets **(see illustrations)**.

11   Position the number one piston at TDC on the compression stroke (see Section 3). On 4A-LC and 4A-FE engines, make sure the small hole in the camshaft sprocket is aligned with the TDC mark on the cam bearing cap **(see illustration)**. On 4A-GE engines, align the marks on the sprockets with the marks on the rear cover **(see illustration)**.

12   Keep the crankshaft from turning with a large screwdriver or a pry bar (see Section 16). Remove the bolt and detach the pulley **(see illustrations)**. Sometimes the pulley can be removed by hand. **Caution:** *Do not use a jaw-type puller!*.

13   Remove the lower timing belt cover(s) and gaskets. It may be necessary to remove the air conditioner idler pulley **(see illustration)**. Slip the belt guide off the crankshaft, noting how it's installed **(see illustration)**.

14   If you plan to reuse the timing belt, paint match marks between each sprocket and the belt and an arrow indicating the belt's direction of travel **(see illustrations)**.

15   Loosen the timing belt idler pulley set bolt **(see illustration)** and push the pulley down (against spring tension) as far as it will go, then temporarily tighten it. Slip the belt off the sprockets.

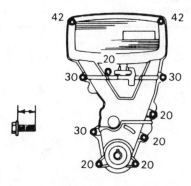

7.10c   4A-GE engine timing belt cover bolt locations – the numbers indicate the various lengths (in millimeters)

16   If a camshaft sprocket is worn or damaged, or if you're replacing the camshaft oil seal(s), remove the camshaft cover, hold the camshaft with a large wrench and remove the bolt, then detach the sprocket **(see illustration)**. Note the locations of the knock pins and/or index marks for correct sprocket installation **(see illustrations)**.

17   On 4A-GE engines, after the camshaft sprockets are removed, the rear cover bolts are accessible **(see illustration)**.

18   The match marks on the crankshaft sprocket and oil pump housing must be aligned **(see illustration)**. If the sprocket is worn or damaged, or if you need to get at the oil pump or front crankshaft oil seal, remove the sprocket from the crankshaft **(see illustration)**.

Inspection

Refer to illustrations 7.19a, 7.19b, 7.21, 7.22 and 7.23

Caution: *Do not bend, twist or turn the timing belt inside out. Do not allow it to come in contact with oil, coolant or fuel. Do not utilize timing belt tension*

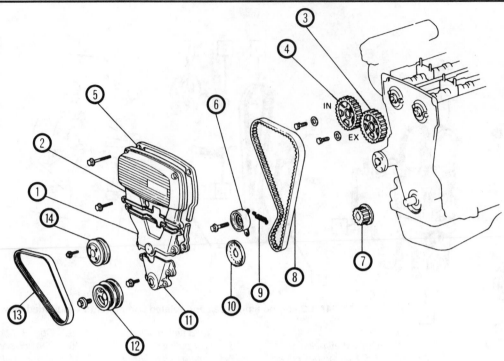

7.10d   4A-GE engine timing belt and related components – exploded view

1	No. 2 timing belt cover	6	Idler pulley	11	No. 1 timing belt cover
2	No. 3 timing belt cover	7	Crankshaft sprocket	12	Crankshaft pulley
3	Exhaust camshaft sprocket	8	Timing belt	13	Drivebelt
4	Intake camshaft sprocket	9	Tension spring	14	Water pump pulley
5	Gasket	10	Timing belt guide		

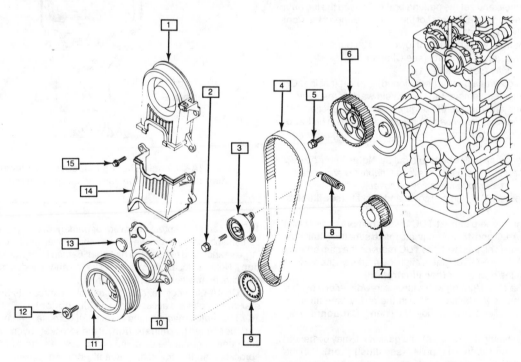

7.10e   4A-FE engine timing belt and related components – exploded view

1	Upper timing belt cover	6	Camshaft sprocket	11	Crankshaft pulley
2	Bolt	7	Crankshaft sprocket	12	Bolt
3	Idler pulley	8	Tension spring	13	Inspection plug
4	Timing belt	9	Timing belt guide	14	Center timing belt cover
5	Bolt	10	Lower timing belt cover	15	Bolt

7.11a   On 4A-LC and 4A-FE engines, align the camshaft sprocket timing hole (arrow) with the center mark on the cylinder head

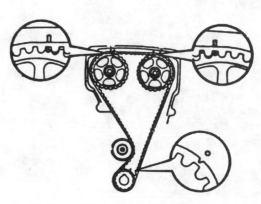

7.11b   On 4A-GE engines, align the marks on the sprockets with the marks on the rear cover, as shown

7.12a   Remove the crankshaft pulley bolt, . . .

7.12b   . . . then use a puller that applies force to the hub to remove the crankshaft pulley – a jaw-type puller will damage the pulley

7.13a   Remove the A/C idler pulley nut (arrow), then detach the pulley

7.13b   The cupped edge (arrow) of the timing belt guide must face out when it's reinstalled

7.14a If you're going to re-use the belt, index it to the camshaft sprocket(s) (4A-GE engine shown)

7.14b Also, be sure to mark the belt's direction of rotation, then index the belt to the crankshaft sprocket

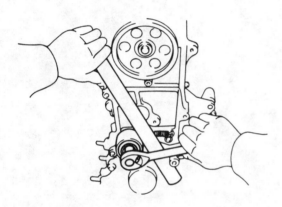

7.15 Temporarily pry the sprocket aside and retighten the bolt

7.16a When removing the camshaft sprocket bolt, hold the camshaft with a large wrench as shown – DO NOT use the timing belt tension to keep the camshaft from turning!

7.16b When removing or installing the camshaft sprockets on a 4A-GE engine, make sure the camshaft sprocket index marks are aligned with the stationary marks on the rear timing belt cover

7.16c On 4A-GE engines, the knock pins (arrows) on the camshafts should be positioned as shown, with the pin on the intake camshaft at 12 o'clock and the pin on the exhaust cam at five o'clock

7.16d   On 4A-FE engines, the knock pin should be at approximately 11 o'clock (arrow)

7.17   On 4A-GE engines, to pull the rear timing belt cover off the cylinder head, remove all seven bolts – the seventh bolt, which isn't visible in this photo, is just below and to the right of the engine mounting bracket (if the cover must be removed, the engine mounting bracket must be disconnected)

7.18a   The match marks on the crankshaft sprocket and oil pump housing must align (arrows)

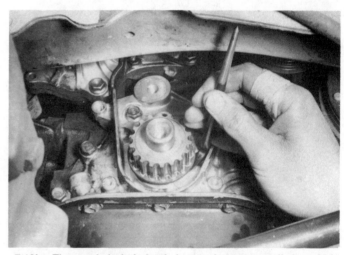

7.18b   The crankshaft timing belt sprocket can usually be pried off with a small pry bar – if the sprocket is stuck, use a puller

7.19a   To remove the timing belt idler pulley, remove the bolt and detach the spring (arrows)

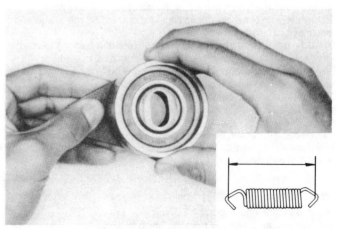

7.19b   Check the idler pulley bearing for smooth operation and measure the free length of the spring

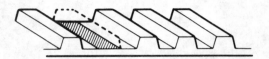

7.21   Check the timing belt for cracked and missing teeth

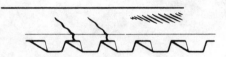

7.22   If the belt is cracked or worn, check the sprockets for nicks and burrs

7.23   Wear on one side of the belt indicates sprocket misalignment

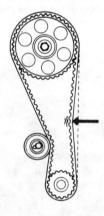

7.35a   On 4A-LC and 4A-FE engines, check the timing belt deflection here (arrow)

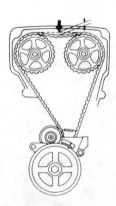

7.35b   On 4A-GE engines, check the timing belt deflection at the top (arrows)

to keep the camshaft or crankshaft from turning when installing the sprocket bolt(s). *Do not turn the crankshaft or camshaft more than a few degrees (necessary for tooth alignment) while the timing belt is removed.*
19   Remove the idler pulley and check the bearings for smooth operation and excessive play **(see illustration)**. Inspect the spring for damage and compare the free length to the Specifications **(see illustration)**.
20   If the timing belt broke during engine operation, the valves and/or pistons may be damaged.
21   If the belt teeth are cracked or pulled off **(see illustration)**, the distributor, water pump, oil pump or camshaft(s) may have seized.
22   If there is noticeable wear or cracks in the belt, check to see if there are nicks or burrs on the sprockets **(see illustration)**.
23   If there is wear or damage on only one side of the belt, check the belt guide and the alignment of all sprockets and the idler pulley **(see illustration)**.
24   Replace the timing belt with a new one if obvious wear or damage is noted or if it's the least bit questionable. Correct any problems which contributed to belt failure prior to belt installation.

Installation

Refer to illustrations 7.35a and 7.35b
25   Remove all dirt and oil from the timing belt area.
26   If it was removed, install the idler pulley and tension spring. The idler should be pulled back against spring tension as far as possible and the bolt temporarily tightened.

27   Recheck the camshaft and crankshaft timing marks to be sure they are properly aligned.
28   Install the timing belt on the crankshaft and camshaft sprockets and idler pulley. If the original belt is being reinstalled, align the marks made during removal.
29   Slip the belt guide onto the crankshaft with the cupped side facing out **(see illustration 7.13b)**.
30   Keep tension on the side nearest the front of the vehicle. If the original belt is being reinstalled, align the marks made during removal.
31   Loosen the idler pulley bolt 1/2-turn, allowing the spring to apply pressure to the idler pulley.
32   Tighten the idler pulley mounting bolt to the torque listed in this Chapter's specifications.
33   Slowly turn the crankshaft clockwise by hand two complete revolutions (720 degrees). If resistance is felt, stop and recheck your work. Don't force the crankshaft to turn – pistons may hit open valves if the valve timing is incorrect.
34   Recheck the timing match marks. If the marks aren't aligned exactly, repeat the belt installation procedure. **Caution:** *DO NOT start the engine until you're absolutely certain the timing belt is installed correctly. Serious and costly engine damage could occur if the belt is installed wrong.*
35   Measure the timing belt deflection **(see illustrations)** and compare it to this Chapter's specifications. If the belt is too loose or tight, repeat the adjustment procedure, then recheck it.
36   Reinstall the remaining parts in the reverse order of removal.
37   Run the engine and check for proper operation.

8.2   Carefully pry the old seal out of the oil pump housing

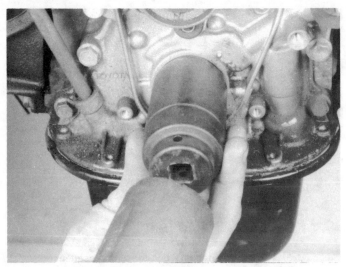

8.4   Gently tap the new seal into place with a hammer and a deep socket

8   Crankshaft front oil seal – replacement

Refer to illustrations 8.2 and 8.4

1   Remove the timing belt and crankshaft sprocket (see Section 7).
2   Note how far the seal is seated in the bore, then carefully pry it out of the oil pump housing with a screwdriver or seal removal tool **(see illustration)**. Don't scratch the housing bore or damage the crankshaft in the process (if the crankshaft is damaged, the new seal will end up leaking).
3   Clean the bore in the housing and coat the outer edge of the new seal with engine oil or multi-purpose grease. Apply moly-base grease to the seal lip.
4   Using a socket with an outside diameter slightly smaller than the outside diameter of the seal, carefully drive the new seal into place with a hammer **(see illustration)**. Make sure it's installed squarely and driven in to the same depth as the original. If a socket isn't available, a short section of large diameter pipe will also work. Check the seal after installation to make sure the garter spring didn't pop out of place.
5   Reinstall the crankshaft sprocket and timing belt (Section 7).
6   Run the engine and check for oil leaks at the front seal.

9   Camshaft oil seal(s) – replacement

Refer to illustrations 9.2 and 9.4

1   Remove the timing belt, camshaft sprocket(s) and rear timing belt cover, if equipped (see Section 7).
2   Note how far the seal is seated in the bore, then carefully pry it out with a small screwdriver **(see illustration)**. Don't scratch the bore or damage the camshaft in the process (if the camshaft is damaged, the new seal will end up leaking).
3   Clean the bore and coat the outer edge of the new seal with engine oil or multi-purpose grease. Apply moly-base grease to the seal lip.
4   Using a socket with an outside diameter slightly smaller than the outside diameter of the seal, carefully drive the new seal into place with a hammer **(see illustration)**. Make sure it's installed squarely and driven in to the same depth as the original. If a socket isn't available, a short section of pipe will also work.
5   Reinstall the camshaft sprocket and timing belt (Section 7).
6   Run the engine and check for oil leaks at the camshaft seal.

9.2   Pry the old seal out with a screwdriver

9.4   Drive the new seal into place with a hammer and a deep socket

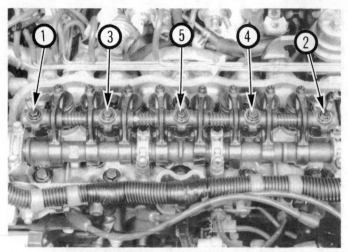

10.5   Rocker arm pedestal bolt loosening sequence

10.6   Leave the bolts in place to hold the rocker arm assembly together as you lift it off the engine

---

10   Camshaft and rocker arms – removal, inspection and installation (4A-LC engine only)

Rocker arm removal

Refer to illustrations 10.5 and 10.6

1   Remove the negative cable from the battery.
2   Set the engine at Top Dead Center (see Section 3).
3   Remove the camshaft cover (see Section 4).
4   Loosen the lock nuts and back off the adjustment screws until they no longer place tension on the valves.
5   Remove the rocker arm shaft by loosening each pedestal bolt a little at a time in the sequence shown **(see illustration)**.
6   Leave the bolts in place to hold the rocker arm assembly together and lift the rocker arm assembly up as a unit **(see illustration)**.

Camshaft removal

Refer to illustrations 10.8, 10.10a and 10.10b

7   Remove the timing belt and the camshaft sprocket (see Section 7).
8   With the camshaft still in the cylinder head, use a dial indicator to check the endplay. Attach the gauge to the end of the head and move the camshaft all the way to the rear. Next, use a screwdriver to pry it all the way forward **(see illustration)**. If the end play exceeds the specified limit, replace the camshaft and/or the cylinder head .

9   Remove the distributor and fuel pump (see Chapters 4 and 5).
10   Mark the bearing caps to ensure reinstallation in the same location. Loosen the bearing cap bolts in the sequence shown **(see illustration)** and lift the bearing caps off. Remove the camshaft from the cylinder head and slip the oil seal off the end **(see illustration)**.

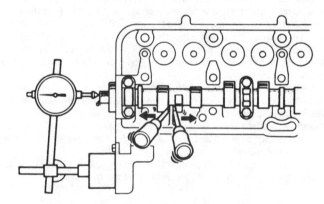

10.8   Using a screwdriver as shown, pry the camshaft back-and-forth to check the endplay (thrust clearance)

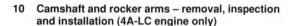

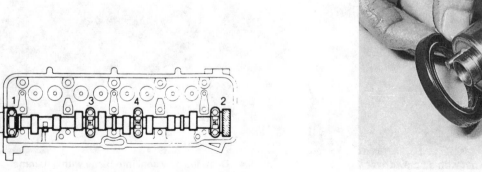

10.10a   Camshaft bearing cap bolt loosening sequence

10.10b   Slip the old oil seal off
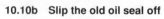

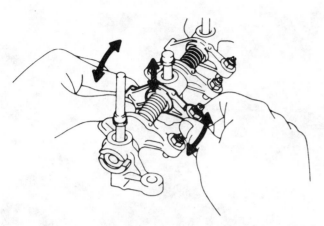

10.11a Move the rocker arms up-and-down and back-and-forth to check for play

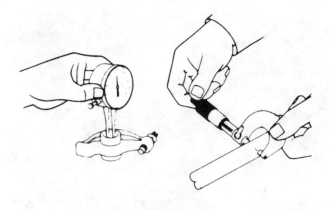

10.11b Measure the diameter of the rocker arm bore and rocker arm shaft

Rocker arm and shaft inspection

Refer to illustrations 10.11a and 10.11b

11   Check the clearance between the rocker arms and shaft by moving the rocker arms as shown **(see illustration)**. Little or no movement should be felt. If movement is felt, disassemble the rocker arm shaft assembly. Lay the components out in order so they can be installed in their original locations. Visually inspect the rocker arm-to-camshaft contact surface. Replace any rockers that are worn excessively. Measure the oil clearance as follows: Using an inside micrometer or dial indicator, measure the inside diameter of the rocker arm, then, using an outside micrometer, measure the diameter of the shaft where the rocker arm rides **(see illustration)**. Subtract the shaft diameter from the rocker arm diameter and compare the result to this Chapter's specifications. Replace the rocker arms and/or shafts as necessary.

Camshaft inspection

Refer to illustrations 10.12, 10.13, 10.14, 10.15a and 10.15b

12   Visually inspect the camshaft journals, lobes and distributor gear. Check for score marks, pitting and evidence of wear or overheating (blue, discolored areas) **(see illustration)**. If wear is excessive or damage is evident, the component will have to be replaced.

13   Using a micrometer, measure the cam lobe height and compare it to this Chapter's specifications. If the lobe height is less than the minimum allowable, the camshaft is worn and must be replaced **(see illustration)**.

14   Using a micrometer, measure the diameter of each journal and compare it to the Specifications **(see illustration)**. If the journals are worn or damaged, replace the camshaft.

10.12 Check the cam lobes for pitting, wear and score marks – if scoring is excessive, as is the case here, replace the camshaft

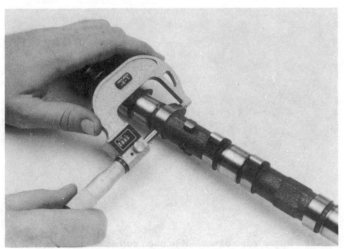

10.13   Measure the lobe heights on each camshaft – if any lobe height is less than the specified allowable minimum, replace that camshaft

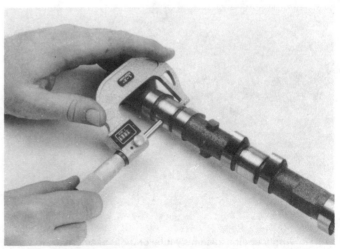

10.14   Measure each journal diameter with a micrometer (if any journal measures less than the specified limit, replace the camshaft)

10.15a   Lay a strip of Plastigage on each camshaft journal

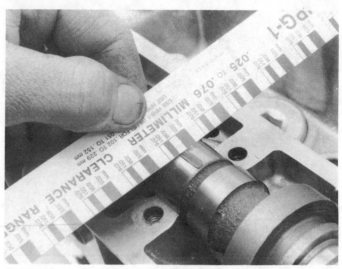

10.15b   Compare the width of the crushed Plastigage to the scale
on the envelope to determine the oil clearance

15   Check the oil clearance for each camshaft journal as follows:
   a) Clean the bearing caps and the camshaft journals with lacquer thin-
      ner or acetone.
   b) Carefully lay the camshaft in place in the head. Don't use any lubri-
      cation.
   c) Lay a strip of Plastigage on each journal (see illustration).
   d) Install the bearing caps with the arrows pointing toward the front
      (timing belt end) of the engine.
   e) Tighten the bolts to the specified torque in 1/4-turn increments.
      Note: Don't turn the camshaft while the Plastigage is in place.
   f) Remove the bolts and detach the caps.
   g) Compare the width of the crushed Plastigage (at its widest point)
      to the scale on the Plastigage envelope (see illustration).
   h) If the clearance is greater than specified, replace the camshaft and/
      or the cylinder head.

   i) Scrape off the Plastigage with your fingernail or the edge of a credit
      card – don't scratch or nick the journals or caps.

Camshaft installation

Refer to illustrations 10.17, 10.18a, 10.18b and 10.18c

16   Installation is basically the reverse of the removal procedure. However, keep the following points in mind:

17   Apply engine assembly lube or moly-base grease to the camshaft
lobes and journals (see illustration). Also apply the same lubricant to the
rocker arms and oil seal lips. Slip a new oil seal over the end of the camshaft with the spring side facing in.

18   Place the camshaft in the cylinder head with the seal correctly positioned. Apply dabs of RTV sealant at the number one cam bearing cap-to-
head joint (see illustration). Install the bearing caps in the original
locations and tighten the bolts in three steps, in the sequence shown (see

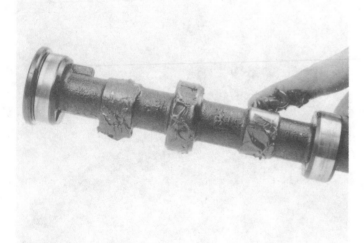

10.17   Apply engine assembly lube or moly-base grease to the
cam lobes and journals before installing the camshaft
in the engine

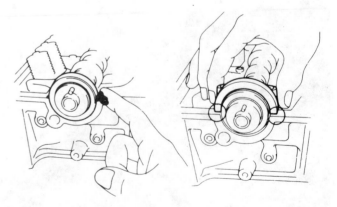

10.18a   Apply a dab of sealant to each corner of the number one
bearing cap

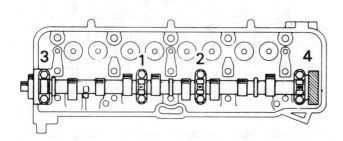

10.18b   Camshaft bearing cap bolt tightening sequence

10.18c   Install the studs in these locations (arrows)

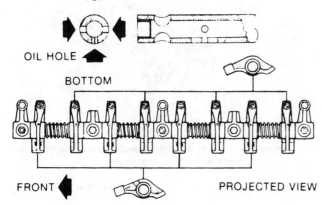

10.19   The rocker arm shaft oil holes must be positioned
as shown

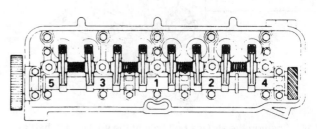

10.20   Rocker arm bolt tightening sequence

illustration), to the specified torque. Be sure the studs that fasten the camshaft cover are in the correct places (see illustration).

Rocker arm installation

Refer to illustrations 10.19 and 10.20

19   If the rocker shaft was disassembled, install the components on the shaft in their original locations. Be sure to apply engine assembly lube or moly-base grease to the moving surfaces. Before installing the shaft on the engine, be sure the oil holes pointing left, right and down, as shown (see illustration).

20   Install and tighten the rocker arm mounting bolts gradually, in three steps, following the sequence shown (see illustration) until the torque specified in this Chapter is reached.

21   Adjust the valve clearances as described in Chapter 1.

22   Reinstall the remaining components in the reverse order of removal.

11   Camshafts and valve lifters – removal, inspection and installation (DOHC engines only)

Camshaft removal (4A-GE engine)

Refer to illustrations 11.4 and 11.5

1   Remove the camshaft covers (see Section 4).

2   Remove the timing belt, camshaft sprockets and rear timing belt cover (see Section 7).

3   Remove the distributor (see Chapter 5).

4   Measure the camshaft endplay with a dial indicator (see illustration). If the play is greater than the specified maximum, replace the camshaft and/or the cylinder head.

5   Check the bearing caps for numbers and mark them, if necessary, for proper reinstallation. Loosen the camshaft bearing cap bolts in the sequence shown (see illustration). Now remove the bearing caps and lift each camshaft from the engine.

Camshaft removal (4A-FE engine)

Refer to illustrations 11.10, 11.11, 11.12, 11.13, 11.14, 11.15, 11.16, 11.17, 11.18 and 11.19

Note: *Before beginning this procedure, obtain three 6 x 1.0 mm bolts, 16 to 20 mm long. They will be referred to as service bolts in the text.*

6   Remove the camshaft cover as described in Section 4.

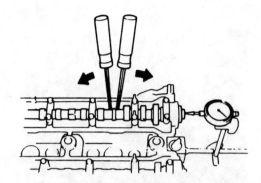

11.4   Pry the camshaft back-and-forth with the dial indicator mounted as shown to measure endplay (4A-GE engine shown)

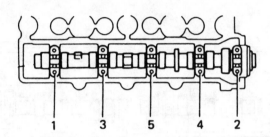

11.5   On 4A-GE engines, loosen the camshaft bearing caps in the sequence shown here

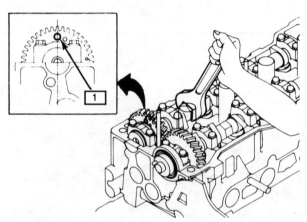

11.10   Position the service bolt hole of the intake camshaft as shown here

1   Service bolt hole

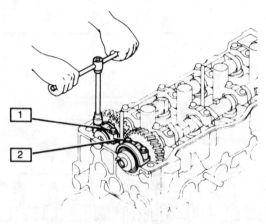

11.11   Loosen the number one intake and exhaust bearing cap bolts in 1/4-turn increments

1   Intake bearing cap bolt   2   Exhaust bearing cap bolt

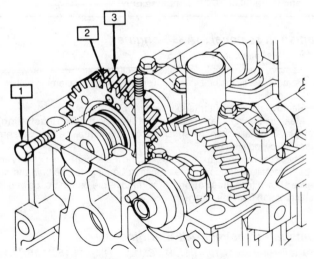

11.12   Install a service bolt

1   Service bolt   3   Main gear
2   Sub-gear

7   Remove the distributor (see Chapter 5).
8   Remove the timing belt and camshaft sprocket (see Section 7).
9   Measure the camshaft thrust clearance (endplay) with a dial indicator **(see illustration 11.4)**. If the clearance is greater than the specified maximum, replace the camshaft and/or the cylinder head.

Intake camshaft
10   Position the service bolt hole of the intake camshaft gear at the top **(see illustration)**.
11   Alternately loosen the number one intake and exhaust bearing cap bolts a little at a time until they can be removed **(see illustration)**.
12   Secure the intake camshaft sub-gear to the main gear with one of the service bolts **(see illustration)**. **Caution:** *When removing the camshaft, make certain the torsional spring force of the sub-gear has been eliminated by the above operation.*
13   Uniformly loosen the intake camshaft bearing cap bolts in 1/4-turn increments in the sequence shown **(see illustration)** until the bolts can be removed by hand. Lift off the bearing caps and remove the camshaft. **Caution:** *As the bearing cap bolts are being loosened, make sure the camshaft is moving up evenly. If one end or the other stops moving and the cam gets cocked, start over by retightening the bolts evenly.*
14   To disassemble the intake camshaft, mount it in a vise with the jaws gripping the large hex on the shaft. Install the two remaining service bolts

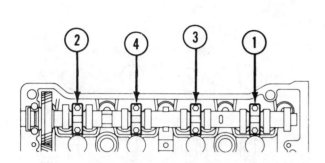

11.13   Loosen the intake camshaft bearing cap bolts in the sequence shown here

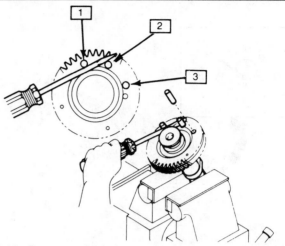

11.14   Pry on service bolts 1 and 2 to remove service bolt 3 (installed in Step 12)

11.15   Remove the sub-gear snap-ring with snap-ring pliers

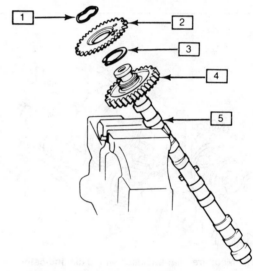

11.16   4A-FE intake camshaft and related components – exploded view

1 *Wave washer*	4 *Camshaft gear*
2 *Camshaft sub-gear*	5 *Camshaft*
3 *Camshaft gear spring*	

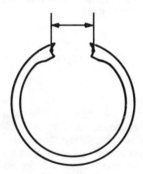

11.17   Measure the distance between the ends of the camshaft gear spring

16   The wave washer, sub-gear and camshaft gear spring and oil seal can now be removed from the camshaft **(see illustration)**.
17   Measure the free length (distance between the ends) of the camshaft gear spring **(see illustration)** and compare it to the Specifications. Replace the spring if the distance isn't within specifications

Exhaust camshaft
18   Turn the exhaust camshaft until the knock pin is near the bottom as shown **(see illustration)**.
19   Loosen the bearing cap bolts in 1/4-turn increments, following the sequence shown **(see illustration)**. **Caution:** *As the bearing cap bolts are being loosened, make sure the camshaft is moving up evenly. If one end or the other stops moving and the cam gets cocked, start over by retightening the bolts evenly.* Detach the bearing caps and lift the camshaft out of the head.

in the unthreaded holes in the camshaft sub-gear. Using a screwdriver positioned against the service bolts just installed, rotate the sub-gear clockwise and remove the number three service bolt (the one installed in Step 12) **(see illustration)**.
15   Remove the sub-gear snap-ring **(see illustration)**.

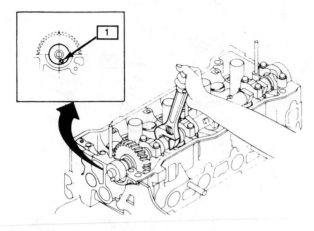

1 KNOCKPIN POSITION

11.18   Turn the exhaust camshaft until the knock pin is in the position shown here

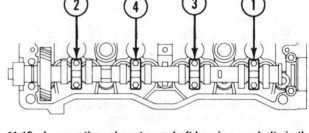

11.19   Loosen the exhaust camshaft bearing cap bolts in the sequence shown here

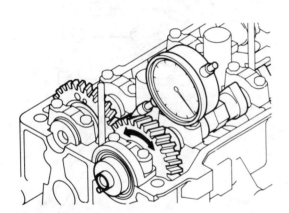

11.21   Measure gear backlash with a dial indicator

11.22   Wipe the oil off the valve shims and mark the intakes I and the exhausts E – a magnetic tool works well for removing the lifters

11.23   Wipe off the oil and inspect each lifter for wear and scuffing

Inspection

Camshaft

Refer to illustration 11.21

20   Refer to Section 10 for camshaft inspection and lobe height and oil clearance measurement procedures.

21   On 4A-FE engines, temporarily install the camshafts without installing the lifters or exhaust camshaft sub-gear. Measure the gear backlash (the freeplay between the gear teeth) with a dial indicator **(see illustration)** and compare it to the Specifications. If the backlash exceeds specifications, replace the camshafts.

Lifters

Refer to illustrations 11.22, 11.23, 11.24a and 11.24b

22   Carefully label, then remove the valve lifters and shims **(see illustration)**.

23   Inspect each lifter for scuffing and score marks **(see illustration)**.

24   Measure the outside diameter of each lifter and the corresponding lifter bore inside diameter **(see illustrations)**. Subtract the lifter diameter from the lifter bore diameter to determine the oil clearance. Compare it to

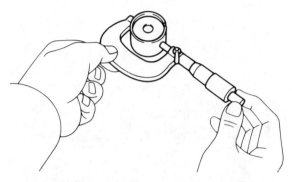

11.24a   Use a micrometer to measure lifter diameter

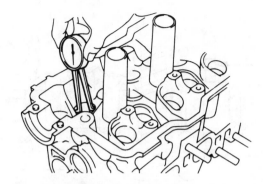

11.24b   Measure the inside diameters of the lifter bores

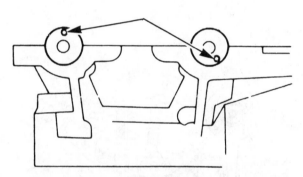

11.28a   On 4A-GE engines, position the knock pins as shown (arrows)

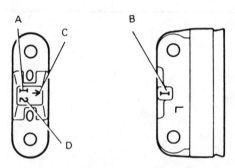

11.28b   4A-GE camshaft bearing cap marks

A   I = intake; E = exhaust   C   Front mark
B   I = intake; E = exhaust   D   Inside diameter for
                                          bearings 2 through 5

the Specifications. If the oil clearance is excessive, a new head and/or new lifters will be required.

25   Store the lifters in a clean box, separated from each other, so they won't be damaged. Make sure the shims stay with the lifters (don't mix them up).

Camshaft installation (4A-GE engine)

Refer to illustrations 11.28a, 11.28b and 11.28c

26   Installation is basically the reverse of the removal procedure. However, keep the following points in mind.

27   Apply engine assembly lube or moly-base grease to the camshaft lobes and journals. Also apply the same lubricant to the sides of the lifters and the lifter shims. Install the lifters and shims in the same positions they were removed from.

28   Lubricate the lip of a new oil seal, then slip it over the end of the camshaft with the spring side facing in. Place the camshaft in the cylinder head with the seal correctly positioned and the knock pin positioned as shown (**see illustration**). Install the bearing caps in the original locations (**see illustration**). Tighten the bolts in three steps, in the sequence shown (**see illustration**) to the specified torque.

Camshaft installation (4A-FE engine)

Refer to illustrations 11.33, 11.34, 11.35, 11.36, 11.37 and 11.39

Exhaust camshaft

29   Apply moly-base grease or engine assembly lube to the lifters, then

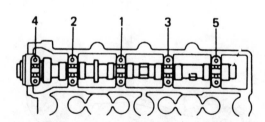

11.28c   On 4A-GE engines, tighten the camshaft bearing cap bolts in the sequence shown here

install them in their original locations. Make sure the valve adjustment shims are in place in the lifters.

30   Apply moly-base grease or engine assembly lube to the camshaft lobes and bearing journals.

31   Reassemble the camshaft subgear assembly in the reverse order of removal.

32   Position the exhaust camshaft in the cylinder head with the knock pin near the bottom (**see illustration 11.18**).

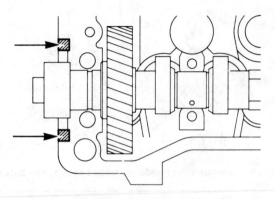

11.33   Apply a dab of RTV sealant to the shaded areas (arrows) adjacent to the oil seal

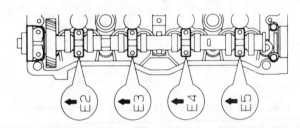

11.34   Install the exhaust camshaft bearing caps with the marks as shown here and the arrows pointing toward the timing belt end of the engine

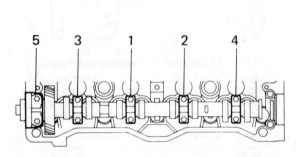

11.35   Tighten the camshaft bearing cap bolts in 1/4-turn increments – follow the sequence shown here

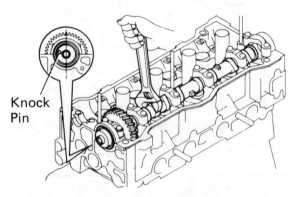

11.36   Turn the exhaust camshaft until the knock pin is positioned as shown here

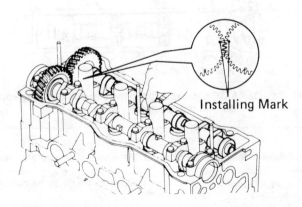

11.37   Mesh the gears with the installing marks aligned

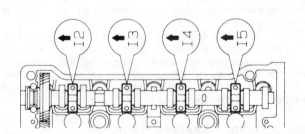

11.39   Install the intake camshaft bearing caps with the marks as shown here and the arrows pointing toward the timing belt end of the engine

33 Apply a thin coat of RTV sealant to the front of the cylinder head at the bearing cap mating surface **(see illustration)**. **Note:** *The cap must be installed immediately or the sealant will dry prematurely.*

34 Install the bearing caps in numerical order with the arrows pointing toward the timing belt end of the engine **(see illustration)**.

35 Tighten the bearing cap bolts in 1/4-turn increments until the specified torque is reached. Follow the factory recommended sequence **(see illustration)**.

Intake camshaft

36 Rotate the exhaust camshaft until the knock pin is located just above the 9 o'clock position **(see illustration)**.

37 Mesh the intake camshaft gear with the exhaust camshaft gear by matching up the installing marks on the gears **(see illustration)**.

38 Roll the intake camshaft down into position. Turn the exhaust camshaft back-and-forth a little until the intake camshaft sits in the bearings evenly.

39 Install the bearing caps (except the one at the timing belt end of the engine) in numerical order with the arrows pointing toward the timing belt end **(see illustration)**.

40 Tighten the bearing cap bolts in 1/4-turn increments until the specified torque is reached. Follow the factory recommended sequence **(see illustration 11.35)**.

41 Remove the service bolt from the camshaft gear.

42 Install the remaining camshaft bearing cap and tighten the bolts to the specified torque.

43 Install the timing belt and sprocket (see Section 7).

44 The remainder of installation is the reverse of the removal procedure.

---

12 Valve springs, retainers and seals – replacement (4A-LC engine only)

Refer to illustrations 12.4, 12.9, 12.15 and 12.17

Note: *Broken valve springs and defective valve stem seals can be replaced without removing the cylinder head. Two special tools and a compressed air source are normally required to perform this operation, so read through this Section carefully and rent or buy the tools before beginning the job. If compressed air isn't available, a length of nylon rope can be used to keep the valves from falling into the cylinder during this procedure.*

1 Refer to Section 10 and remove the rocker arm assembly.

2 Remove the spark plug from the cylinder which has the defective component. If all of the valve stem seals are being replaced, all of the spark plugs sho 'd be removed.

3 Turn the crankshaft until the piston in the affected cylinder is at top dead center on the compression stroke (refer to Section 3 for instructions). If you're replacing all of the valve stem seals, begin with cylinder number one and work on the valves for one cylinder at a time. Move from cylinder-to-cylinder following the firing order sequence (1-3-4-2).

4 Thread an adapter into the spark plug hole **(see illustration)** and connect an air hose from a compressed air source to it. Most auto parts stores can supply the air hose adapter. **Note:** *Many cylinder compression gauges utilize a screw-in fitting that may work with your air hose quick-disconnect fitting.*

5 Apply compressed air to the cylinder. **Warning:** *The piston may be forced down by compressed air, causing the crankshaft to turn suddenly. If the wrench used when positioning the number one piston at TDC is still attached to the bolt in the crankshaft nose, it could cause damage or injury when the crankshaft moves.*

6 The valves should be held in place by the air pressure. If the valve faces or seats are in poor condition, leaks may prevent air pressure from retaining the valves – refer to the alternative procedure below.

7 If you don't have access to compressed air, an alternative method can be used. Position the piston at a point just before TDC on the compression stroke, then feed a long piece of nylon rope through the spark plug hole until it fills the combustion chamber. Be sure to leave the end of the rope hanging out of the engine so it can be removed easily.

8 Use a large ratchet and socket to rotate the crankshaft in the normal direction of rotation (clockwise, viewed from the drivebelt end) until slight resistance is felt.

9 Stuff shop rags into the cylinder head holes above and below the valves to prevent parts and tools from falling into the engine, then use a valve spring compressor to compress the spring. Remove the keepers with small needle-nose pliers or a magnet **(see illustration)**. **Note:** *A couple of different types of tools are available for compressing the valve springs with the head in place. One type grips the lower spring coils and presses on the retainer as the knob is turned. The other type utilizes a lever pulling against the camshaft. Both types work very well.*

10 Remove the spring retainer and valve spring, then remove the stem oil seal. **Note:** *If air pressure fails to hold the valve in the closed position during this operation, the valve face and/or seat is probably damaged. If so, the cylinder head will have to be removed for additional repair operations.*

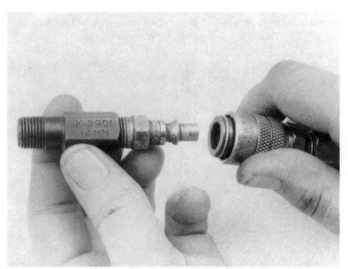

12.4 This is what the air hose adapter that threads into the spark plug hole looks like – they're commonly available from auto parts stores

12.9 This type of spring compressor pulls against the camshaft – use a small magnet (shown) or needle-nose pliers to remove the valve keepers

12.15   Gently tap the seal into place with a hammer and deep socket

12.17   Apply a small dab of grease to each keeper before installation to hold it in place on the valve stem until the spring is released

11   Wrap a rubber band or tape around the top of the valve stem so the valve won't fall into the combustion chamber, then release the air pressure. **Note:** *If a rope was used instead of air pressure, turn the crankshaft slightly in the direction opposite normal rotation.*
12   Inspect the valve stem for damage. Rotate the valve in the guide and check the end for eccentric movement, which would indicate that the valve is bent.
13   Move the valve up-and-down in the guide and make sure it doesn't bind. If the valve stem binds, either the valve is bent or the guide is damaged. In either case, the head will have to be removed for repair.
14   Reapply air pressure to the cylinder to retain the valve in the closed position, then remove the tape or rubber band from the valve stem. If a rope was used instead of air pressure, rotate the crankshaft in the normal direction of rotation until slight resistance is felt.
15   Lubricate the valve stem with engine oil and install a new oil seal **(see illustration)**.
16   Install the spring in position over the valve. Be sure the closely wound coils are next to the head.
17   Install the valve spring retainer. Compress the valve spring and carefully position the keepers in the groove. Apply a small dab of grease to the inside of each keeper to hold it in place if necessary **(see illustration)**.
18   Remove the pressure from the spring tool and make sure the keepers are seated.
19   Disconnect the air hose and remove the adapter from the spark plug hole. If a rope was used in place of air pressure, pull it out of the cylinder.
20   Refer to Section 10 and install the rocker arm assembly.
21   Install the spark plug(s) and connect the wire(s).
22   Start and run the engine, then check for oil leaks and unusual sounds coming from the camshaft cover area.

---

13   Cylinder head – removal and installation

Note: *The engine must be completely cool before beginning this procedure.*

Removal

Refer to illustrations 13.13, 13.14a, 13.14b and 13.15
1   Disconnect the negative cable from the battery.
2   Drain the coolant from the engine block and radiator. Drain the engine oil and remove the oil filter (see Chapter 1).

3   Remove the spark plugs.
4   Remove the carburetor or throttle body and fuel injectors and fuel rail (if equipped) (see Chapter 4).
5   Remove the intake and exhaust manifolds (see Sections 5 and 6). **Note:** *On 4A-LC and 4A-FE engines, the manifolds may be left on the cylinder head until after the head is removed from the engine. However, this makes it more difficult to lift the head.*
6   Remove the camshaft cover(s) as described in Section 4.
7   Remove the timing belt and camshaft sprockets (see Section 7). On 4A-FE engines, remove the rear timing belt cover.
8   On 4A-LC engines, remove the camshaft and rocker arms (see Section 10).
9   On 4A-GE and 4A-FE engines, remove the camshafts and lifters (see Section 11).
10   Remove the alternator and distributor (see Chapter 5).
11   Unbolt the power steering pump (if equipped) and set it aside without disconnecting the hoses (see Chapter 10).
12   Unbolt the engine mount bracket from the engine (below the camshaft sprocket).
13   Check the cylinder head. Label and remove any remaining items, such as coolant lines, tubes, cables, hoses or wires **(see illustration)**. At this point the head should be ready for removal.

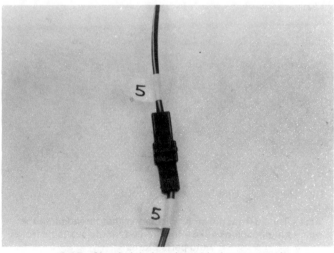

13.13   Clearly label each part before removal

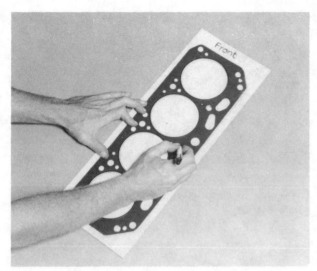

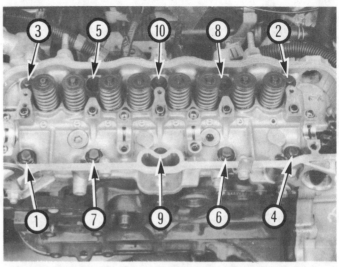

13.14a To avoid mixing up the head bolts, use the new gasket to transfer the bolt pattern to a piece of cardboard, then punch holes in the cardboard to accept the bolts

13.14b Cylinder head bolt loosening sequence (4A-LC shown, others use the same sequence)

14   Using the new head gasket, outline the cylinders and head bolt pattern on a piece of cardboard (see illustration). Be sure to indicate the front or rear of the engine for reference. Punch holes at the bolt locations. Loosen the cylinder head bolts in 1/4-turn increments until they can be removed by hand. Follow the recommended sequence (see illustration) to avoid warping the head. On 4A-FE engines, use a 10 mm 12-point socket. Store the bolts in the cardboard holder as they're removed – this will ensure they are reinstalled in their original locations, which is essential.

15   Lift the cylinder head off the engine block. If it's stuck, very carefully pry up on a protrusion, beyond the gasket surface (see illustration).

16   Remove all external components from the head to allow for thorough cleaning and inspection. See Chapter 2, Part B, for cylinder head servicing procedures.

Installation

Refer to illustrations 13.18, 13.23 and 13.26

17   The mating surfaces of the cylinder head and block must be perfectly clean when the head is installed.

18   Use a gasket scraper to remove all traces of carbon and old gasket material (see illustration), then clean the mating surfaces with lacquer thinner or acetone. If there's oil on the mating surfaces when the head is installed, the gasket may not seal correctly and leaks could develop. When working on the block, stuff the cylinders with clean shop rags to keep out debris. Use a vacuum cleaner to remove material that falls into the cylinders.

19   Check the block and head mating surfaces for nicks, deep scratches and other damage. If damage is slight, it can be removed with a file; if it's excessive, machining may be the only alternative.

20   Use a tap of the correct size to chase the threads in the head bolt holes, then clean the holes with compressed air – make sure that nothing remains in the holes. **Warning:** *Wear eye protection!*

21   Mount each bolt in a vise and run a die down the threads to remove corrosion and restore the threads. Dirt, corrosion, sealant and damaged threads will affect torque readings.

22   Install the components that were removed from the head.

23   Position the new gasket over the dowel pins in the block (see illustration). Be sure to look for marks such as "Top" or "This side up".

24   Carefully set the head on the engine block without disturbing the gasket.

13.15   Use a casting protrusion (arrow) to pry off the head

13.18   Scrape off all the old gasket material

13.23   Position the new gasket over the dowel pins (arrows)

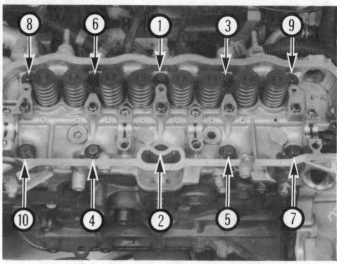

13.26   Cylinder head bolt tightening sequence (4A-LC engine shown, others use same sequence)

25   Before installing the head bolts, apply a small amount of clean engine oil to the threads.

26   Install the bolts in their original locations and tighten them finger-tight. Following the recommended sequence **(see illustration)**, tighten the bolts in several steps to the torque (and angle of rotation, on 4A-GE engines) listed in this Chapter's specifications. **Note:** *On 4A-GE engines, the exhaust side bolts are 4.25-inches long and the intake side bolts are 3.45-inches long.*

27   The remaining installation steps are the reverse of removal.

28   Check and adjust the valves as necessary (see Chapter 1).

29   Refill the cooling system, install a new oil filter and add oil to the engine (see Chapter 1).

30   Run the engine and check for leaks. Set the ignition timing and road test the vehicle.

14   Oil pan – removal and installation

Refer to illustrations 14.7a, 14.7b, 14.11 and 14.14

1   Disconnect the negative cable from the battery.

2   Set the parking brake and block the rear wheels.

3   Raise the front of the vehicle and support it securely on jackstands.

4   Remove the splash shields from under the oil pan.

5   Drain the engine oil and remove the oil filter (see Chapter 1).

6   On DOHC engines, remove the front exhaust pipe (and bracket) from the exhaust manifold and catalytic converter.

7   Remove the bolts **(see illustration)** and detach the oil pan (and baffle plate on 4A-GE engines). If it's stuck, tap it loose with a soft-face hammer **(see illustration)**. Don't pry at the gasket mating surface or you may damage the surfaces and leaks could develop.

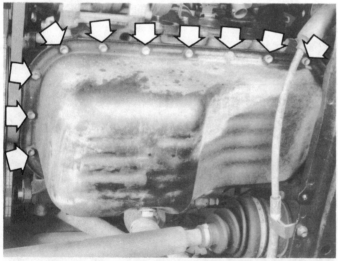

14.7a   Remove the bolt/nuts (arrows) around the perimeter of the oil pan

14.7b   Tap the oil pan with a soft-face hammer to break the gasket seal – don't pry between the pan and block

14.11 The oil pick-up tube assembly is secured by three bolts (arrows)

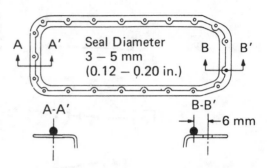

14.14 Apply a bead of sealant to the oil pan flange, to the inside of the bolt holes

8   Use a scraper to remove all traces of old gasket material and sealant from the block and oil pan. Clean the mating surfaces with lacquer thinner or acetone.

9   Make sure the threaded bolt holes in the block are clean.

10   Check the oil pan flange for distortion, particularly around the bolt holes. If necessary, place the pan on a block of wood and use a hammer to flatten and restore the gasket surface.

11   Inspect the oil pump pick-up tube assembly for cracks or a blocked strainer. Remove and replace it, if necessary **(see illustration)**.

12   If the pick-up was removed, install it now, using a new gasket. Tighten the bolts to the torque listed in this Chapter's specifications.

13   If the oil pan was originally installed with a gasket, use a new gasket during assembly. Hold it in place with sealant.

14   If the oil pan was originally installed with sealant only (no gasket), apply a bead of sealant (GM 1050026 or equivalent) to the oil pan flange **(see illustration)**. **Note:** *The oil pan must be installed within 3 minutes once the sealer has been applied.*

15   Carefully position the oil pan on the engine block and install the bolts. Working from the center out, tighten them to the torque listed in this Chapter's specifications in three steps.

16   The remainder of installation is the reverse of removal. Be sure to add oil and install a new oil filter.

17   Run the engine and check for oil pressure and leaks.

15   Oil pump – removal and installation

Removal

Refer to illustrations 15.3, 15.4a, 15.4b, 15.4c, 15.6a, 15.6b and 15.6c

1   Remove the oil pan, oil pick-up tube assembly (and baffle plate on 4A-GE engines) as described in Section 14. **Note:** *Since the oil pan has been removed, the engine must be supported securely from above when removing the following components.*

2   Remove the timing belt and crankshaft sprocket (see Section 7). On 4A-LC engines, remove the timing belt idler pulley. On DOHC engines, temporarily move the idler pulley aside and retighten the adjustment bolt.

3   Remove the dipstick tube **(see illustration)**.

4   Remove the bolts and detach the oil pump body from the engine **(see illustrations)**. You may have to pry carefully between the front main bearing cap and the pump case with a screwdriver **(see illustration)**.

5   Use a scraper to remove all traces of sealant and old gasket material from the pump case and engine block, then clean the mating surfaces with lacquer thinner or acetone.

Installation

Refer to illustrations 15.7 and 15.8

6   Pry the old oil seal out with a screwdriver. Using a deep socket and a hammer, carefully drive a new seal into place. Apply moly-base grease to the seal lip **(see illustrations)**.

7   Apply a light coat of RTV sealant to the gasket mating surfaces **(see illustration)**. Place a new gasket on the engine block (the dowel pins should hold it in place).

8   Position the pump against the block **(see illustration)** and install the mounting bolts.

15.3 The oil dipstick tube is attached to the water pump with a bolt (arrow)

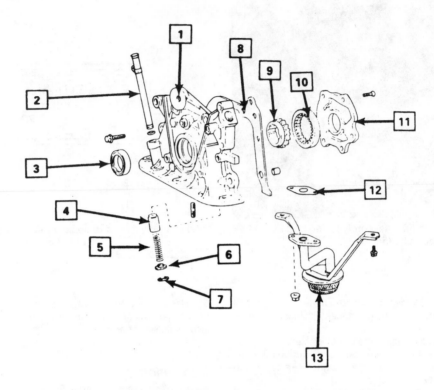

15.4a   Oil pump components – exploded view

1	Oil pump body	6	Retainer	11	Oil pump cover
2	Dipstick tube	7	Snap-ring	12	Gasket
3	Oil seal	8	Gasket	13	Oil pick-up
4	Relief valve piston	9	Drive gear		
5	Spring	10	Driven gear		

15.4b   Remove the oil pump bolts (arrows)

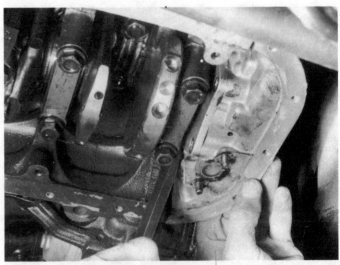

15.4c   To break the bond between the mating surfaces of the oil pump housing and block, insert a pry bar or a large screwdriver between the number one main bearing cap and the pump cover – do not attempt to pry between the actual mating surfaces or you may damage them

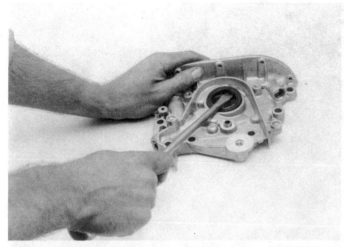

15.6a Lay the housing on a clean work surface and carefully pry the seal out with a screwdriver – if the seal is extremely tight, lay a socket or extension between the screwdriver and pump housing to act as a fulcrum and protect the housing from damage

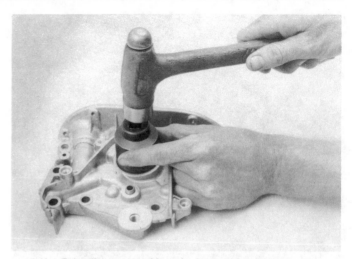

15.6b Drive the new seal into the bore with a hammer and a socket slightly smaller in diameter than the outside of the new seal – make sure the seal doesn't get cocked in the bore or it'll leak

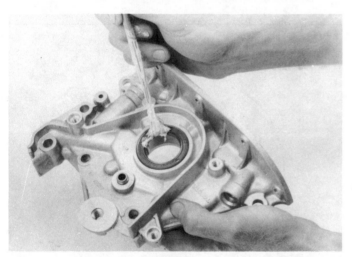

15.6c Coat the lip of the new seal with multi-purpose grease so it won't be damaged by the nose of the crankshaft when the oil pump housing is reinstalled on the block

15.7 It's a good idea to apply gasket sealant to the mating surfaces of the oil pump housing and block

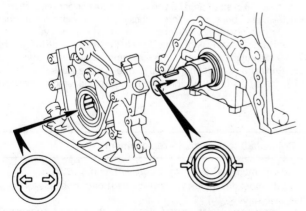

15.8 When installing the oil pump housing on the block, make sure the splines on the drive gear are engaged with the flats on the crankshaft

9   Tighten the bolts to the specified torque in three steps. Follow a criss-cross pattern to avoid warping the case.
10   Reinstall the remaining parts in the reverse order of removal.
11   Add oil, start the engine and check for oil pressure and leaks.
12   Recheck the engine oil level.

16 Flywheel/driveplate – removal and installation

Refer to illustrations 16.3, 16.4, 16.5 and 16.9

1   Raise the vehicle and support it securely on jackstands, then refer to Chapter 7 and remove the transaxle. If it's leaking, now would be a very good time to replace the front pump seal (automatic transaxle only).
2   Remove the pressure plate and clutch disc (see Chapter 8) (manual transaxle equipped vehicles). Now is a good time to check/replace the clutch components.

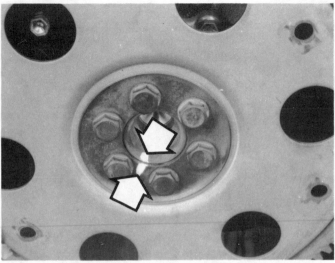

16.3   Make match marks (arrows) to ensure correct alignment during reassembly

16.4   Have an assistant jam a large screwdriver in the ring gear to keep the crankshaft from turning

16.5   Be sure to reinstall the spacers on both sides of the driveplate

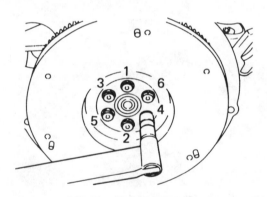

16.9   Tighten the flywheel/driveplate bolts following this sequence

3   Use a center punch or paint to make match marks on the flywheel/driveplate and crankshaft to ensure correct alignment during reinstallation **(see illustration)**.
4   Remove the bolts that secure the flywheel/driveplate to the crankshaft. If the crankshaft turns, wedge a screwdriver in the ring gear teeth to keep the crankshaft from turning **(see illustration)**.
5   Remove the flywheel/driveplate from the crankshaft. Since the flywheel is fairly heavy, be sure to support it while removing the last bolt. Automatic transaxle equipped vehicles have spacers on both sides of the driveplate **(see illustration)**.
6   Clean the flywheel to remove grease and oil. Inspect the surface for cracks, rivet grooves, burned areas and score marks. Light scoring can be removed with emery cloth. Check for cracked and broken ring gear teeth. Lay the flywheel on a flat surface and use a straightedge to check for warpage.
7   Clean and inspect the mating surfaces of the flywheel/driveplate and the crankshaft. If the crankshaft rear seal is leaking, replace it before reinstalling the flywheel/driveplate.
8   Position the flywheel/driveplate against the crankshaft. Be sure to align the marks made during removal. Note that some engines have an

alignment dowel or staggered bolt holes to ensure correct installation. Before installing the bolts, apply thread locking compound to the threads.
9   Wedge a screwdriver in the ring gear teeth to keep the flywheel/driveplate from turning as you tighten the bolts to the torque listed in this Chapter's specifications. Follow the recommended sequence **(see illustration)** and work up to the final torque in three steps.
10   The remainder of installation is the reverse of the removal procedure.

---

17   Crankshaft rear oil seal – replacement

Refer to illustrations 17.2, 17.4a, 17.4b, 17.5 and 17.6

1   The flywheel/driveplate must be removed from the vehicle for this procedure (see Section 16).
2   The seal can be replaced without dropping the oil pan or removing the seal retainer. However, this method isn't recommended because the lip of the seal is quite stiff and it's possible to cock the seal in the retainer bore or damage it during installation. If you want to take the chance, pry out the old

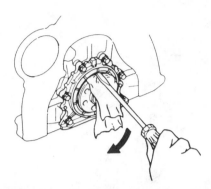

17.4a   Remove the rear engine plate bolts (arrows) . . .

17.2   The quick and dirty way to replace the rear crankshaft oil seal is to simply pry the old one out with a screwdriver, lubricate the crankshaft journal and the lip of the new seal with moly-base grease and push the new seal into place – the trouble is, the seal lip is stiff and can be easily damaged during installation if you're not careful

17.4b   . . . and the seal retainer bolts (arrows)

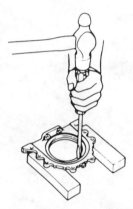

17.5   After removing the seal retainer from the block, support it on a couple of wood blocks and drive out the old seal with a screwdriver and hammer

17.6   Drive the new seal into the retainer with a block of wood or a section of pipe, if you have one large enough – make sure you don't cock the seal in the retainer bore

seal with a screwdriver **(see illustration)**. Apply moly-base grease to the crankshaft seal journal and the lip of the new seal and carefully push the new seal into place. The lip is stiff so carefully work it onto the seal journal of the crankshaft with a smooth object iike the end of an extension as you tap the seal into place. Don't rush it or you may damage the seal.

3   The following method is recommended but requires removal of the oil pan (see Section 15) and the seal retainer.

4   After the oil pan has been removed, remove the bolts, detach the seal retainer **(see illustrations)** and peel off all the old gasket material.

5   Position the seal and retainer assembly on a couple of wood blocks on a workbench and drive the old seal out from the back side with a screwdriver **(see illustration)**.

6   Drive the new seal into the retainer with a block of wood **(see illustration)** or a section of pipe slightly smaller in diameter than the outside diameter of the seal.

7   Lubricate the crankshaft seal journal and the lip of the new seal with moly-base grease. Position a new gasket on the engine block.

8   Slowly and carefully push the seal onto the crankshaft. The seal lip is stiff, so work it onto the crankshaft with a smooth object such as the end of an extension as you push the retainer against the block.

9   Install and tighten the retainer bolts to the torque listed in this Chapter's specifications.

10   The remaining steps are the reverse of removal.

18.8a   Remove the through-bolt (arrow)

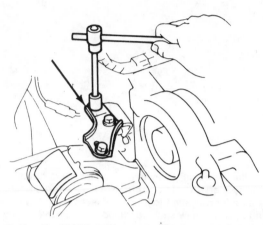

18.8b   On 4A-GE engines, remove the engine mount
brace (arrow)

18.9   The mount is attached to the engine with studs (arrows);
remove the nuts and lift the mount up to remove it

18   Engine mount – check and replacement

Refer to illustrations 18.8a, 18.8b and 18.9

1   The engine mount seldom requires attention, but a broken or deteriorated mount should be replaced immediately or the added strain placed on the driveline components may cause damage or wear.

Check

2   During the check, the engine must be raised slightly to remove the weight from the mount.
3   Raise the vehicle and support it securely on jackstands, then position a jack under the engine oil pan. Place a large block of wood between the jack head and the oil pan, then carefully raise the engine just enough to take the weight off the mount. **Warning:** *DO NOT place any part of your body under the engine when it's supported only by a jack!*
4   Check the mount to see if the rubber is cracked, hardened or separated from the metal plates. Sometimes the rubber will split right down the center.
5   Check for relative movement between the mount plates and the engine or frame (use a large screwdriver or prybar to attempt to move the mount). If movement is noted, lower the engine and tighten the mount fasteners.
6   Rubber preservative should be applied to the mounts to slow deterioration.

Replacement

7   Disconnect the negative battery cable from the battery, then raise the vehicle and support it securely on jackstands (if not already done). Support the engine as described in Step 3.
8   To remove the engine mount, remove the through-bolt from the frame bracket **(see illustration)**. On 4A-FE engines, remove the windshield washer reservoir and engine mount brace **(see illustration)**.
9   Remove the two mount-to-engine bracket nuts and detach the mount **(see illustration)**.
10   Installation is the reverse of removal. Use thread locking compound on the mount bolts/nuts and be sure to tighten them securely.
11   See Chapter 7 for transaxle mount replacement.

Chapter 2 Part B
General engine overhaul procedures

Contents

Specifications

General

Displacement	122 cu in (2.0 liters)
Cylinder compression pressure	
4A-LC engine	
Standard	178 psi
Minimum	128 psi
4A-GE engine	
Standard	179 psi
Minimum	142 psi
4A-FE engine	
Standard	191 psi
Minimum	142 psi
Oil pressure – all models (engine warm)	
At 3000 rpm	36 to 71 psi
At idle	4.3 psi minimum

Warpage limits
4A-LC and 4A-FE engines
  Cylinder head
    Block side .... 0.002 in (0.05 mm)
    Manifold sides .... 0.004 in (0.10 mm)
  Engine block deck surface .... 0.0020 in (0.05 mm)
4A-GE engine
  Cylinder head
    Block side .... 0.002 in (0.05 mm)
    Intake manifold side .... 0.002 in (0.05 mm)
    Exhaust manifold side .... 0.004 in (0.10 mm)
  Engine block deck surface .... 0.0020 in (0.05 mm)

Valves and related components
Minimum valve margin width
  Intake
    4A-LC and 4A-FE engines .... 0.020 in (0.5 mm)
    4A-GE engine .... 0.0315 in (0.8 mm)
  Exhaust
    4A-LC engine .... 0.039 in (1.0 mm)
    4A-GE engine .... 0.0315 in (0.8 mm)
    4A-FE engine .... 0.020 in (0.5 mm)
Intake valve
  Stem diameter
    4A-LC engine .... 0.2744 to 0.2750 in (6.970 to 6.985 mm)
    4A-GE and 4A-FE engines .... 0.2350 to 0.2356 in (5.970 to 5.985 mm)
  Valve stem-to-guide clearance
    Standard .... 0.0010 to 0.0024 in (0.025 to 0.060 mm)
    Service limit .... 0.0031 in (0.08 mm)
  Length
    4A-LC engine
      Standard .... 4.208 in (106.9 mm)
      Minimum .... 4.188 in (106.4 mm)
    4A-GE engine
      Standard .... 3.9213 in (99.60 mm)
      Minimum .... 3.9016 in (99.10 mm)
    4A-FE engine
      Standard .... 3.6004 in (91.45 mm)
      Minimum .... 3.5807 in (90.95 mm)
Exhaust valve
  Stem diameter
    4A-LC engine .... 0.2742 to 0.2748 in (6.965 to 6.980 mm)
    4A-GE and 4A-FE engines .... 0.2348 to 0.2354 in (5.965 to 5.980 mm)
  Valve stem-to-guide clearance
    Standard .... 0.0012 to 0.0026 in (0.030 to 0.065 mm)
    Service limit .... 0.0039 in (0.10 mm)
  Length
    4A-LC engine
      Standard .... 4.2039 in (106.78 mm)
      Minimum .... 4.1839 in (106.28 mm)
    4A-GE engine
      Standard .... 3.9272 in (99.75 mm)
      Minimum .... 3.9075 in (99.25 mm)
    4A-FE engine
      Standard .... 3.6181 in (91.90 mm)
      Minimum .... 3.5984 in (91.40 mm)
Valve spring
  Out-of-square limit
    4A-LC engine .... 0.079 in (2.0 mm)
    4A-GE and 4A-FE engines .... 0.071 in (1.8 mm)
  Free length
    4A-LC engine .... 1.756 in (44.6 mm)
    4A-GE engine .... 1.6177 in (41.09 mm)
    4A-FE engine .... 1.724 in (43.8 mm)
  Installed height
    4A-LC engine .... 1.520 in (38.6 mm)
    4A-GE and 4A-FE engines .... 1.366 in (34.7 mm)

Crankshaft and connecting rods

Connecting rod journal
    Diameter
        4A-LC and 4A-FE engines .... 1.5742 to 1.5748 in (39.985 to 40.000 mm)
        4A-GE engines .... 1.6529 to 1.6535 in (41.989 to 42.000 mm)
    Taper and out-of-round limits .... 0.0008 in (0.02 mm)
    Bearing oil clearance (all)
        Standard .... 0.0008 to 0.0020 in (0.020 to 0.051 mm)
        Service limit .... 0.0031 in (0.08 mm)
Connecting rod side clearance (endplay)
    Standard .... 0.0059 to 0.0098 in (0.15 to 0.25 mm)
    Service limit .... 0.012 in (0.30 mm)
Main bearing journal
    Diameter
        4A-LC engine .... 1.8892 to 1.8898 in (47.985 to 48.000 mm)
        4A-GE and 4A-FE engines .... 1.8891 to 1.8898 in (47.982 to 48.000 mm)
    Taper and out-of-round limit .... 0.0008 in (0.02 mm)
    Oil clearance (4A-LC engine)
        1985 and 1986 (standard) .... 0.0005 to 0.0015 in (0.012 to 0.039 mm)
        1985 (service limit) .... 0.0031 in (0.08 mm)
        1986 (service limit) .... 0.0039 in (0.10 mm)
        1987 and 1988
            Standard .... 0.0006 to 0.0013 in (0.015 to 0.033 mm)
            Service limit .... Not available
    Oil clearance (4A-GE and 4A-FE engines)
        Standard .... 0.0006 to 0.0013 in (0.015 to 0.033 mm)
        Service limit .... 0.0039 in (0.10 mm)
Crankshaft endplay
    4A-LC engine
        Standard .... 0.0008 to 0.0073 in (0.020 to 0.185 mm)
        Service limit .... 0.0118 in (0.30 mm)
    4A-GE and 4A-FE engines
        Standard .... 0.0008 to 0.0087 in (0.022 to 0.185 mm)
        Service limit .... 0.0118 in (0.30 mm)
Thrust bearing thickness .... 0.0961 to 0.0980 in (2.440 to 2.490 mm)

Cylinder bore

Diameter
    Standard .... 3.1890 to 3.1902 in (81.00 to 81.03 mm)
    Service limit .... 3.1980 in (81.23 mm)
Taper and out-of-round limits .... 0.0008 in (0.020 mm)

Pistons and rings

Piston diameter
    4A-LC engine .... 3.1864 to 3.1858 in (80.90 to 80.93 mm)
    4A-GE engine
        1988 .... 3.1846 to 3.1858 in (80.89 to 80.92 mm)
        1989-on
            Size 1 .... 3.1846 to 3.1850 in (80.89 to 80.90 mm)
            Size 2 .... 3.1850 to 3.1854 in (80.90 to 80.91 mm)
            Size 3 .... 3.1854 to 3.1858 in (80.91 to 80.92 mm)
    4A-FE engine
        Size 1 .... 3.1862 to 3.1866 in (80.93 to 80.94 mm)
        Size 2 .... 3.1866 to 3.1870 in (80.94 to 80.95 mm)
        Size 3 .... 3.1870 to 3.1874 in (80.95 to 80.96 mm)
Piston-to-bore clearance
    4A-LC engine .... 0.0035 to 0.0043 in (0.09 to 0.11 mm)
    4A-GE engine .... 0.0039 to 0.0047 in (0.10 to 0.12 mm)
    4A-FE engine .... 0.0024 to 0.0031 in (0.06 to 0.08 mm)
Piston ring end gap
    4A-LC engine
        No. 1 (top) compression ring
            Standard .... 0.0098 to 0.0185 in (0.250 to 0.470 mm)
            Service limit .... 0.0421 in (1.07 mm)

Pistons and rings (continued)

No. 2 (middle) compression ring	
Standard	0.0059 to 0.0165 in (0.150 to 0.420 mm)
Service limit	0.0402 in (1.02 mm)
Oil ring	
Standard	0.0118 to 0.0402 in (0.30 to 1.02 mm)
Service limit	0.0638 in (1.62 mm)
4A-GE engine	
No. 1 (top) compression ring	
1988	0.0098 to 0.0138 in (0.25 to 0.35 mm)
1989-on	0.0098 to 0.0185 in (0.25 to 0.47 mm)
Service limit (all)	0.0421 in (1.07 mm)
No. 2 (middle) compression ring	
1988	0.0078 to 0.0118 in (0.20 to 0.30 mm)
1989-on	0.0079 to 0.0165 in (0.20 to 0.42 mm)
Service limit (all)	0.0402 in (1.02 mm)
Oil ring	
1988	0.0059 to 0.0157 in (0.15 to 0.40 mm)
1989-on	0.0059 to 0.0205 in (0.15 to 0.52 mm)
Service limit (all)	0.0441 in (1.12 mm)
4A-FE engine	
No. 1 (top) compression ring	
Standard	0.0098 to 0.0138 in (0.25 to 0.35 mm)
Service limit	0.0421 in (1.07 mm)
No. 2 (middle) compression ring	
Standard	0.0059 to 0.0118 in (0.15 to 0.30 mm)
Service limit	0.0402 in (1.02 mm)
Oil ring	
Standard	0.0039 to 0.0236 in (0.10 to 0.60 mm)
Service limit	0.0638 in (1.62 mm)
Piston ring side clearance	
No. 1 compression ring	0.0016 to 0.0031 in (0.040 to 0.080 mm)
No. 2 compression ring	0.0012 to 0.0028 in (0.03 to 0.07 mm)

Torque specifications*

	Ft-lbs
Main bearing cap bolts	44
Connecting rod cap nuts	36

* Note: *Refer to Part A for additional torque specifications.*

---

1   General information

Included in this portion of Chapter 2 are the general overhaul procedures for the cylinder head and internal engine components.

The information ranges from advice concerning preparation for an overhaul and the purchase of replacement parts to detailed, step-by step procedures covering removal and installation of the engine, internal engine components and the inspection of parts.

The following Sections have been written based on the assumption the engine has been removed from the vehicle. For information concerning in-vehicle engine repair, as well as removal and installation of the external components necessary for the overhaul, see Part A of this Chapter and Section 7 of this Part.

The Specifications included in this Part are only those necessary for the inspection and overhaul procedures which follow. Refer to Part A for additional Specifications.

2   Engine overhaul – general information

Refer to illustrations 2.4a and 2.4b

It's not always easy to determine when, or if, an engine should be completely overhauled, as a number of factors must be considered.

High mileage is not necessarily an indication that an overhaul is needed, while low mileage doesn't preclude the need for an overhaul. Frequency of servicing is probably the most important consideration. An engine that's had regular and frequent oil and filter changes, as well as other required maintenance, will most likely give many thousands of miles of reliable service. Conversely, a neglected engine may require an overhaul very early in its life.

Excessive oil consumption is an indication that piston rings, valve seals and/or valve guides are in need of attention. Make sure that oil leaks aren't responsible before deciding that the rings and/or guides are bad. Perform a cylinder compression check to determine the extent of the work required (see Section 3).

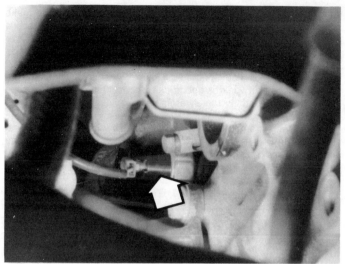

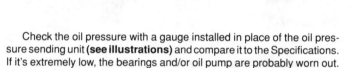

2.4a   The oil pressure sending unit (arrow) is located on the front of the engine block adjacent to the oil filter

2.4b   The oil pressure can be checked by removing the sending unit and installing a pressure gauge in the hole

Check the oil pressure with a gauge installed in place of the oil pressure sending unit **(see illustrations)** and compare it to the Specifications. If it's extremely low, the bearings and/or oil pump are probably worn out.

Loss of power, rough running, knocking or metallic engine noises, excessive valve train noise and high fuel consumption rates may also point to the need for an overhaul, especially if they're all present at the same time. If a complete tune-up doesn't remedy the situation, major mechanical work is the only solution.

An engine overhaul involves restoring the internal parts to the specifications of a new engine. During an overhaul, the piston rings are replaced and the cylinder walls are reconditioned (rebored and/or honed). If a rebore is done by an automotive machine shop, new oversize pistons will also be installed. The main bearings, connecting rod bearings and camshaft bearings are generally replaced with new ones and, if necessary, the crankshaft may be reground to restore the journals. Generally, the valves are serviced as well, since they're usually in less-than-perfect condition at this point. While the engine is being overhauled, other components, such as the distributor, starter and alternator, can be rebuilt as well. The end result should be a like new engine that will give many trouble free miles. **Note:** *Critical cooling system components such as the hoses, drivebelts, thermostat and water pump MUST be replaced with new parts when an engine is overhauled. The radiator should be checked carefully to ensure that it isn't clogged or leaking (see Chapter 3). Also, we don't recommend overhauling the oil pump – always install a new one when an engine is rebuilt.*

Before beginning the engine overhaul, read through the entire procedure to familiarize yourself with the scope and requirements of the job. Overhauling an engine isn't difficult, but it is time consuming. Plan on the vehicle being tied up for a minimum of two weeks, especially if parts must be taken to an automotive machine shop for repair or reconditioning. Check on availability of parts and make sure any necessary special tools and equipment are obtained in advance. Most work can be done with typical hand tools, although a number of precision measuring tools are required for inspecting parts to determine if they must be replaced. Automotive machine shops will often handle the inspection of parts and offer advice concerning reconditioning and replacement. **Note:** *Always wait until the engine has been completely disassembled and all components, especially the engine block, have been inspected before deciding what service and repair operations must be performed by an automotive machine shop. Since the block's condition will be the major factor to consider when determining whether to overhaul the original engine or buy a rebuilt one, never purchase parts or have machine work done on other components until the block has been thoroughly inspected. As a general rule, time is the primary cost of an overhaul, so it doesn't pay to install worn or substandard parts.*

As a final note, to ensure maximum life and minimum trouble from a rebuilt engine, everything must be assembled with care in a spotlessly clean environment.

3   Compression check

Refer to illustration 3.6

1   A compression check will tell you what mechanical condition the upper end (pistons, rings, valves, head gasket) of your engine is in. Specifically, it can tell you if the compression is down due to leakage caused by worn piston rings, defective valves and seats or a blown head gasket. **Note:** *The engine must be at normal operating temperature and the battery must be fully charged for this check.*

2   Begin by cleaning the area around the spark plugs before you remove them (compressed air should be used, if available, otherwise a small brush or even a bicycle tire pump will work). The idea is to prevent dirt from getting into the cylinders as the compression check is being done.

3   Remove all of the spark plugs from the engine (see Chapter 1).

4   Block the throttle wide open.

5   Detach the coil wire from the center of the distributor cap and ground it on the engine block. Use a jumper wire with alligator clips on each end to ensure a good ground. On EFI equipped vehicles, the fuel pump circuit should also be disabled (see Chapter 4).

6   Install the compression gauge in the spark plug hole **(see illustration)**.

7   Crank the engine over at least seven compression strokes and watch the gauge. The compression should build up quickly in a healthy engine. Low compression on the first stroke, followed by gradually increasing pressure on successive strokes, indicates worn piston rings. A low compression reading on the first stroke, which doesn't build up during successive strokes, indicates leaking valves or a blown head gasket (a cracked head could also be the cause). Deposits on the undersides of the valve heads can also cause low compression. Record the highest gauge reading obtained.

8   Repeat the procedure for the remaining cylinders and compare the results to the Specifications listed in this Chapter.

9   Add some engine oil (about three squirts from a plunger-type oil can) to each cylinder, through the spark plug hole, and repeat the test.

10   If the compression increases after the oil is added, the piston rings are definitely worn. If the compression doesn't increase significantly, the leakage is occurring at the valves or head gasket. Leakage past the valves may be caused by burned valve seats and/or faces or warped, cracked or bent valves.

3.6   A compression gauge with a threaded fitting for the spark plug hole is preferred over the type that requires hand pressure to maintain the seal – be sure to open the throttle and choke valve as far as possible during the compression check!

11   If two adjacent cylinders have equally low compression, there's a strong possibility that the head gasket between them is blown. The appearance of coolant in the combustion chambers or the crankcase would verify this condition.

12   If one cylinder is about 20 percent lower than the others, and the engine has a slightly rough idle, a worn exhaust lobe on the camshaft could be the cause.

13   If the compression is unusually high, the combustion chambers are probably coated with carbon deposits. If that's the case, the cylinder head should be removed and decarbonized.

14   If compression is way down or varies greatly between cylinders, it would be a good idea to have a leak-down test performed by an automotive repair shop. This test will pinpoint exactly where the leakage is occurring and how severe it is.

---

4   Engine removal – methods and precautions

If you've decided that an engine must be removed for overhaul or major repair work, several preliminary steps should be taken.

Locating a suitable place to work is extremely important. Adequate work space, along with storage space for the vehicle, will be needed. If a shop or garage isn't available, at the very least a flat, level, clean work surface made of concrete or asphalt is required.

Cleaning the engine compartment and engine before beginning the removal procedure will help keep tools clean and organized.

An engine hoist or A-frame will also be necessary. Make sure the equipment is rated in excess of the combined weight of the engine and transaxle. Safety is of primary importance, considering the potential hazards involved in lifting the engine out of the vehicle.

If the engine is being removed by a novice, a helper should be available. Advice and aid from someone more experienced would also be helpful. There are many instances when one person cannot simultaneously perform all of the operations required when lifting the engine out of the vehicle.

Plan the operation ahead of time. Arrange for or obtain all of the tools and equipment you'll need prior to beginning the job. Some of the equipment necessary to perform engine removal and installation safely and with relative ease are (in addition to an engine hoist) a heavy duty floor jack, complete sets of wrenches and sockets as described in the front of this manual, wooden blocks and plenty of rags and cleaning solvent for mop-

ping up spilled oil, coolant and gasoline. If the hoist must be rented, make sure that you arrange for it in advance and perform all of the operations possible without it beforehand. This will save you money and time.

Plan for the vehicle to be out of use for quite a while. A machine shop will be required to perform some of the work which the do-it-yourselfer can't accomplish without special equipment. These shops often have a busy schedule, so it would be a good idea to consult them before removing the engine in order to accurately estimate the amount of time required to rebuild or repair components that may need work.

Always be extremely careful when removing and installing the engine. Serious injury can result from careless actions. Plan ahead, take your time and a job of this nature, although major, can be accomplished successfully.

---

5   Engine – removal and installation

Refer to illustrations 5.6, 5.11, 5.16, 5.18, 5.19a, 5.19b and 5.20

Note: *Read through the entire Section before beginning this procedure. The engine and transaxle are removed as a unit and then separated outside the vehicle.*

Removal

1   On fuel injected models, relieve the fuel system pressure (see Chapter 4).

2   Remove the battery and coolant reservoir (see Chapters 3 and 5).

3   Place protective covers on the fenders and cowl and remove the hood (see Chapter 11).

4   Remove the air cleaner assembly (see Chapter 4).

5   Raise the vehicle and support it securely on jackstands. Remove the lower splash guards. Drain the cooling system and engine oil and remove the drivebelts (see Chapter 1).

6   Clearly label, then disconnect all vacuum lines, coolant and emissions hoses, wiring harness connectors, ground straps and fuel lines. Masking tape and/or paint work well for marking items **(see illustration)**. Take instant photos or sketch the locations of components and brackets.

7   Remove the cooling fan(s) and radiator (see Chapter 3).

8   Release the residual fuel pressure in the tank by removing the gas cap, then undo the fuel lines connecting the engine to the chassis (see Chapter 4). Plug or cap all open fittings.

9   Disconnect the throttle linkage (and TV linkage and speed control cable/actuator, if equipped) from the engine (see Chapter 4).

10   On power steering equipped vehicles, unbolt the power steering pump. If clearance allows, tie the pump aside without disconnecting the hoses. If necessary, remove the pump (see Chapter 10).

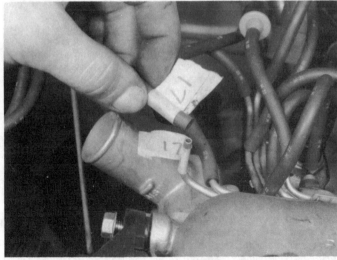

5.6   Label the hoses and wires to ensure correct reassembly

5.11   The air conditioning compressor should be unbolted from the engine with the hoses still connected

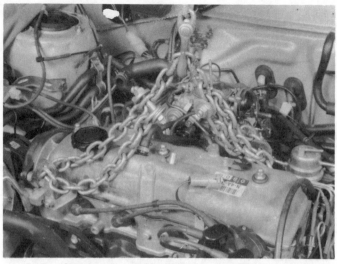

5.16   Attach a sling to the lifting brackets on the engine

11   On air conditioned vehicles, unbolt the compressor and set it aside **(see illustration)**. Do not disconnect the refrigerant hoses.

12   Detach the exhaust pipe from the exhaust manifold.

13   Remove the driveaxles (see Chapter 8), wire harness, shift linkage and speedometer cable from the transaxle (see Chapter 7).

14   On automatic transaxle models, disconnect the two oil cooler lines (see Chapter 7B).

15   On manual transaxle models, unbolt the clutch release cylinder without disconnecting the hose (see Chapter 7A).

16   Attach a lifting sling to the brackets on the engine **(see illustration)**. Position a hoist and connect the sling to it. Take up the slack until there is slight tension on the hoist.

17   Recheck to be sure nothing except the mounts are still connecting the engine/transaxle to the vehicle. Disconnect anything still remaining.

18   Support the transaxle with a floor jack. Place a block of wood on the jack head to prevent damage to the transaxle. Remove the bolts/nuts from the engine and transaxle mounts **(see illustration)**. **Warning:** *Do not place any part of your body under the engine/transaxle when it's supported only by a hoist or other lifting device.*

19   Slowly lift the engine/transaxle out of the vehicle **(see illustrations)**. It may be necessary to pry the mounts away from the frame brackets.

5.18   Remove the through-bolt from the engine mount

5.19a   Guide the engine/transaxle assembly as it's raised to avoid damaging nearby components

5.19b   Tilt the engine/transaxle assembly to clear the battery mount

5.20   When the lowest part of the transaxle has cleared the top of the radiator support, move the engine/transaxle away from the vehicle

20   Move the engine/transaxle away from the vehicle **(see illustration)** and carefully lower the hoist until the transaxle is supported in a level position.

21   On automatic transaxle equipped models, detach the torque converter dust shield from the lower bellhousing. Remove the torque converter-to-driveplate fasteners (see Chapter 7) and push the converter back slightly into the bellhousing.

22   Remove the engine-to-transaxle bolts and separate the engine from the transaxle. The torque converter should remain in the transaxle.

23   Place the engine on the floor or remove the flywheel/driveplate and mount the engine on an engine stand.

Installation

24   Check the engine/transaxle mounts. If they're worn or damaged, replace them.

25   On manual transaxle equipped models, inspect the clutch components (see Chapter 8) and on automatic models inspect the converter seal and bushing.

26   On automatic transaxle equipped models, apply a dab of grease to the nose of the converter and to the seal lips.

27   Carefully guide the transaxle into place, following the procedure outlined in Chapter 7. **Caution:** *Do Not use the bolts to force the engine and transaxle into alignment. It may crack or damage major components.*

28   Install the engine-to-transaxle bolts and tighten them securely.

29   Attach the hoist to the engine and carefully lower the engine/transaxle assembly into the engine compartment.

30   Install the mount bolts and tighten them securely.

31   Reinstall the remaining components and fasteners in the reverse order of removal.

32   Add coolant, oil, power steering and transmission fluids as needed (see Chapter 1).

33   Run the engine and check for proper operation and leaks. Shut off the engine and recheck the fluid levels.

6   Engine rebuilding alternatives

The do-it-yourselfer is faced with a number of options when performing an engine overhaul. The decision to replace the engine block, piston/connecting rod assemblies and crankshaft depends on a number of factors, with the number one consideration being the condition of the block. Other considerations are cost, access to machine shop facilities, parts availability, time required to complete the project and the extent of prior mechanical experience on the part of the do-it-yourselfer.

Some of the rebuilding alternatives include:

Individual parts – If the inspection procedures reveal that the engine block and most engine components are in reusable condition, purchasing individual parts may be the most economical alternative. The block, crankshaft and piston/connecting rod assemblies should all be inspected carefully. Even if the block shows little wear, the cylinder bores should be surface honed.

Short block – A short block consists of an engine block with a crankshaft and piston/connecting rod assemblies already installed. All new bearings are incorporated and all clearances will be correct. The existing camshaft, valve train components, cylinder head and external parts can be bolted to the short block with little or no machine shop work necessary.

Long block – A long block consists of a short block plus an oil pump, oil pan, cylinder head, camshaft cover, camshaft and valve train components, timing sprockets, belt and timing cover. All components are installed with new bearings, seals and gaskets incorporated throughout. The installation of manifolds and external parts is all that's necessary.

Give careful thought to which alternative is best for you and discuss the situation with local automotive machine shops, auto parts dealers and experienced rebuilders before ordering or purchasing replacement parts.

7   Engine overhaul – disassembly sequence

Refer to illustrations 7.5a, 7.5b, 7.5c, 7.5d, 7.5e and 7.5f

1   It's much easier to disassemble and work on the engine if it's mounted on a portable engine stand. A stand can often be rented quite cheaply from an equipment rental yard. Before the engine is mounted on a stand, the flywheel/driveplate and rear oil seal retainer should be removed from the engine.

2   If a stand isn't available, it's possible to disassemble the engine with it blocked up on the floor. Be extra careful not to tip or drop the engine when working without a stand.

3   If you're going to obtain a rebuilt engine, all external components must come off first, to be transferred to the replacement engine, just as they will if you're doing a complete engine overhaul yourself. These include:

   Alternator and brackets
   Emissions control components
   Distributor, spark plug wires and spark plugs
   Thermostat and housing cover
   Water pump
   Carburetor or fuel injection components
   Intake/exhaust manifolds
   Oil filter
   Engine mounts
   Clutch and flywheel or driveplate
   Engine rear plate

Note: *When removing the external components from the engine, pay close attention to details that may be helpful or important during installation. Note the installed position of gaskets, seals, spacers, pins, brackets, washers, bolts and other small items.*

4   If you're obtaining a short block, which consists of the engine block, crankshaft, pistons and connecting rods all assembled, then the cylinder head, oil pan and oil pump will have to be removed as well. See Engine rebuilding alternatives for additional information regarding the different possibilities to be considered.

5   If you're planning a complete overhaul, the engine must be disassembled and the internal components removed in the following order **(see illustrations)**.

   Camshaft cover
   Intake and exhaust manifolds
   Timing belt covers
   Timing belt and sprockets
   Cylinder head
   Oil pan
   Oil pump
   Piston/connecting rod assemblies
   Crankshaft rear oil seal retainer
   Crankshaft and main bearings

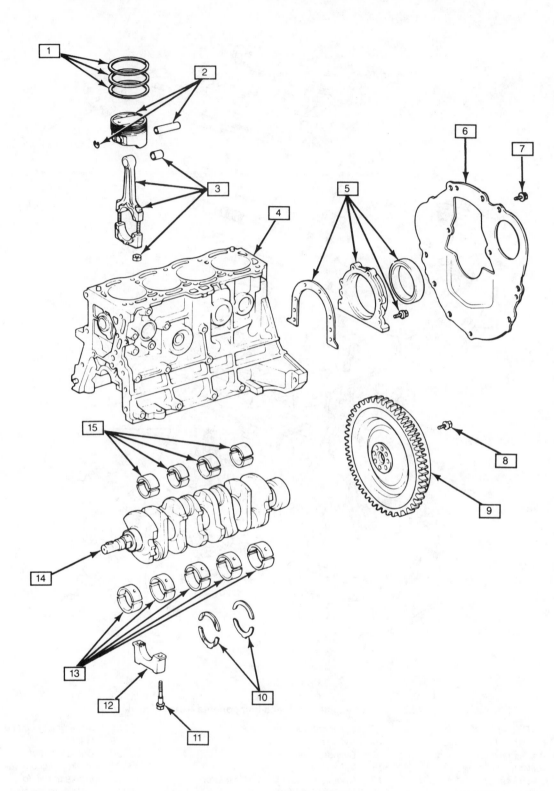

7.5a   Typical lower end components – exploded view

1	Piston rings	6	Rear cover plate	11	Main bearing cap bolt
2	Piston assembly	7	Bolt	12	Main bearing cap
3	Connecting rod assembly	8	Bolt	13	Main bearing
4	Engine block	9	Flywheel	14	Crankshaft
5	Rear crankshaft oil seal, retainer and gasket assembly	10	Crankshaft thrust bearings	15	Connecting rod bearings

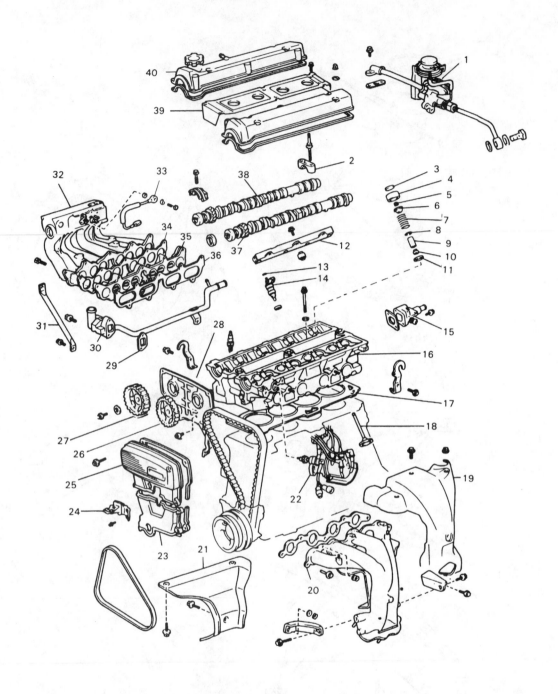

7.5b   4A-GE engine upper end components – exploded view

1	EGR valve	15	Cylinder head rear cover	28	No. 4 timing belt cover
2	Camshaft bearing cap	16	Cylinder head	29	Gasket
3	Adjusting shim	17	Cylinder head gasket	30	Coolant outlet
4	Valve lifter	18	Valve	31	Intake manifold stay
5	Valve keepers	19	Upper exhaust manifold insulator	32	Intake manifold
6	Valve spring retainer	20	Exhaust manifold	33	Cold start injection line
7	Valve spring	21	Lower exhaust manifold insulator	34	Gasket
8	Snap-ring	22	Distributor	35	Air control valve
9	Valve guide bushing	23	No. 2 timing belt cover	36	Gasket
10	Valve stem oil seal	24	Engine mount bracket	37	Exhaust valve camshaft
11	Valve spring seat	25	No. 3 timing belt cover	38	Intake valve camshaft
12	Delivery line	26	Exhaust camshaft sprocket	39	Cylinder head center cover
13	O-ring	27	Intake camshaft sprocket	40	Camshaft cover
14	Injector				

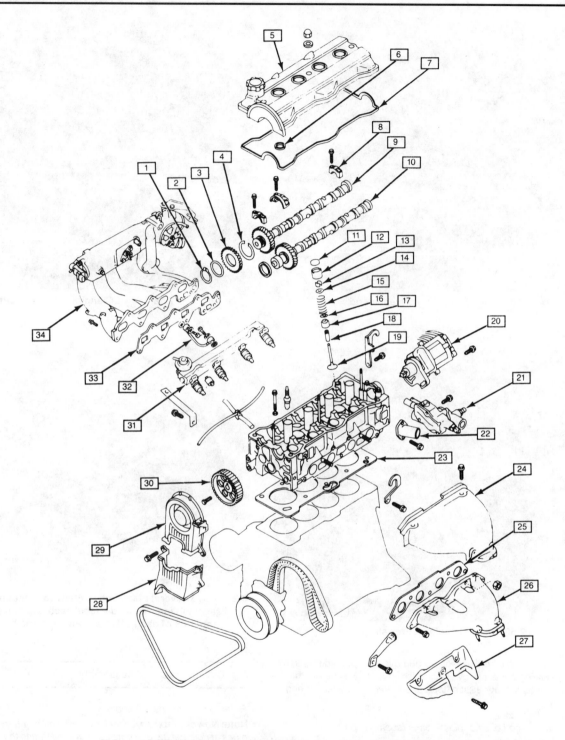

7.5c 4A-FE engine upper end components – exploded view

1	Camshaft snap-ring	13	Valve keepers	25	Exhaust manifold gasket
2	Wave washer	14	Valve spring retainer	26	Exhaust manifold
3	Camshaft sub-gear	15	Valve spring	27	Exhaust manifold lower insulator
4	Camshaft gear spring	16	Valve spring seat	28	Center timing belt cover
5	Camshaft cover	17	Valve stem oil seal	29	Upper timing belt cover
6	Spark plug tube gasket	18	Valve guide bushing	30	Camshaft sprocket
7	Cylinder head cover gasket	19	Valve	31	Fuel rail
8	Camshaft bearing cap	20	Distributor	32	Cold-start injector line
9	Camshaft (intake)	21	Coolant inlet housing	33	Intake manifold gasket
10	Camshaft (exhaust)	22	Coolant outlet housing	34	Intake manifold
11	Adjusting shim	23	Head gasket		
12	Valve lifter	24	Exhaust manifold upper insulator		

7.5d   4A-LC engine – drivebelt end

7.5e   4A-LC engine – radiator side

7.5f   4A-LC engine – firewall side

8.2   Have several plastic bags ready (one for each valve) before disassembling the head – label each bag and put the entire contents of each valve assembly in one bag as shown

6   Before beginning the disassembly and overhaul procedures, make sure the following items are available. Also, refer to Engine overhaul – reassembly sequence for a list of tools and materials needed for engine reassembly.

Common hand tools
Small cardboard boxes or plastic bags for storing parts
Gasket scraper
Ridge reamer
Crankshaft pulley puller
Micrometers
Telescoping gauges
Dial indicator set
Valve spring compressor
Cylinder surfacing hone
Piston ring groove cleaning tool
Electric drill motor
Tap and die set
Wire brushes
Oil gallery brushes
Cleaning solvent

8   Cylinder head – disassembly

Refer to illustrations 8.2 and 8.3

Note: *New and rebuilt cylinder heads are commonly available for most engines at dealerships and auto parts stores. Due to the fact that some specialized tools are necessary for the disassembly and inspection procedures, and replacement parts may not be readily available, it may be more practical and economical for the home mechanic to purchase replacement head rather than taking the time to disassemble, inspect and recondition the original.*

1   Cylinder head disassembly involves removal of the intake and exhaust valves and related components. It's assumed that the lifters or rocker arms and camshaft(s) have already been removed (see Part A as needed).
2   Before the valves are removed, arrange to label and store them, along with their related components, so they can be kept separate and re-installed in the same valve guides they are removed from **(see illustration)**.

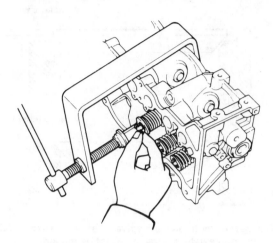

8.3   Use a valve spring compressor to compress the springs, then remove the keepers from the valve stem with a magnet or small needle-nose pliers

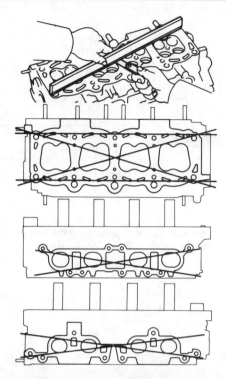

9.12   Check the cylinder head gasket surfaces for warpage by trying to slip a feeler gauge under the precision straightedge (see the Specifications for the maximum warpage allowed and use a feeler gauge of that thickness)

3   Compress the springs on the first valve with a spring compressor and remove the keepers **(see illustration)**. Carefully release the valve spring compressor and remove the retainer, the spring and the spring seat (if used). **Caution:** *Be very careful not to nick or otherwise damage the lifter bores when compressing the valve springs.*

4   Pull the valve out of the head, then remove the oil seal from the guide. If the valve binds in the guide (won't pull through), push it back into the head and deburr the area around the keeper groove with a fine file or whetstone.

5   Repeat the procedure for the remaining valves. Remember to keep all the parts for each valve together so they can be reinstalled in the same locations.

6   Once the valves and related components have been removed and stored in an organized manner, the head should be thoroughly cleaned and inspected. If a complete engine overhaul is being done, finish the engine disassembly procedures before beginning the cylinder head cleaning and inspection process.

9   Cylinder head – cleaning and inspection

Refer to illustrations 9.12, 9.14, 9.16, 9.17 and 9.18

1   Thorough cleaning of the cylinder head and related valve train components, followed by a detailed inspection, will enable you to decide how much valve service work must be done during the engine overhaul. **Note:** *If the engine was severely overheated, the cylinder head is probably warped (see Step 12).*

Cleaning

2   Scrape all traces of old gasket material and sealing compound off the head gasket, intake manifold and exhaust manifold sealing surfaces. Be very careful not to gouge the cylinder head. Special gasket removal solvents that soften gaskets and make removal much easier are available at auto parts stores.

3   Remove all built up scale from the coolant passages.

4   Run a stiff wire brush through the various holes to remove deposits that may have formed in them.

5   Run an appropriate size tap into each of the threaded holes to remove corrosion and thread sealant that may be present. If compressed air is available, use it to clear the holes of debris produced by this operation. **Warning:** *Wear eye protection when using compressed air!*

6   Clean the exhaust and intake manifold stud threads with a wire brush.

7   Clean the cylinder head with solvent and dry it thoroughly. Compressed air will speed the drying process and ensure that all holes and recessed areas are clean. **Note:** *Decarbonizing chemicals are available and may prove very useful when cleaning cylinder heads and valve train components. They are very caustic and should be used with caution. Be sure to follow the instructions on the container.*

8   Clean the lifters or rocker arms with solvent and dry them thoroughly (don't mix them up during the cleaning process). Compressed air will speed the drying process and can be used to clean out the oil passages.

9   Clean all the valve springs, spring seats, keepers and retainers with solvent and dry them thoroughly. Do the components from one valve at a time to avoid mixing up the parts.

10   Scrape off any heavy deposits that may have formed on the valves, then use a motorized wire brush to remove deposits from the valve heads and stems. Again, make sure the valves don't get mixed up.

Inspection

Note: *Be sure to perform all of the following inspection procedures before concluding that machine shop work is required. Make a list of the items that need attention. The inspection procedures for the lifters or rocker arms, as well as the camshaft(s), can be found in Part A.*

Cylinder head

11   Inspect the head very carefully for cracks, evidence of coolant leakage and other damage. If cracks are found, check with an automotive machine shop concerning repair. If repair isn't possible, a new cylinder head should be obtained.

12   Using a straightedge and feeler gauge, check the head gasket mating surfaces for warpage **(see illustration)**. If the warpage exceeds the specified limit, it can be resurfaced at an automotive machine shop.

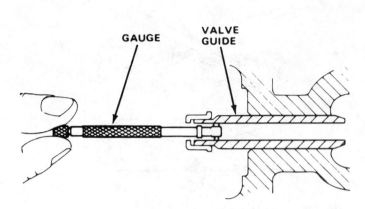

9.14   Use a small hole gauge to determine the inside diameter of the valve guides (the gauge is then measured with a micrometer)

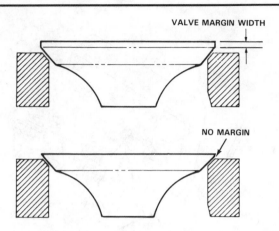

9.16   The margin width on each valve must be as specified (if no margin exists, the valve cannot be reused)

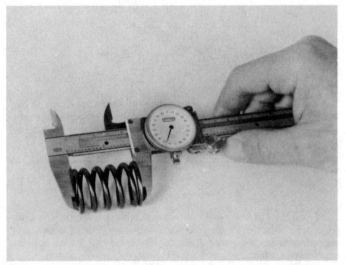

9.17   Measure the free length of each valve spring with a dial or vernier caliper

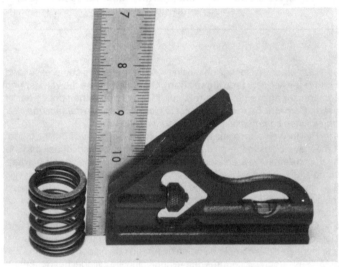

9.18   Check each valve spring for squareness

13   Examine the valve seats in each of the combustion chambers. If they're pitted, cracked or burned, the head will require valve service that's beyond the scope of the home mechanic.

14   Check the valve stem-to-guide clearance with a small hole gauge and micrometer **(see illustration)**. After this is done, if there's still some doubt regarding the condition of the valve guides they should be checked by an automotive machine shop (the cost should be minimal).

Valves

15   Carefully inspect each valve face for uneven wear, deformation, cracks, pits and burned areas. Check the valve stem for scuffing and galling and the neck for cracks. Rotate the valve and check for any obvious indication that it's bent. Look for pits and excessive wear on the end of the stem. The presence of any of these conditions indicates the need for valve service by an automotive machine shop.

16   Measure the margin width on each valve **(see illustration)**. Any valve with a margin narrower than specified will have to be replaced with a new one.

Valve components

17   Check each valve spring for wear (on the ends) and pits. Measure the free length and compare it to the Specifications **(see illustration)**. Any springs that are shorter than specified have sagged and should not be re-used. The tension of all springs should be checked with a special fixture

before deciding they're suitable for use in a rebuilt engine (take the springs to an automotive machine shop for this check).

18   Stand each spring on a flat surface and check it for squareness **(see illustration)**. If any of the springs are distorted or sagged, replace all of them with new parts.

19   Check the spring retainers and keepers for obvious wear and cracks. Any questionable parts should be replaced with new ones, as extensive damage will occur if they fail during engine operation.

20   Any damaged or excessively worn parts must be replaced with new ones.

21   If the inspection process indicates that the valve components are in generally poor condition and worn beyond the limits specified, which is usually the case in an engine that's being overhauled, reassemble the valves in the cylinder head and refer to Section 10 for valve servicing recommendations.

10   Valves – servicing

1   Because of the complex nature of the job and the special tools and equipment needed, servicing of the valves, the valve seats and the valve guides, commonly known as a valve job, should be done by a professional.

11.3   Gently tap the valve seals into place with a deep socket and hammer

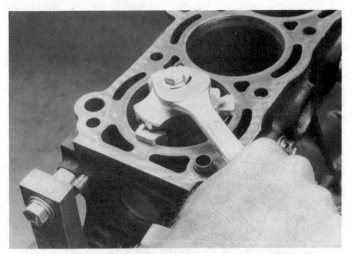

12.1   A ridge reamer is required to remove the ridge from the top of each cylinder – do this before removing the pistons!

2   The home mechanic can remove and disassemble the head, do the initial cleaning and inspection, then reassemble and deliver it to a dealer service department or an automotive machine shop for the actual service work. Doing the inspection will enable you to see what condition the head and valvetrain components are in and will ensure that you know what work and new parts are required when dealing with an automotive machine shop.

3   The dealer service department, or automotive machine shop, will remove the valves and springs, recondition or replace the valves and valve seats, recondition the valve guides, check and replace the valve springs, spring retainers and keepers (as necessary), replace the valve seals with new ones, reassemble the valve components and make sure the installed spring height is correct. The cylinder head gasket surface will also be resurfaced if it's warped.

4   After the valve job has been performed by a professional, the head will be in like new condition. When the head is returned, be sure to clean it again before installation on the engine to remove any metal particles and abrasive grit that may still be present from the valve service or head resurfacing operations. Use compressed air, if available, to blow out all the oil holes and passages. **Warning:** *Wear eye protection!*

11   Cylinder head – reassembly

Refer to illustration 11.3

1   Regardless of whether or not the head was sent to an automotive repair shop for valve servicing, make sure it's clean before beginning reassembly.

2   If the head was sent out for valve servicing, the valves and related components will already be in place.

3   Install new seals on each of the valve guides. **Note:** *Intake and exhaust valves may require different seals – DO NOT mix them up!* **Note:** *The original seals on the 4A-FE engines are color coded. The intake seals are brown and the exhaust seals are black. Check the instructions enclosed with the gasket set to ensure proper installation.* Gently tap each intake valve seal into place until it's seated on the guide **(see illustration)**. **Caution:** *Don't hammer on the valve seals once they're seated or you may damage them. Don't twist or cock the seals during installation or they won't seat properly on the valve stems.*

4   Beginning at one end of the head, lubricate and install the first valve. Apply moly-base grease or clean engine oil to the valve stem.

5   Drop the spring seat or shim(s) over the valve guide and set the valve spring and retainer in place.

6   Compress the springs with a valve spring compressor and carefully install the keepers in the upper groove, then slowly release the compres-

12.3   Check the connecting rod side clearance with a feeler gauge as shown here

sor and make sure the keepers seat properly. Apply a small dab of grease to each keeper to hold it in place if necessary **(see illustration)**.

7   Repeat the procedure for the remaining valves. Be sure to return the components to their original locations – don't mix them up!

12   Pistons/connecting rods – removal

Refer to illustrations 12.1, 12.3, 12.4, and 12.6

Note: *Prior to removing the piston/connecting rod assemblies, remove the cylinder head, the oil pan and the oil pump pick-up tube by referring to the appropriate Sections in Chapter 2.*

1   Use your fingernail to feel if a ridge has formed at the upper limit of ring travel (about 1/4-inch down from the top of each cylinder). If carbon deposits or cylinder wear have produced ridges, they must be completely removed with a special tool **(see illustration)**. Follow the manufacturer's instructions provided with the tool. Failure to remove the ridges before attempting to remove the piston/connecting rod assemblies may result in piston breakage.

2   After the cylinder ridges have been removed, turn the engine upside-down so the crankshaft is facing up.

3   Before the connecting rods are removed, check the endplay with feeler gauges. Slide them between the first connecting rod and the crankshaft throw until the play is removed **(see illustration)**. The endplay is equal to

12.4   The connecting rods and caps should be marked to indicate which cylinder they're installed in – if they aren't, mark them with a center punch to avoid confusion during reassembly

12.6   To prevent damage to the crankshaft journals and cylinder walls, slip sections of hose over the rod bolts before removing the pistons

the thickness of the feeler gauge(s). If the endplay exceeds the service limit, new connecting rods will be required. If new rods (or a new crankshaft) are installed, the endplay may fall under the specified minimum (if it does, the rods will have to be machined to restore it – consult an automotive machine shop for advice if necessary). Repeat the procedure for the remaining connecting rods.

4   Check the connecting rods and caps for identification marks. If they aren't plainly marked, use a small center punch to make the appropriate number of indentations on each rod and cap (1, 2, 3, 4, depending on the cylinder they're associated with) **(see illustration)**. **Note:** *Don't mistake the bearing grade marks for cylinder numbers!*

5   Loosen each of the connecting rod cap nuts 1/2-turn at a time until they can be removed by hand. Remove the number one connecting rod cap and bearing insert. Don't drop the bearing insert out of the cap.

6   Slip a short length of plastic or rubber hose over each connecting rod cap bolt to protect the crankshaft journal and cylinder wall as the piston is removed **(see illustration)**.

7   Remove the bearing insert and push the connecting rod/piston assembly out through the top of the engine. Use a wooden hammer handle to push on the upper bearing surface in the connecting rod. If resistance is felt, double-check to make sure that all of the ridge was removed from the cylinder.

8   Repeat the procedure for the remaining cylinders.

9   After removal, reassemble the connecting rod caps and bearing inserts in their respective connecting rods and install the cap nuts finger tight. Leaving the old bearing inserts in place until reassembly will help prevent the connecting rod bearing surfaces from being accidentally nicked or gouged.

10   Don't separate the pistons from the connecting rods (see Section 17 for additional information).

13   Crankshaft – removal

Refer to illustrations 13.1, 13.3 and 13.4
Note: *The crankshaft can be removed only after the engine has been removed from the vehicle. It's assumed that the flywheel or driveplate, crankshaft pulley, timing belt, oil pan, oil pick-up tube, oil pump and piston/connecting rod assemblies have already been removed. The rear main oil seal retainer must be unbolted and separated from the block before proceeding with crankshaft removal.*

1   Before the crankshaft is removed, check the endplay. Mount a dial indicator with the stem in line with the crankshaft and just touching the end of the crankshaft **(see illustration)**.

2   Push the crankshaft all the way to the rear and zero the dial indicator. Next, pry the crankshaft to the front as far as possible and check the reading on the dial indicator. The distance that it moves is the endplay. If it's greater than specified, check the crankshaft thrust surfaces for wear. If no wear is evident, new thrust bearings should correct the endplay.

3   If a dial indicator isn't available, feeler gauges can be used. Gently pry or push the crankshaft all the way to the front of the engine. Slip feeler gauges between the crankshaft and the front face of the thrust main bearing to determine the clearance **(see illustration)**. The thrust bearing is number three (the center one).

4   Check the main bearing caps to see if they're marked to indicate their locations. They should be numbered consecutively from the front of the engine to the rear. If they aren't, mark them with number stamping dies or a center punch. Main bearing caps generally have a cast-in arrow, which points to the front of the engine. Loosen the main bearing cap bolts 1/4-turn at a time each, in the recommended sequence **(see illustration)**, until they can be removed by hand. Note if any stud bolts are used and make sure they're returned to their original locations when the crankshaft is reinstalled.

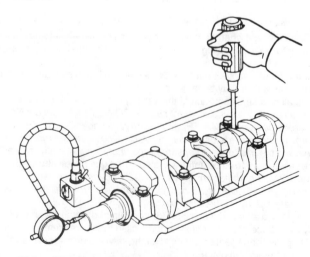

13.1   Check crankshaft endplay with a dial indicator . . .

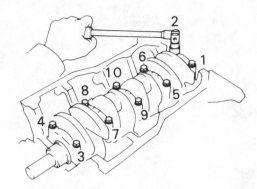

13.3   . . . or slip feeler gauges between the crankshaft and main bearing thrust surfaces – the endplay is equal to the feeler gauge thickness

13.4   Loosen the main bearing cap bolts in this numerical sequence

5   Gently tap the caps with a soft-face hammer, then separate them from the engine block. If necessary, use the bolts as levers to remove the caps. Try not to drop the bearing inserts.
6   Carefully lift the crankshaft out of the engine. It may be a good idea to have an assistant available, since the crankshaft is quite heavy. With the bearing inserts in place in the engine block and main bearing caps or cap assembly, return the caps to their respective locations on the engine block and tighten the bolts finger tight.

14   Engine block – cleaning

Refer to illustrations 14.1, 14.8 and 14.10
Caution: *The core plugs (also known as freeze or soft plugs) may be difficult or impossible to retrieve if they're driven into the block coolant passages.*
1   Drill a small hole in the center of each core plug and pull them out with an auto body type dent puller **(see illustration)**.
2   Using a gasket scraper, remove all traces of gasket material from the engine block. Be very careful not to nick or gouge the gasket sealing surfaces.
3   Remove the main bearing caps or cap assembly and separate the bearing inserts from the caps and the engine block. Tag the bearings, indi-

cating which cylinder they were removed from and whether they were in the cap or the block, then set them aside.
4   Remove all of the threaded oil gallery plugs from the block. The plugs are usually very tight – they may have to be drilled out and the holes re-tapped. Use new plugs when the engine is reassembled.
5   If the engine is extremely dirty it should be taken to an automotive machine shop to be steam cleaned or hot tanked.
6   After the block is returned, clean all oil holes and oil galleries one more time. Brushes specifically designed for this purpose are available at most auto parts stores. Flush the passages with warm water until the water runs clear, dry the block thoroughly and wipe all machined surfaces with a light, rust preventive oil. If you have access to compressed air, use it to speed the drying process and to blow out all the oil holes and galleries. **Warning:** *Wear eye protection when using compressed air!*
7   If the block isn't extremely dirty or sludged up, you can do an adequate cleaning job with hot soapy water and a stiff brush. Take plenty of time and do a thorough job. Regardless of the cleaning method used, be sure to clean all oil holes and galleries very thoroughly, dry the block completely and coat all machined surfaces with light oil.
8   The threaded holes in the block must be clean to ensure accurate torque readings during reassembly. Run the proper size tap into each of the holes to remove rust, corrosion, thread sealant or sludge and restore damaged threads **(see illustration)**. If possible, use compressed air to

14.1   The core plugs should be removed with a puller – if they're driven into the block they may be impossible to retrieve

14.8   All bolt holes in the block – particularly the main bearing cap and head bolt holes – should be cleaned and restored with a tap (be sure to remove debris from the holes after this is done)

14.10   A large socket on an extension can be used to drive the new core plugs into the bores

clear the holes of debris produced by this operation. Now is a good time to clean the threads on the head bolts and the main bearing cap bolts as well.
9   Reinstall the main bearing caps and tighten the bolts finger tight.
10   After coating the sealing surfaces of the new core plugs with Permatex no. 2 sealant, install them in the engine block **(see illustration)**. Make sure they're driven in straight and seated properly or leakage could result. Special tools are available for this purpose, but a large socket, with an outside diameter that will just slip into the core plug, a 1/2-inch drive extension and a hammer will work just as well.
11   Apply non-hardening sealant (such as Permatex no. 2 or Teflon pipe sealant) to the new oil gallery plugs and thread them into the holes in the block. Make sure they're tightened securely.
12   If the engine isn't going to be reassembled right away, cover it with a large plastic trash bag to keep it clean.

---

15   Engine block – inspection

Refer to illustrations 15.4a, 15.4b, 15.4c, 15.12, 15.14a and 15.14b
1   Before the block is inspected, it should be cleaned as described in Section 14.
2   Visually check the block for cracks, rust and corrosion. Look for stripped threads in the threaded holes. It's also a good idea to have the block checked for hidden cracks by an automotive machine shop that has the special equipment to do this type of work. If defects are found, have the block repaired, if possible, or replaced.
3   Check the cylinder bores for scuffing and scoring.
4   Measure the diameter of each cylinder at the top (just under the ridge area), center and bottom of the cylinder bore, parallel to the crankshaft axis **(see illustrations)**. **Note:** *These measurements should not be made with the bare block mounted on an engine stand – the cylinders will be distorted and the measurements will be inaccurate.*
5   Next, measure each cylinder's diameter at the same three locations across the crankshaft axis. Compare the results to the Specifications listed in this Chapter.
6   If the required precision measuring tools aren't available, the piston-to-cylinder clearances can be obtained, though not quite as accurately, using feeler gauge stock. Feeler gauge stock comes in 12-inch lengths and various thicknesses and is generally available at auto parts stores.
7   To check the clearance, select a feeler gauge and slip it into the cylinder along with the matching piston. The piston must be positioned exactly as it normally would be. The feeler gauge must be between the piston and cylinder on one of the thrust faces (90 degrees to the piston pin bore).

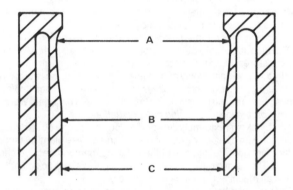

15.4a   Measure the diameter of each cylinder just under the wear ridge (A), at the center (B) and at the bottom (C)

15.4b   The ability to "feel" when the telescoping gauge is at the correct point will be developed over time, so work slowly and repeat the check until you're satisfied the bore measurement is accurate

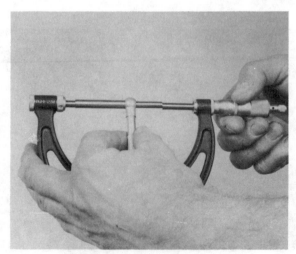

15.4c   The gauge is then measured with a micrometer to determine the bore size

15.12 Lay the straightedge across the block, diagonally and from end-to-end when making the check

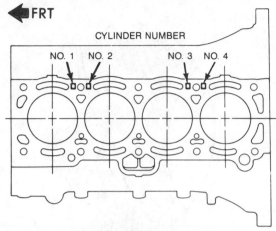

15.14a On 4A-FE engines, the engine block is stamped with a number (1, 2 or 3) adjacent to each cylinder to indicate the original bore size (and consequently the piston size required)

8   The piston should slip through the cylinder (with the feeler gauge in place) with moderate pressure.

9   If it falls through or slides through easily, the clearance is excessive and a new piston will be required. If the piston binds at the lower end of the cylinder and is loose toward the top, the cylinder is tapered. If tight spots are encountered as the piston/feeler gauge is rotated in the cylinder, the cylinder is out-of-round.

10   Repeat the procedure for the remaining pistons and cylinders.

11   If the cylinder walls are badly scuffed or scored, or if they're out of-round or tapered beyond the limits given in the Specifications, have the engine block rebored and honed at an automotive machine shop. If a re-bore is done, oversize pistons and rings will be required.

12   Using a precision straightedge and feeler gauge, check the block deck (the surface that mates with the cylinder head) for distortion **(see illustration)**. If it's distorted beyond the limit specified in this Chapter, it can be resurfaced by an automotive machine shop.

13   If the cylinders are in reasonably good condition and not worn to the outside of the limits, and if the piston-to-cylinder clearances can be maintained properly, then they don't have to be rebored. Honing is all that's necessary (see Section 16).

14   On 4A-FE engines only, the original bores and pistons were available in three sizes. Note the sizes stamped on the block and pistons **(see illustrations)**.

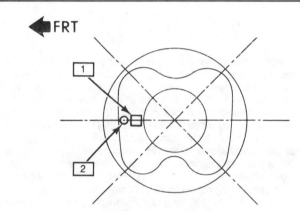

15.14b On 4A-FE engines, the tops of the pistons are marked to indicate size

1 *Piston size mark (1, 2 or 3)*
2 *Indentation (indicates timing belt end)*

16 Cylinder honing

Refer to illustrations 16.3a and 16.3b

1   Prior to engine reassembly, the cylinder bores must be honed so the new piston rings will seat correctly and provide the best possible combustion chamber seal. **Note:** *If you don't have the tools or don't want to tackle the honing operation, most automotive machine shops will do it for a reasonable fee.*

2   Before honing the cylinders, install the main bearing caps or cap assembly (without bearing inserts) and tighten the bolts to the torque listed in this Chapter's specifications.

3   Two types of cylinder hones are commonly available – the flex hone or "bottle brush" type and the more traditional surfacing hone with spring-loaded stones. Both will do the job, but for the less experienced mechanic the "bottle brush" hone will probably be easier to use. You'll also need some kerosene or honing oil, rags and an electric drill motor. Proceed as follows:

   a) Mount the hone in the drill motor, compress the stones and slip it into the first cylinder **(see illustration)**. Be sure to wear safety goggles or a face shield!

16.3a A "bottle brush" hone will produce better results if you've never done cylinder honing before

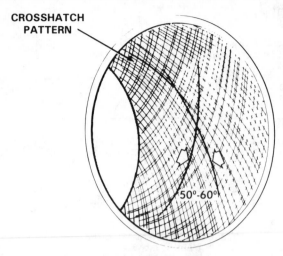

CROSSHATCH
PATTERN

50°-60°

16.3b   The cylinder hone should leave a smooth, crosshatch pattern with the lines intersecting at approximately a 60-degree angle

b) Lubricate the cylinder with plenty of honing oil, turn on the drill and move the hone up-and-down in the cylinder at a pace that will produce a fine crosshatch pattern on the cylinder walls. Ideally, the crosshatch lines should intersect at approximately a 60-degree angle **(see illustration)**. Be sure to use plenty of lubricant and don't take off any more material than is absolutely necessary to produce the desired finish. **Note:** *Piston ring manufacturers may specify a smaller crosshatch angle than the traditional 60-degree – read and follow any instructions included with the new rings.*

c) Don't withdraw the hone from the cylinder while it's running. Instead, shut off the drill and continue moving the hone up-and down in the cylinder until it comes to a complete stop, then compress the stones and withdraw the hone. If you're using a "bottle brush" type hone, stop the drill motor, then turn the chuck in the normal direction of rotation while withdrawing the hone from the cylinder.

d) Wipe the oil out of the cylinder and repeat the procedure for the remaining cylinders.

4   After the honing job is complete, chamfer the top edges of the cylinder bores with a small file so the rings won't catch when the pistons are installed. Be very careful not to nick the cylinder walls with the end of the file.

5   The entire engine block must be washed again very thoroughly with warm, soapy water to remove all traces of the abrasive grit produced during the honing operation. **Note:** *The bores can be considered clean when a lint-free white cloth – dampened with clean engine oil- used to wipe them out doesn't pick up any more honing residue, which will show up as gray areas on the cloth. Be sure to run a brush through all oil holes and galleries and flush them with running water.*

6   After rinsing, dry the block and apply a coat of light rust preventive oil to all machined surfaces. Wrap the block in a plastic trash bag to keep it clean and set it aside until reassembly.

17   Pistons/connecting rods – inspection

Refer to illustrations 17.4a, 17.4b, 17.10, 17.11a and 17.11b

1   Before the inspection process can be carried out, the piston/connecting rod assemblies must be cleaned and the original piston rings removed from the pistons. **Note:** *Always use new piston rings when the engine is reassembled.*

2   Using a piston ring installation tool, carefully remove the rings from the pistons. Be careful not to nick or gouge the pistons in the process.

3   Scrape all traces of carbon from the top of the piston. A handheld wire brush or a piece of fine emery cloth can be used once the majority of the deposits have been scraped away. Do not, under any circumstances, use a wire brush mounted in a drill motor to remove deposits from the pistons. The piston material is soft and may be eroded away by the wire brush.

4   Use a piston ring groove cleaning tool to remove carbon deposits from the ring grooves. If a tool isn't available, a piece broken off the old ring will do the job. Be very careful to remove only the carbon deposits – don't remove any metal and do not nick or scratch the sides of the ring grooves **(see illustrations)**.

5   Once the deposits have been removed, clean the piston/rod assemblies with solvent and dry them with compressed air (if available). Make sure the oil return holes in the back sides of the ring grooves and the oil hole in the lower end of each rod are clear.

6   If the pistons and cylinder walls aren't damaged or worn excessively, and if the engine block is not rebored, new pistons won't be necessary. Normal piston wear appears as even vertical wear on the piston thrust surfaces and slight looseness of the top ring in its groove. New piston rings, however, should always be used when an engine is rebuilt.

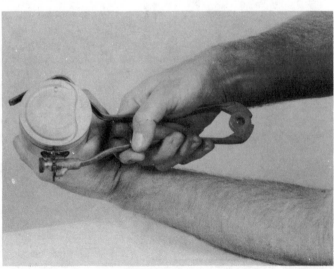

17.4a   The piston ring grooves can be cleaned with a special tool, as shown here, . . .

17.4b   . . . or a section of a broken ring

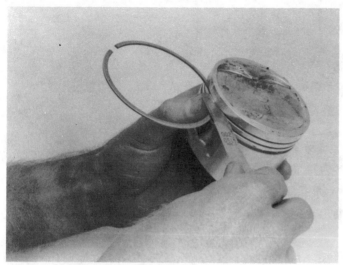

17.10   Check the ring side clearance with a feeler gauge at several points around the groove

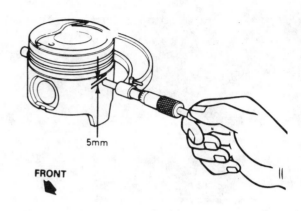

5mm

FRONT

17.11a   On 4A-LC engines, measure the piston diameter 13/64-inch (5 mm) below the oil ring groove

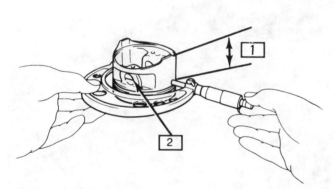

17.11b   4A-GE pistons are measured 1-21/32 inch (42 mm) up from the bottom; 4A-FE pistons are measured 1-33/64 inch (38.5 mm) up from the bottom (piston inverted in illustration)

    1   Distance from the bottom of the piston
        skirt to the measuring point
    2   Piston pin

7   Carefully inspect each piston for cracks around the skirt, at the pin bosses and at the ring lands.

8   Look for scoring and scuffing on the thrust faces of the skirt, holes in the piston crown and burned areas at the edge of the crown. If the skirt is scored or scuffed, the engine may have been suffering from overheating and/or abnormal combustion, which caused excessively high operating temperatures. The cooling and lubrication systems should be checked thoroughly. A hole in the piston crown is an indication that abnormal combustion (preignition) was occurring. Burned areas at the edge of the piston crown are usually evidence of spark knock (detonation). If any of the above problems exist, the causes must be corrected or the damage will occur again. The causes may include intake air leaks, incorrect fuel/air mixture, incorrect ignition timing and EGR system malfunctions.

9   Corrosion of the piston, in the form of small pits, indicates that coolant is leaking into the combustion chamber and/or the crankcase. Again, the cause must be corrected or the problem may persist in the rebuilt engine.

10   Measure the piston ring side clearance by laying a new piston ring in each ring groove and slipping a feeler gauge in beside it **(see illustration)**.

Check the clearance at three or four locations around each groove. Be sure to use the correct ring for each groove – they are different. If the side clearance is greater than specified, new pistons will have to be used.

11   Check the piston-to-bore clearance by measuring the bore (see Section 15) and the piston diameter. Make sure the pistons and bores are correctly matched. Some pistons are available in several standard sizes (or grades). Measure the piston across the skirt, at a 90-degree angle to the piston pin, the specified distance up from the bottom of the piston or down from the lower edge of the oil ring groove **(see illustrations)**. Subtract the piston diameter from the bore diameter to obtain the clearance. If it's greater than specified, the block will have to be rebored and new pistons and rings installed.

12   Check the piston-to-rod clearance by twisting the piston and rod in opposite directions. Any noticeable play indicates excessive wear, which must be corrected. The piston/connecting rod assemblies should be taken to an automotive machine shop to have the pistons and rods resized and new pins installed.

13   If the pistons must be removed from the connecting rods for any reason, they should be taken to an automotive machine shop. While they are there have the connecting rods checked for bend and twist, since automotive machine shops have special equipment for this purpose. **Note:** *Unless new pistons and/or connecting rods must be installed, do not disassemble the pistons and connecting rods.*

14   Check the connecting rods for cracks and other damage. Temporarily remove the rod caps, lift out the old bearing inserts, wipe the rod and cap bearing surfaces clean and inspect them for nicks, gouges and scratches. After checking the rods, replace the old bearings, slip the caps into place and tighten the nuts finger tight. **Note:** *If the engine is being rebuilt because of a connecting rod knock, be sure to install new rods.*

18   Crankshaft – inspection

Refer to illustration 18.1, 18.3, 18.4, 18.6 and 18.8

1   Clean the crankshaft with solvent and dry it with compressed air (if available). Be sure to clean the oil holes with a stiff brush **(see illustration)** and flush them with solvent.

2   Check the main and connecting rod bearing journals for uneven wear, scoring, pits and cracks.

3   Rub a penny across each journal several times **(see illustration)**. If a journal picks up copper from the penny, it's too rough and must be reground.

18.1   Clean the crankshaft oil passages with a wire or stiff plastic bristle brush and flush them out with solvent

18.3   Rubbing a penny lengthwise on each journal will give you a quick idea of its condition – if copper rubs off the penny and adheres to the crankshaft, the journals should be reground

18.4   Chamfer the oil holes to remove sharp edges that might gouge or scratch the new bearings

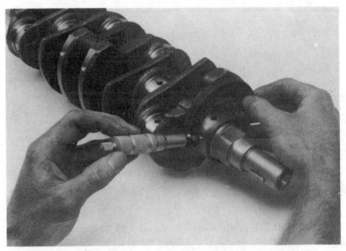

18.6   Measure the diameter of each crankshaft journal at several points to detect taper and out-of-round conditions

18.8   If the seals have worn grooves in the crankshaft journals, or if the seal journals are nicked or scratched, the new seal(s) will leak

4   Remove all burrs from the crankshaft oil holes with a stone, file or scraper (see illustration).
5   Check the rest of the crankshaft for cracks and other damage. It should be magnafluxed to reveal hidden cracks – an automotive machine shop will handle the procedure.
6   Using a micrometer, measure the diameter of the main and connecting rod journals and compare the results to the Specifications (see illustration). By measuring the diameter at a number of points around each journal's circumference, you'll be able to determine whether or not the journal is out-of-round. Take the measurement at each end of the journal, near the crank throws, to determine if the journal is tapered. Crankshaft runout should be checked also, but large V-blocks and a dial indicator are needed to do it correctly. If you don't have the equipment, have a machine shop check the runout.
7   If the crankshaft journals are damaged, tapered, out-of-round or worn beyond the limits given in the Specifications, have the crankshaft reground by an automotive machine shop. Be sure to use the correct size bearing inserts if the crankshaft is reconditioned.

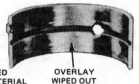

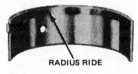

19.1   Typical bearing failures

engine. This will enable you to match any bearing problems with the corresponding crankshaft journal.

4   Dirt and other foreign particles get into the engine in a variety of ways. It may be left in the engine during assembly, or it may pass through filters or the PCV system. It may get into the oil, and from there into the bearings. Metal chips from machining operations and normal engine wear are often present. Abrasives are sometimes left in engine components after reconditioning, especially when parts are not thoroughly cleaned using the proper cleaning methods. Whatever the source, these foreign objects often end up embedded in the soft bearing material and are easily recognized. Large particles will not embed in the bearing and will score or gouge the bearing and journal. The best prevention for this cause of bearing failure is to clean all parts thoroughly and keep everything spotlessly clean during engine assembly. Frequent and regular engine oil and filter changes are also recommended.

5   Lack of lubrication (or lubrication breakdown) has a number of interrelated causes. Excessive heat (which thins the oil), overloading (which squeezes the oil from the bearing face) and oil leakage or throw off (from excessive bearing clearances, worn oil pump or high engine speeds) all contribute to lubrication breakdown. Blocked oil passages, which usually are the result of misaligned oil holes in a bearing shell, will also oil starve a bearing and destroy it. When lack of lubrication is the cause of bearing failure, the bearing material is wiped or extruded from the steel backing of the bearing. Temperatures may increase to the point where the steel backing turns blue from overheating.

6   Driving habits can have a definite effect on bearing life. Full throttle, low speed operation (lugging the engine) puts very high loads on bearings, which tends to squeeze out the oil film. These loads cause the bearings to flex, which produces fine cracks in the bearing face (fatigue failure). Eventually the bearing material will loosen in pieces and tear away from the steel backing. Short trip driving leads to corrosion of bearings because insufficient engine heat is produced to drive off the condensed water and corrosive gases. These products collect in the engine oil, forming acid and sludge. As the oil is carried to the engine bearings, the acid attacks and corrodes the bearing material.

7   Incorrect bearing installation during engine assembly will lead to bearing failure as well. Tight fitting bearings leave insufficient bearing oil clearance and will result in oil starvation. Dirt or foreign particles trapped behind a bearing insert result in high spots on the bearing which lead to failure.

8   Check the oil seal journals at each end of the crankshaft for wear and damage **(see illustration)**. If the seal has worn a groove in the journal, or if it's nicked or scratched, the new seal may leak when the engine is reassembled. In some cases, an automotive machine shop may be able to repair the journal by pressing on a thin sleeve. If repair isn't feasible, a new or different crankshaft should be installed.

9   Refer to Section 19 and examine the main and rod bearing inserts.

Bearing selection

Refer to illustrations 19.9, 19.10, 19.11, 19.12a, 19.12b, 19.12c, 19.13a and 19.13b

8   If the original bearings are worn or damaged, or if the oil clearances are incorrect (see Section 22 or 24), the following procedures should be used to select the correct new bearings for engine reassembly. However, if the crankshaft has been reground, new undersize bearings must be installed – the following procedure should not be used if undersize bearings are required! The automotive machine shop that reconditions the crankshaft will provide or help you select the correct size bearings. **Note:** *Undersize main bearings are not supplied by the factory for 4A-LC engines. Regardless of how the bearing sizes are determined, use the oil clearance, measured with Plastigage, as a guide to ensure the bearings are the right size.*

Main bearings

9   If you need a STANDARD size main bearing, install one that has the same number as the original bearing **(see illustration)**.

10   If you're working on a 1985 or 1986 model and the number on the original main bearing has been obscured, install one that has the same number as the number stamped into the block at the corresponding cap location **(see illustration)**.

19   Main and connecting rod bearings – inspection and bearing selection

Inspection

Refer to illustration 19.1

1   Even though the main and connecting rod bearings should be replaced with new ones during the engine overhaul, the old bearings should be retained for close examination, as they may reveal valuable information about the condition of the engine **(see illustration)**.

2   Bearing failure occurs because of lack of lubrication, the presence of dirt or other foreign particles, overloading the engine and corrosion. Regardless of the cause of bearing failure, it must be corrected before the engine is reassembled to prevent it from happening again.

3   When examining the bearings, remove them from the engine block, the main bearing caps, the connecting rods and the rod caps and lay them out on a clean surface in the same general position as their location in the

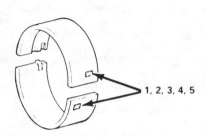

19.9   The main bearings are stamped with grade numbers

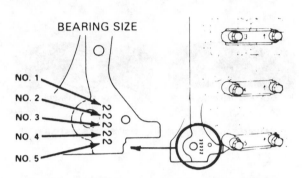

19.10   On 1985 and 1986 models, if the number on the original main bearing isn't clear, install a new bearing with a number that matches the number stamped into the block – different journals may require different size bearings

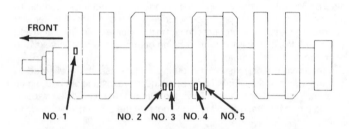

19.11   On 1987 and later models, the grade numbers are stamped on the crankshaft as well as the block – use the applicable table to select the correct main bearings

Cylinder Block	No.	1	2	3	1	2	3	1	2	3
Crankshaft	No.	0	0	0	1	1	1	2	2	2
Bearing	No.	1	2	3	2	3	4	3	4	5

EXAMPLE: CYLINDER BLOCK NO. 2, CRANKSHAFT NO. 1 = BEARING NO. 3

19.12a   1987 and later 4A-LC and 4A-GE main bearing selection table

mm (in.)

No.	Cylinder Block Bearing Housing	No.	Crankshaft Diameter	No.	Bearing Thickness
1	52.025-52.031 (2.0482-2.0485)	0	47.994-48.000 (1.8895-1.8898)	1	2.002-2.005 (0.0788-0.0789)
				2	2.005-2.008 (0.0789-0.0791)
2	52.031-52.037 (2.0485-2.0487)	1	47.994-47.988 (1.8895-1.8893)	3	2.008-2.011 (0.0791-0.0792)
				4	2.011-2.014 (0.0792-0.0793)
3	52.037-52.043 (2.0487-2.0489)	2	47.988-47.982 (1.8893-1.8891)	5	2.014-2.017 (0.0793-0.0794)

19.12b   1987 and later 4A-LC and 4A-GE main bearing sizes

BEARING SELECTION TABLE

Crankshaft Block Mark	1	2	3	1	2	3	1	2	3
Crankshaft Mark	0	0	0	1	1	1	2	2	2
Bearing Mark	1	2	3	3	2	4	3	4	5

19.12c   1987 and later 4A-FE main bearing selection table

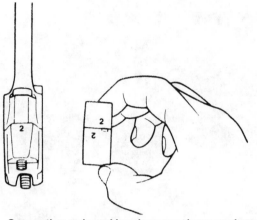

19.13a   Connecting rods and bearings may have grade marks like this . . .

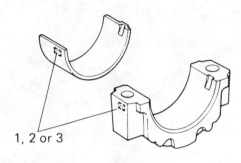

1, 2 or 3

19.13b   . . . or this – DO NOT confuse them with the cylinder numbers

11   If you're working on a 1987 or later model and the number on the original main bearing has been obscured, locate the main journal grade numbers stamped into the oil pan mating surface on the engine block and on the crankshaft **(see illustration)**.

12   Use the accompanying tables to determine the correct bearings for each journal **(see illustrations)**.

Connecting rod bearings

13   If you need a STANDARD size rod bearing, install one that has the same number as the number stamped into the connecting rod cap **(see illustrations)**. *Note: Some 4A-FE engines have only one standard size bearing available.*

All bearings

14   Remember, the oil clearance is the final judge when selecting new bearing sizes. If you have any questions or are unsure which bearings to use, get help from your dealer parts or service department.

---

20   Engine overhaul – reassembly sequence

---

1   Before beginning engine reassembly, make sure you have all the necessary new parts, gaskets and seals as well as the following items on hand:

Common hand tools
A 1/2-inch drive torque wrench
Piston ring installation tool
Piston ring compressor
Short lengths of rubber or plastic hose to fit over connecting rod bolts
Plastigage
Feeler gauges
A fine-tooth file
New engine oil
Engine assembly lube or moly-base grease
Gasket sealer
Thread locking compound

2   In order to save time and avoid problems, engine reassembly must be done in the following general order:

Piston rings (Part B)
Crankshaft and main bearings (Part B)
Piston/connecting rod assemblies (Part B)
Rear crankshaft oil seal (Part B)
Cylinder head and rocker arms or lifters (Part A)
Camshaft (Part A)
Timing belt, sprockets and cover(s) (Part A)

Oil pump (Part A)
Oil pan and pick-up (Part A)
Intake and exhaust manifolds (Part A)
Camshaft cover(s) (Part A)
Flywheel/driveplate (Part A)

---

21   Piston rings – installation

Refer to illustrations 21.3, 21.4, 21.9a, 21.9b and 21.12

1   Before installing the new piston rings, the ring end gaps must be checked. It's assumed that the piston ring side clearance has been checked and verified correct (see Section 17).

2   Lay out the piston/connecting rod assemblies and the new ring sets so the ring sets will be matched with the same piston and cylinder during the end gap measurement and engine assembly.

3   Insert the top (number one) ring into the first cylinder and square it up with the cylinder walls by pushing it in with the top of the piston **(see illustration)**. The ring should be near the bottom of the cylinder, at the lower limit of ring travel.

21.3   When checking piston ring end gap, the ring must be square in the cylinder bore – this is done by pushing the ring down with the top of a piston as shown

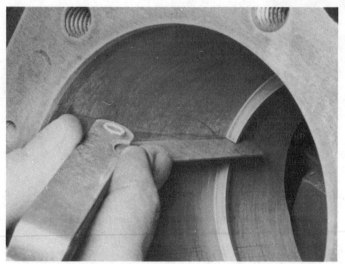

21.4   With the ring square in the cylinder, measure the end gap with a feeler gauge

21.9a   Installing the spacer/expander in the oil control ring groove

21.9b   DO NOT use a piston ring installation tool when installing the oil ring side rails

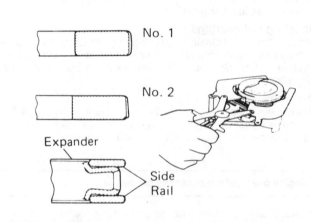

21.12   Install the compression rings with an expander – the beveled edge on the number two piston ring faces down

4   To measure the end gap, slip feeler gauges between the ends of the ring until a gauge equal to the gap width is found **(see illustration)**. The feeler gauge should slide between the ring ends with a slight amount of drag. Compare the measurement to the Specifications listed in this Chapter. If the gap is larger or smaller than specified, double-check to make sure you have the correct rings before proceeding.

5   If the gap is too small, replace the rings – DO NOT file the ends to increase the clearance.

6   Excess end gap isn't critical unless it's greater than 0.040-inch. Again, double-check to make sure you have the correct rings for your engine.

7   Repeat the procedure for each ring that will be installed in the first cylinder and for each ring in the remaining cylinders. Remember to keep rings, pistons and cylinders matched up.

8   Once the ring end gaps have been checked/corrected, the rings can be installed on the pistons.

9   The oil control ring (lowest one on the piston) is usually installed first. It's composed of three separate components. Slip the spacer/expander into the groove **(see illustration)**. If an anti-rotation tang is used, make sure it's inserted into the drilled hole in the ring groove. Next, install the lower side rail. Don't use a piston ring installation tool on the oil ring side rails, as they may be damaged. Instead, place one end of the side rail into the groove between the spacer/expander and the ring land, hold it firmly in place and slide a finger around the piston while pushing the rail into the groove **(see illustration)**. Next, install the upper side rail in the same manner.

10   After the three oil ring components have been installed, check to make sure that both the upper and lower side rails can be turned smoothly in the ring groove.

11   The number two (middle) ring is installed next. It's usually stamped with a mark which must face up, toward the top of the piston. **Note:** *Always follow the instructions printed on the ring package or box – different man-*

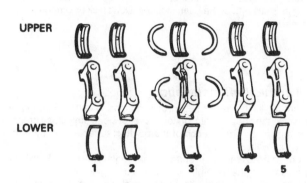

22.5   Install the main and thrust bearings as shown – the bearings marked UPPER are installed in the block; the ones marked LOWER are installed in the bearing caps

22.10   Lay the Plastigage strips (arrow) on the main bearing journals parallel to the crankshaft centerline

ufacturers may require different approaches. Do not mix up the top and middle rings, as they have different cross sections.

12   Use a piston ring installation tool and make sure the identification mark is facing the top of the piston, then slip the ring into the middle groove on the piston **(see illustration)**. Don't expand the ring any more than necessary to slide it over the piston.

13   Install the number one (top) ring in the same manner. Make sure the mark is facing up. Be careful not to confuse the number one and number two rings.

14   Repeat the procedure for the remaining pistons and rings.

---

22   Crankshaft – installation and main bearing oil clearance check

---

Refer to illustrations 22.5, 22.10, 22.12, 22.14, 22.19a and 22.19b

1   Crankshaft installation is the first major step in engine reassembly. It's assumed at this point that the engine block and crankshaft have been cleaned, inspected and repaired or reconditioned.

2   Position the engine with the bottom facing up.

3   Remove the main bearing cap bolts and lift out the caps or cap assembly. Lay the caps out in the proper order to ensure correct installation.

4   If they're still in place, remove the old bearing inserts from the block and the main bearing caps. Wipe the main bearing surfaces of the block and caps with a clean, lint free cloth. They must be kept spotlessly clean!

Main bearing oil clearance check

5   Clean the back sides of the new main bearing inserts and lay the bearing half with the oil groove in each main bearing saddle in the block **(see illustration)**. Lay the other bearing half from each bearing set in the corresponding main bearing cap. Make sure the tab on each bearing insert fits into the recess in the block or cap. Also, the oil holes in the block must line up with the oil holes in the bearing insert. **Caution:** *Do not hammer the bearings into place and don't nick or gouge the bearing faces. No lubrication should be used at this time.*

6   The thrust bearings must be installed in the number three (center) cap.

7   Clean the faces of the bearings in the block and the crankshaft main bearing journals with a clean, lint free cloth. Check or clean the oil holes in the crankshaft, as any dirt here can go only one way – straight through the new bearings.

8   Once you're certain the crankshaft is clean, carefully lay it in position in the main bearings.

9   Before the crankshaft can be permanently installed, the main bearing oil clearance must be checked.

10   Trim several pieces of the appropriate size Plastigage (they must be slightly shorter than the width of the main bearings) and place one piece on each crankshaft main bearing journal, parallel with the journal axis **(see illustration)**.

11   Clean the faces of the bearings in the caps and install the caps in their respective positions (don't mix them up) with the arrows pointing toward the front of the engine.

12   Following the recommended sequence **(see illustration)**, tighten the

22.12   Main bearing cap bolt tightening sequence

22.14   Compare the width of the crushed Plastigage to the scale on the envelope to determine the main bearing oil clearance (always take the measurement at the widest point of the Plastigage) – be sure to use the correct scale; standard and metric scales are included

main bearing cap bolts, in three steps, to the specified torque. Don't rotate the crankshaft at any time during this operation!

13   Remove the bolts and carefully lift off the main bearing caps or cap assembly. Keep them in order. Don't disturb the Plastigage or rotate the crankshaft. If any of the main bearing caps are difficult to remove, tap them gently from side-to-side with a soft-face hammer to loosen them.

14   Compare the width of the crushed Plastigage on each journal to the scale printed on the Plastigage envelope to obtain the main bearing oil clearance **(see illustration)**. Check the Specifications to make sure it's correct.

15   If the clearance is not as specified, the bearing inserts may be the wrong size (which means different ones will be required – see Section 19).

Before deciding that different inserts are needed, make sure that no dirt or oil was between the bearing inserts and the caps or block when the clearance was measured. If the Plastigage is noticeably wider at one end than the other, the journal may be tapered (see Section 18).

16   Carefully scrape all traces of the Plastigage material off the main bearing journals and/or the bearing faces. Don't nick or scratch the bearing faces.

Final crankshaft installation

17   Carefully lift the crankshaft out of the engine. Clean the bearing faces in the block, then apply a thin, uniform layer of clean moly-base grease or engine assembly lube to each of the bearing surfaces. Coat the thrust bearings as well.

18   Lubricate the crankshaft surfaces that contact the oil seals with moly-base grease, engine assembly lube or clean engine oil.

19   Make sure the crankshaft journals are clean, then lay the crankshaft back in place in the block. Clean the faces of the bearings in the caps or cap assembly, then apply lubricant to them. Install the caps in their respective positions with the arrows pointing toward the front of the engine. **Note:** *Be sure to install the thrust bearings* **(see illustrations)**.

20   Apply a light coat of oil to the bolt threads and the under sides of the bolt heads, then install them. Tighten all except the center (number three) cap bolts (the one with the thrust bearings) to the specified torque (work from the center out and approach the final torque in three steps). Tighten the center cap bolts to 10-to-12 ft-lbs. Tap the ends of the crankshaft forward and backward with a lead or brass hammer to line up the thrust washer and crankshaft surfaces. Retighten all main bearing cap bolts to the torque listed in this Chapter's specifications, following the recommended sequence.

21   Rotate the crankshaft a number of times by hand to check for any obvious binding.

22   Check the crankshaft endplay with a feeler gauge or a dial indicator as described in Section 13. The endplay should be correct if the crankshaft thrust faces aren't worn or damaged and new thrust bearings have been installed.

23   Install a new rear main oil seal, then bolt the retainer to the block (see Section 23).

22.19a   Rotate the thrust bearing into position on the number three crankshaft journal with the oil grooves facing OUT

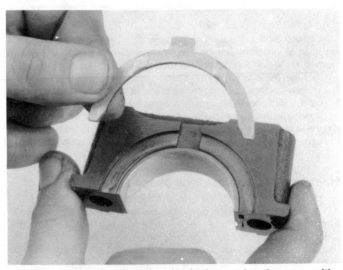

22.19b   Install the thrust bearing in the number three cap with the oil grooves facing OUT

23.3   After removing the retainer from the block, support it on a couple of wood blocks and drive out the old seal with a punch or screwdriver and hammer

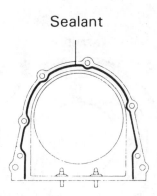

Sealant

23.6   Apply sealant to the retainer before bolting it to the block

23   Rear main oil seal installation

Refer to illustrations 23.3 and 23.6

1   The crankshaft must be installed first and the main bearing caps bolted in place, then the new seal should be installed in the retainer and the retainer bolted to the block.

2   Check the seal contact surface on the crankshaft very carefully for scratches and nicks that could damage the new seal lip and cause oil leaks. If the crankshaft is damaged, the only alternative is a new or different crankshaft.

3   The old seal can be removed from the retainer by driving it out from the back side with a hammer and punch **(see illustration)**. Be sure to note how far it's recessed into the bore before removing it; the new seal will have to be recessed an equal amount. Be very careful not to scratch or otherwise damage the bore in the retainer or oil leaks could develop.

4   Make sure the retainer is clean, then apply a thin coat of engine oil to the outer edge of the new seal. The seal must be pressed squarely into the bore, so hammering it into place isn't recommended. If you don't have access to a press, sandwich the retainer and seal between two smooth pieces of wood and press the seal into place with the jaws of a large vise. The pieces of wood must be thick enough to distribute the force evenly around the entire circumference of the seal. Work slowly and make sure the seal enters the bore squarely.

5   As a last resort, the seal can be tapped into the retainer with a hammer. Use a block of wood to distribute the force evenly and make sure the seal is driven in squarely.

6   The seal lips must be lubricated with clean engine oil or moly-based grease before the seal/retainer is slipped over the crankshaft and bolted to the block. Use a new gasket – and sealant – and make sure the dowel pins are in place before installing the retainer **(see illustration)**.

7   Tighten the bolts a little at a time until they're all at the torque listed in this Chapter's specifications.

24   Pistons/connecting rods – installation and rod bearing oil clearance check

Refer to illustrations 24.3, 24.5, 24.9, 24.11, 24.13, 24.14 and 24.17

1   Before installing the piston/connecting rod assemblies, the cylinder

walls must be perfectly clean, the top edge of each cylinder must be chamfered, and the crankshaft must be in place.

2   Remove the cap from the end of the number one connecting rod (refer to the marks made during removal). Remove the original bearing inserts and wipe the bearing surfaces of the connecting rod and cap with a clean, lint-free cloth. They must be kept spotlessly clean.

Connecting rod bearing oil clearance check

3   Clean the back side of the new upper bearing insert, then lay it in place in the connecting rod. Make sure the tab on the bearing fits into the recess in the rod so the oil holes line up **(see illustration)**. Don't hammer the bearing insert into place and be very careful not to nick or gouge the bearing face. Don't lubricate the bearing at this time.

4   Clean the back side of the other bearing insert and install it in the rod cap. Again, make sure the tab on the bearing fits into the recess in the cap, and don't apply any lubricant. It's critically important that the mating surfaces of the bearing and connecting rod are perfectly clean and oil free when they're assembled.

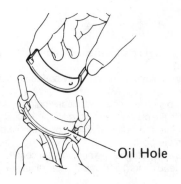

Oil Hole

24.3   Align the oil hole in the bearing with the oil hole in the rod

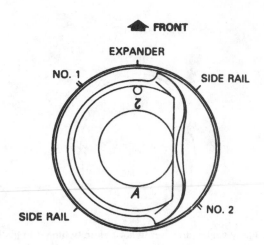

24.5   Stagger the ring end gaps before installing the pistons

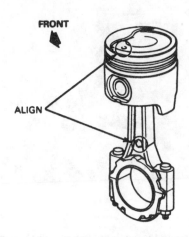

24.9   Check to be sure both the mark on the piston and the mark on the connecting rod are aligned as shown

24.11   The piston can be driven (gently) into the cylinder bore with the end of a wooden or plastic hammer handle

24.13   Lay the Plastigage strips on each rod bearing journal, parallel to the crankshaft centerline

5   Position the piston ring gaps at staggered intervals around the piston **(see illustration)**.

6   Slip a section of plastic or rubber hose over each connecting rod cap bolt.

7   Lubricate the piston and rings with clean engine oil and attach a piston ring compressor to the piston. Leave the skirt protruding about 1/4-inch to guide the piston into the cylinder. The rings must be compressed until they're flush with the piston.

8   Rotate the crankshaft until the number one connecting rod journal is at BDC (bottom dead center) and apply a coat of engine oil to the cylinder walls.

9   With the marks on the piston and connecting rod **(see illustration)** facing the timing belt end of the engine, gently insert the piston/connecting

rod assembly into the number one cylinder bore and rest the bottom edge of the ring compressor on the engine block.

10   Tap the top edge of the ring compressor to make sure it's contacting the block around its entire circumference.

11   Gently tap on the top of the piston with the end of a wooden or plastic hammer handle **(see illustration)** while guiding the end of the connecting rod into place on the crankshaft journal. The piston rings may try to pop out of the ring compressor just before entering the cylinder bore, so keep some downward pressure on the ring compressor. Work slowly, and if any resistance is felt as the piston enters the cylinder, stop immediately. Find out what's hanging up and fix it before proceeding. Do not, for any reason, force the piston into the cylinder – you might break a ring and/or the piston.

12   Once the piston/connecting rod assembly is installed, the connecting

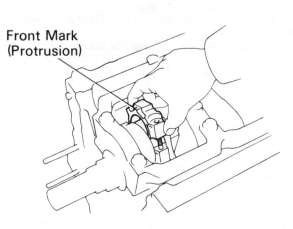

24.14 **Install the connecting rod caps with the front mark facing the timing belt end of the engine**

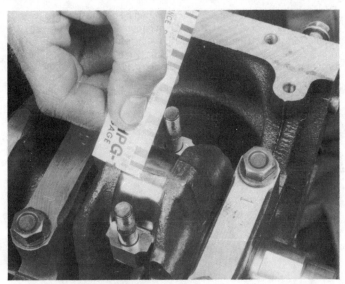

24.17 **Measure the width of the crushed Plastigage to determine the rod bearing oil clearance (be sure to use the correct scale – standard and metric scales are included)**

rod bearing oil clearance must be checked before the rod cap is permanently bolted in place.

13　Cut a piece of the appropriate size Plastigage slightly shorter than the width of the connecting rod bearing and lay it in place on the number one connecting rod journal, parallel with the journal axis **(see illustration)**.

14　Clean the connecting rod cap bearing face, remove the protective hoses from the connecting rod bolts and install the rod cap. Make sure the mating mark on the cap is on the same side as the mark on the connecting rod **(see illustration 12.4)**. Some engines also have a protrusion on the rod cap which faces the timing belt end of the engine **(see illustration)**.

15　Apply a light coat of oil to the undersides of the nuts, then install and tighten them to the specified torque, working up to it in three steps. Use a thin-wall socket to avoid erroneous torque readings that can result if the socket is wedged between the rod cap and nut. If the socket tends to wedge itself between the nut and the cap, lift up on it slightly until it no longer contacts the cap. Do not rotate the crankshaft at any time during this operation.

16　Remove the nuts and detach the rod cap, being very careful not to disturb the Plastigage.

17　Compare the width of the crushed Plastigage to the scale printed on the Plastigage envelope to obtain the oil clearance **(see illustration)**. Compare it to the Specifications to make sure the clearance is correct.

18　If the clearance is not as specified, the bearing inserts may be the wrong size (which means different ones will be required). Before deciding that different inserts are needed, make sure that no dirt or oil was between the bearing inserts and the connecting rod or cap when the clearance was measured. Also, recheck the journal diameter. If the Plastigage was wider at one end than the other, the journal may be tapered (refer to Section 18).

Final connecting rod installation

19　Carefully scrape all traces of the Plastigage material off the rod journal and/or bearing face. Be very careful not to scratch the bearing – use your fingernail or the edge of a credit card.

20　Make sure the bearing faces are perfectly clean, then apply a uniform layer of clean moly-base grease or engine assembly lube to both of them. You'll have to push the piston into the cylinder to expose the face of the bearing insert in the connecting rod – be sure to slip the protective hoses over the rod bolts first.

21　Slide the connecting rod back into place on the journal, remove the protective hoses from the rod cap bolts, install the rod cap and tighten the nuts to the specified torque. Again, work up to the torque in three steps.

22　Repeat the entire procedure for the remaining pistons/connecting rods.

23　The important points to remember are . . .
　a)　Keep the back sides of the bearing inserts and the insides of the connecting rods and caps perfectly clean when assembling them.
　b)　Make sure you have the correct piston/rod assembly for each cylinder.
　c)　The dimple on the piston must face the front (timing belt end) of the engine.
　d)　Lubricate the cylinder walls with clean oil.
　e)　Lubricate the bearing faces when installing the rod caps after the oil clearance has been checked.

24　After all the piston/connecting rod assemblies have been properly installed, rotate the crankshaft a number of times by hand to check for any obvious binding.

25　As a final step, the connecting rod endplay must be checked. Refer to Section 12 for this procedure.

26　Compare the measured endplay to the Specifications to make sure it's correct. If it was correct before disassembly and the original crankshaft and rods were reinstalled, it should still be right. If new rods or a new crankshaft were installed, the endplay may be inadequate. If so, the rods will have to be removed and taken to an automotive machine shop for resizing.

25　Initial start-up and break-in after overhaul

Warning: *Have a fire extinguisher handy when starting the engine for the first time.*

1　Once the engine has been installed in the vehicle, double-check the engine oil and coolant levels.

2　With the spark plugs out of the engine and the ignition system disabled (see Section 3), crank the engine until oil pressure registers on the gauge or the warning light goes out.

3　Install the spark plugs, connect the plug wires and restore the ignition system functions (Section 3).

4　Start the engine. It may take a few moments for the fuel system to build up pressure, but the engine should start without a great deal of effort.

5　After the engine starts, it should be allowed to warm up to normal operating temperature. While the engine is warming up, make a thorough check for fuel, oil and coolant leaks.

6   Shut the engine off and recheck the engine oil and coolant levels.
7   Drive the vehicle to an area with minimum traffic, accelerate at full throttle from 30 to 50 mph, then allow the vehicle to slow to 30 mph with the throttle closed. Repeat the procedure 10 or 12 times. This will load the piston rings and cause them to seat properly against the cylinder walls. Check again for oil and coolant leaks.
8   Drive the vehicle gently for the first 500 miles (no sustained high speeds) and keep a constant check on the oil level. It is not unusual for an engine to use oil during the break-in period.
9   At approximately 500 to 600 miles, change the oil and filter.
10   For the next few hundred miles, drive the vehicle normally. Do not pamper it or abuse it.
11   After 2000 miles, change the oil and filter again and consider the engine broken in.

Chapter 3   Cooling, heating and air conditioning systems

Contents

Specifications

General

Radiator cap pressure rating .... 13 psi
Thermostat rating (opening temperature) .... 180-degrees F (82-degrees C)
Cooling system capacity .... See Chapter 1
Refrigerant capacity .... 1.3 to 1.7 lbs

Torque specifications   Ft-lbs

Water pump-to-engine block bolts 11
Water pump pulley bolts 17
Thermostat housing bolts 20
Coolant inlet pipe nuts 14

1   General information

Engine cooling system

All vehicles covered by this manual employ a pressurized engine cooling system with thermostatically controlled coolant circulation. An impeller type water pump mounted on the drivebelt end of the block pumps coolant through the engine. The coolant flows around each cylinder and toward the transaxle end of the engine. Cast-in coolant passages direct coolant around the intake and exhaust ports, near the spark plug areas and in close proximity to the exhaust valve guides.

A wax pellet type thermostat is located in a housing near the transaxle end of the engine. During warm up, the closed thermostat prevents coolant from circulating through the radiator. As the engine nears normal operating temperature, the thermostat opens and allows hot coolant to travel through the radiator, where it's cooled before returning to the engine.

The cooling system is sealed by a pressure type radiator cap, which raises the boiling point of the coolant and increases the cooling efficiency of the radiator. If the system pressure exceeds the cap pressure relief value, the excess pressure in the system forces the spring-loaded valve inside the cap off its seat and allows the coolant to escape through the overflow tube into a coolant reservoir. When the system cools, the excess coolant is automatically drawn from the reservoir back into the radiator.

The coolant reservoir does double duty as both the point at which fresh coolant is added to the cooling system to maintain the proper fluid level and as a holding tank for overheated coolant.

This type of cooling system is known as a closed design because coolant that escapes past the pressure cap is saved and reused.

Heating system

The heating system consists of a blower fan and heater core located in the heater box, the hoses connecting the heater core to the engine cooling system and the heater/air conditioning control head on the dashboard. Hot engine coolant is circulated through the heater core. When the heater mode is activated, a flap door opens to expose the heater box to the passenger compartment. A fan switch on the control head activates the blower motor, which forces air through the core, heating the air.

Air conditioning system

The air conditioning system consists of a condenser mounted in front of the radiator, an evaporator mounted adjacent to the heater core, a compressor mounted on the engine, a filter-drier which contains a high pressure relief valve and the plumbing connecting all of the above components.

A blower fan forces the warmer air of the passenger compartment through the evaporator core (sort of a radiator-in-reverse), transferring the heat from the air to the refrigerant. The liquid refrigerant boils off into low pressure vapor, taking the heat with it when it leaves the evaporator.

---

2   Antifreeze – general information

Warning: *Do not allow antifreeze to come in contact with your skin or painted surfaces of the vehicle. Rinse off spills immediately with plenty of water. NEVER leave antifreeze lying around in an open container or in a puddle in the driveway or on the garage floor. Children and pets are attracted by it's sweet smell. Antifreeze is fatal if ingested.*

The cooling system should be filled with a water/ethylene glycol based antifreeze solution, which will prevent freezing down to at least -20-degrees F, or lower if local climate requires it. It also provides protection against corrosion and increases the coolant boiling point.

The cooling system should be drained, flushed and refilled at the specified intervals (see Chapter 1). Old or contaminated antifreeze solutions are likely to cause damage and encourage the formation of corrosion and scale in the system. Use distilled water with the antifreeze.

Before adding antifreeze, check all hose connections, because antifreeze tends to search out and leak through very minute openings. Engines don't normally consume coolant, so if the level goes down, find the cause and correct it.

The exact mixture of antifreeze-to-water which you should use depends on the relative weather conditions. The mixture should contain at least 50 percent antifreeze, but should never contain more than 70 percent antifreeze. Consult the mixture ratio chart on the antifreeze container before adding coolant. Hydrometers are available at most auto parts stores to test the coolant. Use antifreeze which meets the vehicle manufacturer's specifications.

---

3   Thermostat – check and replacement

Warning: *Do not remove the radiator cap, drain the coolant or replace the thermostat until the engine has cooled completely.*

Check

1   Before assuming the thermostat is to blame for a cooling system problem, check the coolant level, drivebelt tension (see Chapter 1) and temperature gauge operation.

2   If the engine seems to be taking a long time to warm up (based on heater output or temperature gauge operation), the thermostat is probably stuck open. Replace the thermostat with a new one.

3   If the engine runs hot, use your hand to check the temperature of the upper radiator hose. If the hose isn't hot, but the engine is, the thermostat is probably stuck closed, preventing the coolant inside the engine from escaping to the radiator. Replace the thermostat. **Caution:** *Don't drive the vehicle without a thermostat. The lack of a thermostat will cause coolant to bypass the radiator and the computer may stay in open loop causing emissions and fuel economy to suffer.*

4   If the upper radiator hose is hot, it means that the coolant is flowing and the thermostat is open. Consult the Troubleshooting Section at the front of this manual for cooling system diagnosis.

Replacement

Refer to illustrations 3.10, 3.11a, 3.11b, 3.13 and 3.14

5   Disconnect the negative battery cable from the battery.

6   Drain the cooling system (see Chapter 1). If the coolant is relatively new or in good condition, save it and reuse it.

7   Follow the lower radiator hose to the engine to locate the thermostat housing.

8   Loosen the hose clamp, then detach the hose from the fitting. If it's stuck, grasp it near the end with a pair of adjustable pliers and twist it to break the seal, then pull it off. If the hose is old or deteriorated, cut it off and install a new one.

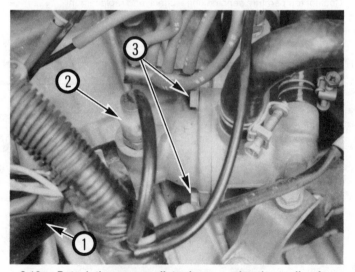

3.10   Detach the upper radiator hose, unplug the cooling fan switch connector and remove the mounting bolts/nuts (SOHC engine shown, DOHC similar)

1 Upper radiator hose	3 Mounting bolts/nuts
2 Cooling fan switch connector	

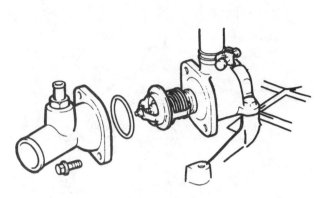

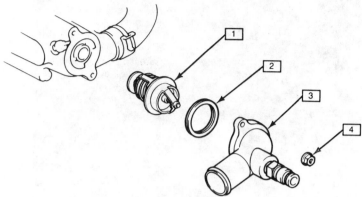

**3.11a   Nova thermostat and related components –
exploded view**

**3.11b   Prizm thermostat and related components –
exploded view**

1	Thermostat	3	Thermostat housing
2	Gasket	4	Retaining nut

9   If the outer surface of the large fitting that mates with the hose is deteriorated (corroded, pitted, etc.) it may be damaged further by hose removal. If it is, the thermostat housing cover will have to be replaced.

10   Unplug the engine cooling fan switch connector **(see illustration)**.

11   Remove the bolts/nuts and detach the housing cover **(see illustrations)**. If the cover is stuck, tap it with a soft-face hammer to jar it loose. Be prepared for some coolant to spill as the gasket seal is broken.

12   Note how it's installed (which end is facing the engine), then remove the thermostat. Thoroughly clean the sealing surfaces.

13   Fit a new gasket over the thermostat **(see illustration)**.

14   Install the new thermostat in the housing. Make sure the air bleed faces up and the spring end is directed into the engine **(see illustration)**.

15   Install the cover and bolts. Tighten the bolts to the specified torque.

16   Reattach the hose to the fitting and tighten the hose clamp securely.

17   Refill the cooling system (see Chapter 1).

18   Start the engine and allow it to reach normal operating temperature, then check for leaks and proper thermostat operation (as described in Steps 2 through 4).

---

4   Engine cooling fan – check and replacement

Refer to illustrations 4.3, 4.5, 4.7a, 4.7b and 4.8

Check

1   The engine cooling fan is controlled by a temperature switch mounted into the thermostat cover. When the coolant reaches a predetermined temperature, the switch opens the ground return for the fan motor relay, completing the circuit.

2   First, check the fuses (see Chapter 12).

3.13   The thermostat gasket fits over the edge of the thermostat

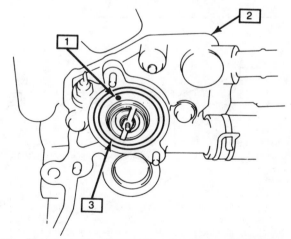

3.14   The air bleed valve must be near the top (Prizm shown, Nova similar)

1	Air bleed valve	3	Thermostat
2	Cylinder head		

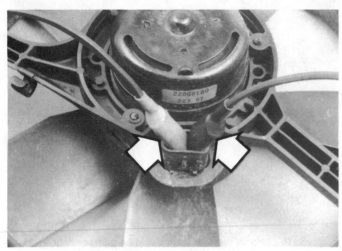

4.3   Connect jumper wires directly to the motor (arrows)

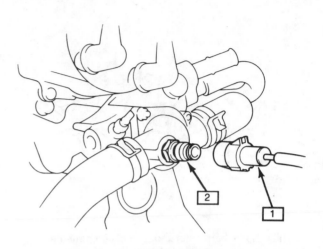

4.5   Engine cooling fan switch location

1   Connector   2   Switch

4.7a   Engine cooling fan mounting details

1   Hose   2   Mounting bolt (upper)

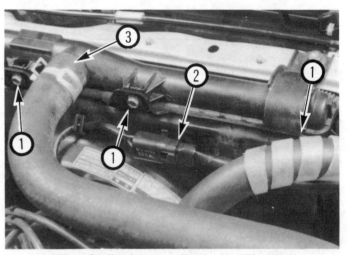

4.7b   Cooling fan mounting details (HD option)

1   Mounting bolts (upper)   3   Hose
2   Electrical connector

4.8   Cooling fan components – exploded view

1 Radiator	*5 Shroud retaining bolt*
2 Fan retaining nut	*6 Cooling fan motor*
3 Cooling fan	*7 Motor retaining bolt*
4 Shroud	

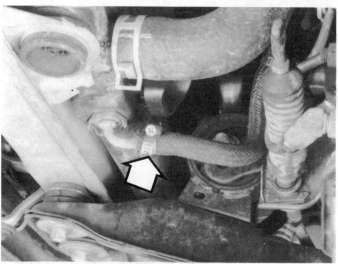

5.7   On automatic transaxle models, disconnect the cooler lines (arrow) on either side of the longitudinal crossmember (viewed from below)

5.8   Remove the bolt (arrow) and upper mounting bracket from each side of the radiator

3   To test the fan motor, unplug the motor connector and use fused jumper wires **(see illustration)** to connect the fan directly to the battery. If the fan still does not work, replace the motor.

4   If the motor tested okay, the fault lies in the coolant temperature switch, the relay or the wiring harness (see Chapter 12).

5   Test the temperature switch by unplugging the connector **(see illustration)** with the ignition switch on.

6   If the fan does not operate, check the wiring (see Chapter 12).

Replacement

7   Unplug the wires and detach the hoses, then unbolt the fan shroud **(see illustrations)**. Be sure to remove the lower shroud bolts. **Note:** *Refer to Chapter 1 and drain the coolant before removing the upper radiator hose.*

8   Remove the nut and detach the fan blade assembly from the motor shaft **(see illustration)**.

9   Take out the screws holding the fan motor to the bracket and detach the motor.

10   Installation is the reverse of removal. **Note:** *Air conditioned vehicles have an additional fan on the right side of the radiator. It can be checked by following Steps 2, 3 and 6. For replacement, follow Steps 7 through 10.*

---

5   Radiator – removal and installation

Refer to illustrations 5.7, 5.8 and 5.12

Warning: *Wait until the engine is completely cool before beginning this procedure.*

Removal

1   Disconnect the negative battery cable from the battery.

2   Raise the front of the vehicle and support it securely on jackstands. Remove the lower splash pans.

3   Drain the cooling system (see Chapter 1). If the coolant is relatively new or in good condition, save it and reuse it.

4   Loosen the hose clamps, then detach the radiator hoses from the fittings. If they're stuck, grasp each hose near the end with a pair of adjustable pliers and twist it to break the seal, then pull it off – be careful not to damage the radiator fittings! If the hoses are old or deteriorated, cut them off and install new ones.

5   Disconnect the coolant reservoir hose from the radiator filler neck.

6   Remove the cooling fan(s) as described in Section 4.

7   If the vehicle is equipped with an automatic transaxle, disconnect the cooler lines **(see illustration)** and plug the lines and fittings.

8   Remove the radiator mounting bolts **(see illustration)**.

9   Carefully lift out the radiator. Don't spill coolant on the vehicle or scratch the paint.

10   With the radiator removed, it can be inspected for leaks and damage. If it needs repair, have a radiator shop or dealer service department perform the work as special techniques are required.

11   Bugs and dirt can be removed from the radiator with a garden hose or a soft brush. Don't bend the cooling fins as this is done.

Installation

12   Installation is the reverse of the removal procedure. Be sure the rubber cushions are seated properly **(see illustration)**.

13   After installation, fill the cooling system with the proper mixture of antifreeze and water. Refer to Chapter 1 if necessary.

14   Start the engine and check for leaks. Allow the engine to reach normal operating temperature, indicated by the upper radiator hose becoming hot. Recheck the coolant level and add more if required.

15   If you're working on an automatic transaxle equipped vehicle, check and add fluid as needed.

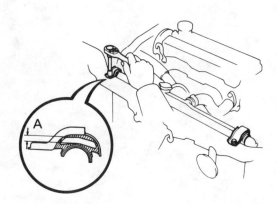

5.12   After installation, confirm that the rubber cushion (A) is seated properly

6.1   Remove the battery hold-down bracket (arrow) for access

6.3   The reservoir is slipped onto a bracket – pull straight up to
remove it

6   Coolant reservoir – removal and installation

Refer to illustrations 6.1 and 6.3

1   Remove the battery hold-down bolt and move the bracket aside **(see illustration)**. **Note:** *This step is not necessary on some Geo models.*
2   Lift the cap off the coolant reservoir and withdraw the overflow hose.
3   Lift the coolant reservoir straight up to remove it **(see illustration)**.
4   Installation is the reverse of removal.

7   Water pump – check

Refer to illustrations 7.4 and 7.5
1   A failure in the water pump can cause serious engine damage due to overheating.
2   There are three ways to check the operation of the water pump while it's installed on the engine. If the pump is defective, it should be replaced with a new or rebuilt unit.

3   With the engine running at normal operating temperature, squeeze the upper radiator hose. If the water pump is working properly, a pressure surge should be felt as the hose is released. **Warning:** *Keep your hands away from the fan blades!*
4   Water pumps are equipped with weep or vent holes. If a failure occurs in the pump seal, coolant will leak from the hole. In most cases you'll need a flashlight to find the hole on the water pump from underneath to check for leaks **(see illustration)**.
5   If the water pump shaft bearings fail there may be a howling sound at the drivebelt end of the engine while it's running. Shaft wear can be felt if the water pump pulley is rocked up and down **(see illustration)**. Don't mistake drivebelt slippage, which causes a squealing sound, for water pump bearing failure.

8   Water pump – removal and installation

Refer to illustrations 8.3, 8.7, 8.9, 8.10a, 8.10b and 8.14
Warning: *Wait until the engine is completely cool before beginning this procedure.*

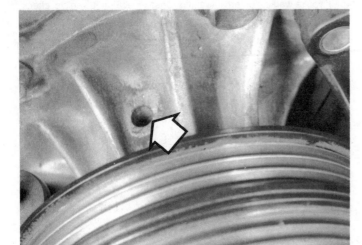

7.4   If coolant is leaking from the weep hole (arrow) the water
pump must be replaced

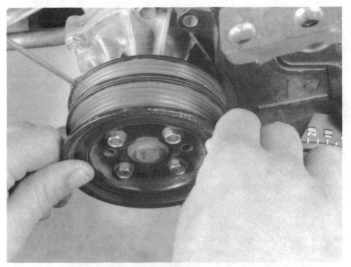

7.5   If there's play in the shaft, replace the water pump

4A-LC and 4A-GE engines

1   Disconnect the negative battery cable from the battery.
2   Drain the cooling system (see Chapter 1). If the coolant is relatively new or in good condition, save it and reuse it.
3   Loosen the water pump pulley bolts **(see illustration)**.
4   Refer to Chapter 1 and remove the alternator (and power steering drivebelts, if equipped). Remove the pulley at the end of the water pump shaft. **Note:** *On some models the pulley may not have sufficient clearance for removal; follow the engine jacking procedure listed below for the 4A-FE engine.*
5   Remove the power steering pump adjustment bracket (if equipped) and move the pump aside.
6   Set the parking brake and block the rear wheels. Raise the front of the vehicle and support it securely on jackstands. Remove the lower splash pans.
7   Detach the coolant hose(s) from the coolant inlet pipe and unbolt the pipe **(see illustration)**.
8   On 4A-LC engines, remove the upper timing belt cover. On 4A-GE engines, remove the lower and middle timing belt covers.
9   Remove the mounting bolt for the dipstick tube and pull the tube out **(see illustration)**. Plug the hole to prevent dirt or coolant from getting in the oil.
10   Remove the bolts **(see illustrations)** and detach the water pump from the engine. Note the locations of the various brackets and lengths and different diameters of bolts as they're removed to ensure correct installation.
11   Clean the bolt threads and the threaded holes in the engine to remove corrosion and sealant.
12   Compare the new pump to the old one to make sure they're identical.

13   Remove all traces of old O-rings and gasket material from the sealing surfaces.
14   Install new O-rings on the dipstick tube, in the engine block **(see illustration)** and behind the water pump. Use a dab of RTV sealant to hold the pump O-rings in place. Wet the dipstick O-ring with engine oil.
15   Carefully mate the pump to the engine. Slip a couple of bolts through the pump mounting holes to hold the O-rings in place.

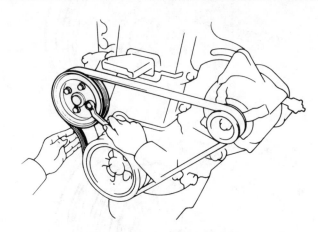

8.3   Use the drivebelt to keep the pulley from turning when loosening the bolts

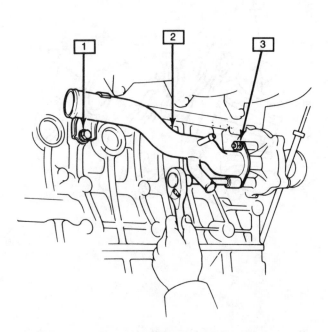

8.7   Remove the coolant inlet pipe (Several versions of this pipe are used with different hose fittings)

1   Pipe retaining brace
2   Inlet pipe
3   Pipe retaining nuts

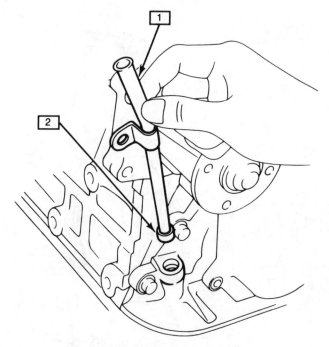

8.9   Unbolt the dipstick and pull it up

1   Oil dipstick tube
2   O-ring

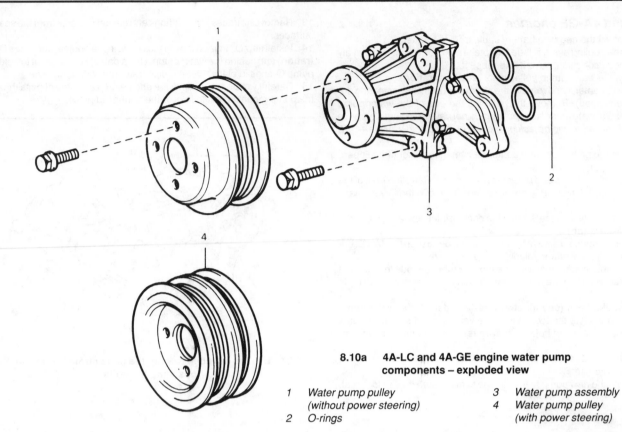

8.10a   **4A-LC and 4A-GE engine water pump components – exploded view**

1	Water pump pulley (without power steering)	3	Water pump assembly
2	O-rings	4	Water pump pulley (with power steering)

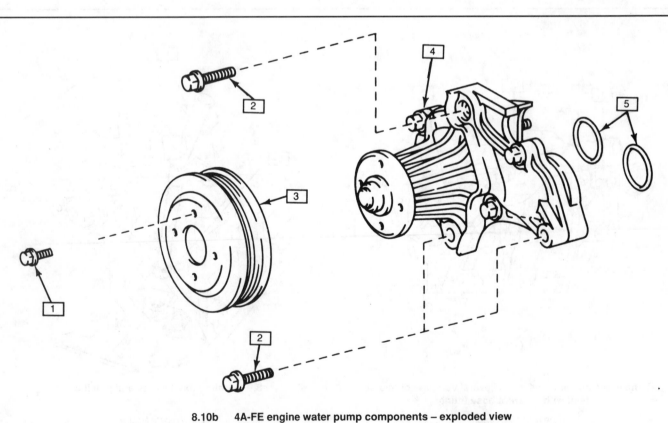

8.10b   **4A-FE engine water pump components – exploded view**

1	Pulley retaining bolt	4	Water pump
2	Water pump retaining bolt	5	O-rings
3	Water pump pulley		

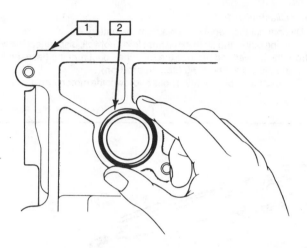

8.14   Install new O-rings in the engine block and in back of the water pump

1   Engine block   2   O-ring

9.3   The coolant temperature gauge sending unit (arrow) is located in the cylinder head at the drivebelt end of the engine – it has only one wire going to it

16   Install the remaining bolts. Tighten them to the torque listed in this Chapter's specifications in 1/4-turn increments. Don't overtighten them or the pump may be damaged.
17   Reinstall all parts removed for access to the pump.
18   Refill the cooling system and check the drivebelt tension (see Chapter 1). Run the engine and check for leaks.

4A-FE engine

19   Disconnect the negative battery cable from the battery.
20   Drain the cooling system (see Chapter 1). If the coolant is relatively new or in good condition, save it and reuse it.
21   Set the parking brake and block the rear wheels. Raise the front of the vehicle and support it securely on jackstands. Remove the lower splash pans.
22   Remove the two nuts from the rear engine mount.
23   Remove the coolant reservoir (see Section 6).
24   Remove the cruise control module and bracket (if equipped).
25   Support the engine with a floor jack. Place a block of wood on the jack pad to prevent damage to the oil pan.
26   Remove the right engine mount through bolt.
27   Raise the engine slightly for access to the water pump pulley bolts.
28   Loosen the water pump pulley bolts **(see illustration 8.10b)**.
29   Remove the alternator drivebelt (and power steering belt, if equipped).
30   Lower the engine to its normal level.
31   Remove the upper timing belt covers.
32   Follow Steps 9 through 18 listed above to complete the procedure.

9   Coolant temperature sending unit – check and replacement

Refer to illustration 9.3
Warning: *The engine must be completely cool before removing the sending unit.*

Check

1   If the coolant temperature gauge is inoperative, check the fuses first (see Chapter 12).

2   If the temperature indicator shows excessive temperature after running a while, see the Troubleshooting Section in the front of the manual.
3   If the temperature gauge indicates Hot shortly after the engine is started cold, disconnect the wire at the coolant temperature sending unit **(see illustration)**. If the gauge reading drops, replace the sending unit. If the reading remains high, the wire to the gauge may be shorted to ground or the gauge is faulty.
4   If the coolant temperature gauge fails to indicate after the engine has been warmed up (approximately 10 minutes) and the fuses checked out okay, shut off the engine. Disconnect the wire at the sending unit and using a jumper wire, connect it to a clean ground on the engine. Turn on the ignition without starting the engine. If the gauge now indicates Hot, replace the sending unit.
5   If the gauge still does not work, the circuit may be open or the gauge may be faulty. See Chapter 12 for additional information.

Replacement

6   With the engine completely cool, remove the cap from the radiator to release any pressure, then reinstall the cap. This reduces coolant loss during sending unit replacement.
7   Disconnect the wiring harness from the sending unit.
8   Prepare the new sending unit for installation by applying a light coat of sealant to the threads.
9   Unscrew the sending unit from the engine and quickly install the new one to prevent coolant loss.
10   Tighten the sending unit securely and connect the wiring harness.
11   Refill the cooling system and run the engine. Check for leaks and proper gauge operation.

10   Blower unit – removal and installation

Nova

Refer to illustrations 10.2, 10.3, 10.4a and 10.4b
1   Disconnect the negative cable from the battery.
2   Remove the glove compartment and adjacent panels **(see illustration)** (see Chapter 11, if necessary).
3   Disconnect the wiring from the blower and remove the rubber air duct running between the motor and the blower housing **(see illustration)**.

4   Remove the nuts and screws holding the blower housing to the vehicle and lower the unit from the dash **(see illustrations)**.
5   Remove the three mounting bolts and lift the motor out of the housing.
6   If you are replacing the motor, detach the fan and transfer it to the new
motor.
7   Installation is the reverse of removal. Run the blower and check for
proper operation.

Prizm

Refer to illustration 10.9

8   Disconnect the negative cable from the battery.
9   Working below the dash in the right front footwell, disconnect the wiring from the blower and remove the rubber air duct running between the
motor and the blower housing **(see illustration)**.
10   Remove the three mounting bolts and lower the motor out of the housing.

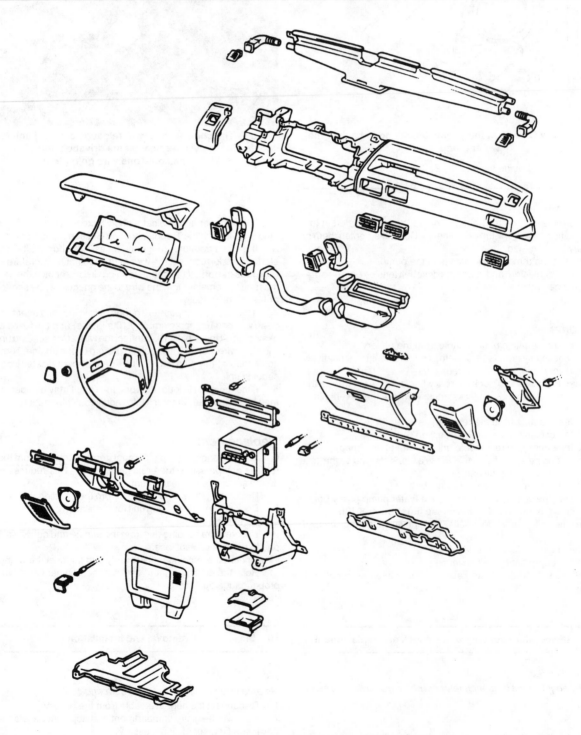

10.2   Typical instrument panel components – exploded view

10.3   Remove the wiring and air duct

1   Wiring connector   2   Air duct

10.4a   Remove the blower housing fasteners from the sides . . .

10.4b   . . . and top

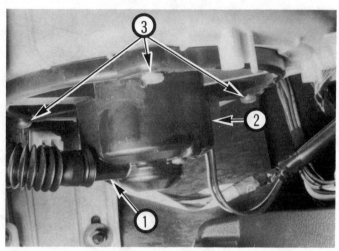

10.9   Blower unit

1   Flexible tube   3   Retaining screws
2   Wiring connector

11   If you are replacing the motor, detach the fan and transfer it to the new motor.

12   Installation is the reverse of removal. Run the blower and check for proper operation.

11   Heater core – removal and installation

Refer to illustrations 11.3, 11.6a, 11.6b and 11.7

1   Disconnect the negative cable from the battery.

2   Drain the cooling system (see Chapter 1).

3   Working in the engine compartment, disconnect the heater hoses where they enter the firewall **(see illustration)**.

4   Remove the instrument panel and the center console (Chapter 11).

5   Remove the heater controls (see Section 12). Be sure to mark the locations of the cable clamps on the cables to ensure correct adjustment upon reinstallation.

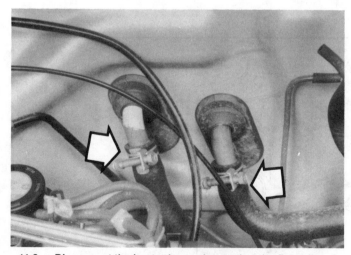

11.3   Disconnect the heater hoses (arrows) at the firewall and remove the rubber grommets

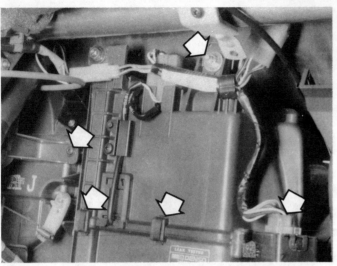

11.6a   Remove the various clips, screws and wires (arrows)

6   Label and detach the air ducts, wiring and controls still attached to the heater housing **(see illustrations)**.
7   Remove the screws and clips and separate the two halves of the heater assembly **(see illustration)**. Take out the the old heater core and install the new unit.
8   Reassemble the heater unit and check the operation of the control flaps. If any parts bind, correct the problem before installation.
9   Reinstall the remaining parts in the reverse order of removal.
10   Refill the cooling system, reconnect the battery and run the engine. Check for leaks and proper system operation.

---

12   Air conditioner and heater control assembly – removal, installation and cable adjustment

---

Removal and installation

Refer to illustrations 12.3, 12.4 and 12.5

1   Disconnect the negative cable from the battery.
2   Remove the radio (see Chapter 12) and the trim panels which surround the radio and heater control assembly **(see illustration 10.2)**.

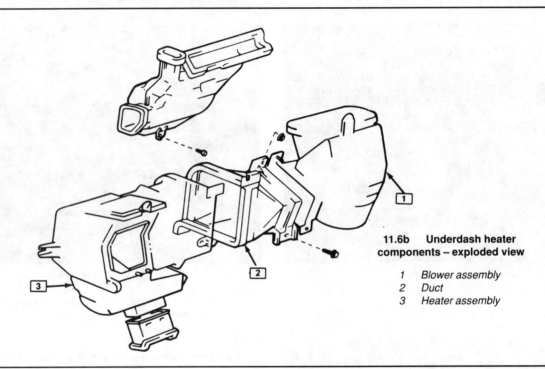

11.6b   Underdash heater components – exploded view

1   Blower assembly
2   Duct
3   Heater assembly

11.7   The heater core is located inside the heater assembly

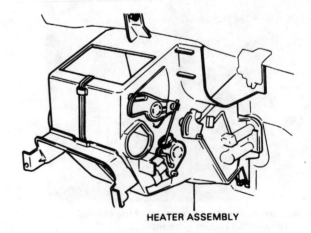

HEATER ASSEMBLY

3   Remove the glove compartment **(see illustration)** and the covers on the sides of the console under the dash.

4   Remove the control mounting screws **(see illustration)**.

5   Carefully pull and tilt the unit out of the dash **(see illustration)**.

6   Check the outer sheath of the cables for indentations where the clamps grip them. Mark the cable sheath with paint if no indentation is visible. Remove the clamps and detach the control cables. If necessary, disconnect the control cables at the ends opposite from the control by detaching the cable clamps and separating the cables from the operating levers (see below).

7   Unplug the wiring connectors and lift the control from the vehicle.

8   Installation is the reverse of removal.

Cable adjustment

Refer to illustrations 12.9a, 12.9b, 12.9c, 12.9d

9   Normally, if a control cable is reattached where the clamp mark is, the lever will be adjusted properly. If the lever requires adjustment, remove the clamp **(see illustrations)** and move the cable until the control lever moves freely through its normal range of motion.

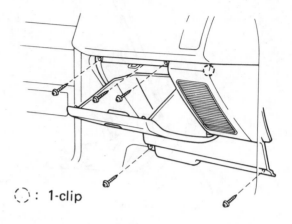

⬡ : 1-clip

12.3   Remove the glove compartment screws

12.4   Remove the four mounting screws (arrows)

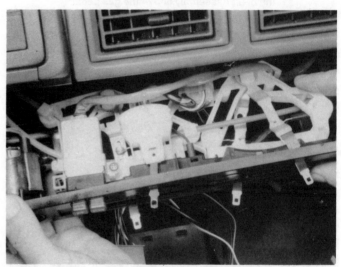

12.5   Pull the control assembly out slightly and tilt it to gain access to the components

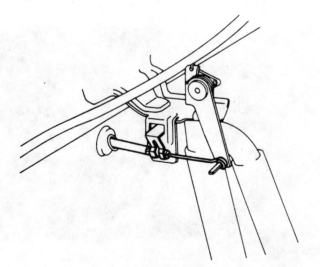

12.9a   The water valve is mounted on the firewall in the engine compartment, adjacent to the brake master cylinder

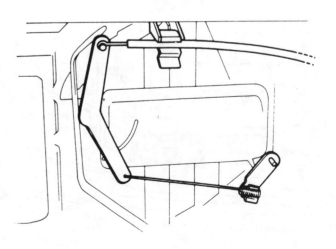

12.9b   The air-mix damper is located just forward of the heater control

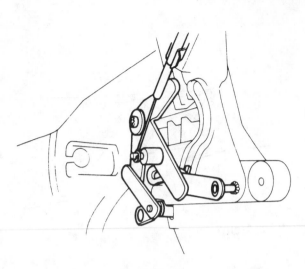

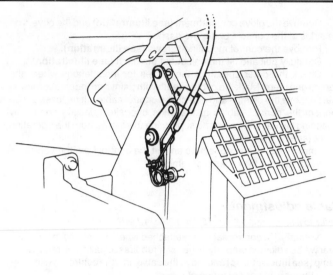

12.9c   The mode selector damper is located on the left side of the heater assembly above the gas pedal

12.9d   The air inlet damper is located forward of the glove compartment

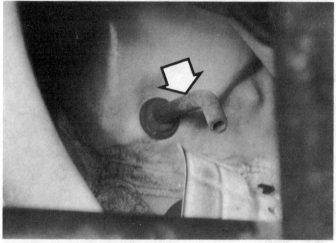

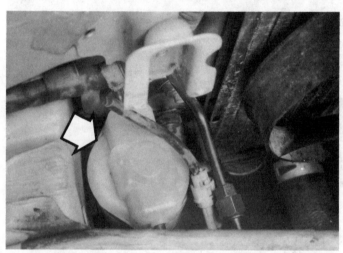

13.1   The evaporator housing drain tube (arrow) is located on the lower portion of the firewall in the engine compartment – insert a wire to clear it

13.7a   On Novas, the receiver-drier is located under the coolant reservoir – pull off the plastic cap to view the sight glass

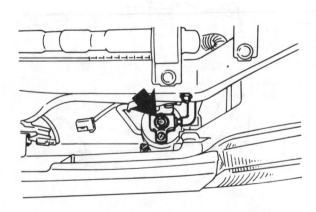

13.7b   On Prizms, the receiver-drier (arrow) is mounted between the grille and radiator

13.7c   The sight glass (arrow) is mounted in the top of the receiver-drier

13.9   Connect the charging kit to the low pressure port – easily identified because the tubing is larger in diameter than the high pressure side

13.11   Place the thermometer in the dash vent

13   Air conditioning system – check and maintenance

Refer to illustrations 13.1, 13.7a, 13.7b, 13.7c, 13.9 and 13.11

Warning: *The air conditioning system is under high pressure. Do not loosen any hose fittings or remove any components until after the system has been discharged by a dealer service department or service station. Always wear eye protection when disconnecting air conditioning system fittings.*

Check

1   The following maintenance checks should be performed on a regular basis to ensure that the air conditioner continues to operate at peak efficiency.

   a) Check the compressor drivebelt. If it's worn or deteriorated, replace it (see Chapter 1).

   b) Check the drivebelt tension and, if necessary, adjust it (see Chapter 1).

   c) Check the system hoses. Look for cracks, bubbles, hard spots and deterioration. Inspect the hoses and all fittings for oil bubbles and seepage. If there's any evidence of wear, damage or leaks, replace the hose(s).

   d) Inspect the condenser fins for leaves, bugs and other debris. Use a "fin comb" or compressed air to clean the condenser.

   e) Make sure the system has the correct refrigerant charge.

   f) Check the evaporator housing drain tube for blockage **(see illustration)**.

2   It's a good idea to operate the system for about 10 minutes at least once a month, particularly during the winter. Long term non-use can cause hardening, and subsequent failure, of the seals.

3   Because of the complexity of the air conditioning system and the special equipment necessary to service it, in-depth troubleshooting and repairs are not included in this manual. However, simple checks and component replacement procedures are provided in this Chapter.

4   The most common cause of poor cooling is simply a low system refrigerant charge. If a noticeable drop in cool air output occurs, one of the following quick checks will help you determine if the refrigerant level is low.

5   Warm the engine up to normal operating temperature.

6   Place the air conditioning temperature selector at the coldest setting and put the blower at the highest setting. Open the doors (to make sure the air conditioning system doesn't cycle off as soon as it cools the passenger compartment).

7   When the compressor engages the clutch will make an audible click and the center of the clutch will rotate – inspect the sight glass **(see illustrations)**. If the refrigerant looks foamy, it's low. Charge the system as described later in this Section.

Adding refrigerant

8   Buy an automotive charging kit at an auto parts store. A charging kit includes a 14-ounce can of refrigerant, a tap valve and a short section of hose that can be attached between the tap valve and the system low side service valve. Because one can of refrigerant may not be sufficient to bring the system charge up to the proper level, it's a good idea to buy a few additional cans. Make sure that the first can contains red refrigerant dye. If the system is leaking, the red dye will leak out with the refrigerant and help you pinpoint the location of the leak. **Warning:** *Never add more than three cans of refrigerant to the system.*

9   Connect the charging kit by following the manufacturer's instructions. On carbureted Novas, the charging port is on the right side of the engine compartment **(see illustration)**. The port is on the firewall of fuel injected Novas. On Prizms, connect directly to the "S" port on the compressor. **Warning:** *DO NOT connect the charging kit hose to the system high side! Wear eye protection.*

10   Warm up the engine and turn on the air conditioner. Keep the charging kit hose away from the fan and other moving parts.

11   Place a thermometer in the dashboard vent nearest the evaporator **(see illustration)** and add refrigerant until the indicated temperature is around 40 to 45-degrees F.

14   Air conditioning receiver/drier – removal and installation

Refer to illustrations 14.3, 14.6a and 14.6b

Warning: *The air conditioning system is under high pressure. Do not loosen any fittings or remove any components until after the system has been discharged by a dealer service department or service station. Always wear eye protection when disconnecting air conditioning system fittings.*

1   The receiver/drier, which acts as a reservoir and filter for the refrigerant, is located in the left front corner of the engine compartment. On Novas it is below the coolant reservoir, on Prizms it is mounted between the grille and radiator.

2   On Novas, remove the coolant reservoir for access (see Section 7). On Prizms, remove the grille (see Chapter 11).

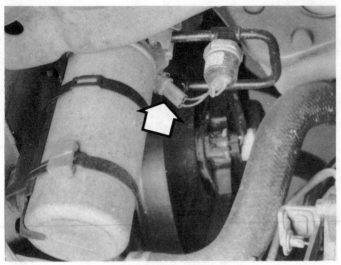

14.3   Unplug the electrical connector (arrow) – Nova, viewed from below

14.6a   Remove the bracket bolts (arrows) – Nova, viewed from below

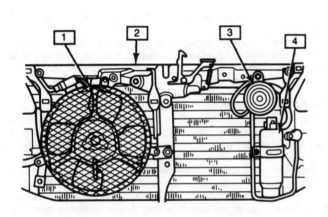

14.6b   Prizm receiver-drier mounting details

1   *Condenser fan*   3   *Horn*
2   *Condenser*   4   *Receiver/drier*

15.6   Unbolt the refrigerant lines (arrows) from the back of the compressor

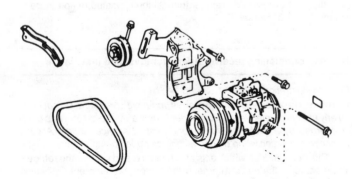

15.7a   4A-LC engine compressor mounting details – exploded view

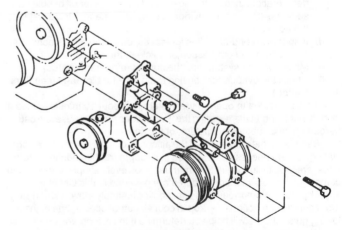

15.7b   4A-GE engine compressor mounting details – exploded view

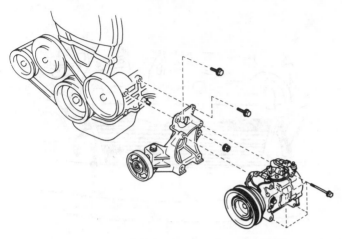

15.7c   4A-FE engine compressor mounting details – exploded view

3   Unplug the electrical connector from the pressure switch **(see illustration)**.

4   Detach the two refrigerant lines from the receiver/drier.

5   Immediately cap the open fittings to prevent the entry of dirt and moisture.

6   Unbolt the receiver/drier **(see illustrations)** and lift it from the vehicle.

7   Install new O-rings on the lines and lubricate them with clean refrigerant oil.

8   Installation is the reverse of removal. **Note:** *Do not remove the sealing caps until you are ready to reconnect the lines. Do not mistake the inlet (marked IN) and the outlet (marked OUT) connections.*

9   If a new receiver/drier is installed, add 0.7 US fluid ounces (20 cc) of refrigerant oil to the system.

10   Have the system evacuated, charged and leak tested by the shop that discharged it.

15   Air conditioning compressor – removal and installation

Refer to illustrations 15.6, 15.7a, 15.7b and 15.7c

Warning: *The air conditioning system is under high pressure. Do not loos-en any fittings or remove any components until after the system has been discharged by a dealer service department or service station. Always wear eye protection when disconnecting air conditioning system fittings.*

1   Disconnect the negative cable from the battery.

2   Set the parking brake and block the rear tires.

3   Raise the front of the vehicle and support it securely on jackstands.

4   Unbolt the lower splash shield and remove the compressor drivebelt (see Chapter 1). Detach the fan shroud, if necessary.

5   Disconnect the clutch wire from the compressor.

6   Detach the refrigerant lines from the back of the compressor **(see illustration)** and immediately cap the open fittings to prevent the entry of dirt and moisture.

7   Remove the mounting bolts **(see illustrations)** and lower the compressor from the engine compartment. **Note:** *Keep the compressor level during handling and storage. If the compressor seized or you find metal particles in the refrigerant lines, the system must be flushed out by an air conditioning technician and the receiver/drier must be replaced.*

8   Prior to installation, turn the center of the clutch six times to disperse any oil that has collected in the head.

9   Install the compressor in the reverse order of removal.

10   If you are installing a new compressor, refer to the manufacturer's instructions for adding refrigerant oil to the system.

11   Have the system evacuated, charged and leak tested by the shop that discharged it.

16   Air conditioning condenser – removal and installation

Refer to illustrations 16.2, 16.3a, 16.3b and 16.5

Warning: *The air conditioning system is under high pressure. Do not loos-en any fittings or remove any components until after the system has been discharged by a dealer service department or service station. Always wear eye protection when disconnecting air conditioning system fittings.*

1   Remove the grille (also the headlight assemblies on Novas and the bumper on Prizms) – see Chapter 11.

2   Remove the hood latch and vertical brace **(see illustration)**.

16.2   Remove the hood latch and vertical brace bolts (arrows) – don't forget the bottom one (not shown)

16.3a   Use two wrenches to avoid twisting the refrigerant lines

16.3b   Disconnect the lines on both sides (Nova shown, Prizm similar)

16.5   Remove the condenser mounting bolts (arrows)

3   Disconnect the refrigerant lines from the condenser. Be sure to use a back-up wrench to avoid twisting the lines **(see illustrations)**.
4   Immediately cap the open fittings to prevent the entry of dirt and moisture.
5   Unbolt the condenser **(see illustration)** and lift it out of the vehicle. Store it upright to prevent oil loss.

6   Installation is the reverse of removal.
7   If a new condenser was installed, add 1.4 to 1.7 ounces (40 to 50 cc) of refrigerant oil to the system.
8   Have the system evacuated, charged and leak tested by the shop that discharged it.

Chapter 4   Fuel and exhaust systems

Contents

Specifications

Torque specifications
                                                                       Ft-lbs

Throttle body mounting bolts .... 14 to 16
Carburetor mounting bolts 18

---

1   General information

The fuel system consists of a rear mounted tank, combination metal and rubber fuel hoses, an engine-mounted mechanical pump or an electric pump, and either a two-stage, two venturi carburetor or an electronic fuel injection system.

The exhaust system is composed of an exhaust manifold, the catalytic converter and a combination muffler and tailpipe assembly.

The emission control systems modify the functions of both the exhaust and fuel systems. There may be some cross-references throughout this Chapter to sections in Chapter 6 because the emissions control systems are integral with the induction and exhaust systems.

Extreme caution should be exercised when dealing with either the fuel or exhaust system. Fuel is a primary element for combustion. Be very careful! The exhaust system is also an area for exercising caution as it operates at very high temperatures. Serious burns can result from even momentary contact with any part of the exhaust system and the fire potential is ever present.

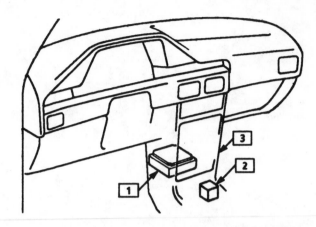

2.3   To relieve the fuel pressure, remove the center console and unplug the circuit opening relay – start the engine and allow it to run until it stalls, then crank it over a few times

1	ECM	3	Console
2	Circuit opening relay		

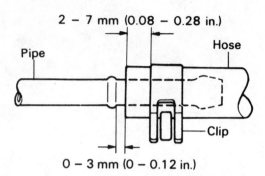

3.6   When attaching a section of rubber hose to a metal fuel line, be sure to overlap the hose as shown and secure it to the line with a new hose clamp of the proper type

2   Fuel pressure relief procedure

Warning: *Gasoline is extremely flammable, so extra precautions must be taken when working on any part of the fuel system. Do not smoke or allow open flames or bare light bulbs near the work area. Also, do not work in a garage if a natural gas-type appliance with a pilot light is present. Always keep a dry chemical (Class B) fire extinguisher near the work area.*

1   Always relieve the fuel pressure before disconnecting any fuel system component to minimize the risk of fire and personal injury.

All vehicles

2   Unscrew the fuel filler cap to release the pressure caused by fuel vapor.

Fuel injected vehicles

Refer to illustration 2.3

3   Remove the center console (see Chapter 11 if necessary). Remove the circuit opening relay **(see illustration)** and start the engine, allowing it to run until it stalls. Crank it over five or six times. Reinstall the relay, but don't turn the ignition key on until after all work to the fuel system has been performed, otherwise the fuel system will pressure-up again.

4   Even though fuel pressure should now be safely relieved, it's always a good idea to place a shop rag over any fuel fitting before loosening it.

3   Fuel lines and fittings – inspection and replacement

Warning: *Gasoline is extremely flammable, so extra precautions must be taken when working on any part of the fuel system. Do not smoke or allow open flames or bare light bulbs near the work area. Also, do not work in a garage if a natural gas-type appliance with a pilot light is present. Always keep a dry chemical (Class B) fire extinguisher near the work area.*

Inspection

1   Once in a while, you will have to raise the vehicle to service or replace some component (an exhaust pipe hanger, for example). Whenever you work under the vehicle, always inspect fuel lines and all fittings and connections for damage or deterioration.

2   Check all hoses and pipes for cracks, kinks, deformation or obstructions.

3   Make sure all hoses and pipe clips attach their associated hoses or pipes securely to the underside of the vehicle.

4   Verify all hose clamps attaching rubber hoses to metal fuel lines or pipes are snug enough to assure a tight fit between the hoses and pipes.

Replacement

Refer to illustration 3.6

5   If you must replace any damaged sections, use original equipment replacement hoses or pipes constructed from exactly the same material as the section you are replacing. Do not install substitutes constructed from inferior or inappropriate material or you could cause a fuel leak or a fire.

6   Always, before detaching or disassembling any part of the fuel line system, note the routing of all hoses and pipes and the orientation of all clamps and clips to assure that replacement sections are installed in exactly the same manner. When attaching hoses to metal lines, overlap them as shown **(see illustration)**.

7   Before detaching any part of the fuel system, be sure to relieve the fuel line and tank pressure (see Section 2).

8   While you're under the vehicle, it's a good idea to check the condition of the fuel filter – make sure that it's not clogged or damaged (see Chapter 1).

4   Fuel pump – check

Warning: *Gasoline is extremely flammable, so extra precautions must be taken when working on any part of the fuel system. Do not smoke or allow open flames or bare light bulbs near the work area. Also, do not work in a garage if a natural gas-type appliance with a pilot light is present. Always keep a dry chemical (Class B) fire extinguisher near the work area.*

Note: *The following checks assume the fuel filter is in good condition. If you doubt it's condition, install a new one (see Chapter 1).*

1   Check that there is adequate fuel in the fuel tank. If you doubt the reading on the gauge, insert a long wooden dowel at the filler opening; it will serve as a dipstick.

Mechanical pump (carbureted vehicles)

Refer to illustration 4.3

2   Raise the vehicle and support is securely on jackstands. With the engine running, examine all fuel lines between the fuel tank and fuel pump for leaks, loose connections, kinks or distortion of the rubber hoses. Do this quickly, before the engine gets hot. Air leaks upstream of the fuel pump can seriously affect the pump's output.

3   Check the body of the pump for leaks **(see illustration)**. Shut off the engine.

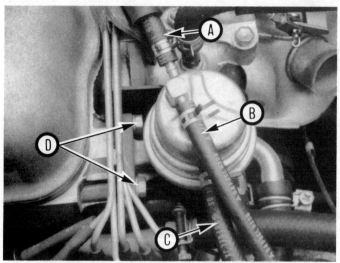

4.3   The fuel pump on carburetor-equipped models is mounted
on the left rear corner of the cylinder head

| A | Fuel outlet hose | C | Fuel inlet hose |
| B | Fuel return hose | D | Mounting bolts |

4   Remove the fuel filler cap to relieve the fuel tank pressure. Disconnect
the fuel line at the carburetor. Disconnect the wiring connectors to the distributor so the engine can be cranked without it firing. Place an approved
gasoline container at the end of the detached fuel line and have an assistant crank the engine for several seconds. There should be a strong spurt
of gasoline from the line on every second revolution.

5   If little or no gasoline emerges from the line during engine cranking,
either the fuel line is clogged or the fuel pump is not working properly. Disconnect the fuel feed line from the pump and blow air through it to be sure
that the line is clear. If the line is not clogged, then pump should be replaced with a new one.

Electric pump (fuel injected vehicles)

Refer to illustrations 4.8a and 4.8b

6   Although the best way to check the operation of the fuel pump is with a
fuel pressure gauge, to do so on these fuel injected vehicles requires the
use of special adapters not normally available to the home mechanic. It is
possible, however, to determine if the fuel pump is receiving power and
rotating, which is usually a pretty good indication that it is pumping fuel.

7   Turn the ignition key to the Off position and remove the fuel filler cap.
With the help of an assistant, put your ear next to the opening, crank the
engine over and listen for the fuel pump working, which is characterized by
a whirring sound. After listening, turn the ignition switch to Off.

8   If the fuel pump is not working, check the ignition fuse, the EFI fuse,
the stop fuse and the fusible links (see Chapter 12). If the fuse is okay, find
the fuel pump circuit test connector (**see illustrations**). Using a jumper
wire, bridge the indicated terminals. Turn the ignition switch to On. If the
fuel pump now works, replace the fuel pump relay.

9   If the fuel pump is still not working, a problem could exist with the wiring harness to the pump or the pump itself. Any further checks should be
done by a dealer service department or automotive repair shop.

---

5   Fuel pump – removal and installation

Warning: *Gasoline is extremely flammable, so extra precautions must be
taken when working on any part of the fuel system. Do not smoke or allow
open flames or bare light bulbs in the work area. Also, do not work in garage if a natural gas-type appliance that has a pilot light is present. Always
keep a dry chemical (Class B) fire extinguisher near the work area.*

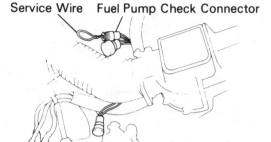

4.8a   To check the fuel pump on 1988 models, turn on the
ignition switch (but don't start the engine) and bridge both
terminals of the fuel pump check connector with a jumper wire –
the test connector is located near the windshield wiper motor

4.8b   To check the fuel pump on 1989 and 1990 models, turn on
the ignition switch (but don't start the engine) and bridge
terminals +B and Fp of the service connector

1   Disconnect the cable from the negative terminal of the battery.

2   Relieve the fuel system pressure (see Section 2).

Mechanical pump (carbureted vehicles)

3   Relieve the fuel tank pressure by removing the fuel filler cap.

4   Locate the fuel pump mounted on the left rear corner of the cylinder
head (**see illustration 4.3**). Place rags underneath the pump to catch any
spilled fuel.

5   Loosen hose clamps and slide them down the hoses, past the fittings.
Disconnect the hoses from the pump, using a twisting motion as you pull
them from the fittings. Immediately plug the hoses to prevent leakage of
fuel and the entry of dirt.

6   Unscrew the fasteners that retain the pump to the cylinder head, then
detach the pump from the head. Inspect the fuel pump arm for wear. Coat it
with clean engine oil before installing it.

7   Using a gasket scraper or putty knife, remove all traces of old gasket
material from the mating surfaces on the cylinder head (and the fuel pump,
if the same one will be reinstalled). While scraping, be careful not to gouge
the soft aluminum surfaces.

8   Installation is the reverse of the removal procedure, but be sure to use
a new gasket and tighten the mounting fasteners securely.

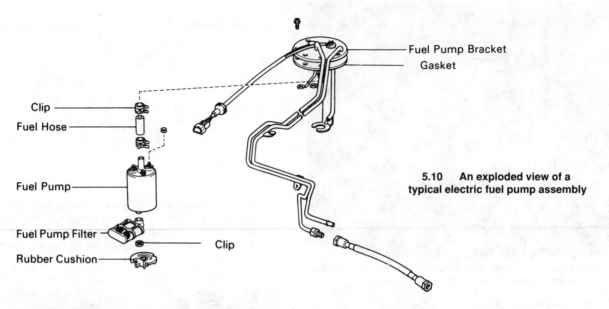

Clip

Fuel Hose

Fuel Pump

Fuel Pump Filter

Rubber Cushion

Clip

Fuel Pump Bracket

Gasket

**5.10   An exploded view of a
typical electric fuel pump assembly**

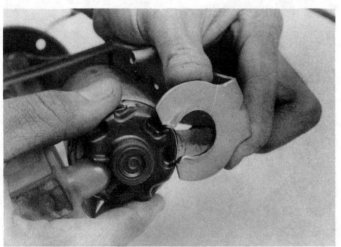

**5.11   Pull the lower end of the fuel pump loose from the bracket
and remove the rubber cushion that insulates the bottom of
the pump**

**5.13   Pry off the clip that holds the filter to the fuel pump and
pull the filter off – replace the clip if it's a loose fit**

**5.14   Pull the fuel pump loose from the hose far enough to get
at the electrical lead near the bracket**

Electric pump (fuel injected vehicles)

Refer to illustration 5.10, 5.11, 5.13 and 5.14

9   Remove the fuel tank following the procedure described in Section 6.
10   Remove the retaining screws, then lift the assembly out of the fuel tank **(see illustration)**.
11   Pull the lower end of the fuel pump loose from the bracket **(see illustration)**.
12   Remove the rubber cushion from the lower end of the fuel pump.
13   Remove the clip securing the filter to the pump **(see illustration)**. Pull out the filter and inspect it for contamination. If it is dirty, replace it.
14   Loosen the hose clamp at the upper end of the pump, disconnect the pump from the hose, then disconnect the electrical wires from the pump terminals **(see illustration)**.
15   The remainder of installation is the reverse of the removal procedure. Be sure to replace the pump unit gasket if it shows any signs of deterioration.

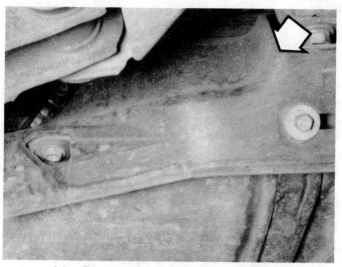

6.6   Remove the fuel tank protectors (arrow)

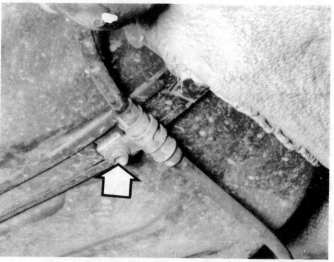

6.7   Remove the bracket bolt (arrow) and detach the parking brake cable from the fuel tank strap

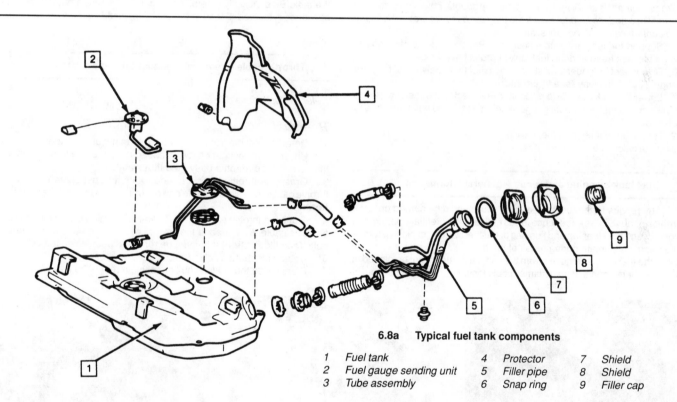

6.8a   Typical fuel tank components

1	Fuel tank	4	Protector	7	Shield
2	Fuel gauge sending unit	5	Filler pipe	8	Shield
3	Tube assembly	6	Snap ring	9	Filler cap

6   Fuel tank – removal and installation

Refer to illustrations 6.6, 6.7, 6.8a, 6.8b and 6.10

Warning: *Gasoline is extremely flammable, so extra precautions must be taken when working on any part of the fuel system. Do not smoke or allow open flames or bare light bulbs near the work area. Also, do not work in a garage if a natural gas-type appliance with a pilot light is present. While performing any work on the fuel tank, wear safety glasses and have a dry chemical (Class B) fire extinguisher on hand. If you spill any fuel on your skin, rinse it off immediately with soap and water.*

Note: *The following procedure is much easier to perform if the fuel tank is*
empty. *Some tanks have a drain plug for this purpose. If the tank does not have drain plug, simply run the engine until the tank is empty.*

1   Remove the fuel filler cap to relieve fuel tank pressure.
2   Relieve the fuel pressure (see Section 2).
3   Detach the cable from the negative terminal of the battery.
4   If the tank has a drain plug, remove it and allow the fuel to drain into an approved gasoline container.
5   Raise the vehicle and place it securely on jackstands.
6   Remove the fuel tank protectors **(see illustration)**.
7   Detach the parking brake cable from the fuel tank strap **(see illustration)**.
8   Disconnect the fuel lines, the vapor return lines and the fuel filler neck **(see illustrations)**. **Note:** *The fuel lines are usually different diameters,*

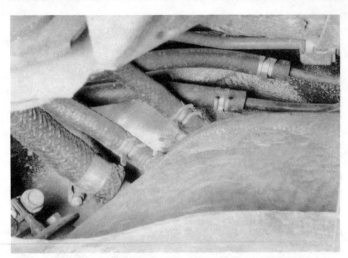

6.8b   Label and disconnect the fuel lines

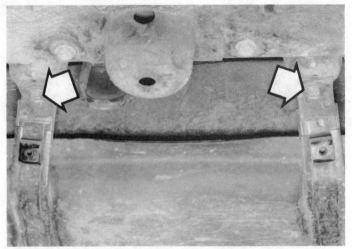

6.10   Remove the fuel tank strap bolts (arrows) and swing the
strap down out of the way

so reattachment is simplified. If you have any doubts, however, clearly label the lines and the fittings. Be sure to plug the hoses to prevent leakage
and contamination of the fuel system.

9   Support the fuel tank with a floor jack. Position a piece of wood between the jack head and the fuel tank to protect the tank.
10   Disconnect both fuel tank straps and pivot them down until they are
hanging out of the way **(see illustration)**.
11   Lower the tank enough to disconnect the electrical wires and ground
strap from the fuel pump/fuel gauge sending unit, if you have not already
done so.
12   Remove the tank from the vehicle.
13   Installation is the reverse of removal.

7   Fuel tank cleaning and repair – general information

1   Any repairs to the fuel tank or filler neck should be carried out by a
professional who has experience in this critical and potentially dangerous
work. Even after cleaning and flushing of the fuel system, explosive fumes
can remain and ignite during repair of the tank.
2   If the fuel tank is removed from the vehicle, it should not be placed in
an area where sparks or open flames could ignite the fumes coming out of

the tank. Be especially careful inside garages where a natural gas-type
appliance is located, because the pilot light could cause an explosion.

8   Throttle cable – removal, installation and adjustment

Refer to illustrations 8.2, 8.3 and 8.5

Removal

1   Detach the cable from the negative terminal of the battery.
2   Unscrew the locknut on the threaded portion of the throttle cable at
the carburetor or throttle body **(see illustration)**.
3   Grasp the throttle lever arm and rotate it to put some slack in the
throttle cable, then slip the cable end out of its slot in the arm **(see illustration)**.
4   Trace the throttle cable to the firewall, detaching it from all brackets.
5   The cable is secured to the firewall with a flange and two mounting
bolts **(see illustration)** that must be removed from inside the vehicle.
6   Detach the throttle cable from the accelerator pedal.
7   From inside the vehicle, pull the cable through the firewall.

8.2   Unscrew the locknut (arrow) on
the threaded portion of
the cable

8.3   Grasp the throttle lever arm and
rotate it to put some slack in the cable,
then slip the cable end out of the slot in
the arm

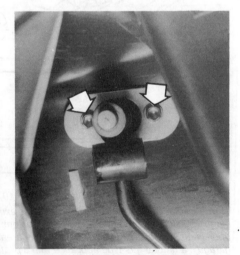

8.5   To detach the cable ferrule and
mounting flange from the firewall,
remove the bolts (arrows) from inside
the vehicle

Installation and adjustment

8   Installation is the reverse of removal.
9   To adjust the cable, fully depress the accelerator pedal and check that the throttle is fully opened.
10   If not fully opened, loosen the locknuts, depress accelerator pedal and adjust the cable.
11   Tighten the locknuts and recheck the adjustment. Make sure the throttle closes fully when the pedal isn't depressed.

9   Electronic Fuel Injection system – general information

Refer to illustration 9.1

Non-carbureted engines are equipped with an Electronic Fuel Injection (EFI) system. The EFI system is composed of three basic sub systems: fuel system, air system and electronic control system **(see illustration)**.

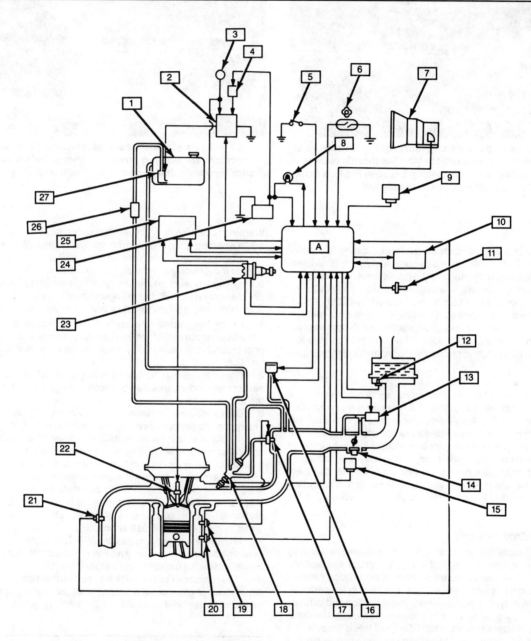

9.1   Typical fuel injection system components (VIN code 6)

A	Engine control module	8	Check engine warning light	14	Air valve	22	Spark plug
1	Fuel tank	9	A/C amplifier	15	Throttle position sensor	23	Distributor
2	Circuit opening relay	10	EGR vacuum switching valve (California only)	16	Manifold pressure sensor	24	Battery
3	Ignition switch			17	Cold-start injector	25	Igniter
4	EFI main relay	11	EGR temperature switch (California only)	18	Injector	26	Fuel filter
5	Check connector			19	Start injector time switch	27	Fuel pump
6	Vehicle speed sensor	12	Intake temperature sensor	20	Coolant temperature sensor		
7	Neutral start switch	13	Air control valve	21	Oxygen sensor		

10.6   Clean the throttle body casting thoroughly with solvent or carburetor cleaner – the area right behind the throttle plate is particularly susceptible to sludge buildup because the PCV hose vents crankcase vapors to the plenum

10.7   Use a stethoscope or screwdriver to determine if the injectors are working properly – they should make a steady clicking sound that rises and falls with engine speed changes

Fuel system

An electric fuel pump located inside the fuel tank supplies fuel under constant pressure to the fuel rail, which distributes fuel evenly to all injectors. From the fuel rail, fuel is injected into the intake ports, just above the intake valves, by four fuel injectors. The amount of fuel supplied by the injectors is precisely controlled by an Electronic Control Unit (ECU). An additional injector, known as the cold start injector, supplies extra fuel into the intake manifold for starting. A pressure regulator controls system pressure in relation to intake manifold vacuum. A fuel filter between the fuel pump and the fuel rail filters fuel to protect the components of the system.

Air system

The air system consists of an air filter housing, some models will have an air flow meter and a throttle body. The air flow meter is an information gathering device for the ECU. A potentiometer measures intake air flow and a temperature sensor measures intake air temperature. This information helps the ECU determine the amount (duration) of fuel to be injected by the injectors. The throttle plate inside the throttle body is controlled by the driver. As the throttle plate opens, the amount of air that can pass through the system increases, so the potentiometer opens further and the ECU signals the injectors to increase the amount of fuel delivered to the intake ports.

Electronic control system

The Computer Control System controls the EFI and other systems by means of an Electronic Control Unit (ECU), which employs a microcomputer. The ECU receives signals from a number of information sensors which monitor such variables as intake air volume, intake air temperature, coolant temperature, engine rpm, acceleration/deceleration and exhaust oxygen content. These signals help the ECU determine the injection duration necessary for the optimum air/fuel ratio. Some of these sensors and their corresponding ECU-controlled relays are not contained within EFI components, but are located throughout the engine compartment. For further information regarding the ECU and its relationship to the engine electrical and ignition system, refer to Chapter 6.

---

10   Electronic Fuel Injection system – check

Refer to illustrations 10.6 and 10.7

Warning: *Gasoline is extremely flammable, so extra precautions must be taken when working on any part of the fuel system. Do not smoke or allow open flames or bare light bulbs near the work area. Also, do not work in a garage if a natural gas-type appliance with a pilot light is present. While performing any work on the fuel system, wear safety glasses and have a dry chemical (Class B) fire extinguisher on hand. If you spill any fuel on your skin, rinse it off immediately with soap and water.*

1   Check the ground wire connections for tightness. Check all wiring harness connectors that are related to the system. Loose connectors and poor grounds can cause many problems that resemble more serious malfunctions.

2   Check to see that the battery is fully charged, as the control unit and sensors depend on an accurate supply voltage in order to properly meter the fuel.

3   Check the air filter element – a dirty or partially blocked filter will severely impede performance and economy (see Chapter 1).

4   If a blown fuse is found, replace it and see if it blows again. If it does, search for a grounded wire in the harness related to the system.

5   Check the air intake duct from the air mass sensor to the intake manifold for leaks, which will result in an excessively lean mixture. Also check the condition of the vacuum hoses connected to the intake manifold.

6   Remove the air intake duct from the throttle body and check for dirt, carbon or other residue build-up. If it's dirty, clean with carburetor cleaner and a toothbrush **(see illustration)**.

7   With the engine running, place a screwdriver or a stethoscope against each injector, one at a time, and listen through the handle for a clicking sound, indicating operation **(see illustration)**.

8   The remainder of the system checks should be left to a GM service department or other qualified repair shop, as there is a chance that the control unit may be damaged if not performed properly.

---

11   Electronic Fuel Injection system – component removal and installation

Warning: *Gasoline is extremely flammable, so extra precautions must be taken when working on any part of the fuel system. Do not smoke or allow open flames or bare light bulbs near the work area. Also, do not work in a garage if a natural gas-type appliance with a pilot light is present. While performing any work on the fuel system, wear safety glasses and have a dry chemical (Class B) fire extinguisher on hand. If you spill any fuel on your skin, rinse it off immediately with soap and water.*

11.6   Label and detach all vacuum hoses from the throttle body

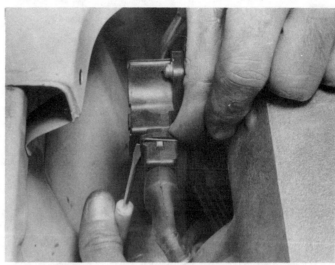

11.7   Pry the spring clip up far enough to release the electrical connector plug from the throttle position sensor (TPS) and unplug the connector

11.8   Remove the bolts (arrows) to detach the throttle body from the air intake chamber – DOHC engine (VIN code 6) shown, others similar

11.16   To detach the fuel pressure regulator from the fuel rail, remove the banjo bolt (arrow) and crush washers, detach the fuel line, remove the two regulator mounting bolts (arrows), then separate the regulator from the fuel rail

Throttle body

Refer to illustrations 11.6, 11.7 and 11.8

1   Detach the cable from the negative terminal of the battery.
2   On 1988 models, drain about a gallon of engine coolant from the radiator (see Chapter 1).
3   Loosen the hose clamps and remove the air intake duct.
4   Detach the throttle cable from the throttle lever arm (see Section 8), then detach the throttle cable bracket and set it aside (it's not necessary to detach the throttle cable from the bracket).
5   If your vehicle is equipped with an automatic transaxle, detach the throttle valve (TV) cable from the throttle linkage (see Chapter 7B), detach the TV cable brackets from the engine and set the cable and brackets aside.
6   Clearly label, then detach, all vacuum and coolant hoses from the throttle body **(see illustration)**.
7   Unplug the electrical connector from the throttle position sensor **(see illustration)**.
8   Remove the throttle body mounting bolts **(see illustration)** and de-

tach the throttle body and gasket from the air intake chamber.
9   Using a soft brush and carburetor cleaner, thoroughly clean the throttle body casting, then blow out all passages with compressed air.
Caution: *Do not clean the throttle position sensor with anything. Just wipe it off carefully with a clean soft cloth.*
10   Installation of the throttle body is the reverse of removal. Be sure to tighten the throttle body mounting bolts to the specified torque.

Fuel pressure regulator

Refer to illustrations 11.16 and 11.17

11   Relieve the fuel pressure (see Section 2).
12   Detach the cable from the negative terminal of the battery.
13   Detach the vacuum sensing hose.
14   Place a metal container or shop towel under the fuel return line banjo fitting.
15   Slowly loosen the banjo bolt, then remove it along with the crush washers and discard the crush washers.
16   Remove the pressure regulator mounting bolts **(see illustration)** and detach the pressure regulator from the fuel rail.

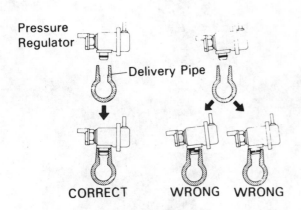

Pressure Regulator

Delivery Pipe

CORRECT   WRONG   WRONG

11.17   If the fuel pressure regulator is cocked during installation, it will not seal properly

11.23   Unplug the electrical connector, remove the banjo bolt (arrow) and crush washers, then separate the line from the cold start injector

11.24   The injector connectors can be tricky to unplug – firmly depress the tang (arrow) to unlock each connector

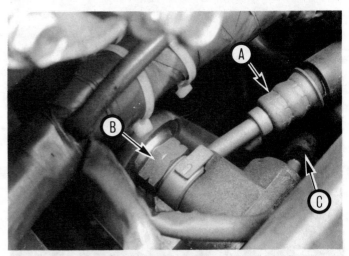

11.25   To detach the fuel feed line (A) from the fuel rail, remove the pulsation damper (B) – discard the crush washers – the fuel return line (C) is also visible in the lower right corner of this photo but you can't detach it until the fuel rail is detached from the head

11.27   Unless you are only removing one fuel injector at a time, it's a good practice to place the injectors in a clearly labelled container, like an egg carton, to prevent mixing up the injectors when it's time to install them in the fuel rail

11.28   Carefully remove the fuel rail assembly through the space between the cam covers and the air intake chamber

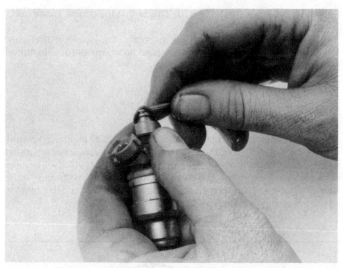

11.30a   Even if you plan to reinstall the same injector(s), be sure to remove and discard the old O-rings and replace them with new ones

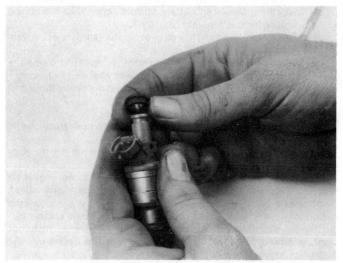

11.30b   Also remove and discard the old grommets and replace them with new ones

17   Installation is the reverse of removal. Be sure to use new crush washers and make sure that the pressure regulator is installed properly on the fuel rail **(see illustration)**.

Fuel rail and fuel injectors

Refer to illustrations 11.23, 11.24, 11.25, 11.27, 11.28, 11.30a and 11.30b

18   Remove the fuel filler cap to relieve the fuel tank pressure.
19   Relieve the system fuel pressure (see Section 2).
20   Detach the cable from the negative terminal of the battery.
21   Detach the accelerator cable from the throttle linkage and from its bracket on the air intake (see Section 9).
22   Detach the vacuum sensing hose from the fuel pressure regulator (see above).
23   Unplug the cold start injector connector and remove the cold start injector pipe bolt **(see illustration)**.
24   Unplug the four fuel injector electrical connectors **(see illustration)** and set the injector wire harness aside.
25   Remove the pulsation damper and detach the fuel feed line **(see illustration)**.
26   Remove the two fuel rail mounting bolts and detach the fuel rail/injector assembly from the cylinder head by pulling on it while wiggling it back and forth.
27   Remove the fuel injectors from the fuel rail and set them aside in a clearly labelled storage container **(see illustration)**.
28   Remove the fuel rail **(see illustration)**.
29   Remove the four fuel rail insulators from the cylinder head and set them aside.
30   If you are replacing the injector(s), discard the old injector, the grommet and the O-ring. If you are simply replacing leaking injector O-rings, and intend to re-use the same injectors, remove the old grommet and O-ring **(see illustrations)** and discard them.
31   Further testing of the injector(s) is beyond the scope of the home mechanic. If you are in doubt as to the status of any injector(s), it can be bench tested for volume and leakage at a dealer service department.
32   Installation of the fuel injectors is the reverse of removal. Be sure to use new grommets and O-rings on the injector(s).

12   Carburetor – diagnosis and overhaul

Warning: *Gasoline is extremely flammable, so extra precautions must be taken when working on any part of the fuel system. Do not smoke or allow open flames or bare light bulbs near the work area. Also, do not work in a garage if a natural gas-type appliance with a pilot light is present. While performing any work on the fuel system, wear safety glasses and have a dry chemical (Class B) fire extinguisher on hand. If you spill any fuel on your skin, rinse it off immediately with soap and water.*

General diagnosis

1   A thorough road test and check of carburetor adjustments should be done before any major carburetor service work. Specifications for some adjustments are listed on the Vehicle Emissions Control Information (VECI) label found in the engine compartment.
2   Carburetor problems usually show up as flooding, hard starting, stalling, severe backfiring and poor acceleration. A carburetor that's leaking fuel and/or covered with wet looking deposits definitely needs attention.
3   Some performance complaints directed at the carburetor are actually a result of loose, out-of-adjustment or malfunctioning engine or electrical components. Others develop when vacuum hoses leak, are disconnected or are incorrectly routed. The proper approach to analyzing carburetor problems should include the following items:

   a) Inspect all vacuum hoses and actuators for leaks and correct installation (see Chapters 1 and 6).
   b) Tighten the intake manifold and carburetor mounting nuts/bolts evenly and securely.
   c) Perform a cylinder compression test (see Chapter 2).
   d) Clean or replace the spark plugs as necessary (see Chapter 1).
   e) Check the spark plug wires (see Chapter 1).
   f) Inspect the ignition primary wires.
   g) Check the ignition timing (follow the instructions printed on the Emissions Control Information label).
   h) Check the fuel pump (see Section 4).
   i) Check the heat control valve in the air cleaner for proper operation (see Chapter 1).
   j) Check/replace the air filter element (see Chapter 1).
   k) Check the PCV system (see Chapters 1 and 6).
   l) Check/replace the fuel filter (see Chapter 1). Also, the strainer in the tank could be restricted.
   m) Check for a plugged exhaust system.
   n) Check EGR valve operation (see Chapter 6).

o) Check the choke – it should be completely open at normal engine operating temperature (see Chapter 1).

p) Check for fuel leaks and kinked or dented fuel lines (see Chapters 1 and 4).

q) Check accelerator pump operation with the engine off (remove the air cleaner cover and operate the throttle as you look into the carburetor throat – you should see a stream of gasoline enter the carburetor).

r) Check for incorrect fuel or bad gasoline.

s) Check the valve clearances (if applicable) and camshaft lobe lift (see Chapters 1 and 2)

t) Have a dealer service department or repair shop check the electronic engine and carburetor controls.

4   Diagnosing carburetor problems may require that the engine be started and run with the air cleaner off. While running the engine without the air cleaner, backfires are possible. This situation is likely to occur if the carburetor is malfunctioning, but just the removal of the air cleaner can lean the fuel/air mixture enough to produce an engine backfire. **Warning:** *Don't position any part of your body, especially your face, directly over the carburetor during inspection and servicing procedures. Wear eye protection!*

Feedback carburetor inspection

Refer to illustrations 12.5a, 12.5b and 12.6

5   Check the Thermostatic Vacuum Switching Valve (TVSV) with a cold engine.

a) The coolant temperature should be below 45-degrees Fahrenheit.

b) Disconnect the vacuum hose from the vacuum switch **(see illustrations)**.

c) Start the engine and check that no vacuum is felt at the hose.

d) Reconnect the vacuum hose.

6   Check the Electronic Air Bleed Control Valve (EBCV).

a) Warm up the engine to normal operating temperature.

b) Disconnect the EBCV connector **(see illustration)**.

c) Maintain engine speed at 2,500 rpm.

d) Reconnect the EBCV connector and the engine rpm should drop about 300 rpm momentarily.

e) With the engine idling repeat steps (b) and (d).

f) Check that the engine speed does not change.

g) Disconnect the vacuum hose from the vacuum switch **(see illustration 12.5a or 12.5b).**

h) Repeat steps (b), (c) and (d). Check that the engine speed does not change.

7   If no problems is found with this inspection the system is okay. Any further check should be done by dealer service department or automotive repair shop.

Overhaul

Refer to illustration 12.9

8   Once it's determined that the carburetor needs an overhaul, several options are available. If you're going to attempt to overhaul the carburetor yourself, first obtain a good quality carburetor rebuild kit (which will include all necessary gaskets, internal parts, instructions and a parts list). You'll also need some special solvent and a means of blowing out the internal passages of the carburetor with air.

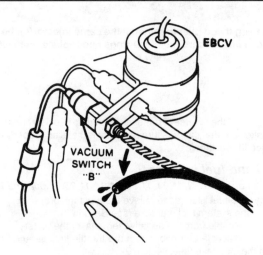

12.5a   On 1985, 1986 and 1988 models, remove the vacuum hose from vacuum switch B

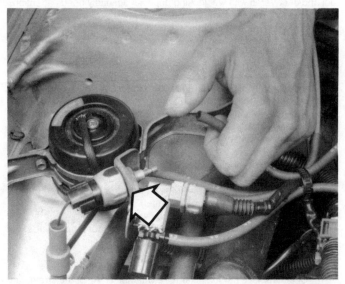

12.5b   On 1987 models only, remove the vacuum hose from the vacuum switch (arrow)

12.6   Typical EBCV and connector (arrows)

12.9   Before buying a carburetor rebuild kit, look for a tag like this and write the number down – it will ensure that you get the correct rebuild kit for the carburetor

9   An alternative is to obtain a new or rebuilt carburetor. They're readily available from dealers and auto parts stores. Make absolutely sure the exchange carburetor is identical to the original. A tag is usually attached to the top of the carburetor or a number is stamped on the float bowl **(see illustration)**. It'll help determine the exact type of carburetor you have. When obtaining a rebuilt carburetor or a rebuild kit, make sure the kit or carburetor matches your application exactly. Seemingly insignificant differences can make a large difference in engine performance.

10   If you choose to overhaul your own carburetor, allow enough time to disassemble it carefully, soak the necessary parts in the cleaning solvent (usually for at least one-half day or according to the instructions listed on the carburetor cleaner) and reassemble it, which will usually take much longer than disassembly. When disassembling the carburetor, match each part with the illustration in the carburetor kit and lay the parts out in order on a clean work surface. Overhauls by inexperienced mechanics can result in an engine which runs poorly or not at all. To avoid this, use care and patience when disassembling the carburetor so you can reassemble it correctly.

11   Because carburetor designs are constantly modified by the manufacturer in order to meet increasingly more stringent emissions regulations, the overhaul procedures in this Chapter may not apply exactly to your vehicle. You'll receive a detailed, well illustrated set of instructions with any carburetor overhaul kit; they'll apply in a more specific manner to the carburetor on your vehicle.

13   Carburetor – removal and installation

Warning: *Gasoline is extremely flammable, so extra precautions must be taken when working on any part of the fuel system. Do not smoke or allow open flames or bare light bulbs near the work area. Also, do not work in a garage if a natural gas-type appliance with a pilot light is present. While performing any work on the fuel system, wear safety glasses and have a dry chemical (Class B) fire extinguisher on hand. If you spill any fuel on your skin, rinse it off immediately with soap and water.*

Removal

Refer to illustrations 13.5 and 13.7

1   Remove the fuel tank cap to relieve the tank pressure.
2   Remove the air cleaner from the carburetor. Be sure to label all vacuum hoses attached to the air cleaner housing.
3   Disconnect the throttle cable from the throttle lever (see Section 8).
4   If the vehicle is equipped with an automatic transmission, disconnect the TV cable from the throttle lever.
5   Clearly label all vacuum hoses and fittings, then disconnect the hoses **(see illustration)**.
6   Disconnect the fuel line from the carburetor.
7   Label the wires and terminals, then unplug all wire harness connectors **(see illustration)**.
8   Remove the mounting fasteners, remove the EGR modulator bracket out of the way and lift the carburetor from the intake manifold. Remove the carburetor mounting gasket. Do not remove the cold mixture heater. Stuff a shop rag into the intake manifold openings.

Installation

9   Use a gasket scraper to remove all traces of gasket material and sealant from the cold mixture heater, being careful not to damage the heater, (and the carburetor, if it's being reinstalled), then remove the shop rag from the manifold openings. Clean the mating surfaces with lacquer thinner or acetone.
10   Place a new gasket on the cold mixture heater.
11   Position the carburetor on the gasket, attach the EGR modulator bracket then install the mounting fasteners.
12   To prevent carburetor distortion or damage, tighten the fasteners, in a criss-cross pattern, 1/4-turn at a time.
13   The remaining installation steps are the reverse of removal.
14   Check and, if necessary, adjust the idle speed (see Chapter 1).
15   If the vehicle is equipped with an automatic transmission, refer to Chapter 7, Part B, for the TV cable adjustment procedure.
16   Start the engine and check carefully for fuel leaks.

13.5   Clearly label all vacuum hoses before disconnecting them

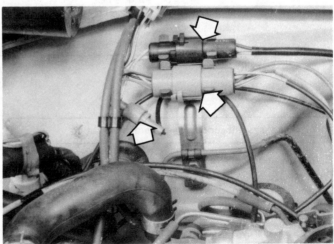

13.7   Label and unplug the electrical connectors from the carburetor (arrows)

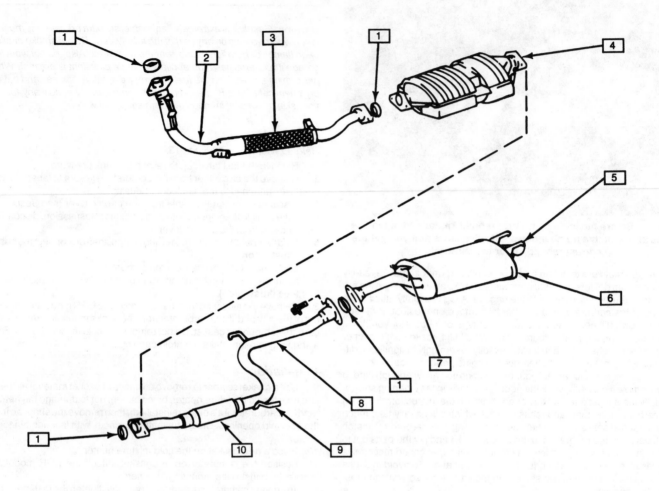

14.1a   Typical exhaust system components

1	Gasket	6	Muffler/tailpipe assembly
2	Forward pipe	7	Front muffler hanger
3	Flexible pipe	8	Intermediate pipe
4	Catalytic converter	9	Hanger bracket
5	Rear muffler hanger	10	Integral resonator

14   Exhaust system servicing – general information

Refer to illustrations 14.1a, 14.1b, 14.1c and 14.1d

Warning: *Inspection and repair of exhaust system components should be done only after enough time has elapsed after driving the vehicle to allow the system components to cool completely. Also, when working under the vehicle, make sure it is securely supported on jackstands.*

1   The exhaust system consists of the exhaust manifold, catalytic converter, the muffler, the tailpipe and all connecting pipes, brackets, hangers and clamps **(see illustrations)**. The exhaust system is attached to the body with mounting brackets and rubber hangers. If any of these parts are damaged or deteriorated, excessive noise and vibration will be transmitted to the body.

2   Conduct regular inspections of the exhaust system will keep it safe and quiet. Look for any damaged or bent parts, open seams, holes, loose connections, excessive corrosion or other defects which could allow exhaust fumes to enter the vehicle. Deteriorated exhaust system components should not be repaired – they should be replaced with new parts.

3   If the exhaust system components are extremely corroded or rusted together, they will probably have to be cut from the exhaust system. The convenient way to accomplish this is to have a muffler repair shop remove the corroded sections with a cutting torch. If, however, you want to save money by doing it yourself and you don't have an oxy/acetylene welding outfit with a cutting torch), simply cut off the old components with a hack-

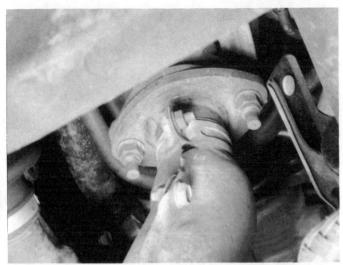

14.1b   the exhaust pipe is connected to the exhaust manifold with two nuts – there is a sealing ring under the flange which should be replaced whenever the pipe is unbolted from the manifold

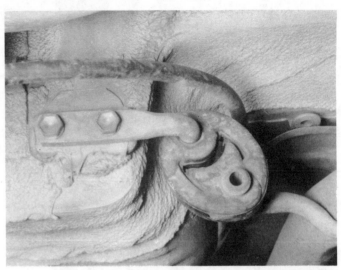

14.1c   Here's a typical exhaust system hanger – they should be inspected for cracks and replaced if deteriorated

saw. If you have compressed air, special pneumatic cutting chisels can also be used. If you do decide to tackle the job at home, be sure to wear eye protection to protect your eyes from metal chips and work gloves to protect your hands.

4   Here are some simple guidelines to apply when repairing the exhaust system:

  a) Work from the back to the front when removing exhaust system components.

  b) Apply penetrating oil to the exhaust system component fasteners to make them easier to remove.

  c) Use new gaskets, hangers and clamps when installing exhaust system components.

  d) Apply anti-seize compound to the threads of all exhaust system fasteners during reassembly.

  e) Be sure to allow sufficient clearance between newly installed parts and all points on the underbody to avoid overheating the floor pan and possibly damaging the interior carpet and insulation. Pay particularly close attention to the catalytic converter and its heat shield. **Warning:** *The catalytic converter operates at very high temperatures and takes about 30 minutes to cool. Wait half an hour before attempting to remove the converter. Failure to do so could result in serious burns.*

14.1d   Exhaust system bolts and nuts, particularly those on the exhaust manifold and catalytic converters, can be very difficult to loosen – spraying them with a penetrant will free up the threads

Chapter 5   Engine electrical systems

Contents

Specifications

Ignition coil

Primary resistance
    4A-LC (SOHC) engine .... 0.4 to 0.5 ohms
    4A-GE (DOHC) engine (VIN 5)
        1988 .... 0.5 to 0.7 ohms
        1990 .... 0.4 to 0.5 ohms
    4A-FE (DOHC) engine (VIN 6) .... 1.3 to 1.6 ohms
Secondary resistance
    4A-LC (SOHC) engine .... 7.5 to 10.4 k-ohms
    4A-GE (DOHC) engine (VIN 5)
        1988 .... 11 to 16 k-ohms
        1990 .... 10.2 to 13.8 k-ohms
    4A-FE (DOHC) engine (VIN 6) .... 10.4 to 14 k-ohms

Distributor air gap . . . . 0.008 to 0.016 in

Charging system
Charging voltage . . . . 13.5 to 15.1 volts
Alternator brush length
   Standard . . . . 0.413 in (10.5 mm)
   Minimum . . . . 0.177 in (4.5 mm)

1 General information

The engine electrical systems include all ignition, charging and starting components. Because of their engine-related functions, these components are discussed separately from chassis electrical devices such as the lights, the instruments, etc. (which are included in Chapter 12).

Always observe the following precautions when working on the electrical systems:

a) Be extremely careful when servicing engine electrical components. They are easily damaged if checked, connected or handled improperly.

b) Never leave the ignition switch on for long periods of time with the engine off.

c) Don't disconnect the battery cables while the engine is running.

d) Maintain correct polarity when connecting a battery cable from another vehicle during jump starting.

e) Always disconnect the negative cable first and hook it up last or the battery may be shorted by the tool being used to loosen the cable clamps.

It's also a good idea to review the safety-related information regarding the engine electrical systems located in the *Safety first* section near the front of this manual before beginning any operation included in this Chapter.

2 Battery – removal and installation

Refer to illustrations 2.1 and 2.2

1 **Warning:** *Always disconnect the negative cable first and hook it up last or the battery may be shorted by the tool being used to loosen the*

cable clamps. Disconnect both cables from the battery terminals **(see illustration)**.

2 Remove the battery hold down clamp **(see illustration)**.

3 Lift out the battery. Be careful – it's heavy.

4 While the battery is out, inspect the carrier (tray) for corrosion (see Chapter 1).

5 If you are replacing the battery, make sure that you get one that's identical, with the same dimensions, amperage rating, cold cranking rating, etc.

6 Installation is the reverse of removal.

3 Battery – emergency jump starting

Refer to the Booster battery (jump) starting procedure at the front of this manual.

4 Battery cables – check and replacement

1 Periodically inspect the entire length of each battery cable for damage, cracked or burned insulation and corrosion. Poor battery cable connections can cause starting problems and decreased engine performance.

2 Check the cable-to-terminal connections at the ends of the cables for cracks, loose wire strands and corrosion. The presence of white, fluffy deposits under the insulation at the cable terminal connection is a sign that the cable is corroded and should be replaced. Check the terminals for distortion, missing mounting bolts and corrosion.

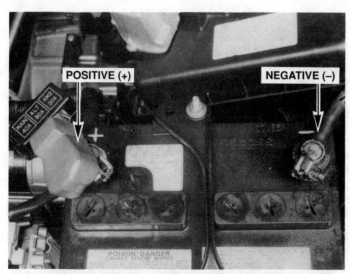

2.1 When detaching the cables from the battery, be sure to ALWAYS disconnect the negative cable (the one with the minus sign) first – when reattaching the cables, hook up the positive cable (the one with the plus sign) first

2.2 To remove the battery, detach the cables, remove the hold-down strap bolt (arrow), nut (arrow) and strap, then carefully lift the battery out of the engine compartment

3   When removing the cables, always disconnect the negative cable first and hook it up last or the battery may be shorted by the tool used to loosen the cable clamps. Even if only the positive cable is being replaced, be sure to disconnect the negative cable from the battery first (see Chapter 1 for further information regarding battery cable removal).

4   Disconnect the old cables from the battery, then trace each of them to their opposite ends and detach them from the starter solenoid and ground terminals. Note the routing of each cable to ensure correct installation.

5   If you are replacing either or both of the old cables, take them with you when buying new cables. It is vitally important that you replace the cables with identical parts. Cables have characteristics that make them easy to identify: positive cables are usually red, larger in cross section and have a larger diameter battery post clamp; ground cables are usually black, smaller in cross-section and have a slightly smaller diameter clamp for the negative post.

6   Clean the threads of the solenoid or ground connection with a wire brush to remove rust and corrosion. Apply a light coat of battery terminal corrosion inhibitor, or petroleum jelly, to the threads to prevent future corrosion.

7   Attach the cable to the solenoid or ground connection and tighten the mounting nut/bolt securely.

8   Before connecting a new cable to the battery, make sure that it reaches the battery post without having to be stretched.

9   Connect the positive cable first, followed by the negative cable.

5   Ignition system – general information and precautions

The ignition system includes the ignition switch, the battery, the igniter, the coil, the primary (low voltage) and secondary (high voltage) wiring circuits, the distributor and the spark plugs. On fuel injected models, the ignition system is controlled by the Electronic Control Unit (ECU). Using data provided by information sensors which monitor various engine functions (such as rpm, intake air volume, engine temperature, etc.), the ECU ensures a perfectly timed spark under all conditions. This system is known as Electronic Spark Advance (ESA). On models with carburetors, the spark advance is controlled by vacuum and centrifugal advance units.

When working on the ignition system, take the following precautions:

a) Do not keep the ignition switch on for more than 10 seconds if the engine will not start.

b) Always connect a tachometer in accordance with the manufacturer's instructions. Some tachometers may be incompatible with this ignition system. Consult a dealer service department before buying a tachometer for use with this vehicle.

c) Never allow the ignition coil terminals to touch ground. Grounding the coil could result in damage to the igniter and/or the ignition coil.

d) Do not disconnect the battery when the engine is running.

e) Make sure that the igniter is properly grounded.

6   Ignition system – check

Warning: *Because of the high voltage generated by the ignition system, extreme care should be taken whenever an operation is performed involving ignition components. This includes the igniter, coil, distributor and spark plug wires, but related components such as plug connectors, tachometer and other test equipment.*

1   If the engine won't start, the following quick checks should pinpoint the problem.

2   Attach an inductive timing light to each plug wire, one at a time, and crank the engine.

a) If the light flashes, voltage is reaching the plug.

b) If the light does not flash, proceed to the next step.

3   Inspect the spark plug wire(s), distributor cap, rotor and spark plug(s) (see Chapter 1).

4   If the engine still won't start, check the ignition coil (see Section 7).

7   Ignition coil – check and replacement

Check

1   Detach the cable from the negative terminal of the battery.

Coil in cap

Refer to illustrations 7.3a and 7.3b

2   Remove the distributor cap (see Chapter 1).

3   Using an ohmmeter, check the coil:

a) Measure the resistance between the positive and negative terminals **(see illustration)**. Compare your reading with the specified primary coil resistance.

b) Measure the resistance between the positive terminal and the high tension terminal **(see illustration)**. Compare your reading with the specified secondary coil resistance.

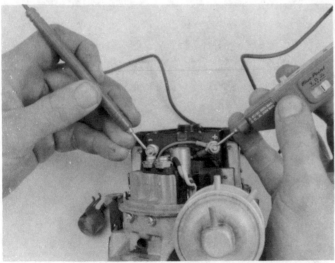

7.3a   **To check the primary resistance of the coil used on coil-in-cap models, measure between the positive and negative terminals**

7.3b   **To check the secondary resistance of the coil used on coil-in-cap models, measure between the positive terminal and the high tension terminal**

4   If either of the above tests yield resistance values outside the specified amount, replace the coil.

Remote mounted coil

Refer to illustrations 7.6a, 7.6b, 7.6c and 7.6d

5   Locate the coil in the engine compartment.
6   Using an ohmmeter, check the coil:
   a) Measure the resistance between the positive and negative terminals **(see illustrations)**. Compare your reading with the specified primary coil resistance.
   b) Detach the high tension lead from the coil. Measure the resistance between the positive terminal and high tension terminal **(see illustrations)**. Compare your reading with the specified secondary coil resistance.

7   If either of the above tests yield resistance values outside the specified resistance, replace the coil.

Replacement

Remote mounted coil

8   Label and remove the coil terminal connector or nuts and wires.
9   On 1988 models, unplug the connector to the igniter.
10   Remove the coil bracket bolts.
11   On 1988 models, separate the coil and the igniter, then attach the new coil to the old igniter.
12   Installation is the reverse of removal.

Coil in cap

Refer to illustrations 7.16 and 7.17

13   Detach the cable from the negative terminal of the battery.
14   Remove the distributor (see Section 8).
15   Remove the coil dust cover.

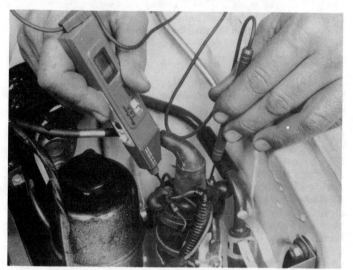

7.6a   To check the primary resistance of the coil used with the 1988 DOHC engine (VIN code 5), measure between the positive and negative terminals as shown

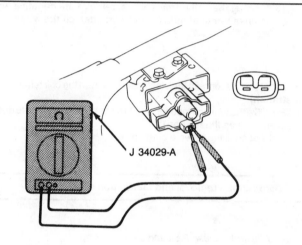

7.6b   To check the primary resistance of the coil used with the 1990 DOHC engine (VIN code 5), measure between the positive and negative terminals as shown

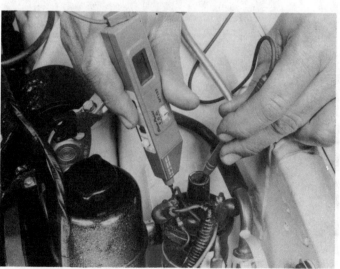

7.6c   To check the secondary resistance of the coil used with the 1988 DOHC engine (VIN code 5), measure between the positive and high-tension terminals

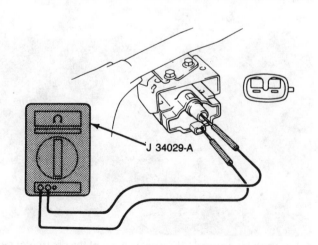

7.6d   To check the secondary resistance of the coil used with the 1990 DOHC engine (VIN code 5), measure between the positive and high tension terminals

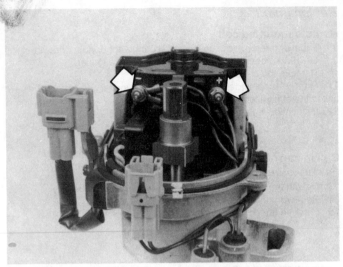

7.16   Label the coil primary wires, remove the negative and positive terminal nuts (arrows) and detach the wires

7.17   Remove the four coil mounting screws to separate the coil from the distributor assembly

16   Label and disconnect the electrical wires from the coil terminals **(see illustration)**.
17   Remove the four coil mounting bolts and separate it from the distributor assembly **(see illustration)**.
18   Installation is the reverse of removal.

8   Distributor – removal and installation

Removal

Refer to illustrations 8.4, 8.6a and 8.6b
1   Detach the cable from the negative battery terminal.
2   Unplug the electrical connectors from the distributor.

3   If equipped, detach the vacuum hose(s) from the advance unit.
4   Look for a raised "1" on the distributor cap **(see illustration)**. This marks the location for the number one cylinder spark plug wire terminal. If the cap does not have a mark for the number one terminal, locate the number one spark plug and trace the wire back to the terminal on the cap.
5   Remove the distributor cap (see Chapter 1) and turn the engine over until the rotor is pointing toward the number one spark plug terminal (see locating TDC procedure in Chapter 2).
6   Make a mark on the edge of the distributor base directly below the rotor tip and in line with it. Also, mark the distributor base and the engine block to ensure that the distributor is installed correctly **(see illustrations)**.
7   Remove the distributor hold down bolt(s), then pull the distributor straight out to remove it. **Caution:** *DO NOT turn the crankshaft while the distributor is out of the engine, or the alignment marks will be useless.*

8.4   Look for a raised "1" (arrow) on top of the distributor cap to find the number one spark plug terminal (if there is no raised "1" indicating the number one terminal, trace the plug lead from the number one spark plug back to the terminal)

8.6a   Use a permanent felt-tip pen or scribe to mark the edge of the distributor housing (arrow) immediately below the rotor tip to ensure the rotor is pointing in the same direction when the distributor is reinstalled

8.6b   Make another mark across one of the distributor adjustment bolt flanges and the cylinder head (arrow) to ensure the distributor is aligned correctly when it's reinstalled

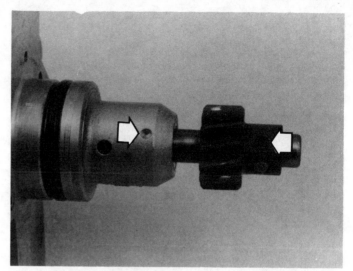

8.9a   On SOHC engines, align the protrusion on the distributor housing with the one on the spiral gear before installing the distributor

Installation

Refer to illustrations 8.9a, 8.9b and 8.10

Note: *If the crankshaft has been moved while the distributor is out, locate Top Dead Center (TDC) for the number one piston (see Chapter 2) and position the distributor and the rotor accordingly.*

8   Insert the distributor into the engine in exactly the same relationship to the block that it was in when removed.

9   On models with gear driven distributors, align the dimples on the driven gear and distributor housing **(see illustrations)**. To mesh the helical gears on the camshaft and the distributor, it may be necessary to turn the rotor slightly.

10   On models with lug driven distributors, align the distributor match marks **(see illustration)**.

11   If the distributor does not seat completely, recheck the alignment marks between the distributor base and the block to verify that the distributor is in the same position it was in before removal. Also check the rotor to see if it's aligned with the mark you made on the edge of the distributor base.

12   Loosely install the distributor hold-down bolt(s).

13   Installation is the reverse of removal.

14   Check the ignition timing (see Section 9) and tighten the distributor hold down bolt securely.

9   Ignition timing – check and adjustment

Note: *The following ignition timing procedure should apply to all vehicles covered by this manual. However, if the procedure specified on the VECI label of your vehicle differs from this one, use the one contained on the VECI label.*

1   Warm up the engine and allow it to reach its normal operating temperature.

2   Hook up a timing light in accordance with the manufacturer's instructions.

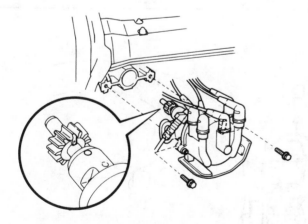

8.9b   On the DOHC engine (VIN code 5), align the protrusion on the distributor housing with the one on the spiral gear before installing the distributor

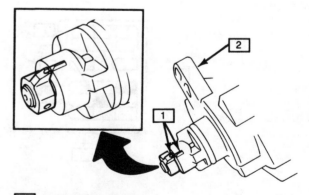

| 1 | ALIGNMENT MARKS |
| 2 | DISTRIBUTOR HOUSING |

8.10   On the DOHC engine (VIN code 6), the mark on the lug and the protrusion on the distributor housing must be in alignment before installing the distributor

9.4   Typical SOHC engine ignition timing marks

4A-LC (SOHC) engine

Refer to illustration 9.4

3   Detach the vacuum hose(s) from the vacuum advance diaphragm on the distributor.

4   Locate the timing marks on the timing cover and crankshaft pulley **(see illustration)**.

5   Using the timing light, check the ignition timing and compare it to the specified timing on the VECI label.

6   If necessary, loosen the distributor hold-down bolts and turn the distributor slightly to align the timing marks.

7   Recheck the timing to make sure that the distributor did not move when the bolts were tightened.

8   Reattach the vacuum hose(s) to the vacuum advance diaphragm.

9   Set the engine idle speed (see Chapter 1).

10   Recheck the ignition timing and compare it to the specified timing. If the ignition timing deviates from the specified value, repeat the timing procedure.

1988 4A-GE (DOHC) engine (VIN code 5)

Refer to illustrations 9.11 and 9.13

11   Locate the check engine connector near the windshield wiper motor. Using a jumper wire, bridge the terminals **(see illustration)**.

12   Set the engine idle speed (see Chapter 1).

13   Using a timing light, set the timing to specifications with the engine idling and the transmission in neutral. If necessary, loosen the distributor hold down bolt and turn it until the marks are aligned. Recheck the timing after tightening the distributor **(see illustration)**.

14   Remove the jumper wire from the connector.

15   Recheck the timing with the engine idling and the transmission in neutral. Models with automatic transmissions should show more than 16-degrees BTDC and models with manual transmissions should show more than 12-degrees BTDC. If necessary, repeat the timing procedure.

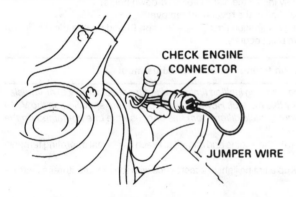

9.11   On 1988 DOHC engine models (VIN code 5), use a jumper wire to bridge both terminals

9.13   Typical DOHC engine (VIN code 5) timing marks

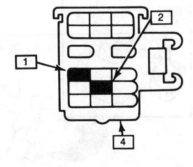

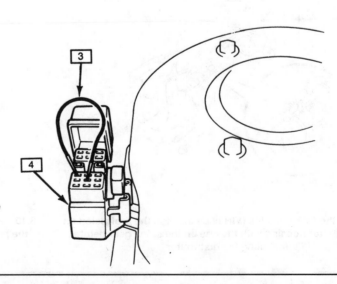

9.18   On DOHC engine (VIN code 6) models, bridge terminals T and E1 of the diagnostic connector

1	E1 terminal	3	Jumper wire
2	T terminal	4	Diagnostic connector

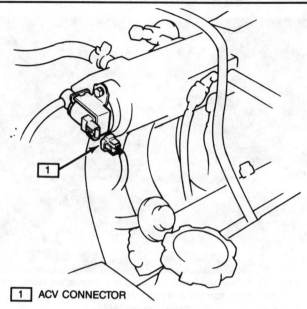

1 ACV CONNECTOR

9.21   Unplug the Air Control Valve (ACV) connector

1989 and 1990 4A-FE (DOHC) engine (VIN code 6)

Refer to illustrations 9.18 and 9.21

16   Set the engine idle speed (see Chapter 1).
17   With the ignition switch off, connect a timing light in accordance with manufactures instructions.
18   Locate the diagnostic connector and insert a jumper wire between E1 and T terminals **(see illustration)**.
19   Locate the timing marks on the timing cover and the crankshaft pulley.
20   Start the engine and aim the timing light at the mark. If necessary, loosen the distributor and slowly turn it until the timing marks indicates specified value from the VECI label. Tighten the hold down bolt and recheck the timing.
21   Remove the jumper wire from the diagnostic connector, then unplug the Air Control Valve (ACV) connector **(see illustration)**.
22   Recheck the timing and it should be 10-degrees BTDC.

23   Turn the engine off, reconnect the ACV connector and remove the timing light.

1990 4A-GE (DOHC) engine (VIN code 5)

24   Set the engine idle speed (see Chapter 1).
25   With the ignition switch off, connect a timing light in accordance with manufacturer's instructions.
26   Locate the diagnostic connector and insert a jumper wire between E1 and T terminals **(see illustration 9.18).**
27   Locate the the timing marks on the timing cover and the crankshaft pulley.
28   Start the engine and aim the timing light at the mark. It should be 10-degrees BTDC. If necessary, loosen the distributor and slowly align the marks. Tighten the distributor and recheck the timing.
29   Turn the engine off, remove the jumper wire and the timing light.

---

10   Vacuum advance unit – check and replacement

Check

Refer to illustration 10.4

1   Detach the negative cable of the battery.
2   Remove the distributor cap (see Chapter 1).
3   Disconnect the vacuum hoses from the vacuum advance unit and, using a T-fitting and two hoses, connect a vacuum pump to both diaphragms.
4   Apply vacuum and verify that the vacuum advancer moves **(see illustration)**.
5   If the vacuum advancer does not work, replace it.

Replacement

Refer to illustration 10.10

6   Remove the distributor (see Section 8).
7   Carefully clamp the distributor in a bench vise. Pad the jaws of the vise to avoid damage to the housing. Do not overtighten the vise – the distributor housing is an aluminum casting and will crack if squeezed too hard.
8   Pull the rotor off the shaft (see Chapter 1).
9   Remove the vacuum unit mounting screws.
10   Remove the controller link from the pin on the breaker base **(see illustration)**, then detach the vacuum unit.
11   Installation is the reverse of removal.

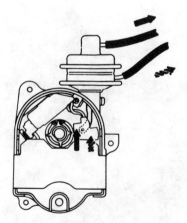

10.4   To check the vacuum advance unit, connect a vacuum pump to both diaphragms, apply vacuum and verify that the vacuum advancer moves

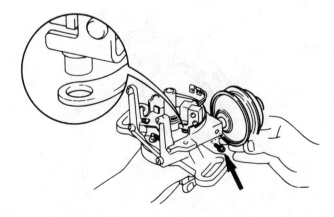

10.10   To detach the vacuum advance unit from the distributor, remove the small mounting screw (arrow) and disconnect the advancer link rod from the breaker plate

11.4   Label and disconnect the wires (arrows), then remove the two mounting screws (arrows)

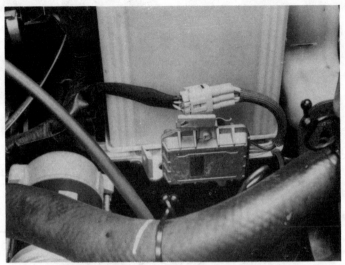

11.6   To detach the igniter, unplug the connector, remove the mounting screws and separate the igniter from the mounting bracket

11   Igniter – replacement

1   Detach the cable from the negative terminal of the battery.

Distributor mounted igniter

Refer to illustration 11.4

2   Remove the distributor (see Section 8).
3   Remove the rotor and the igniter dust cover.
4   Label and disconnect the wires from the igniter, then remove the two igniter mounting screws and detach it from the distributor **(see illustration)**.
5   Installation is the reverse of removal.

Remote mounted igniter

Refer to illustration 11.6

Note: *See Chapter 6 for component location charts.*

6   Unplug the electrical connector from the igniter **(see illustration)**.
7   Remove the mounting screws from the igniter and detach it from its mounting bracket.
8   Installation is the reverse of removal.

12   Centrifugal advance mechanism – check and component replacement

1   Detach the cable from the negative terminal of the battery.
2   Remove the distributor cap (see Chapter 1).

Check

Refer to illustration 12.3

3   Turn the rotor clockwise, release it and verify that the rotor returns slightly counterclockwise **(see illustration)**.
4   Verify that the rotor is not excessively loose.
5   If the centrifugal advance does not work as described, repair or replace as necessary.

Replacement

Refer to illustrations 12.9, 12.11, 12.13a, 12.13b, 12.14 and 12.16

6   Remove the distributor (see Section 8).
7   Remove the coil (see Section 7).
8   Remove the igniter (see Section 11).
9   Remove the signal rotor **(see illustration)**.

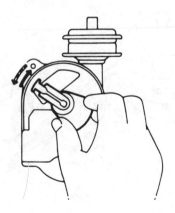

12.3   To check the centrifugal advance unit, turn the rotor and shaft clockwise, release it and verify that the rotor returns slightly in a counterclockwise direction

12.9   Carefully pry off the signal rotor with a screwdriver – the rotor is retained by a spring clip – be careful not to lose it

12.11   To detach the breaker plate, remove the two retaining
screws (arrows)

12.13a   Mark the governor shaft and the stopper (arrows) to
ensure correct installation

10   Remove the vacuum advance unit (see Section 10).
11   Remove the breaker plate assembly **(see illustration)**.
12   Mark the governor springs to insure their proper installation. Using a
pair of needle-nose pliers, remove the two governor springs.
13   Mark the governor shaft and the stopper to insure their proper installation **(see illustration)**. Remove the grease stopper and the screw at the
end of the governor shaft **(see illustration)**, then remove the governor
shaft.
14   Using a small screwdriver, remove the C-clips and pull out the two
governor weights **(see illustration)**.
15   Apply a very small amount of lightweight grease to the pivot pins, then
install the governor weights.
16   Inspect the breaker plate **(see illustration)**.
17   Reassembly is the reverse of removal.

13   Air gap – check

Refer to illustrations 13.3a, 13.3b and 13.3c
1   Detach the cable from the negative terminal of the battery.

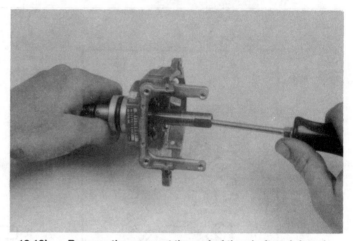

12.13b   Remove the screw at the end of the shaft and detach
the shaft

12.14   Using a small screwdriver, pop off the governor weight
E-clips and remove the governor weights

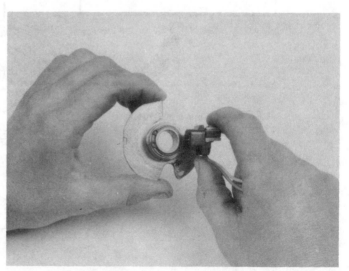

12.16   To inspect the breaker plate, turn it and make sure there's
a slight drag – if strong resistance or binding is felt, replace the
breaker plate and the pick-up coil assembly

13.3a   On SOHC engines, measure the air gap between the signal rotor and pick-up coil projection – if the gap is not as specified, replace the distributor

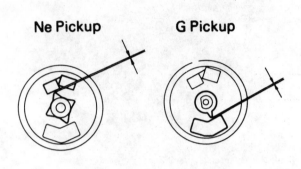

13.3b   On DOHC engine (VIN code 6) models, use a feeler gauge to measure the air gap between the signal rotor and pick-up coil projection – if the gap is not as specified, replace the distributor

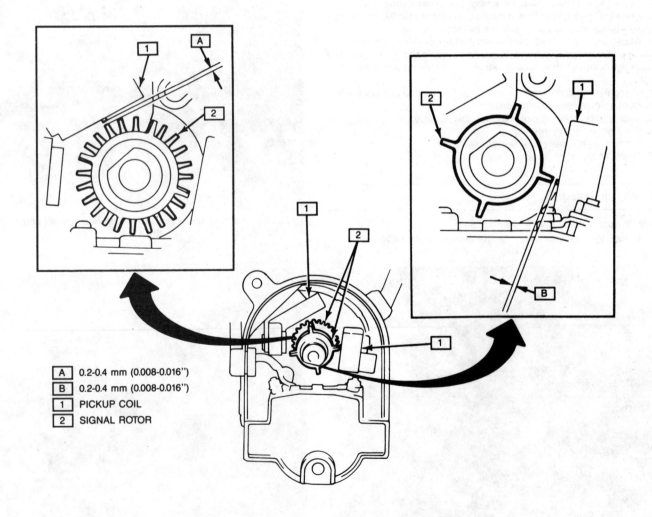

A	0.2-0.4 mm (0.008-0.016")
B	0.2-0.4 mm (0.008-0.016")
1	PICKUP COIL
2	SIGNAL ROTOR

13.3c   On DOHC engine (VIN code 5) models, check the air gap between the signal rotor and pick-up coil – if the gap is not as specified, replace the distributor

2   Remove the distributor cap (see Chapter 1).

3   Using a feeler gauge, measure the gap between the signal rotor and the pick-up coil projection **(see illustrations)**. Compare your measurement to the specified air gap. If the air gap is not as specified, replace the distributor, as the air gap is not adjustable.

14   Charging system – general information and precautions

The charging system includes the alternator, an internal voltage regulator, a charge indicator, the battery, a fusible link and the wiring between all the components. The charging system supplies electrical power for the ignition system, the lights, the radio, etc. The alternator is driven by a drivebelt at the front (right end) of the engine.

The purpose of the voltage regulator is to limit the alternator's voltage to a preset value. This prevents power surges, circuit overloads, etc., during peak voltage output.

The fusible link is a short length of insulated wire integral with the engine compartment wiring harness. The link is several wire gauges smaller in diameter than the circuit it protects. Production fusible links and their identification flags are identified by the flag color. See Chapter 12 for additional information regarding fusible links.

The charging system doesn't ordinarily require periodic maintenance. However, the drivebelt, battery and wires and connections should be inspected at the intervals outlined in Chapter 1.

The dashboard warning light should come on when the ignition key is turned to Start, then should go off immediately. If it remains on, there is a malfunction in the charging system (see Section 13). Some vehicles are also equipped with a voltage gauge. If the voltage gauge indicates abnormally high or low voltage, check the charging system (see Section 13).

Be very careful when making electrical circuit connections to a vehicle equipped with an alternator and note the following:

a) When reconnecting wires to the alternator from the battery, be sure to note the polarity.

b) Before using arc welding equipment to repair any part of the vehicle, disconnect the wires from the alternator and the battery terminals.

c) Never start the engine with a battery charger connected.

d) Always disconnect both battery leads before using a battery charger.

e) The alternator is driven by an engine drivebelt which could cause serious injury if your hand, hair or clothes become entangled in it with the engine running.

f) Because the alternator is connected directly to the battery, it could arc or cause a fire if overloaded or shorted out.

g) Wrap a plastic bag over the alternator and secure it with rubber bands before steam cleaning the engine.

15   Charging system – check

Refer to illustrations 15.7, 15.8a and 15.8b

1   If a malfunction occurs in the charging circuit, don't automatically assume that the alternator is causing the problem. First check the following items:

a) Check the drivebelt tension and its condition. Replace it if worn or deteriorated.

b) Make sure the alternator mounting and adjustment bolts are tight.

c) Inspect the alternator wiring harness and the connectors at the alternator and voltage regulator. They must be in good condition and tight.

d) Check the fusible link (if equipped) located between the starter solenoid and the alternator. If it's burned, determine the cause, repair the circuit and replace the link (the vehicle won't start and/or the accessories won't work if the fusible link blows).

e) Start the engine and check the alternator for abnormal noises (a shrieking or squealing sound indicates a bad bushing).

f) Check the specific gravity of the battery electrolyte. If it's low, charge the battery (doesn't apply to maintenance free batteries).

g) Make suer that the battery is fully charged (one bad cell in a battery can cause overcharging by the alternator).

h) Disconnect the battery cables (negative first, then positive). Inspect the battery posts and the cable clamps for corrosion. Clean them thoroughly if necessary (see Section 4 and Chapter 1). Reconnect the cable to the negative terminal.

i) With the key off, insert a test light between the negative battery post and the disconnected negative cable clamp.

   1) If the test light does not come on, reattach the clamp and proceed to the next step.

   2) If the test light comes on, there is a short in the electrical system of the vehicle. The short must be repaired before the charging system can be checked.

   3) Disconnect the alternator wiring harness.

      (a) If the light goes out, the alternator is bad.

      (b) If the light stays on, pull each fuse until the light goes out (this will tell you which component is shorted).

2   Using a voltmeter, check the battery voltage with the engine off. It should be approximately 12 volts.

3   Start the engine and check the battery voltage again. It should now be approximately 13.5 to 15.1 volts.

4   Turn on the headlights. The voltage should drop and then come back up, if the charging system is working properly.

5   If the voltage reading is greater than the specified charging voltage, replace the voltage regulator (see Section 15).

6   If the voltmeter reading is less than standard voltage, check the regulator and alternator as follows.

7   Ground terminal F, start the engine, check the voltage at terminal B **(see illustration)** and compare your reading to the standard voltage.

a) If the voltmeter reading is greater than standard voltage, replace the regulator.

b) If the voltmeter reading is less than standard voltage, check the alternator (or have it checked by a dealer service department if you do not have an ammeter).

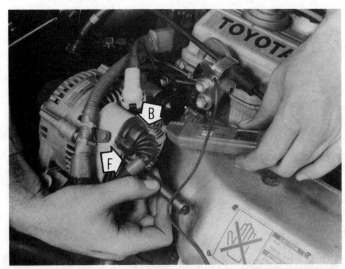

15.7   If the alternator is putting out less than standard voltage, ground terminal F, start the engine and check the voltage at terminal B – if the reading is greater than standard voltage, replace the regulator; if the reading is less than standard, check the alternator or have it checked by a dealer service department or service station

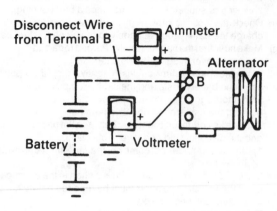

15.8a   Hook up an ammeter as shown to check alternator output

15.8b   An inductive type ammeter like this one, which is available at most auto parts stores, is much cheaper than a professional ammeter, but it's accurate enough for a quick check of the charging system and is quite easy to use: Simply place it on the alternator output lead, start the engine and check charging amperage

8   If you have an ammeter, hook it up to the charging system as shown **(see illustration)**. If you don't have a professional ammeter, you can also use an inductive-type current indicator **(see illustration)**. This device is inexpensive, readily available at auto parts stores and accurate enough to perform simple amperage checks like the following test.

9   With the engine running at 2000 rpm, turn on the high beam headlights, turn the heater blower switch to the HI position, check the reading on the ammeter and compare your reading to the standard amperage.

10   If the ammeter reading is less than standard amperage, repair or replace the alternator.

16   Alternator – removal and installation

Refer to illustrations 16.2 and 16.3

1   Detach the cable from the negative terminal of the battery.

2   Detach the electrical connectors from the alternator **(see illustration)**.

3   Loosen the alternator adjustment and pivot bolts **(see illustration)** and detach the drivebelt.

4   Remove the adjustment and pivot bolts and separate the alternator from the engine.

16.2   Before removing the alternator, detach the cable from the negative terminal of the battery, then unplug or disconnect the electrical connectors (arrows) from the alternator – to remove the drivebelt, loosen the adjustment bolts (arrows)

16.3   To remove the alternator, loosen the adjustment bolts shown on the other side of the adjustment bracket in the previous illustration, then remove the adjustment bolt and pivot bolt (arrows) shown here

5 If you are replacing the alternator, take the old alternator with you when purchasing a replacement unit. Make sure that the new/rebuilt unit is identical to the old alternator. Look at the terminals – they should be the same in number, size and locations as the terminals on the old alternator. Finally, look at the identification markings – they will be stamped in the housing or printed on a tag or plaque affixed to the housing. Make sure that these numbers are the same on both alternators.

6 Many new/rebuilt alternators do not have a pulley installed, so you may have to switch the pulley from the old unit to the new/rebuilt one. When buying an alternator, find out the shop's policy regarding installation of pulleys – some shops will perform this service free of charge.

7 Installation is the reverse of removal.

8 After the alternator is installed, adjust the drivebelt tension (see Chapter 1).

9 Check the charging voltage to verify proper operation of the alternator (see Section 15).

17 Voltage regulator and alternator brushes – replacement

Refer to illustrations 17.2a, 17.2b, 17.3, 17.4a, 17.4b, 17.5 and 17.7

1 Remove the alternator (see Section 16) and place it on a clean workbench.

2 Remove the three rear cover nuts, the nut and terminal insulator and the rear cover **(see illustrations)**.

3 Remove the five voltage regulator and brush holder mounting screws **(see illustration)**.

4 Remove the brush holder and the regulator from the rear end frame **(see illustrations)**. If you are only replacing the regulator, proceed to Step 8, install the new unit, reassemble the alternator and install it on the engine (see Section 16). If you are going to replace the brushes, proceed with the next Step.

17.2a Remove the three nuts from the rear cover

17.2b Take the nut, washer and insulator off terminal B and remove the alternator end cover

17.3 Once the rear cover is removed, remove the five screws (arrows) that retain the voltage regulator and brush holder

17.4a Remove the brush holder

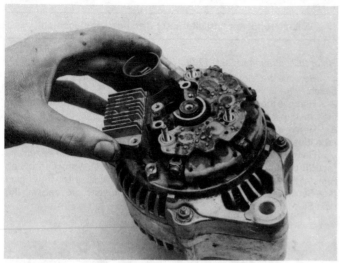

17.4b   Remove the regulator

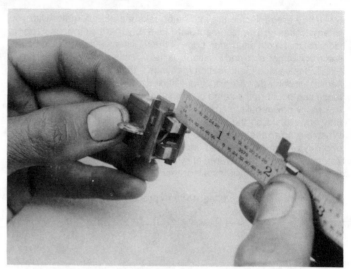

17.5   Measure the exposed length of the brushes and compare your measurements to the specified minimum length to determine whether they should be replaced

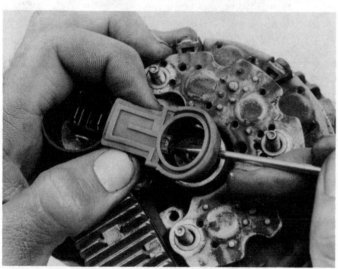

17.7   To facilitate installation of the brush holder, depress each brush with a small screwdriver to clear the shaft

5   Measure the exposed length of each brush **(see illustration)** and compare it to the specified minimum length. If the length of either brush is less than the specified minimum, replace the brushes.

6   Make sure that each brush moves smoothly in the brush holder.

7   Install the brush holder by depressing each brush with a small screwdriver to clear the shaft **(see illustration)**.

8   Install the voltage regulator and brush holder screws into the rear frame.

9   Install the rear cover and tighten the three nuts securely.

10   Install the terminal insulator and tighten it with the nut.

11   Install the alternator (see Section 16).

18   Starting system – general information and precautions

The sole function of the starting system is to turn over the engine quickly enough to allow it to start.

The starting system consists of the battery, the starter motor, the starter solenoid and the wires connecting them. The solenoid is mounted directly on the starter motor.

The solenoid/starter motor assembly is installed on the lower part of the engine, next to the transaxle bellhousing.

When the ignition key is turned to the Start position, the starter solenoid is actuated through the starter control circuit. The starter solenoid then connects the battery to the starter. The battery supplies the electrical energy to the starter motor, which does the actual work of cranking the engine.

The starter motor on a vehicle equipped with a manual transaxle can be operated only when the clutch pedal is depressed; the starter on a vehicle equipped with an automatic transaxle can be operated only when the transaxle selector lever is in Park or Neutral.

Always observe the following precautions when working on the starting system:

a) Excessive cranking of the starter motor can overheat it and cause serious damage. Never operate the starter motor for more than 15 seconds at a time without pausing to allow it to cool for at least two minutes.

b) The starter is connected directly to the battery and could arc or cause a fire if mishandled, overloaded or shorted out.

c) Always detach the cable from the negative terminal of the battery before working on the starting system.

19   Starter motor – testing in vehicle

Note: *Before diagnosing starter problems, make sure that the battery is fully charged.*

1   If the starter motor does not turn at all when the switch is operated, make sure that the shift lever is in Neutral or Park (automatic transaxle) or that the clutch pedal is depressed (manual transaxle).

2   Make sure that the battery is charged and that all cables, both at the battery and starter solenoid terminals, are clean and secure.

20.2   To remove the starter motor/solenoid assembly, detach the cable from the negative terminal of the battery, then disconnect the electrical connectors (arrows) from the starter/solenoid assembly

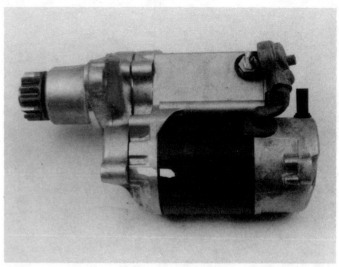

21.2   Before disassembling the starter motor, solenoid and gear reduction assembly, make an alignment mark across the starter motor and gear reduction assembly

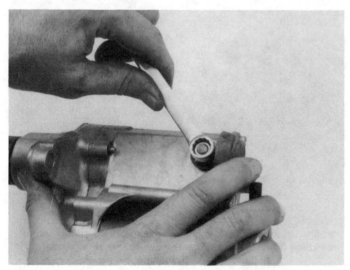

21.3   To disconnect the strap that connects the starter to the solenoid, remove this nut

3   If the starter motor spins but the engine is not cranking, the overrunning clutch in the starter motor is slipping and the starter motor must be replaced.

4   If, when the switch is actuated, the starter motor does not operate at all but the solenoid clicks, then the problem lies with either the battery, the main solenoid contacts or the starter motor itself (or the engine is seized).

5   If the solenoid plunger cannot be heard when the switch is actuated, the battery is bad, the fusible link is burned (the circuit is open) or the solenoid itself is defective.

6   To check the solenoid, connect a jumper lead between the battery (+) and the ignition switch terminal (the small terminal) on the solenoid. If the starter motor now operates, the solenoid is OK and the problem is in the ignition switch, Neutral start switch or in the wiring.

7   If the starter motor still does not operate, remove the starter/solenoid assembly for disassembly, testing and repair.

8   If the starter motor cranks the engine at an abnormally slow speed, first make sure that the battery is charged and that all terminal connections

are tight. If the engine is partially seized, or has the wrong viscosity oil in it, it will crank slowly.

9   Run the engine until normal operating temperature is reached, then disconnect the coil wire from the distributor cap and ground it on the engine.

10   Connect a voltmeter positive lead to the battery positive post and connect the negative lead to the negative post.

11   Crank the engine and take the voltmeter readings as soon as a steady figure is indicated. Do not allow the starter motor to turn for more than 15 seconds at a time. A reading of nine volts or more, with the starter motor turning at normal cranking speed, is normal. If the reading is nine volts or more but the cranking speed is slow, the motor is faulty. If the reading is less than nine volts and the cranking speed is slow, the solenoid contacts are probably burned, the starter motor is bad, the battery is discharged or there is a bad connection.

20   Starter motor – removal and installation

Refer to illustration 20.2

1   Detach the cable from the negative terminal of the battery.

2   Detach the electrical connectors from the starter/solenoid assembly **(see illustration)**.

3   Remove the starter motor mounting bolts. On some models it may be necessary to remove the shift cable bracket to gain access to the mounting bolts (see Chapter 7). Remove the starter.

4   Installation is the reverse of removal.

21   Starter solenoid – removal and installation

Refer to illustrations 21.2, 21.3, 21.4, 21.5, 21.6a and 21.6b

1   Remove the starter motor (see Section 20).

2   Scribe or paint a mark across the starter motor and gear reduction assembly **(see illustration)**.

3   Disconnect the strap from the solenoid to the starter motor terminal **(see illustration)**.

21.4   To detach the solenoid from the starter motor, remove the screws (arrows) which secure the gear reduction assembly to the solenoid, . . .

21.5   . . . then remove the through-bolts (arrows) which secure the starter motor

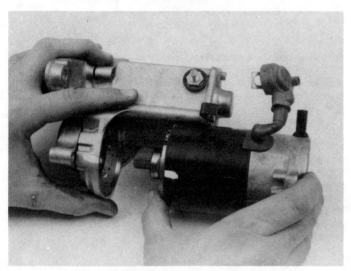

21.6a   Separate the starter from the gear reduction assembly, . . .

21.6b   . . . then separate the solenoid (note the return spring protruding from the solenoid assembly – make sure this spring is installed before reattaching the solenoid)

4   Remove the screws **(see illustration)** which secure the gear reduction assembly to the solenoid.
5   Remove the through-bolts **(see illustration)** which secure the starter motor to the gear reduction assembly.
6   Separate the motor from the gear reduction and solenoid assembly

then remove the solenoid from the gear reduction assembly **(see illustrations)**.
7   Installation is the reverse of removal. Be sure to align the paint or scribe mark.

Chapter 6   Emissions control systems

Contents

1   General information

Refer to illustrations 1.1a, 1.1b, 1.1c, 1.1d, 1.1e, 1.1f, 1.1g, 1.1h, 1.1i, 1.1j, 1.1k, 1.1l, 1.1m and 1.6

To minimize pollution of the atmosphere from incompletely burned and evaporating gases and to maintain good driveability and fuel economy, a number of emission control systems are used on these vehicles **(see illustrations)**. They include the:

Positive Crankcase Ventilation (PCV) system, which reduces hydrocarbons from crankcase blowby
Evaporative Emission Control (EVAP) system, which reduces evaporative hydrocarbons
Feedback carburetor system (some models), which reduces hydrocarbons and carbon monoxide by regulating the operating conditions of the engine
Exhaust Gas Recirculation (EGR) system, which reduces oxides of nitrogen emissions
Catalytic converter, which reduces hydrocarbons, carbon monoxide and oxides of nitrogen
Electronic Fuel Injection (EFI) system (some models), which reduces all exhaust emissions by regulating the operating conditions of the engine

The sections in this chapter include general descriptions, checking procedures within the scope of the home mechanic and component replacement procedures (when possible) for each of the systems listed above.

Before assuming an emissions control system is malfunctioning, check the fuel and ignition systems carefully (see Chapters 4 and 5). The diagnosis of some emission control devices requires specialized tools, equipment and training. If checking and servicing become too difficult or if a procedure is beyond the scope of your skills, consult your dealer service department.

This doesn't mean, however, that emission control systems are particularly difficult to maintain and repair. You can quickly and easily perform many checks and do most of the regular maintenance at home with common tune-up and hand tools. **Note:** *The most frequent cause of emissions problems is simply a loose or broken electrical connector or vacuum hose, so always check the electrical connectors and vacuum hoses first.*

Pay close attention to any special precautions outlined in this chapter. It should be noted that the illustrations of the various systems may not exactly match the system installed on your vehicle because of changes made by the manufacturer during production or from year to-year.

The Vehicle Emissions Control Information (VECI) label is located in the engine compartment **(see illustration)**. This label contains important emissions specifications and setting procedures, and a vacuum hose schematic with emissions components identified. When servicing the engine or emissions systems, the VECI label in your particular vehicle should always be checked for up-to-date information.

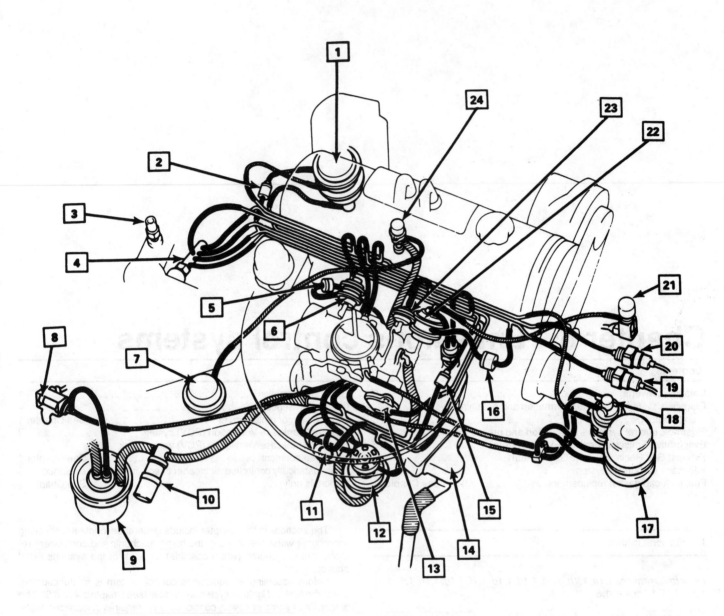

1.1a   Typical emissions control system component locations (1985 Federal models)

1	Distributor	13	Auxiliary acceleration pump
2	Check valve	14	Air suction valve
3	Thermo switch	15	Check valve
4	Thermostatic vacuum switching valve	16	Delay valve
5	Jet	17	Electric air bleed control valve
6	Choke	18	High altitude compensation valve
7	Hot air intake diaphragm	19	Vacuum switch (A)
8	Vacuum switching valve	20	Vacuum switch (B)
9	Charcoal canister	21	Vacuum switching valve
10	Outer vent control valve	22	Throttle positioner
11	EGR valve	23	Choke opener
12	EGR vacuum modulator	24	Hot idle compensator

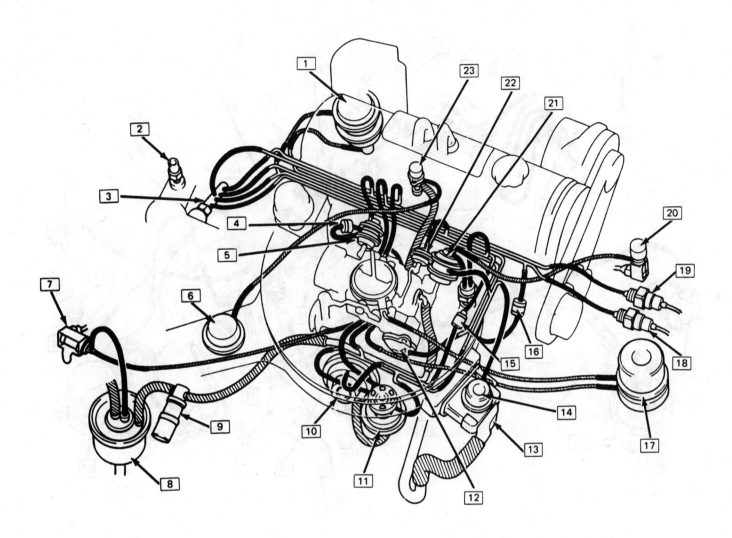

1.1b   Typical emissions control system component locations (1985 California models)

1	Distributor	13	Air suction valve (reed valve)
2	Thermo switch	14	Air suction valve (shut-off valve)
3	Thermostatic vacuum switching valve	15	Check valve
4	Jet	16	Delay valve
5	Choke breaker	17	Electric air bleed control valve
6	Hot air intake diaphragm	18	Vacuum switch (A)
7	Vacuum switching valve	19	Vacuum switch (B)
8	Charcoal canister	20	Vacuum switching valve
9	Outer vent control valve	21	Throttle positioner
10	EGR valve	22	Choke opener
11	EGR vacuum modulator	23	Hot idle compensator
12	Auxiliary acceleration pump		

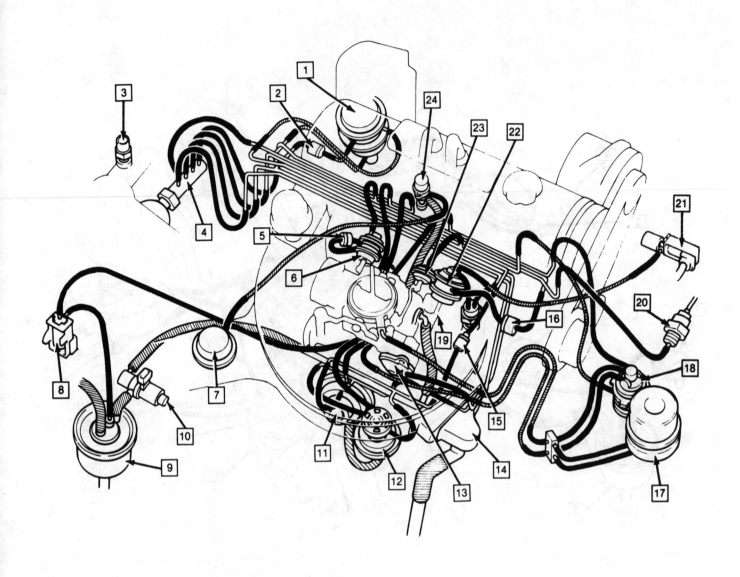

1.1c   Typical emissions control system component locations (1986 Federal models)

1	Distributor	13	Auxiliary acceleration pump
2	Check valve	14	Air suction valve
3	Thermo switch	15	Check valve
4	Thermostatic vacuum switching valve	16	Delay valve
5	Jet	17	Electric air bleed control
6	Choke breaker	18	High altitude compensation valve
7	Hot air intake diaphragm	19	Throttle position switch
8	Vacuum switching valve	20	Vacuum switch
9	Charcoal canister	21	Vacuum switching valve
10	Outer vent control valve	22	Throttle positioner
11	EGR valve	23	Choke opener
12	EGR vacuum modulator	24	Hot idle compensator

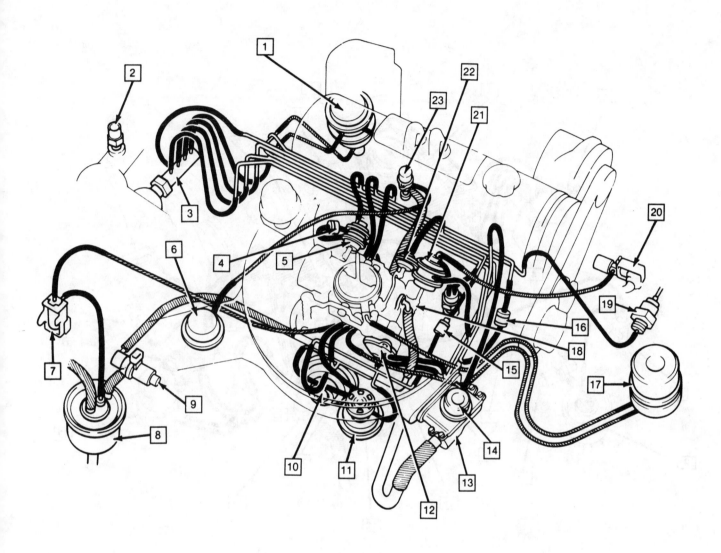

1.1d   Typical emissions control system component locations (1986 California models)

1	Distributor	13	Air suction valve (reed valve)
2	Thermo switch	14	Air suction valve (shut-off valve)
3	Thermostatic vacuum switching valve	15	Check valve
4	Jet	16	Delay valve
5	Choke breaker	17	Electric air bleed control valve
6	Hot air intake diaphragm	18	Throttle position switch
7	Vacuum switching valve	19	Vacuum switch
8	Charcoal canister	20	Vacuum switching valve
9	Outer vent control valve	21	Throttle positioner
10	EGR valve	22	Choke opener
11	EGR vacuum modulator	23	Hot idle compensator
12	Auxiliary acceleration pump		

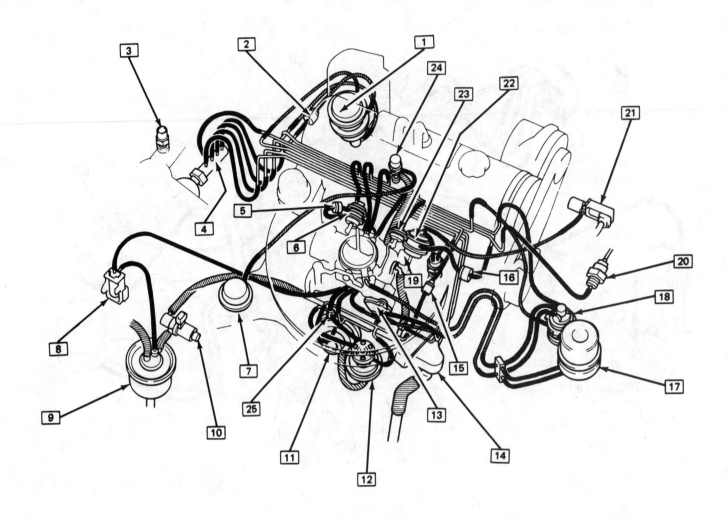

1.1e   Typical emissions control system component locations (1987 Federal models)

1 Distributor	14 Air suction valve
2 Check valve	15 Check valve
3 Thermo switch	16 Delay valve
4 Thermostatic vacuum switching valve	17 Electric air bleed control valve
5 Jet	18 High altitude compensation valve
6 Choke breaker	19 Throttle position switch
7 Hot air intake diaphragm	20 Vacuum switch
8 Vacuum switching valve	21 Vacuum switching valve
9 Charcoal canister	22 Throttle positioner
10 Outer vent control valve	23 Choke opener
11 EGR valve	24 Hot idle compensator
12 EGR vacuum modulator	25 Jet
13 Auxiliary acceleration pump	

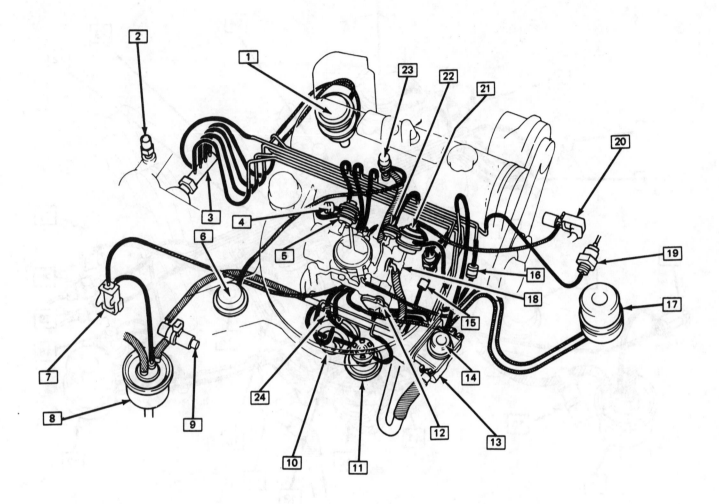

1.1f   Typical emissions control system component locations (1987 California models)

1	Distributor	13	Air suction valve (reed)
2	Thermo switch	14	Air suction valve (shut-off valve)
3	Thermostatic vacuum switching valve	15	Check valve
4	Jet	16	Delay valve
5	Choke breaker	17	Electric air bleed control valve
6	Hot air intake diaphragm	18	Throttle position switch
7	Vacuum switching valve	19	Vacuum switch
8	Charcoal canister	20	Vacuum switching valve
9	Outer vent control valve	21	Throttle positioner
10	EGR valve	22	Choke opener
11	EGR vacuum modulator	23	Hot idle compensator
12	Auxiliary acceleration pump	24	Jet

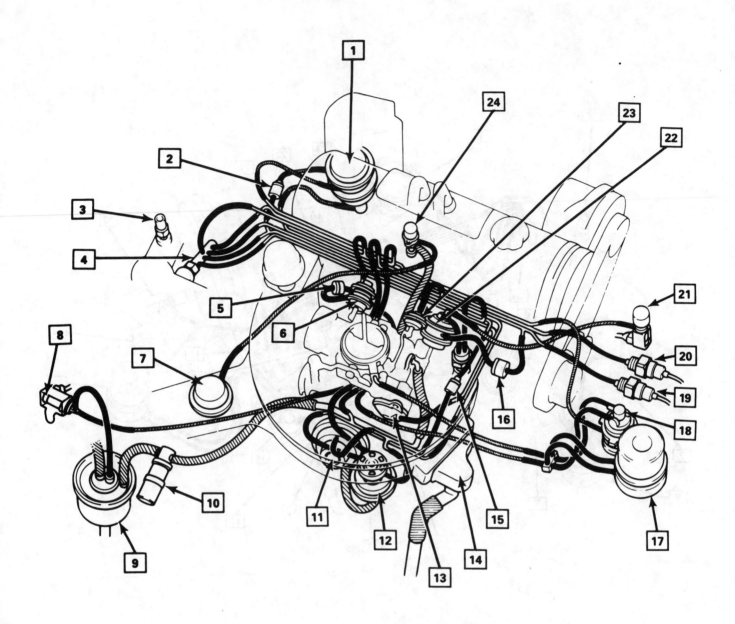

1.1g   Typical emissions control system component locations (1988 Federal manual transaxle models)

1	Distributor	13	Auxiliary acceleration pump
2	Check valve	14	Air suction valve
3	Thermo switch	15	Check valve
4	Thermostatic vacuum switching valve	16	Delay valve
5	Jet	17	Electric air bleed control valve
6	Choke breaker	18	High altitude compensation valve
7	Hot air intake diaphragm	19	Vacuum switch (A)
8	Vacuum switching valve	20	Vacuum switch (B)
9	Charcoal canister	21	Vacuum switching valve
10	Outer vent control valve	22	Throttle positioner
11	EGR valve	23	Choke opener
12	EGR vacuum modulator	24	Hot idle compensator

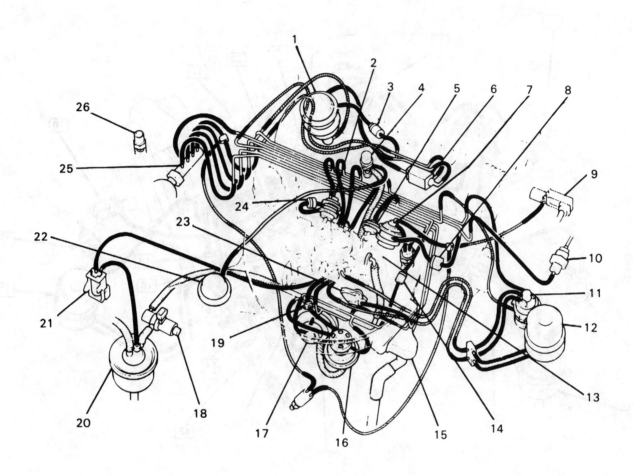

1.1h   Typical emissions control system component locations (1988 Federal and Canada automatic transaxle models)

1	Distributor	14	Check valve
2	CB	15	AS reed valve
3	Check valve	16	EGR vacuum modulator
4	HIC valve	17	EGR valve
5	Choke opener	18	Outer vent control valve
6	VSV	19	Jet
7	TP	20	Fuel vapor canister
8	VTV	21	VSV
9	VSV	22	HAI diaphragm
10	Vacuum switch	23	AAP
11	HAC valve	24	Jet
12	EBCV	25	TVSV
13	Throttle position switch	26	Thermo switch

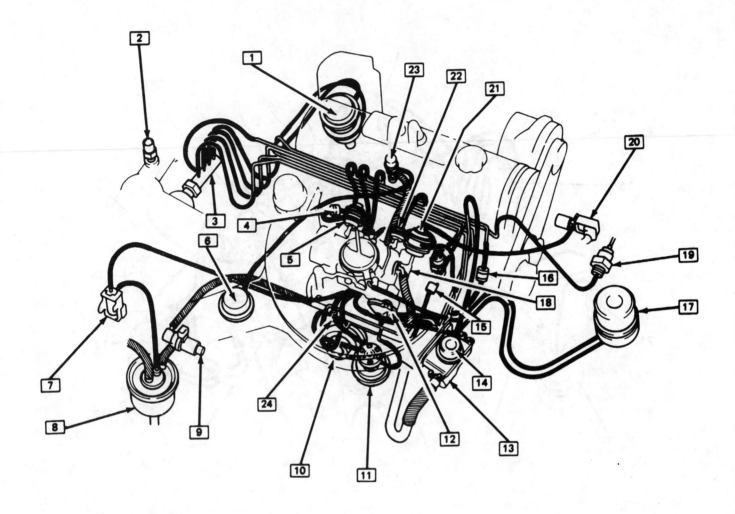

1.1i   Typical emissions control system component locations (1988 California manual transaxle models)

1 Distributor	13 Air suction valve (reed valve)
2 Thermo switch	14 Air suction valve (shut-off valve)
3 Thermostatic vacuum switching valve	15 Check valve
4 Jet	16 Delay valve
5 Choke breaker	17 Electric air bleed control valve
6 Hot air intake diaphragm	18 Throttle position switch
7 Vacuum switching valve	19 Vacuum switch
8 Fuel vapor canister	20 Vacuum switching valve
9 Outer vent control valve	21 Throttle positioner
10 EGR valve	22 Choke opener
11 EGR vacuum modulator	23 Hot idle compensator
12 Auxiliary acceleration pump	24 Jet

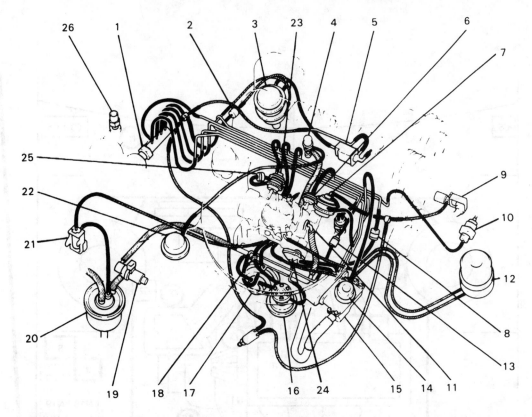

1.1j   Typical emissions control system component locations (1988 California automatic transaxle models)

1	TVSV	10	Vacuum switch	19	Outer vent control valve
2	Check valve	11	Throttle position switch	20	Fuel vapor canister
3	Distributor	12	EBCV	21	VSV
4	HIC valve	13	Check valve	22	HAI diaphragm
5	VSV	14	AS shut-off valve	23	CB
6	Choke opener	15	AS reed valve	24	AAP
7	TP	16	EGR vacuum modulator	25	Jet
8	VTV	17	EGR valve	26	Thermo switch
9	VSV	18	Jet		

1.1k   Typical emissions control system component locations – 1988 DOHC (VIN code 5) models

101   EGR vacuum modulator
102   Diaphragm (for T-VIS)
103   VSV
104   Vacuum tank
105   Exhaust oxygen sensor
106   Check valve
107   DP (W/VTV)
108   Fuel vapor canister
109   BVSV (for EGR)
110   EGR valve
111   BVSV (for EVAP)
112   EGR temp. switch (for Calif.)

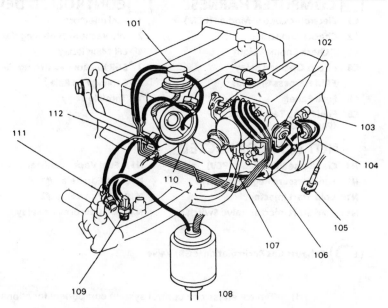

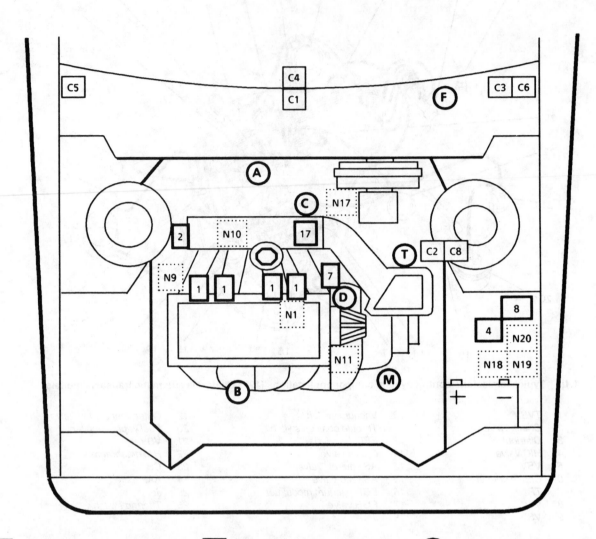

COMPUTER HARNESS

C1	Electronic Control Module (ECM)
C2	Check Connector
C3	"Check Engine" Light
C4	Circuit Opening Relay
C5	ECM Harness Grounds
C6	Fuse Panel
C8	Fuel Pump Test Connector (Part of C2)

NOT ECM CONNECTED

N1	Crankcase Vent Valve (PCV)	N17	Fuel Vapor Canister
N9	Fuel Pressure Regulator Valve	N18	A/C Fan Relay #1
N10	Cold Start Injector	N19	A/C Fan Relay #2
N11	Cold Start Injector Valve Switch	N20	A/C Compressor Relay

Exhaust Gas Recirculation (EGR) Valve

CONTROLLED DEVICES

1	Fuel Injectors
2	Idle Vacuum Switching Valve (VSV)
4	EFI Main Relay
7	*EGR Vacuum Switching Valve (VSV)
8	Cooling Fan Relay
17	Throttle Body

INFORMATION SENSORS

A	Manifold Absolute Pressure (MAP) Sensor
B	Oxygen (O$_2$) Sensor
C	Throttle Switch (TS)
D	Coolant Temperature Sensor (CTS)
F	Vehicle Speed Sensor (VSS)
M	Park/Neutral (P/N) Switch
T	Manifold Air Temperature (MAT) Sensor

* California Only

1.1l   Typical emissions control system component locations – 1989 and 1990 DOHC (VIN code 6) models

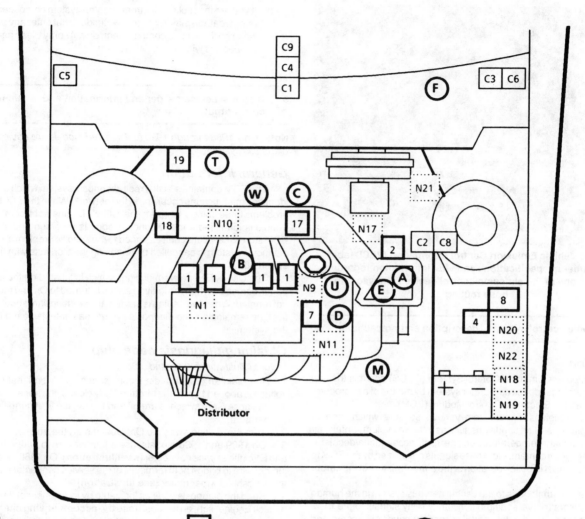

Distributor

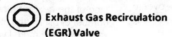

COMPUTER HARNESS

C1	Electronic Control Module (ECM)
C2	Check Connector
C3	"Check Engine" Light
C4	Circuit Opening Relay
C5	ECM Harness Grounds
C6	Fuse Panel
C8	Fuel Pump Test Connector (Part of C2)
C9	Electronic Controlled Transaxle (ECT)

NOT ECM CONNECTED

N1	Crankcase Vent Valve (PCV)
N9	Fuel Pressure Regulator Valve
N10	Cold Start Injector
N11	Cold Start Injector Valve Switch
N17	Fuel Vapor Canister
N18	A/C Fan Relay #1
N19	A/C Fan Relay #2
N20	A/C Compressor Relay
N21	A/C Actuator
N22	Cooling Fan Relay

CONTROLLED DEVICES

1	Fuel Injectors
2	Idle Up (VSV)
4	EFI Main Relay
7	EGR Vacuum Switching Valve (VSV)
17	Throttle Body
18	Fuel Pressure Regulator (VSV)
19	Distributor Igniter

Exhaust Gas Recirculation (EGR) Valve

INFORMATION SENSORS

A	Mass Air Flow Sensor (MAF)
• B	Oxygen (O_2) Sensor Heated
C	Throttle Position Sensor
D	Coolant Temperature Sensor (CTS)
E	Manifold Air Temperature (MAT) Part of (MAF)
F	Vehicle Speed Sensor (VSS)
M	Park/Neutral (P/N) Switch
T	*Sub Oxygen Sensor (After Exhaust Converter)
U	*EGR Temperature Sensor
W	Knock Sensor

• Located in exhaust pipe after exhaust manifold.
* California Only

1.1m   Typical emissions control system component locations – 1990 DOHC (VIN code 5) models

1.6   The Vehicle Emission Control Information (VECI) label contains tune-up specifications and vital information regarding the locations of the emission control devices and vacuum hose routing

2   Electronic control system – description and precautions

Description

The Computer Command Control System (CCCS) controls the fuel injection system or feedback carburetor system by means of a microcomputer known as the Electronic Control Module (ECM).

The ECM receives signals from various sensors which monitor changing engine operating conditions such as intake air volume, intake air temperature, coolant temperature, engine rpm, acceleration/deceleration, exhaust oxygen content, etc. These signals are utilized by the ECM to determine the correct injection duration or the air/fuel mixture in the carburetor.

The system is analogous to the central nervous system in the human body: The sensors (nerve endings) constantly relay signals to the ECM (brain), which processes the data and, if necessary, sends out a command to change the operating parameters of the engine (body).

Here's a specific example of how one portion of this system operates: An oxygen sensor, located in the exhaust manifold, constantly monitors the oxygen content of the exhaust gas. If the percentage of oxygen in the exhaust gas is incorrect, an electrical signal is sent to the ECM. The ECM takes this information, processes it and then sends a command to the fuel injection system or feedback carburetor telling it to change the air/fuel mixture. This happens in a fraction of a second and it goes on continuously when the engine is running. The end result is an air/fuel mixture ratio which is constantly maintained at a predetermined ratio, regardless of driving conditions.

In the event of a sensor malfunction, a backup circuit will take over to provide driveability until the problem is identified and fixed.

Precautions

a) Always disconnect the power by either turning off the ignition switch or disconnecting the battery terminals before removing CCCS wiring connectors.

b) When installing a battery, be particularly careful to avoid reversing the positive and negative battery cables.

c) Do not subject EFI, emissions related components, feedback carburetor components or the ECM to severe impact during removal or installation.

d) Do not be careless during troubleshooting. Even slight terminal contact can invalidate a testing procedure and damage one of the numerous transistor circuits.

e) Never attempt to work on the ECM or open the ECM cover. The ECM is protected by a government mandated extended warranty that will be nullified if you tamper with or damage the ECM.

f) If you are inspecting electronic control system components during rainy weather, make sure that water does not enter any part. When washing the engine compartment, do not spray these parts or their connectors with water.

3   Diagnosis system – general information and obtaining code output

Note: *Only 1988 through 1990 fuel injected models are equipped with a diagnosis system.*

General information

The ECM contains a built-in self-diagnosis system which detects and identifies malfunctions occurring in the network. When the ECM detects a problem, three things happen: the Check Engine light comes on, the trouble is identified and a diagnostic code is recorded and stored. The ECM stores the failure code assigned to the specific problem area until the diagnosis system is cancelled by removing the stop fuse with the ignition switch off.

The Check Engine warning light, which is located on the instrument panel, comes on when the ignition switch is turned to On and the engine is not running. When the engine is started, the warning light should go out. If the light remains on, the diagnosis system has detected a malfunction in the system.

Obtaining diagnosis code output

Refer to illustrations 3.3a and 3.3b

1   To obtain an output of diagnostic codes, verify first that the battery voltage is above 11 volts, the throttle is fully closed, the transaxle is in Neutral, the accessory switches are off and the engine is at normal operating temperature.

2   Turn the ignition switch to On. Do not start the engine.

3   On 1989 and 1990 models, use a jumper wire to bridge terminals T and E1 of the service connector (**see illustration**). On 1988 models, use a jumper wire to bridge both terminals of the service connector located near the windshield wiper motor (**see illustration**).

4   Read the diagnosis code as indicated by the number of flashes of the "Check Engine" light on the dash (**see the accompanying chart**). Normal system operation is indicated by Code No. 1 (no malfunctions) for all models. The "Check Engine" light displays a Code No. 1 by blinking once every few seconds.

5   If there are any malfunctions in the system, their corresponding trouble codes are stored in computer memory and the light will blink the requisite number of times for the indicated trouble codes. If there's more than one trouble code in the memory, they'll be displayed in numerical order (from lowest to highest) with a pause interval between each one. After the code with the largest number flashes has been displayed, there will be another pause and then the sequence will begin all over again.

6   To ensure correct interpretation of the blinking "Check Engine" light, watch carefully for the interval between the end of one code and the beginning of the next (otherwise, you will become confused by the apparent number of blinks and misinterpret the display). The length of this interval varies with the model year.

Cancelling a diagnostic code

7   After the malfunctioning component has been repaired/replaced, the trouble code(s) stored in computer memory must be cancelled. To accomplish this, simply remove the 15A stop fuse for at least ten seconds with the ignition switch off (the lower the temperature, the longer the fuse must be left out). The location of this fuse varies with the model year.

8   Cancellation can also be affected by removing the cable from the battery negative terminal, but other memory systems (such as the clock) will also be cancelled.

9   If the diagnosis code is not cancelled it will be stored by the ECM and appear with any new codes in the event of future trouble.

10   Should it become necessary to work on engine components requiring removal of the battery terminal, first check to see if a diagnostic code has been recorded.

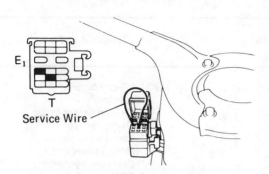

3.3a   To display the diagnostic codes on a 1989 or 1990 model, use a jumper wire to bridge terminals T and E1 of the service connector (located in the engine compartment)

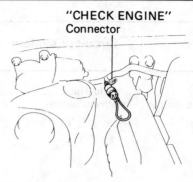

3.3b   On 1988 models, use a jumper wire to bridge both terminals of the CHECK ENGINE connector located near the windshield wiper motor

Code	Circuit or system	Diagnosis	Trouble area
Code 1 . . . . 1 Flash, Pause, 1 Flash	Normal	This appears when none of the other codes are identified	
Code 12 . . . . 1 flash, Pause, 2 flashes	RPM signal	* No "Ne" signal to the ECM . . . . . within 2 seconds after the engine is cranked. * No "G" signal to the ECM two times in succession when engine speed is between 500 rpm and 4000 rpm.	* Distributor circuit * Distributor * Starter signal circuit * Igniter circuit * Igniter * ECM
Code 13 . . . . 1 flash, Pause, 3 flashes	RPM signal	No "Ne" signal to the ECM . . . . when the engine speed is above 1500 rpm	* Distributor circuit * Distributor * ECM
Code 14 . . . . 1 flash, Pause, 4 flashes	Ignition signal	No "IGF" signal to the ECM . . . . . . 4 times in succession	* Igniter circuit * Igniter * ECM
Code 21 . . . . 2 Flashes, Pause, 1 Flash	Oxygen sensor	Problem in the oxygen sensor . . . . circuit	* Oxygen sensor circuit * ECM
Code 22 . . . . 2 Flashes, Pause, 2 Flashes	Coolant temperature . . . . sensor circuit	Open or short in the coolant . . . . . . temperature sensor	* Coolant temperature sensor circuit * Coolant temperature sensor * ECM
Code 24 . . . . 2 Flashes, Pause, 4 Flashes	Manifold air temperature sensor . .	Open or short in the . . . . Manifold Air Temperature (MAT) sensor circuit	* Manifold air temperature sensor * Manifold air temperature sensor circuit * ECM
Code 25 . . . . 2 Flashes, Pause, 5 Flashes	Air/fuel ratio . . . . lean malfunction	The air/fuel ratio feedback . . . . compensation valve or additive control valve continues at the upper (lean) or lower (rich) limit for a certain period of time	* Injector circuit * Injector * Oxygen sensor circuit * Oxygen sensor * ECM * Fuel line pressure * Air leak * Mass air-flow meter * Air intake system * Ignition system

Code	Circuit or system	Diagnosis	Trouble area
Code 26 2 Flashes, Pause 6 Flashes	Air/fuel ratio rich malfunction	The air/fuel ratio is overly rich	* Injector circuit * Injector * Oxygen sensor circuit * Oxygen sensor * Fuel line pressure * Mass air-flow meter * Cold start injector * ECM
Code 27 2 Flashes, Pause, 7 Flashes	Sub-oxygen sensor	Open or shorted circuit	* Sub-oxygen sensor circuit * Sub oxygen sensor * ECM
Code 31 3 Flashes, Pause, 1 Flash	Manifold Absolute Pressure (MAP) sensor (VIN code 6)	Open or short circuit	* MAP sensor circuit * MAP Sensor * No vacuum to sensor
Code 31 3 Flashes, Pause, 1 Flash	Mass Air Flow (MAF) meter (VIN code 5)	Open or short circuit	* Mass Air Flow circuit * Mass Air Flow meter * ECM
Code 41 4 Flashes, Pause, 1 Flash	Throttle position sensor	Open or short in the throttle position sensor circuit	* Throttle Position sensor * Throttle Position sensor circuit * ECM
Code 42 4 Flashes, Pause, 2 Flashes	Vehicle speed sensor	No "SPD" signal for 5 seconds when the engine speed is above 2800 rpm	* Vehicle speed sensor circuit * Vehicle speed sensor * ECM
Code 43 4 Flashes, Pause, 3 Flashes	Starter signal	No "STA" signal to the ECM until engine speed reaches 800 rpm with the vehicle not moving	* Starter signal circuit * Ignition switch * Main relay * ECM
Code 51 5 Flashes, Pause, 1 Flash	A/C switch signal	Air conditioner switch on, idle switch off during diagnosis check	* A/C switch circuit * A/C switch * A/C amplifier * Throttle position sensor circuit * Throttle position sensor * ECM
Code 52 5 Flashes, Pause, 2 Flashes	Knock sensor	Open or short circuit	* Knock sensor circuit * Knock sensor * ECM
Code 53 5 Flashes, Pause, 3 Flashes	Knock control signal	ECM	* ECM connectors * ECM
Code 71 7 Flashes, Pause, 1 Flash	EGR	EGR gas temperature signal is too low	* EGR system (EGR valve, hoses, etc.) * EGR gas temperature sensor circuit * EGR gas temperature sensor * Vacuum switching valve for the EGR circuit * ECM

4.6a To check the coolant temperature sensor, use an ohmmeter to measure the resistance between the two sensor terminals

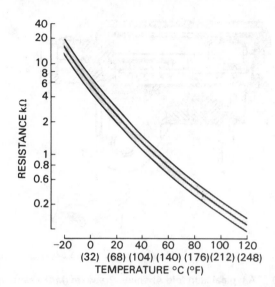

4.6b Compare the indicated resistance to the resistance values specified on this graph – note that as the temperature increases (as the engine warms up), resistance decreases

4 Information sensors

Note: *Most of the components described in this section are protected by a Federally-mandated extended warranty. See your dealer for the details regarding your vehicle. It therefore makes little sense to either check or replace any of these parts yourself as long as they are still under warranty. However, once the warranty has expired, you may wish to perform some of the component checks and\or replacement procedures in this Chapter to save money.*

Oxygen sensor (all models)

1   The oxygen sensor is located in the exhaust manifold. It's purpose is to detect the concentration of oxygen in the exhaust gases. On some models, a second oxygen sensor is located in the catalytic converter. This sensor rechecks the emission level after the exhaust gases pass through the converter and feeds the results back to the main oxygen sensor so the air\fuel ratio is maintained as precisely as possible.

2   An open or shorted oxygen circuit will set a code 21 or 27.

3   See Chapter 1 for the oxygen sensor replacement procedure.

Carburetor-equipped models

4   See Section 8 for information on the feedback carburetor system.

Fuel injected models

Coolant temperature sensor

Refer to illustrations 4.6a and 4.6b

5   The coolant temperature sensor is a thermistor (a resistor which varies the value of its voltage output in accordance with temperature changes). A failure in the coolant sensor or circuit will set a code 22. The coolant temperature sensor is located in the thermostat housing or behind the distributor housing.

6   To check the coolant temperature sensor, unplug the electrical connector and use an ohmmeter to measure the resistance between the two terminals **(see illustrations)**.

7   If the indicated resistance is not as specified, replace the sensor. Be sure to use Teflon tape or thread sealant on the threads of the new sensor to prevent leaks.

Manifold Air Temperature (MAT) sensor

8   The manifold air temperature (MAT) sensor, located in the side of the air cleaner housing, is a thermistor which constantly measures the temperature of the air entering the intake manifold. As air temperature varies, the ECM, by monitoring the MAT sensor, adjusts the amount of fuel according to the air temperature. A failure in the MAT sensor or circuit will set a code 24. The diagnosis of the MAT sensor should be left to a dealer service department.

Mass Air Flow (MAF) sensor (VIN code 5)

Refer to illustration 4.9

9   The mass air flow (MAF) sensor, which is located near the battery **(see illustration)**, measures the amount of air which passes through it in a given time. The ECM uses this information to control fuel delivery. A large quantity of air indicates acceleration, while a small quantity indicates deceleration or idle. A failure in the sensor or its circuit will set a code 31. Diagnosis of the MAF sensor should be left to a dealer service department.

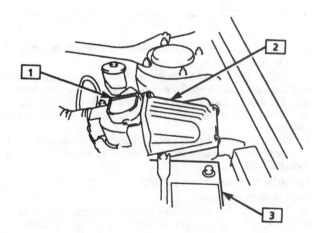

4.9   Typical Mass Air Flow (MAF) sensor installation

1   *Mass air flow sensor*   3   *Battery*
2   *Air filter housing*

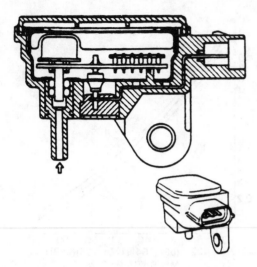

4.10   A typical Manifold Absolute Pressure (MAP) sensor

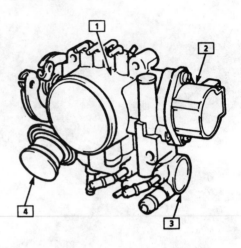

4.12   The Throttle Position Sensor (TPS) is mounted on the throttle body

1 Throttle body	3 Auxiliary air valve
2 Throttle position sensor	4 Dashpot

4.18   A typical Electronic Spark Control (ESC) knock sensor

Manifold Absolute Pressure (MAP) sensor (VIN code 6)

Refer to illustration 4.10

10   The Manifold Absolute Pressure (MAP) sensor **(see illustration)** monitors the intake manifold pressure changes resulting from changes in engine load and speed, then converts the information into a voltage reading. The ECM uses the MAP sensor to control fuel delivery and ignition timing.

11   Other than checking for vacuum, hose connection or electrical connectors the only service possible is unit replacement should diagnosis show the sensor faulty.

Throttle Position Sensor (TPS)

Refer to illustration 4.12

12   The Throttle Position sensor (TPS) is located on the throttle body **(see illustration)**. By monitoring the output voltage from the TPS, the ECM can determine fuel delivery based on throttle valve angle (driver demand). A failure in the TPS sensor or circuit will set a code 41. If the TPS requires diagnosis or replacement, it should be done by a dealer service department (because of the need for special tools and test equipment).

Park/Neutral switch (automatic transaxle equipped vehicles only)

13   The Park/Neutral switch, located on the automatic transaxle, indi-

cates to the ECM when the transaxle is in park or neutral. The ECM uses this information to control the fuel injectors and the ISC solenoid valve.

Air conditioner (A/C) signal

14   The A/C amplifier supplies a signal to the ECM when the air conditioning is turned on. This signal allows the ECM to adjust engine speed to compensate for the additional load on the engine. A code 51 will set if this signal is not present. Diagnosis should be left to a dealer service department.

Vehicle Speed Sensor (VSS)

15   The Vehicle Speed Sensor (VSS) consists of the lead switch and magnet that's built into the speedometer. As the magnet turns with the speedometer cable, its magnetic force causes the lead switch to turn on and off. This pulsing voltage signal is sent to the ECM which is converted into miles per hour. If a failure occurs, a code 42 will be set. Diagnosis and repair should be left to a dealer service department.

Crank angle sensor

16   The Crank Angle Sensor is located in the distributor and consists of a signal generator and signal rotor. As the signal rotor turns, pulsing AC voltage is generated in the pick-up coil. This pulse signal is sent to the ECM where it is used to calculate the engine speed and also as one of the signals to control various devices.

Engine start signal

17   This signal is sent from the engine starter circuit. Receiving it, the ECM detects that the engine is cranking and uses it as one of the signals to control the fuel injectors.

Electronic Spark Control (ESC) system

Refer to illustration 4.18

18   The Electronic Spark Control (ESC) system has two major components: the ESC module, which is part of the ECM, and the ESC knock sensor **(see illustration)**.

19   The ESC knock sensor detects abnormal detonation in the engine. The sensor is mounted in the engine block near the cylinders, or in the intake manifold at the rear of the engine. The ESC module receives the knock sensor information and sends a signal to the ECM. Then the ECM adjusts the timing to reduce detonation. If a failure should occur, a code 52 or 53 will be set. The repair of this system should be left to a dealer service department.

5   Evaporative Emission Control (EVAP) system

General description
Refer to illustrations 5.2a, 5.2b and 5.2c

1   This system is designed to trap and store fuel that evaporates from the fuel tank, carburetor and intake manifold that would normally enter the atmosphere in the form of hydrocarbon (HC) emissions.

2   The Evaporative Emission Control (EVAP) system consists of a charcoal-filled canister, the lines connecting the canister to the fuel tank and a thermo switch or an ECM-controlled solenoid valve **(see illustrations)**.

3   Fuel vapors are transferred from the fuel tank and carburetor to a canister where they're stored when the engine isn't running. When the engine is running, the fuel vapors are purged from the canister by intake air flow and consumed in the normal combustion process.

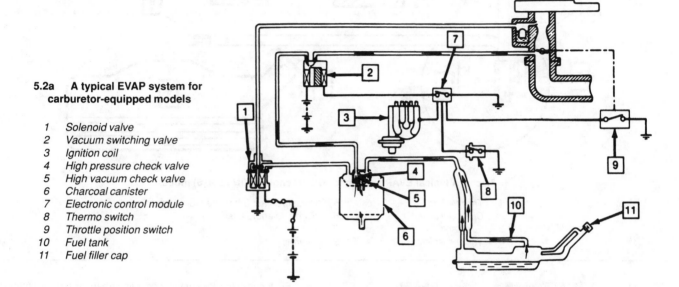

5.2a   A typical EVAP system for carburetor-equipped models

1   Solenoid valve
2   Vacuum switching valve
3   Ignition coil
4   High pressure check valve
5   High vacuum check valve
6   Charcoal canister
7   Electronic control module
8   Thermo switch
9   Throttle position switch
10   Fuel tank
11   Fuel filler cap

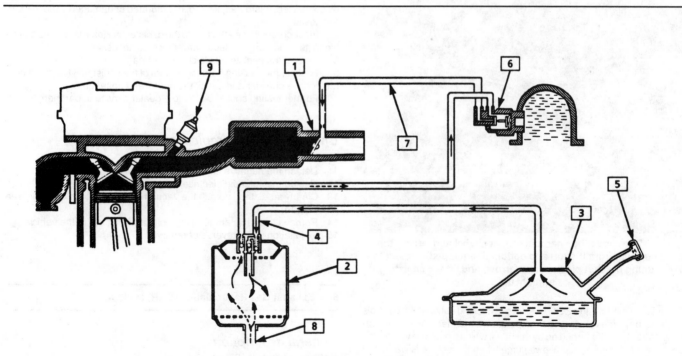

5.2b   A typical EVAP system for DOHC engine (VIN code 5) models

1	*Throttle valve*	*4*	*Canister check valve*	*7*	*Purge line*
2	*Charcoal canister*	*5*	*Pressure/vacuum vented fuel filler cap*	*8*	*Air inlet*
3	*Fuel tank*	*6*	*Bimetal vacuum switching valve*	*9*	*Fuel Injector*

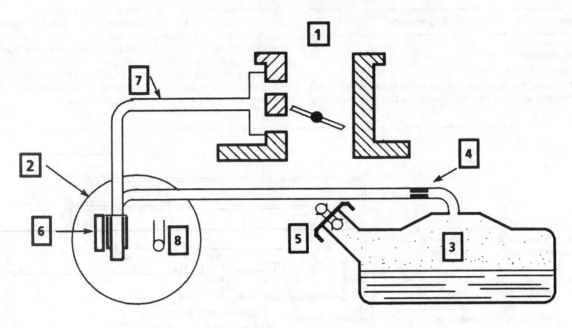

5.2c   A typical EVAP system for DOHC engine (VIN code 6) models

1	Throttle body	5	Pressure/vacuum vented fuel filler cap
2	Charcoal canister	6	Purge solenoid assembly
3	Fuel tank	7	Purge line
4	Vapor restrictor	8	Air inlet

5.13   To remove the charcoal canister, label and detach the hoses (arrows) from the top and bottom (if equipped), loosen the mounting bracket pinch screw (arrow) and lift the canister straight up

4   On some models, the ECM operates a solenoid valve which controls vacuum to the purge valve in the charcoal canister. Under cold engine conditions, the solenoid is turned on by the ECM, which closes the valve. The ECM turns off the valve and allows purge when the engine is warm. On some models, a bi-metal thermo switch controls the canister purge.

Checking

5   Poor idle, stalling and poor driveability can be caused by an inoperative purge valve, a damaged canister, split or cracked hoses or hoses connected to the wrong fittings. Check the fuel filler cap for a damaged or deformed gasket (see Chapter 1).

6   Evidence of fuel loss or fuel odor can be caused by liquid fuel leaking from fuel lines, a cracked or damaged canister, an inoperative purge valve, disconnected, misrouted, kinked, deteriorated or damaged vapor or control hoses.
7   Inspect each hose attached to the canister for kinks, leaks and cracks along its entire length. Repair or replace as necessary.
8   Inspect the canister. If it's cracked or damaged, replace it.
9   Look for fuel leaking from the bottom of the canister. If fuel is leaking, replace the canister and check the hoses and hose routing.
10   Further testing should be left to a dealer service department.

Charcoal canister replacement

Refer to illustration 5.13

11   Detach the negative cable from the battery.
12   Unplug the solenoid electrical connectors, if equipped.
13   Clearly label, then detach the vacuum hoses from the canister (**see illustration**).
14   Remove the canister mounting bolts and lift it out of the vehicle.
15   Installation is the reverse of removal.

6   Exhaust Gas Recirculation (EGR) system

General description

Refer to illustrations 6.2 and 6.3

1   To reduce oxides of nitrogen emissions, some of the exhaust gases are recirculated through the EGR valve to the intake manifold to lower combustion temperatures.
2   On carburetor-equipped vehicles, the EGR system (**see illustration**) consists of the EGR valve, EGR vacuum modulator, a check valve and a thermovalve. The EGR valve, which is operated by ported vacuum recir-

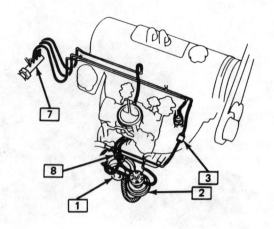

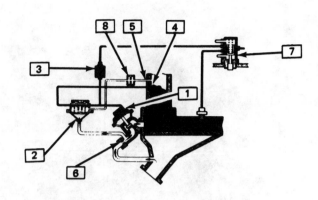

6.2 Typical EGR system diagram (carburetor-equipped models)

1 EGR valve
2 EGR vacuum modulator
3 Check valve
4 EGR port
5 EGR "R" port
6 Pressure chamber
7 Thermostatic vacuum
switching valve
8 Jet

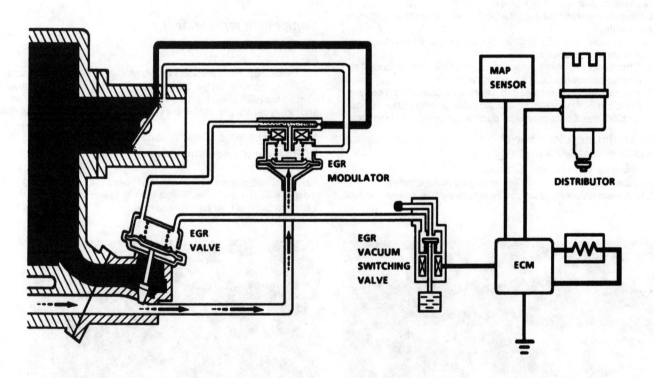

6.3 Typical EGR system diagram (fuel injected models)

culates gases in accordance with engine load (intake air volume). To eliminate recirculation at idle, the vacuum signal is ported above the idle throttle position. During cold engine operation, the thermovalve opens, bleeding off ported vacuum and keeping the EGR valve closed. When the engine coolant temperature exceeds the set temperature of the thermovalve, it closes and ported vacuum is applied to the EGR valve. The EGR vacuum modulator controls the EGR valve by controlling the vacuum signal to the EGR valve with an atmospheric bleed. This bleed is controlled by the amount of exhaust pressure which acts on the bottom of the EGR vacuum modulator.

3   On fuel-injected vehicles, the EGR system **(see illustration)** consists of the EGR valve, the EGR modulator, vacuum switching valve, the Electronic Control Module (ECM) and various sensors. The ECM memory is programmed to produce the ideal EGR valve lift for each operating condition.

6.8a To remove the EGR vacuum modulator filters for cleaning, remove this cap, . . .

6.8b   . . . then pull out the two filters and blow them out with compressed air – be sure the coarse side of the outer filter faces the atmosphere (out) when reinstalling the filters

Checking

EGR valve

4   Start the engine and allow it to idle.
5   Detach the vacuum hose from the EGR valve and attach a hand vacuum pump in its place.
6   Apply vacuum to the EGR valve. Vacuum should remain steady and the engine should run poorly.
   a) If the vacuum doesn't remain steady and the engine doesn't run poorly, replace the EGR valve and recheck it.
   b) If the vacuum remains steady but the engine doesn't run poorly, remove the EGR valve and check the valve and the intake manifold for blockage. Clean or replace parts as necessary and recheck.

EGR vacuum modulator valve

Refer to illustrations 6.8a and 6.8b

7   Remove the valve (see Step 13 below).
8   Pull the cover off and check the filters **(see illustrations)**.
9   Clean them with compressed air, reinstall the cover and the modulator.

EGR system

10   Any further checking of the EGR systems requires special tools and test equipment. Take the vehicle to a dealer service department for checking.

Component replacement

EGR valve

Refer to illustration 6.11

11   Disconnect the threaded fitting that attaches the EGR pipe to the EGR valve, remove the two EGR valve mounting bolts **(see illustration)**, remove the EGR valve from the intake manifold and check it for sticking and heavy carbon deposits. If the valve is sticking or clogged with deposits, clean or replace it.
12   Installation is the reverse of removal.

EGR vacuum modulator valve

Refer to illustration 6.13

13   Label and disconnect the vacuum hoses **(see illustration)** and remove the EGR vacuum modulator from its bracket.
14   Installation is the reverse of removal.

6.11   The EGR valve is mounted on the intake manifold – carburetor-equipped model shown, others similar

A   Mounting bolts   B   EGR pipe

6.13   Location of the EGR vacuum modulator valve on a carburetor-equipped model (arrow)

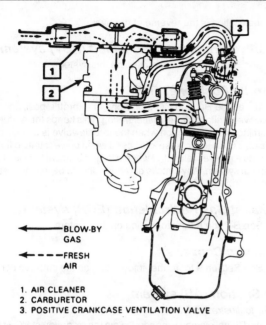

BLOW-BY GAS
FRESH AIR

1. AIR CLEANER
2. CARBURETOR
3. POSITIVE CRANKCASE VENTILATION VALVE

7.1a   The Positive Crankcase Ventilation (PCV) system used on carburetor-equipped models

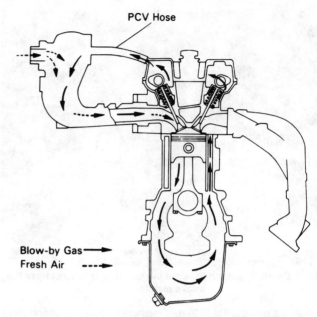

PCV Hose

Blow-by Gas
Fresh Air

7.1b   The Positive Crankcase Ventilation (PCV) system used on fuel injected models

7   Positive Crankcase Ventilation (PCV) system

Refer to illustrations 7.1a and 7.1b

1   To reduce hydrocarbon (HC) emissions, crankcase blow-by gas is routed to the intake manifold for combustion in the cylinders **(see illustrations)**.

2   On carburetor-equipped models, the main components of the PCV system are the PCV valve, a fresh air filtered inlet and the vacuum hoses connecting these components with the engine. On fuel injected models, the system consists only of a PCV hose between the valve cover and the intake manifold.

3   On carburetor-equipped models, to maintain idle quality, the PCV valve restricts the flow when the intake manifold vacuum is high. If abnormal operating conditions arise, the system is designed to allow excessive amounts of blow-by gases to flow back through the crankcase vent tube into the air cleaner to be consumed by normal combustion.

4   Checking and replacement of the PCV valve (carburetor-equipped models) is covered in Chapter 1.

8   Feedback carburetor system

Note: *The Feedback Carburetor system and all components related to the system is covered by a Federally mandated extended warranty. Check with a dealer service department before replacing or repairing the system components at your own expense.*

1   The feedback carburetor (FBC) system maintains the air/fuel ratio at the desired 14.7-to-1 during normal operation. The system is designed to operate somewhat richer than desired. This sets up the rich limit of the system operation. When a more lean operation is desired, the Electronic Control Module (ECM) commands air to be bled into the carburetor's main metering system and into the carburetor primary bore. A lean operating condition is therefore easily obtained.

2   The various sub-systems and components of the feedback system are discussed below. Checking and component replacement information is provided, where possible.

Evaporative Emission Control (EVAP) system

3   See Section 5 for information on this system.

Feedback control system

4   See Chapter 4 for information on this system.

Deceleration Fuel Cut system

Refer to illustration 8.7

5   During deceleration, this system cuts off part of the fuel flow in the idle circuit of the carburetor to prevent overheating and afterburning in the exhaust system. The fuel cut solenoid is kept energized by the ECM whenever the engine is running, except when the throttle is closed with the rpm above 2290.

6   To check the system, hook up a tachometer in accordance with manufacturer's instructions and start the engine.

7   Disconnect the throttle position switch connector **(see illustration)**, raise the engine speed to 2300 rpm and check that the engine speed is fluctuating.

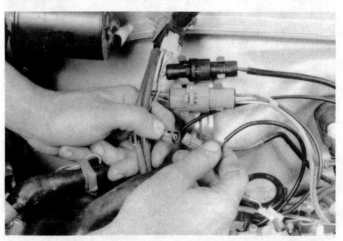

8.7   Unplug the connector from the throttle position switch, raise the engine speed to 2300 rpm and make sure the engine speed is fluctuating

8.13   Carefully detach the cold mixture heater (arrow) from the intake manifold

8   With the speed still at 2300 rpm, reconnect the connector and check that engine operation returns to normal.

9   If no problems are found, the system is okay. Any further checks or repairs should be left to a dealer service department.

Cold Mixture Heater (CMH) system

Refer to illustration 8.13

10   The Cold Mixture Heater (CMH) system reduces cold engine emissions and improves driveability during engine warm up. The intake manifold is heated during cold engine operation to accelerate vaporization of the liquid fuel. The ECM will turn the CMH on and off according to engine coolant temperature.

11   To check the cold mixture heater, locate the connector, unplug it and, using an ohmmeter, measure the resistance between the terminals. It should be between 0.5 and 2.0 ohms. If the readings are not within specification, replace the heater. Any further checks should be done by a dealer service department.

12   To replace the cold mixture heater, first remove the carburetor (see Chapter 4).

13   Unplug the cold mixture heater connector, remove the PCV hose and lift the heater from the intake manifold **(see illustration)**.

14   Installation is the reverse of removal.

Positive Crankcase Ventilation (PCV) system

15   See Section 7 for information on this system.

Throttle Positioner (TP)

16   To reduce HC and CO emissions, the throttle positioner opens the throttle valve slightly when decelerating. This keeps the air/fuel ratio from becoming excessively rich when the throttle valve is quickly closed. The TP is also used to increase idle speed when power stefluid fluid pressure exceeds a pre-set value and when a large electrical load is placed on the electrical system. Any checks or repairs should be left to a dealer service department.

Exhaust Gas Recirculation (EGR) system

17   See Section 6 for information on this system .

Catalytic Converter

18   See Section 9 for further information on the catalytic converter.

Air Suction (AS) system

Refer to illustration 8.21

19   Additional oxygen is needed to aid the oxidation of HC and CO in the catalytic converter. The air suction valve is a simple reed-type valve that opens when vacuum is present in the exhaust system. When open, oxygen-rich air is drawn into the exhaust to aid the converter with the oxidation process.

20   To check the system, first check the hoses and fittings for cracks, kinks, damage or loose connections.

21   Remove the air cleaner top cover and, with the engine idling, check that a burbling noise is heard from the air suction valve inlet **(see illustration)**. Any further checks or repairs should be left to a dealer service department.

High Altitude Compensation (HAC) system (Federal models only)

Refer to illustration 8.24

22   As altitude increases, air density decreases so that the air/fuel mixture becomes richer. The High Altitude Compensation (HAC) system insures proper air/fuel mixture by supplying additional air to the primary and high-speed circuit of the carburetor. The system also advances the ignition timing to improve driveability at high altitudes.

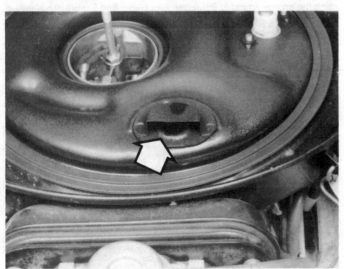

8.21   With the engine running, listen for a burbling noise from the air suction valve inlet (arrow)

8.24   Remove the HAC cover, peel the filter out, clean it with compressed air, inspect it and, if necessary, replace it

8.28   Label and detach the vacuum hoses from the HIC valve, then remove the mounting screws (arrows)

23   To check the system, first inspect all hoses for cracks, kinks, damage or loose connections.

24   Check and clean the air filter in the HAC valve **(see illustration)**. Any further checks or repairs should be left to a dealer service department.

Thermostatic Air Cleaner (TAC) system

25   This system directs hot air to the carburetor in cold weather to improve driveability and to prevent carburetor icing in extremely cold weather.

26   See Chapter 1 for the TAC system check.

Hot Idle Compensation (HIC) system

Refer to illustrations 8.28 and 8.29

27   The Hot Idle Compensation (HIC) system allows additional air to enter the intake manifold to maintain proper air/fuel mixture during high temperatures at idle.

28   To check the system, remove the HIC valve from the air cleaner housing **(see illustration)**.

29   With the temperature above 72-degrees F, check the operation of the valve by placing a finger over the atmospheric port and blowing into the port for the HIC diaphragm **(see illustration)**. Air should flow from the port normally connected to the carburetor.

30   At temperatures below 72-degrees F, carry out a similar air flow test. Place a finger over the port normally connected to the carburetor. Blow through the port for the HIC diaphragm and make sure that air does not pass out of the atmospheric port.

Automatic Choke

31   The automatic choke system temporarily supplies a rich air/fuel mixture to the engine by closing the choke valve when the engine is cold. It automatically opens the choke as the engine warms up. See Chapter 1 for the choke check procedure. Any further checks or repairs should be left to a dealer service department.

Auxiliary Acceleration Pump (APP)

32   When accelerating with a cold engine, the main acceleration pump's capacity is insufficient. The auxiliary acceleration pump system compensates for this by forcing more fuel into the acceleration nozzle to obtain better cold engine performance. A thermostatic control valve controls the APP system. After the engine is warmed up, the valve lets the main acceleration pump take over. Any checks or repairs should be left to a dealer service department.

Heat Control Valve

Refer to illustration 8.34

33   When the engine is cold, the heat control valve improves fuel vaporization for better driveability by quickly heating the intake manifold. Once the engine has warmed up, the valve helps to keep the intake manifold at the proper temperature. The valve is located in the exhaust manifold and can be seen best from under the vehicle.

34   Check the heat control valve when the engine is cold. The counterweight of the heat control valve should be in it's upper position **(see illustration)**. After warm-up, check that the counterweight is in it's lower position.

35   If the valve is stuck, apply some penetrating oil to the shaft – this will normally free it up.

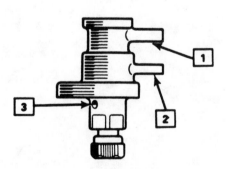

8.29   A typical HIC valve

1 Carburetor port	3 Atmospheric port
2 Hot air intake diaphragm port	

8.34   When the engine is cold, make sure the valve is in the upper position – when the engine is hot, make sure the valve is in the lower position

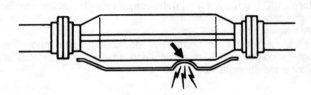

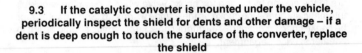

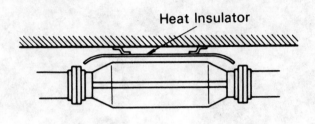

9.3   If the catalytic converter is mounted under the vehicle, periodically inspect the shield for dents and other damage – if a dent is deep enough to touch the surface of the converter, replace the shield

9.4   If the catalytic converter is mounted under the vehicle, periodically inspect the heat insulator to make sure there's adequate clearance between it and the converter

9   Catalytic converter

Note: *Because of a federally mandated extended warranty which covers emissions-related components such as the catalytic converter, check with a dealer service department before replacing the converter at your own expense.*

General description

1   To reduce hydrocarbon, carbon monoxide and oxides of nitrogen emissions, all vehicles are equipped with a three-way catalyst system which oxidizes and reduces these chemicals, converting them into harmless nitrogen, carbon dioxide and water.

Checking

Refer to illustrations 9.3 and 9.4

2   Periodically inspect the catalytic converter-to-exhaust pipe mating flanges and bolts. Make sure that there are no loose bolts and no leaks between the flanges.

3   Look for dents in or damage to the catalytic converter protector (**see illustration**). If any part of the protector is damaged or dented enough to touch the converter, repair or replace it.

4   Inspect the heat insulator for damage. Make sure that there is adequate clearance between the heat insulator and the catalytic converter (**see illustration**).

Replacement

5   To replace the catalytic converter, refer to Chapter 4.

Chapter 7 Part A   Manual transaxle

Contents

Specifications

Lubricant type .... See Chapter 1

Torque specifications   **Ft-lbs**
Transaxle-to-engine bolts 37
Back-up light switch 30

---

1   General information

The vehicles covered by this manual are equipped with either a five-speed manual or a three or four-speed automatic transaxle. Information on the manual transaxle is in this Part of Chapter 7. Service procedures for the automatic transaxle are in Chapter 7, Part B.

The manual transaxle is a compact, two-piece, lightweight aluminum alloy housing containing both the transmission and differential assemblies.

Because of the complexity, unavailability of replacement parts and special tools necessary, internal repair procedures for the manual transaxle are not recommended for the home mechanic. For readers who wish to tackle a transaxle rebuild, exploded views are provided. The bulk of information in this Chapter is devoted to removal and installation procedures.

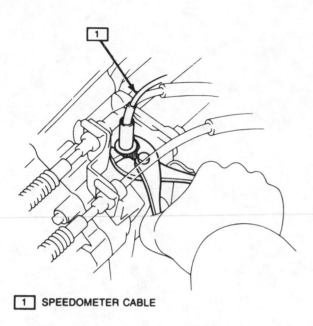

1 SPEEDOMETER CABLE

2.9   Use a pair of pliers to loosen the speedometer cable fitting

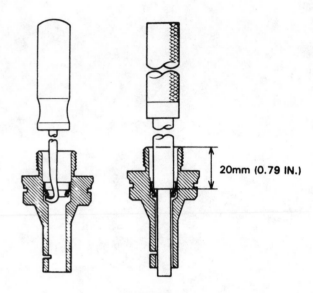

20mm (0.79 IN.)

2.10   Use a hooked tool to pull the old speedometer cable seal out of the driven gear housing – use a small hammer and socket to tap the new seal into place (make sure the seal is recessed the same amount)

2   Oil seal replacement

Driveaxle seals

1   Oil leaks frequently occur due to wear of the differential side gear shaft seals and/or the speedometer driven gear oil seal and O-rings. Replacement of these seals is relatively easy, since the repairs can usually be performed without removing the transaxle from the vehicle.

2   The differential side gear shaft oil seals are located at the sides of the transaxle, where the side gear shafts are attached. If leakage at the seal is suspected, raise the vehicle and support it securely on jackstands. If the seal is leaking, lubricant will be found on the side of the transaxle.

3   Refer to Chapter 8 and remove the driveaxles and side gear shafts.

4   Using a screwdriver or pry bar, carefully pry the oil seal out of the transaxle bore (see Section 7 in Part B).

5   If the oil seal cannot be removed with a screwdriver or pry bar, a special oil seal removal tool (available at auto parts stores) will be required.

6   Using a large section of pipe or a large deep socket as a drift, install the new oil seal. Drive it into the bore squarely and make sure it's completely seated. Lubricate the lip of the new seal with multi-purpose grease.

7   Install the driveaxle(s) and side gear shaft(s). Be careful not to damage the lip of the new seal.

Speedometer cable O-ring

Refer to illustrations 2.9 and 2.10

8   The speedometer cable and driven gear housing are located on the transaxle near the shift cable linkage. Look for lubricant around the cable housing to determine if the seal and O-ring are leaking.

9   Disconnect the speedometer cable and remove the driven gear housing from the transaxle **(see illustration)**.

10   Using a hook, remove the seal from the driven gear housing **(see illustration)**.

11   Using a small socket of the appropriate diameter or other similar tool as a drift, install the new seal.

12   Install a new O-ring on the driven gear housing and reattach the speedometer cable assembly to the housing.

3   Shift lever – removal and installation

Refer to illustration 3.3

1   Remove the shifter boot and center console.
2   Detach the shift cables (see Section 4).
3   Remove the bolts and detach the shift lever **(see illustration)**.
4   Installation is the reverse of removal.

4   Shift cables – removal and installation

1   Detach the cable from the negative battery terminal.

Nova

Refer to illustration 4.2

2   Remove the retaining clips and disconnect the shift cables from the transaxle linkage **(see illustration)**.
3   Remove the console and shifter boot.
4   Remove the cable retainers from the shift lever assembly **(see illustration 3.3)**.
5   Disconnect the shift cables from the shift lever assembly **(see illustration 3.3)**.
6   Remove the left front sill plate and pull the carpet back to gain access to the cables.
7   Remove the shift cable retainer screws at the floor pan and detach the cables.

Prizm

8   Remove the shift lever knob and boot.
9   Remove the front and rear center console halves.
10   Remove the center air duct.
11   Remove the ECM-to-floor mounting nuts and remove the ECM from under the dash.
12   Remove the shift cable hold-down bracket.

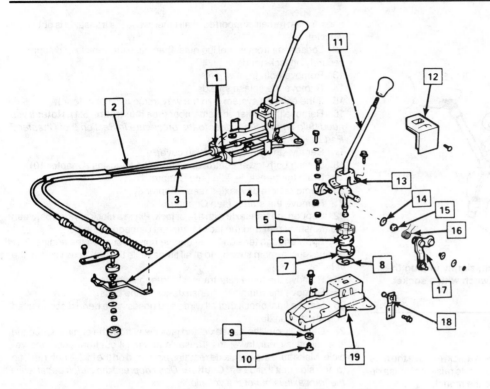

3.3 Manual transaxle shift lever and cable assembly components – exploded view (Nova shown, Prizm similar)

1   Retainer
2   Shift control cable
3   Shift select cable
4   Bellcrank
5   Spacer
6   Upper seat
7   Lower seat
8   Adjusting shim
9   Bushing no. 2
10 Bushing no. 1
11 Shift lever
12 Shift lever cover
13 Shift lever cap
14 Washer
15 Bushing
16 Torsion spring
17 Bellcrank
18 Spring holder
19 Shift lever retainer

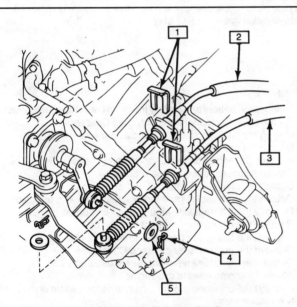

4.2   Shift cable/linkage details

1   Cable retainers
2   Shift control cable
3   Shift select cable
4   Retaining clips
5   Cable end washer

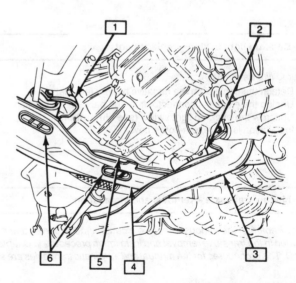

5.1   Transaxle mount locations (Prizm shown, Nova similar)

1   Front transaxle mount
2   Rear transaxle mount
3   Main crossmember
4   Center crossmember
5   Center transaxle mount
6   Mount bolt shields

13 Disconnect the shift cables from the control assembly (see illustration 3.3).
14 Remove the shift cable retainers at the transaxle and disconnect the shift cables from the transaxle linkage (see illustration 4.2).
15 Pull the shift cables through from the inside of the vehicle to remove them.

All models

16 Installation is the reverse of removal.

5   Transaxle mounts – check and replacement

Refer to illustration 5.1

1   Insert a large screwdriver or pry bar between each mount and the transaxle and pry up while watching the mount (see illustration).
2   If the rubber separates from the metal plate on the mount, or the case moves up, but not down (mount bottomed out), replace the mount.

6.3   To replace the back-up light switch, simply unplug the electrical connector and unscrew the switch with a socket and ratchet

3   To replace a mount, support the transaxle with a jack, remove the nuts and bolts and detach the mount. It may be necessary to raise the transaxle slightly to provide enough clearance to remove the mount.
4   Installation is the reverse of removal.

6   Back-up light switch – replacement

Refer to illustration 6.3
1   Detach the cable from the negative battery terminal.
2   Unplug the electrical connector from the back-up light switch.
3   Unscrew the back-up light switch **(see illustration)**.
4   Installation is the reverse of removal.

7   Manual transaxle – removal and installation

Note: *Photos of the various transaxle mounts and the center beam are included in the transaxle removal and installation procedure in Chapter 7, Part B. The procedures for the manual and automatic transaxles are similar.*

Nova

1   Detach the negative cable from the battery.
2   Remove the air inlet tube (see Chapter 4).
3   Disconnect the speedometer cable **(see illustration 2.9).**
4   Disconnect the thermostat housing from the transaxle bellhousing.
5   Disconnect the ground strap from the transaxle.
6   Remove the clutch slave cylinder (see Chapter 8) and set it aside.
7   Unplug the back-up light switch wire harness.
8   Disconnect the shift linkage from the transaxle.
9   Remove the two upper transaxle-to-engine bolts.
10   Remove the left upper transaxle mount through-bolt.
11   Attach an engine hoist to the engine. If you don't have a hoist, place a jack (with a block of wood as an insulator) under the engine oil pan. The

engine must remain supported at all times while the transaxle is out of the vehicle!
12   Loosen the front wheel lug nuts, then raise the vehicle and support it securely on jackstands.
13   Remove both front wheels.
14   Remove the splash shields.
15   If the exhaust system is in the way, remove it (Chapter 4).
16   Remove the center crossmember **(see illustration 5.1). Note:** *If you need help on this Step, refer to the procedure in Section 9 of Chapter 7 Part B.*
17   Remove the clutch inspection cover.
18   Detach both lower control arms from the knuckles (Chapter 10).
19   Drain the transaxle fluid (see Chapter 1).
20   Remove both driveaxles (see Chapter 8).
21   Remove the starter (see Chapter 5).
22   Support the transaxle with a floor jack. Place a block of wood between the transaxle pan and the jack to prevent damage to the pan.
23   Apply enough tension to the engine hoist to support the engine. The engine must remain supported at all times while the transaxle is out of the vehicle.
24   Remove the three rear transaxle-to-engine bolts.
25   Remove the remaining transaxle-to-engine bolts.
26   Make a final check that all wires and hoses have been disconnected from the transaxle.
27   Carefully pull the transaxle and jack away from the engine. Once the input shaft is clear, lower the transaxle and roll it out from under the vehicle. Make sure the transaxle remains balanced on the jack – don't let it tip to one side or it'll slide off. **Caution:** *Don't depress the clutch pedal while the transaxle is out of the vehicle.*
28   Inspect the clutch components (see Chapter 8). It's a good idea to install new clutch components each time the transaxle is removed.
29   Installation is the reverse of removal.

Prizm

30   Remove the battery and battery tray from the vehicle (see Chapter 5).
31   Remove the air cleaner assembly (see Chapter 4).
32   Unplug the back-up switch electrical connector.
33   Detach the ground strap.
34   Remove the two clutch actuator mounting bolts.
35   Detach the clutch actuator line bracket.
36   Detach the shift cable retainers and end clips.
37   Detach the shift cables from the brackets and lay them aside.
38   Remove the left transaxle mount cover and brace.
39   Remove the left transaxle mount through bolt.
40   Remove the two upper transaxle-to-engine bolts.
41   Remove the upper starter bolt (see Chapter 5).
42   Detach the speedometer cable **(see illustration 2.9).**
43   Attach an engine hoist to the engine.
44   Loosen the front wheel lug nuts, then raise the vehicle and place it securely on jackstands.
45   Remove both front wheels.
46   Remove the left and right splash shields.
47   Detach the starter electrical connections (see Chapter 5).
48   Remove both driveaxles (see Chapter 8).
49   Remove the three center crossmember-to-radiator support bolts.
50   Remove the front and center mount bolt shields **(see illustration 5.1).**
51   Remove the two front mount nuts.
52   Remove the two center mount nuts.
53   Remove the two rear mount nuts.
54   Remove the two center crossmember-to-main crossmember bolts.
55   Remove the three exhaust hanger bracket nuts and exhaust hanger (see Chapter 4).
56   Support the main crossmember with a floor jack.
57   Remove the eight main crossmember-to-underbody bolts.
58   Remove the two lower control arm bracket-to-underbody bolts.

59   Lower the main crossmember slowly while holding onto the center crossmember. **Warning:** *The center crossmember is free to fall at this time and could cause serious injury.*
60   Remove the front mount through-bolt and mount.
61   Remove the front mount bracket from the transaxle.
62   Remove the center mount from the transaxle.
63   Remove the clutch inspection cover.
64   Remove the two lower transaxle bracket-to-mount nuts.
65   Lower the vehicle.
66   Remove the remaining transaxle mount-to-bracket bolt.
67   Lower the engine/transaxle assembly enough to provide clearance to remove the transaxle.
68   Remove the transaxle mount.
69   Raise the vehicle again and support it securely on jackstands.
70   Support the transaxle with a floor jack. Place a wooden block between the jack and transaxle pan to protect the pan from damage.
71   Remove the front and rear lower transaxle-to-engine bolts.
72   Remove the remaining transaxle mount-to-bracket bolt.
73   Make a final check that all wires and hoses have been disconnected from the transaxle.
74   Move the transaxle and jack toward the side of the vehicle until the transaxle is clear of the engine. Make sure the transaxle remains balanced on the jack – don't let it tip to one side or it'll slide off.
75   Carefully lower the transaxle and remove it from under the vehicle. **Caution:** *Don't depress the clutch pedal while the transaxle is out of the vehicle.*
76   Inspect the clutch components (see Chapter 8). It's a good idea to install new clutch components each time the transaxle is removed.
77   Installation is the reverse of removal.

8   Manual transaxle overhaul – general information

Refer to illustrations 8.4a, 8.4b, 8.4c, 8.4d, 8.4e and 8.4f

Overhauling a manual transaxle is a difficult job for the do-it-yourselfer. It involves the disassembly and reassembly of many small parts. Numerous clearances must be precisely measured and, if necessary, changed with select fit spacers and snap-rings. As a result, if transaxle problems arise, it can be removed and installed by a competent do-it-yourselfer, but overhaul should be left to a transmission repair shop. Rebuilt transaxles may be available – check with a dealer parts department and auto parts stores. At any rate, the time and money involved in an overhaul is almost sure to exceed the cost of a rebuilt unit.

Nevertheless, it's not impossible for an inexperienced mechanic to rebuild a transaxle if the special tools are available and the job is done in a deliberate step-by-step manner so nothing is overlooked.

The tools necessary for an overhaul include internal and external snap-ring pliers, a bearing puller, a slide hammer, a set of pin punches, a dial indicator and possibly a hydraulic press. In addition, a large, sturdy workbench and a vise or transaxle stand will be required.

During disassembly of the transaxle, make careful notes of how each piece comes off, where it fits in relation to other pieces and what holds it in place. Exploded views are included **(see illustrations)** to show where the parts go – but actually noting how they're installed when you remove the parts will make it much easier to get the transaxle back together.

Before taking the transaxle apart for repair, it will help if you have some idea what area of the transaxle is malfunctioning. Certain problems can be closely tied to specific areas in the transaxle, which can make component examination and replacement easier. Refer to the Troubleshooting section at the front of this manual for information regarding possible sources of trouble.

Illustrations for Section 8
begin on next page

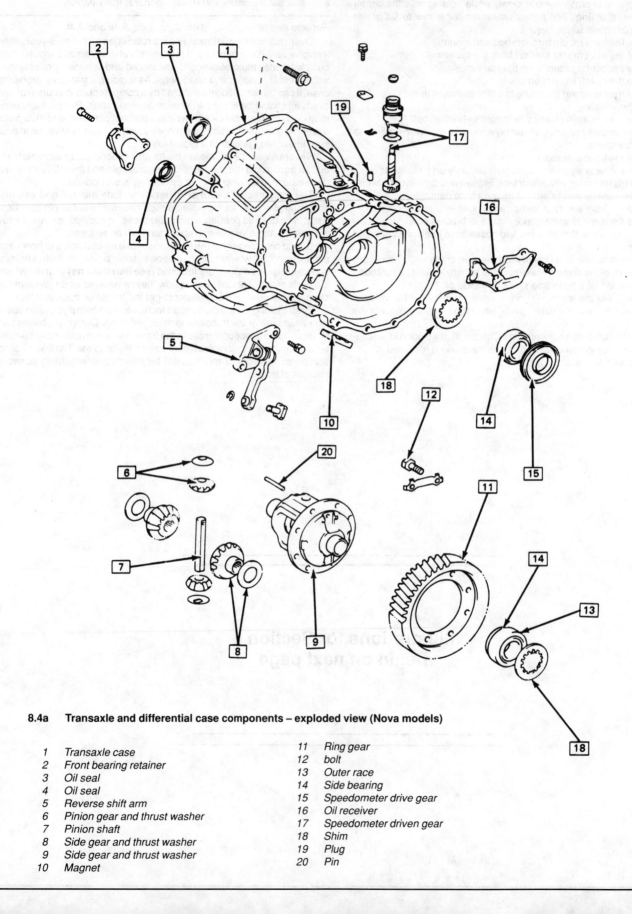

8.4a   Transaxle and differential case components – exploded view (Nova models)

1	Transaxle case	11	Ring gear
2	Front bearing retainer	12	bolt
3	Oil seal	13	Outer race
4	Oil seal	14	Side bearing
5	Reverse shift arm	15	Speedometer drive gear
6	Pinion gear and thrust washer	16	Oil receiver
7	Pinion shaft	17	Speedometer driven gear
8	Side gear and thrust washer	18	Shim
9	Side gear and thrust washer	19	Plug
10	Magnet	20	Pin

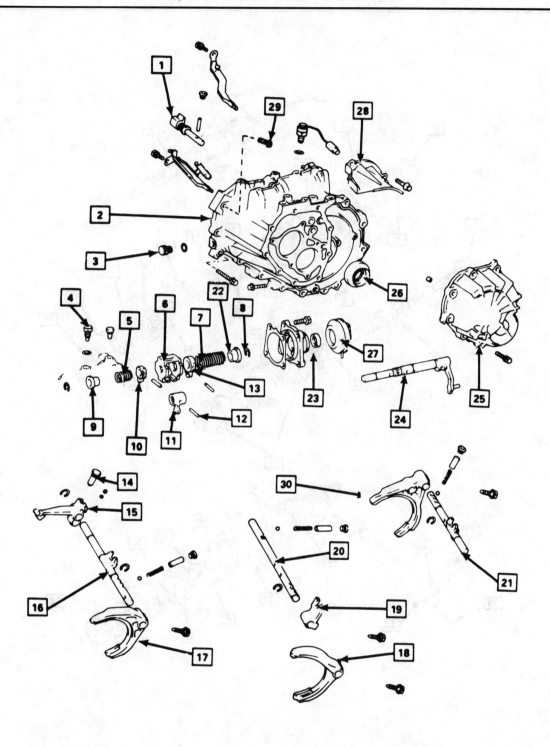

8.4b   Shift mechanism components – exploded view (Nova models)

1	Reverse restrict pin	11	Shift inner no. 1 lever	21	Shift fork shaft no. 1
2	Transmission case	12	Roll pin	22	Select spring seat
3	Plug	13	Select inner lever	23	Oil seal
4	Lock bolt	14	Lock ball assembly	24	Shift and select lever
5	Spring	15	Reverse shift fork	25	Transmission case cover
6	Shift interlock plate	16	Shift fork shaft no. 3	26	Oil seal
7	Spring	17	Shift fork no. 3	27	Boot
8	Snap-ring	18	Shift fork no. 2	28	Protector
9	Select no. 2 seat	19	Shift head	29	Bolt
10	Shift inner no. 2 lever	20	Shift fork shaft no. 2	30	Shift fork no. 1

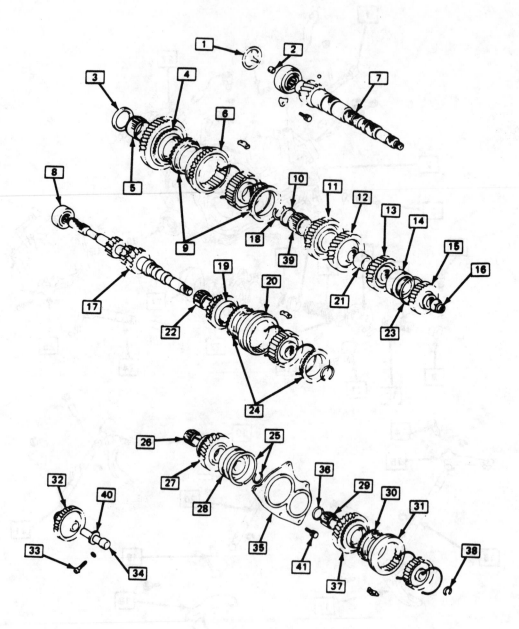

8.4c   Input and output shaft components – exploded view (Nova models)

1	Output shaft cover	12	Third driven gear	22	Needle roller bearing	32	Reverse idler gear
2	Roll pin	13	Fourth driven gear	23	Snap-ring	33	Bolt
3	Thrust gear	14	Rear bearing	24	Synchronizer ring	34	Idler gear shaft
4	First gear	15	Fifth driven gear	25	Snap-ring	35	Rear bearing retainer
5	Needle roller bearing	16	Locknut	26	Needle roller bearing	36	Spacer
6	Hub sleeve no. 1	17	Input shaft	27	Fourth gear	37	Fifth gear
7	Output shaft	18	Snap-ring	28	Rear bearing	38	Snap-ring
8	Input shaft front bearing	19	Third gear	29	Needle roller bearing	39	Needle roller bearing
9	Synchronizer rings	20	Hub sleeve no. 2	30	Synchronizer ring	40	Thrust washer
10	Spacer	21	Output gear spacer	31	Hub sleeve no. 3	41	Bolt
11	Second gear						

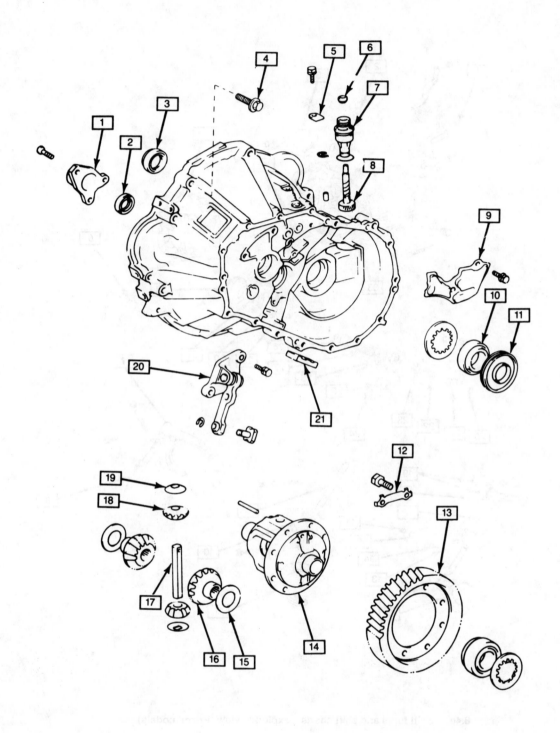

8.4d   Differential components – exploded view (Prizm models)

1	Front bearing retainer	8	Speedometer driven gear	15
2	Retainer seal	9	Oil receiver	16
3	Driveaxle seal	10	Side bearing	17
4	Transaxle mounting bolt	11	Speedometer drive gear	18
5	Speedometer housing hold-down	12	Bolt lock plate	19
6	Speedometer gear seal	13	Ring gear	20
7	Speedometer housing	14	Differential case	21

1 Front bearing retainer
2 Retainer seal
3 Driveaxle seal
4 Transaxle mounting bolt
5 Speedometer housing hold-down
6 Speedometer gear seal
7 Speedometer housing

8 Speedometer driven gear
9 Oil receiver
10 Side bearing
11 Speedometer drive gear
12 Bolt lock plate
13 Ring gear
14 Differential case

15 Thrust washer
16 Side gear
17 Pinion shaft
18 Pinion gear
19 Thrust washer
20 Reverse shift arm
21 Magnet

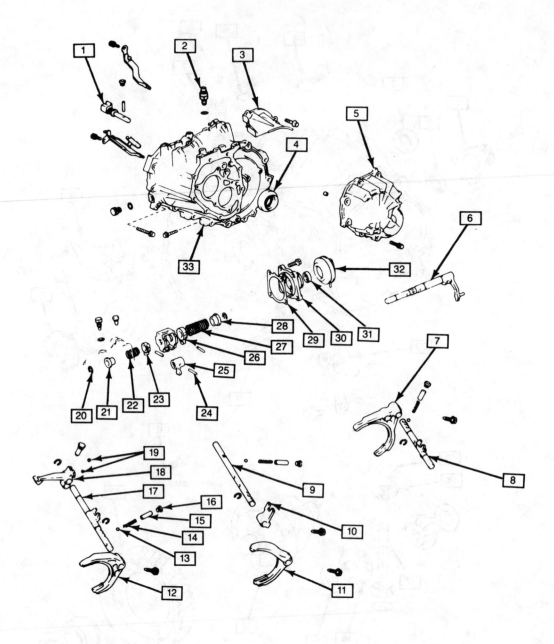

8.4e   Shift forks and shift shafts – exploded view (Prizm models)

1	Reverse restrict pin	12	No. 3 shift fork	23	No. 2 inner shift lever
2	Reverse light switch	13	Ball	24	Slotted spring pin
3	Protector	14	Spring	25	No. 1 inner shift lever
4	Driveaxle seal	15	Seat	26	Select inner lever
5	Transmission case cover	16	Plug	27	Spring
6	Shift and select lever shaft	17	No. 3 shift fork shaft	28	Select spring seat
7	No. 1 shift fork	18	Reverse shift fork	29	Gasket
8	No. 1 Shift fork shaft	19	Fork lock balls	30	Control shaft cover
9	No. 2 shift fork shaft	20	E-clip	31	Oil seal
10	Shift head	21	No. 2 select spring seat	32	Boot
11	No. 2 shift fork	22	Spring	33	Transaxle case

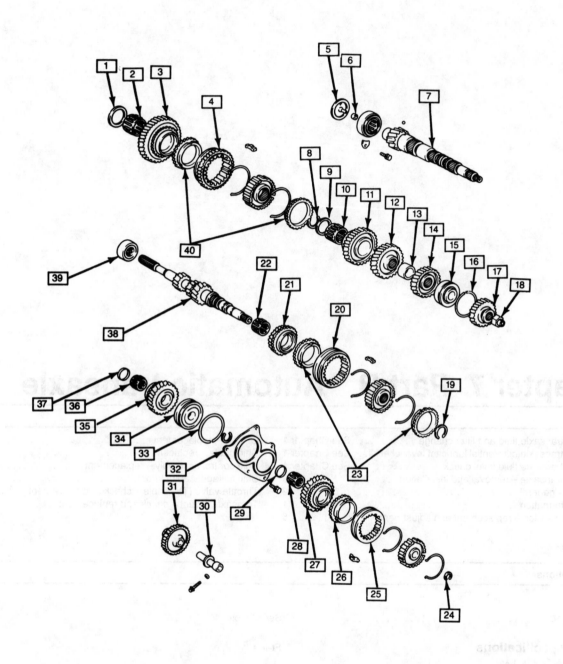

8.4f   Input and output shaft components – exploded view (Prizm models)

1	Thrust washer	11	Second gear	21	Third gear	31	Reverse idler gear
2	Needle roller bearing	12	Third driven gear	22	Needle roller bearing	32	Rear bearing retainer
3	First gear	13	Output gear spacer	23	Synchronizer ring	33	Snap-ring
4	No. 1 hub sleeve	14	Fourth driven gear	24	Snap-ring	34	Ring bearing
5	Output shaft cover	15	Rear bearing	25	No. 3 hub sleeve	35	Fourth gear
6	Roll pin	16	Snap-ring	26	Syncrhonizer ring	36	Needle roller bearing
7	Output shaft	17	Fifth driven gear	27	Fifth gear	37	Spacer
8	Snap-ring	18	Locknut	28	Needle roller bearing	38	Input shaft
9	Spacer	19	Snap-ring	29	Spacer	39	Input shaft front bearing
10	Needle roller bearing	20	No. 2 hub sleeve	30	Idler gear shaft	40	Synchronizer ring

Chapter 7 Part B   Automatic transaxle

Contents

Specifications

Fluid type .... See Chapter 1

Torque specifications   Ft-lbs
Transaxle-to-engine bolts
   10 mm 34
   12 mm 47
Torque converter-to-driveplate bolts
   Three-speed transaxle 13
   Four-speed transaxle 20

1   General information

All vehicles covered in this manual come equipped with either a five-speed manual or a three or four-speed automatic transaxle. All information on the automatic transaxle is included in this Part of Chapter 7. Information for the manual transaxle can be found in Part A of this Chapter.

Due to the complexity of the automatic transaxles covered in this manual and the need for special equipment to perform most service operations, this Chapter contains only general diagnosis, routine maintenance, adjustment and removal and installation procedures.

If the transaxle requires major repair work, it should be left to a dealer service department or an automotive or transmission repair shop. You can, however, remove and install the transaxle yourself and save the expense, even if the repair work is done by a transmission shop.

2   Diagnosis – general

Note: *Automatic transaxle malfunctions may be caused by five general conditions: poor engine performance, improper adjustments, hydraulic malfunctions, mechanical malfunctions or malfunctions in the computer or its signal network. Diagnosis of these problems should always begin with a check of the easily repaired items: fluid level and condition (Chapter 1), shift linkage adjustment and throttle linkage adjustment. Next, perform a road test to determine if the problem has been corrected or if more diagnosis is necessary. If the problem persists after the preliminary tests and corrections are completed, additional diagnosis should be done by a dealer service department or transmission repair shop. Refer to the Troubleshooting Section at the front of this manual for information on symptoms of transaxle problems.*

Preliminary checks

1   Drive the vehicle to warm the transaxle to normal operating temperature.
2   Check the fluid level as described in Chapter 1:
   a) If the fluid level is unusually low, add enough fluid to bring the level within the designated area of the dipstick, then check for external leaks (see below).
   b) If the fluid level is abnormally high, drain off the excess, then check the drained fluid for contamination by coolant. The presence of engine coolant in the automatic transmission fluid indicates that a failure has occurred in the internal radiator walls that separate the coolant from the transmission fluid (see Chapter 3).
   c) If the fluid is foaming, drain it and refill the transaxle, then check for coolant in the fluid, or a high fluid level.
3   Check the engine idle speed. **Note:** *If the engine is malfunctioning, do not proceed with the preliminary checks until it has been repaired and runs normally.*
4   Check the throttle valve cable for freedom of movement. Adjust it if necessary (Section 4). **Note:** *The throttle cable may function properly when the engine is shut off and cold, but it may malfunction once the engine is hot. Check it cold and at normal engine operating temperature.*
5   Inspect the shift control linkage (Section 3). Make sure that it's properly adjusted and that the linkage operates smoothly.

Fluid leak diagnosis

6   Most fluid leaks are easy to locate visually. Repair usually consists of replacing a seal or gasket. If a leak is difficult to find, the following procedure may help.
7   Identify the fluid. Make sure it's transmission fluid and not engine oil or brake fluid (automatic transmission fluid is a deep red color).
8   Try to pinpoint the source of the leak. Drive the vehicle several miles, then park it over a large sheet of cardboard. After a minute or two, you should be able to locate the leak by determining the source of the fluid dripping onto the cardboard.
9   Make a careful visual inspection of the suspected component and the area immediately around it. Pay particular attention to gasket mating surfaces. A mirror is often helpful for finding leaks in areas that are hard to see.
10   If the leak still cannot be found, clean the suspected area thoroughly with a degreaser or solvent, then dry it.
11   Drive the vehicle for several miles at normal operating temperature and varying speeds. After driving the vehicle, visually inspect the suspected component again.
12   Once the leak has been located, the cause must be determined before it can be properly repaired. If a gasket is replaced but the sealing flange is bent, the new gasket will not stop the leak. The bent flange must be straightened.
13   Before attempting to repair a leak, check to make sure that the following conditions are corrected or they may cause another leak. **Note:** *Some of the following conditions cannot be fixed without highly specialized tools and expertise. Such problems must be referred to a transmission shop or a dealer service department.*

Gasket leaks

14   Check the pan periodically. Make sure the bolts are tight, no bolts are missing, the gasket is in good condition and the pan is flat (dents in the pan may indicate damage to the valve body inside).
15   If the pan gasket is leaking, the fluid level or the fluid pressure may be too high, the vent may be plugged, the pan bolts may be too tight, the pan sealing flange may be warped, the sealing surface of the transaxle housing may be damaged, the gasket may be damaged or the transaxle casting may be cracked or porous. If sealant instead of gasket material has been used to form a seal between the pan and the transaxle housing, it may be the wrong sealant.

Seal leaks

16   If a transaxle seal is leaking, the fluid level or pressure may be too high, the vent may be plugged, the seal bore may be damaged, the seal itself may be damaged or improperly installed, the surface of the shaft protruding through the seal may be damaged or a loose bearing may be causing excessive shaft movement.
17   Make sure the dipstick tube seal is in good condition and the tube is properly seated. Periodically check the area around the speedometer gear or sensor for leakage. If transmission fluid is evident, check the O-ring for damage.

Case leaks

18   If the case itself appears to be leaking, the casting is porous and will have to be repaired or replaced.
19   Make sure the oil cooler hose fittings are tight and in good condition.

Fluid comes out vent pipe or fill tube

20   If this condition occurs, the transaxle is overfilled, there is coolant in the fluid, the case is porous, the dipstick is incorrect, the vent is plugged or the drain back holes are plugged.

3   Shift linkage – adjustment

Refer to illustration 3.5
1   Raise the vehicle and support it securely on jackstands.
2   Loosen the swivel nut on the manual shift lever at the transaxle.
3   Push the lever toward the right side of the vehicle and then return it two notches to the Neutral position.
4   Move the shift lever inside the vehicle to the Neutral position.
5   While holding the lever with slight pressure toward the Reverse position, tighten the swivel nut securely **(see illustration)**.
6   Check the operation of the transaxle in each shift lever position (try to start the engine in each gear – the starter should operate in the Park and Neutral positions only).

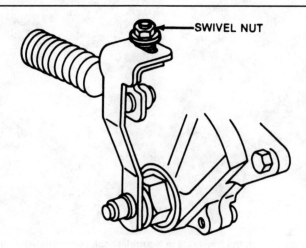

3.5   While pushing the lever gently toward Reverse, tighten the swivel nut securely

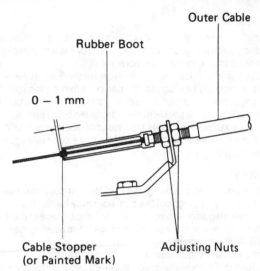

4.3   Loosen the adjusting nuts and adjust the cable housing position until the stopper or painted mark is the specified distance from the boot end

5.3   To replace the Neutral start switch, remove the shift lever nut, detach the shift lever, unplug the electrical connector and remove the switch mounting bolts (arrows)

4   Throttle valve (TV) cable – check and adjustment

Refer to illustration 4.3

1   Remove the air cleaner duct assembly.
2   Have an assistant hold the throttle pedal down while you watch the TV link in the engine compartment to make sure it opens fully.
3   If the link doesn't open all the way, have the assistant continue to hold the pedal down, loosen the adjusting nuts and adjust the cable until the mark or stopper is the specified distance from the boot end **(see illustration)**.
4   Tighten the adjusting nuts securely, recheck the clearance and make sure the link opens all the way when the throttle is depressed.

5   Neutral start switch – replacement and adjustment

Replacement
Refer to illustration 5.3

1   Disconnect the negative cable from the battery.
2   Shift the transaxle into Neutral.
3   Remove the nut and lift off the shift lever **(see illustration)**.
4   Unplug the electrical connector.
5   Remove the bolts and detach the switch from the shift shaft.
6   To install the switch, line up the flats on the shift shaft with the flats in the switch and push the switch onto the shaft.
7   Install the bolts, but leave them loose and follow the adjustment procedure below. The remainder of installation is the reverse of removal.

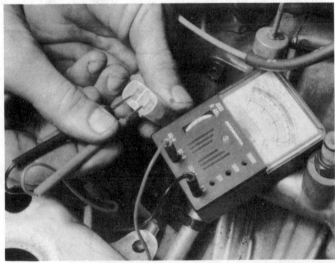

5.9a   With the transaxle in Neutral, check continuity with an ohmmeter as shown . . .

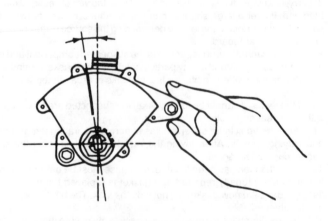

5.9b   . . . and rotate the Neutral start switch until continuity exists between the switch terminals, then tighten the bolts

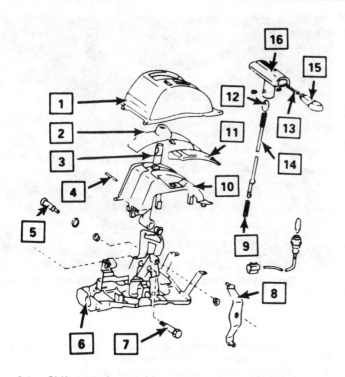

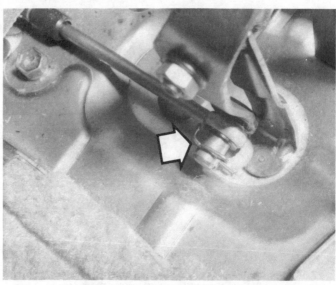

6.2 Pull out the retaining clip and pin, then detach the shift cable from the shift control assembly

6.1 Shift control assembly components – exploded view

1	Center console	9	Spring
2	Shift indicator	10	Housing
3	Lever	11	Plate
4	Pin	12	Sleeve
5	Shaft	13	Spring
6	Plate	14	Rod
7	Shaft	15	Button
8	Lever	16	Knob

6.3 Remove the mounting bolts (arrows) and detach the shift control assembly from the floorpan

Adjustment (1983 through 1985 models only)

Refer to illustrations 5.9a and 5.9b

8   Make sure the switch connector is unplugged.
9   Connect an ohmmeter to the switch terminals and rotate the switch until there's continuity between the terminals, indicating that it's now in the Neutral position **(see illustrations)**. Tighten the switch bolts.
10   Connect the negative battery cable and verify that the engine will start only in Neutral or Park.

6   Shift control assembly – replacement

Refer to illustrations 6.1, 6.2 and 6.3

1   Remove the shift control knob, the center console, the shift indicator and the housing **(see illustration)**.
2   Remove the shift cable end clip, pull out the pin and detach the cable from the shift control assembly **(see illustration)**.
3   Remove the four shift control assembly mounting bolts **(see illustration)**.
4   Remove the shift control assembly.
5   Installation is the reverse of removal.

7   Shift cable – replacement

Refer to illustrations 7.8 and 7.9

1   Detach the cable from the negative battery terminal.
2   Remove the shift control knob, center console, shift indicator and housing (see Section 6).
3   Detach the shift cable from the shift control assembly (see Section 6).
4   Remove the ECM.
5   Trace the shift cable to the grommet retainer where the cable goes through the lower firewall. Detach this retainer.
6   Raise the vehicle and place it securely on jackstands.
7   Detach the shift cable from the Neutral start switch (see Section 5).

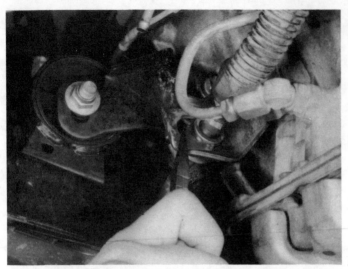

7.8   Pry off the clip with a pair of needle-nose pliers, then separate the shift cable from the bracket

7.9   Detach both of the shift cable clips from the crossmember

8   Detach the shift cable from the bracket on the transaxle, next to the Neutral start switch **(see illustration)**.

9   Detach the shift cable from the cable clips on the crossmember **(see illustration)**.

10   Pull the cable through the firewall from inside the vehicle.

11   Installation is the reverse of removal.

8   Oil seal – replacement

Refer to illustrations 8.4 and 8.6

1   Oil leaks frequently occur due to wear of the driveaxle oil seals, and/or the speedometer drive gear O-ring. Replacement of these seals is relatively easy, since the repairs can usually be performed without removing the transaxle from the vehicle.

2   The driveaxle oil seals are located at the sides of the transaxle, where the driveaxles are attached. If leakage at the seal is suspected, raise the vehicle and support it securely on jackstands. If the seal is leaking, lubricant will be found on the sides of the transaxle.

3   Refer to Chapter 8 and remove the driveaxles.

4   Using a screwdriver or pry bar, carefully pry the oil seal out of the transaxle bore **(see illustration)**.

5   If the oil seal cannot be removed with a screwdriver or pry bar, a special oil seal removal tool (available at auto parts stores) will be required.

6   Using a large section of pipe or a large deep socket as a drift, install the new oil seal **(see illustration)**. Drive it into the bore squarely and make sure it's completely seated.

7   Install the driveaxle(s). Be careful not to damage the lip of the new seal.

8   The speedometer cable and driven gear housing is located on the transaxle housing. Look for lubricant around the cable housing to determine if the O-ring is leaking.

9   Disconnect the speedometer cable from the transaxle.

10   Install a new O-ring on the driven gear housing and reinstall the speedometer cable assembly.

8.4   Pry out the old differential oil seal with a screwdriver – don't scratch the seal bore

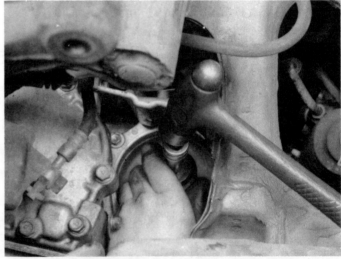

8.6   To install a new differential oil seal, simply drive it into place with a large socket that has a slightly smaller diameter than the seal

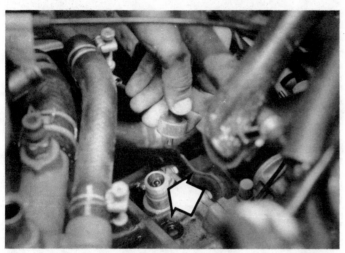

9.3 Detach the speedometer cable from the speedometer driven gear housing (arrow) on the transaxle

9.4 Remove the bolts (arrows) and detach the thermostat assembly from the transaxle

9 Automatic transaxle – removal and installation

Removal

Refer to illustrations 9.3, 9.4, 9.7, 9.10, 9.11, 9.17, 9.19, 9.24a, 9.24b, 9.24c, 9.24d, 9.24e, 9.26a and 9.26b

1   Disconnect the negative cable from the battery.
2   Remove the air cleaner tube (see Chapter 4).
3   Detach the speedometer cable **(see illustration)**.
4   Detach the thermostat housing from the transaxle **(see illustration)**.
5   Detach the ground cable from the transaxle.
6   Unplug the electrical connector from the Neutral start switch (see Section 5).
7   Remove the upper transaxle mount-to-bracket bolt **(see illustration)**.
8   Disconnect any electrical connectors.
9   Detach the throttle valve (TV) cable from the carburetor or throttle body (see Section 4).
10 Remove the two upper mounting bolts **(see illustration)**.
11 Support the engine with an engine hoist. If you don't have a hoist, place a 4 x 4 between the firewall and the upper crossmember and hang the engine from it with a heavy chain **(see illustration)**.

9.7 Remove the through-bolt (arrow) from the upper transaxle mount

9.10 Remove the upper transaxle-to-engine bolts (arrows)

9.11 If you don't have a regular engine hoist, lay a 4 x 4 across the engine compartment like this and support the engine with a heavy chain

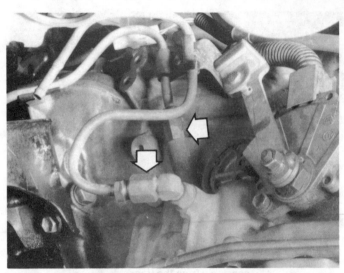

9.17   Disconnect the oil cooler lines at the fittings (arrows) and plug them to prevent leakage

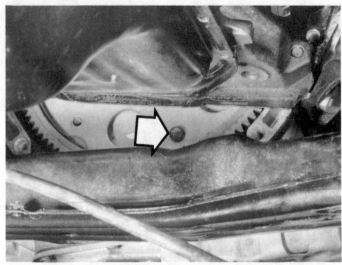

9.19   Mark the torque converter and driveplate so they can be reinstalled in the same relative positions, then remove each of the torque converter-to-driveplate bolts (arrow)

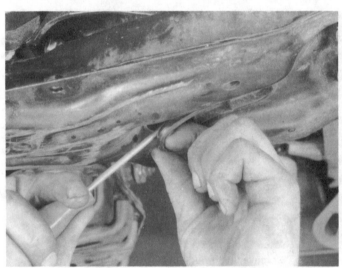

9.24a   Pry off the protective plastic covers from the front and rear recesses in the center beam (front shown, rear similar), . . .

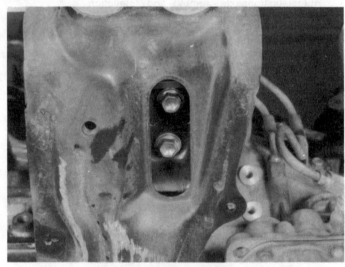

9.24b   . . . remove the front transaxle mount bolts, . . .

9.24c   . . . remove the rear transaxle mount bolts, . . .

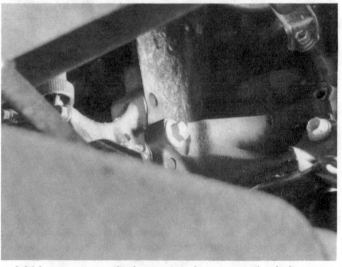

9.24d   . . . remove the front center beam mounting bolts, . . .

9.24e ... remove the rear center beam mounting bolts and detach the center beam from the vehicle

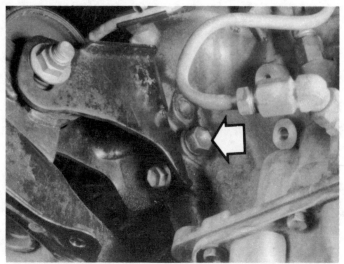

9.26a   Remove the front lower bellhousing bolt (arrow) ...

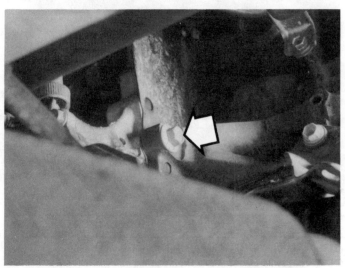

9.26b ... and the rear lower bellhousing bolt (arrow)

12   Loosen – but don't remove – the front wheel lug nuts.
13   Raise the vehicle and support it securely on jackstands.
14   Remove the front wheels.
15   Remove the left, right and center splash shields.
16   Disconnect the shift cable from the Neutral start switch and from the two shift cable clips (see Section 5).
17   Disconnect the cooler line fittings from the transaxle **(see illustration)**. Cap the lines to prevent leakage. Detach the bracket that attaches the lines to the transaxle.

18   Remove the torque converter cover.
19   Mark the torque converter and driveplate so they can be installed in the same position **(see illustration)**.
20   Remove the torque converter-to-driveplate bolts. Turn the crankshaft pulley bolt for access to each bolt.
21   Drain the transaxle fluid (see Chapter 1).
22   Disconnect the driveaxles from the transaxle (see Chapter 8).
23   Remove the starter motor (see Chapter 5).
24   Remove the center beam **(see illustrations)**.
25   Support the transaxle with a jack – preferably a special jack made for this purpose. Safety chains will help steady the transaxle on the jack. If you don't have a transmission jack, support the transaxle with a floor jack. Be sure to put a block of wood between the jack and the transaxle.
26   Remove the rest of the mounting bolts **(see illustrations)**.
27   Grasp the transaxle firmly and disengage it from the engine block dowel pins. Make sure the torque converter is detached from the driveplate. Slowly lower the transaxle until it clears the vehicle. Secure the torque converter to the transaxle so it will not fall out during removal.

Installation

28   Prior to installation, make sure the torque converter hub is securely engaged in the pump.
29   With the transaxle secured to the jack, raise it into position. Be sure to keep it level so the torque converter doesn't slide out. Connect the fluid cooler lines.
30   Turn the torque converter to line up the holes with the holes in the driveplate. The marks must line up.
31   Move the transaxle forward carefully until the dowel pins and the torque converter are engaged.
32   Install the transaxle-to-engine bolts. Tighten them securely.
33   The remainder of installation is the reverse of removal.

Chapter 8 Clutch and driveaxles

Contents

Specifications

Clutch

Fluid type . . . .   See Chapter 1
Pedal freeplay . . . .   See Chapter 1
Pedal height . . . .   See Chapter 1

Driveaxle length (standard)

Automatic transaxle
  Left . . . . 16.54 ± 0.20 in
  Right . . . . 27.56 ± 0.20 in
Manual transaxle
  Left . . . . 16.54 ± 0.20 in
  Right . . . . 27.48 ± 0.20 in

Torque specifications

	Ft-lbs
Brake caliper bracket-to-knuckle bolts	65
Clutch master cylinder mounting nuts	11
Clutch pressure plate-to-flywheel bolts	14
Clutch release cylinder mounting bolts	9
Driveaxle/hub nut	137
Driveaxle inner CV joint-to-differential side gear shaft flange	27
Control arm-to-balljoint nuts and bolts	47
Tie-rod end-to-steering knuckle nut	38
Wheel lug nuts	See Chapter 1

1   General information

The information in this Chapter deals with the components from the rear of the engine to the front wheels, except for the transaxle, which is dealt with in the previous Chapter. For the purposes of this Chapter, these components are grouped into two categories: Clutch and driveaxles. Separate Sections within this Chapter offer general descriptions and checking procedures for both groups.

Since nearly all the procedures covered in this Chapter involve working under the vehicle, make sure it's securely supported on sturdy jackstands or a hoist where the vehicle can be easily raised and lowered.

2   Clutch – description and check

Refer to illustration 2.1

All vehicles with a manual transaxle use a single dry plate, diaphragm spring type clutch **(see illustration)**. The clutch disc has a splined hub which allows it to slide along the splines of the transaxle input shaft. The clutch and pressure plate are held in contact by spring pressure exerted by the diaphragm in the pressure plate.

The clutch release system is operated by hydraulic pressure. The hydraulic release system consists of the clutch pedal, a master cylinder and fluid reservoir, the hydraulic line, a slave cylinder which actuates the clutch release lever and the clutch release (or throwout) bearing.

When pressure is applied to the clutch pedal to release the clutch, hydraulic pressure is exerted against the outer end of the clutch release lever. As the lever pivots, the shaft fingers push against the release bearing. The bearing pushes against the fingers of the diaphragm spring of the pressure plate assembly, which in turn releases the clutch plate.

Terminology can be a problem regarding the clutch components because common names have in some cases changed from that used by the manufacturer. For example, the driven plate is also called the clutch plate or disc, the pressure plate assembly is sometimes referred to as the clutch cover, the clutch release bearing is sometimes called a throwout bearing, and the release cylinder is sometimes called the operating or slave cylinder.

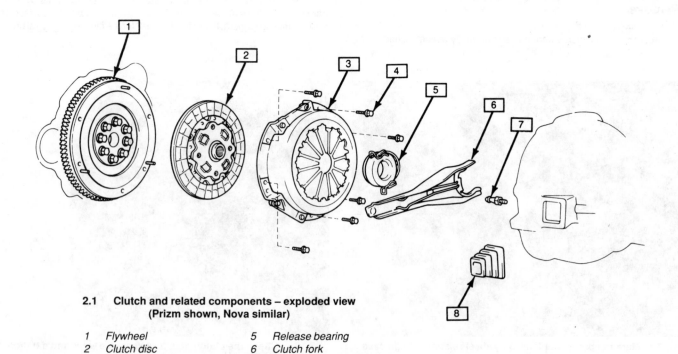

**2.1   Clutch and related components – exploded view
(Prizm shown, Nova similar)**

1	Flywheel	5	Release bearing
2	Clutch disc	6	Clutch fork
3	Clutch cover	7	Clutch fork ball stud
4	Clutch cover bolts	8	Fork boot

Other than replacing components that have obvious damage, some preliminary checks should be performed to diagnose a clutch system failure.

a) The first check should be of the fluid level in the clutch master cylinder (see Chapter 1). If the fluid level is low, add fluid as necessary and inspect the hydraulic clutch system for leaks. If the master cylinder reservoir has run dry, bleed the system as described in Section 7 and re-test the clutch operation.

b) To check "clutch spin down time," run the engine at normal idle speed with the transaxle in Neutral (clutch pedal up – engaged). Disengage the clutch (pedal down), wait nine seconds and shift the transaxle into Reverse. No grinding noise should be heard. A grinding noise would most likely indicate a problem in the pressure plate or the clutch disc.

c) To check for complete clutch release, run the engine (with the parking brake applied to prevent movement) and hold the clutch pedal approximately 1/2-inch from the floor. Shift the transaxle between 1st gear and Reverse several times. If the shift is not smooth, component failure is indicated. Check the release cylinder pushrod travel. With the clutch pedal depressed completely the release cylinder pushrod should extend substantially. If it doesn't, check the fluid level in the clutch master cylinder.

d) Visually inspect the clutch pedal bushing at the top of the clutch pedal to make sure there is no sticking or excessive wear.

e) Under the vehicle, check that the clutch release lever is solidly mounted on the ball stud.

3   Clutch components – removal, inspection and installation

Warning: *Dust produced by clutch wear and deposited on clutch components may contain asbestos, which is hazardous to your health. DO NOT blow it out with compressed air and DO NOT inhale it. DO NOT use gasoline or petroleum-based solvents to remove the dust. Brake system cleaner should be used to flush the dust into a drain pan. After the clutch components are wiped clean with a rag, dispose of the contaminated rags and cleaner in a labeled, covered container.*

Removal

Refer to illustration 3.6

1   Access to the clutch components is normally accomplished by re-moving the transaxle, leaving the engine in the vehicle. If, of course, the engine is being removed for major overhaul, then the opportunity should always be taken to check the clutch for wear and replace worn components as necessary. However, the relatively low cost of the clutch components compared to the time and labor involved in gaining access to them warrants their replacement any time the engine or transaxle is removed, unless they are new or in near-perfect condition. The following procedures assume that the engine will stay in place.

2   Remove the release cylinder (see Section 6). Hang it out of the way with a piece of wire – it's not necessary to disconnect the hose.

3   Referring to Chapter 7 Part A, remove the transaxle from the vehicle. Support the engine while the transaxle is out. Preferably, an engine hoist should be used to support it from above. However, if a jack is used underneath the engine, make sure a piece of wood is used between the jack and oil pan to spread the load. **Caution:** *The pickup for the oil pump is very close to the bottom of the oil pan. If the pan is bent or distorted in any way, engine oil starvation could occur.*

4   The release fork and release bearing can remain attached to the transaxle for the time being.

5   To support the clutch disc during removal, install a clutch alignment tool through the clutch disc hub.

6   Carefully inspect the flywheel and pressure plate for indexing marks. The marks are usually an X, an O or a white letter. If they cannot be found, scribe marks yourself so the pressure plate and the flywheel will be in the same alignment during installation **(see illustration)**.

7   Turning each bolt only 1/2-turn at a time, slowly loosen the pressure plate-to-flywheel bolts. Work in a diagonal pattern and loosen each bolt a little at a time until all spring pressure is relieved. Then hold the pressure plate securely and completely remove the bolts, followed by the pressure plate and clutch disc.

Inspection

Refer to illustrations 3.10, 3.12a and 3.12b

8   Ordinarily, when a problem occurs in the clutch, it can be attributed to wear of the clutch driven plate assembly (clutch disc). However, all components should be inspected at this time.

9   Inspect the flywheel for cracks, heat checking, score marks and other damage. If the imperfections are slight, a machine shop can resurface it to make it flat and smooth. Refer to Chapter 2 for the flywheel removal procedure.

3.6   **Mark the pressure plate-to-flywheel relationship (in case you're going to reuse the same pressure plate)**

3.10   **Check the clutch disc for excessive wear and damage such as distorted lining material, chewed up rivets, worn hub splines and distorted damper cushions or springs**

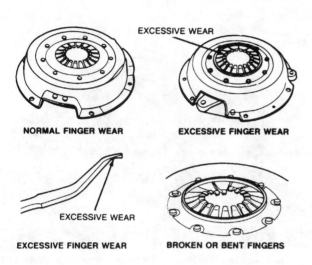

3.12a   Replace the pressure plate if any of these conditions are noted

3.12b   Check the pressure plate friction surface for score marks, cracks and evidence of overheating (blue spots)

10   Inspect the lining on the clutch disc. There should be at least 1/16-inch of lining above the rivet heads. Check for loose rivets, distortion, cracks, broken springs and other obvious damage **(see illustration)**. As mentioned above, ordinarily the clutch disc is replaced as a matter of course, so if in doubt about the condition, replace it with a new one.

11   The release bearing should be replaced along with the clutch disc (see Section 4).

12   Check the machined surface and the diaphragm spring fingers of the pressure plate **(see illustrations)**. If the surface is grooved or otherwise damaged, replace the pressure plate assembly. Also check for obvious damage, distortion, cracking, etc. Light glazing can be removed with emery cloth or sandpaper. If a new pressure plate is indicated, new or factory-rebuilt units are available.

Installation

Refer to illustration 3.14

13   Before installation, carefully wipe the flywheel and pressure plate ma-

3.14   Center the clutch disc in the pressure plate with a clutch alignment tool

chined surfaces clean. It's important that no oil or grease is on these surfaces or the lining of the clutch disc. Handle these parts only with clean hands.

14   Position the clutch disc and pressure plate with the clutch held in place with an alignment tool **(see illustration)**. Make sure it's installed properly (most replacement clutch plates will be marked "flywheel side" or something similar – if not marked, install the clutch disc with the damper springs or cushion toward the transaxle).

15   Tighten the pressure plate-to-flywheel bolts only finger-tight, working around the pressure plate.

16   Center the clutch disc by ensuring the alignment tool is through the splined hub and into the recess in the crankshaft. Wiggle the tool up, down or side-to-side as needed to bottom the tool. Tighten the pressure plate-to-flywheel bolts a little at a time, working in a criss-cross pattern to prevent distortion of the cover. After all of the bolts are snug, tighten them to the specified torque. Remove the alignment tool.

17   Using high-temperature grease, lubricate the inner groove of the release bearing (refer to Section 4). Also place grease on the release lever contact areas and the transaxle input shaft bearing retainer.

18   Install the clutch release bearing as described in Section 4.

19   Install the transaxle, slave cylinder and all components removed previously, tightening all fasteners to the proper torque specifications.

---

4   Clutch release bearing and fork – removal, inspection and installation

---

Warning: *Dust produced by clutch wear and deposited on clutch components may contain asbestos, which is hazardous to your health. DO NOT blow it out with compressed air and DO NOT inhale it. DO NOT use gasoline or petroleum-based solvents to remove the dust. Brake system cleaner should be used to flush it into a drain pan. After the clutch components are wiped clean with a rag, dispose of the contaminated rags and cleaner in a labeled, covered container.*

Removal

Refer to illustration 4.3

1   Disconnect the negative cable from the battery.

2   Remove the transaxle (see Chapter 7).

3   Remove the clutch release fork from the ball stud, then remove the bearing from the fork **(see illustration)**.

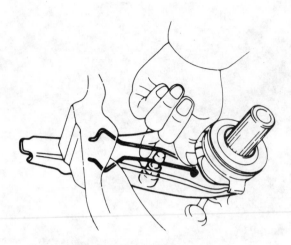

4.3   Reach behind the release lever and disengage the lever from the ball stud by pulling on the retention spring, then remove the lever and bearing

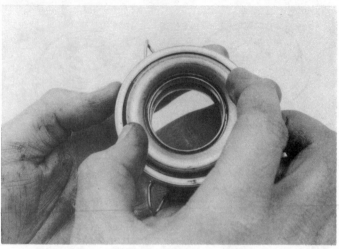

4.4   To check the bearing, hold it by the outer cage (hub) and turn the inner race while applying pressure – the bearing should turn smoothly – if it doesn't, replace it

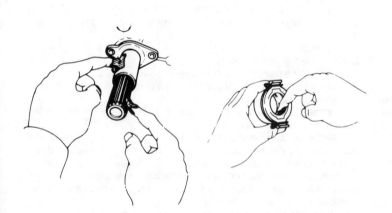

4.5   Apply a light coat of high-temperature grease to the transaxle bearing retainer and fill the release bearing groove

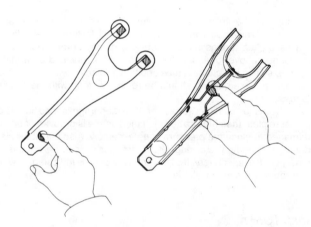

4.6   Apply high-temperature grease to the release fork in the areas indicated

Inspection

Refer to illustration 4.4

4   Hold the bearing by the outer race and rotate the inner race while applying pressure **(see illustration)**. If the bearing doesn't turn smoothly or if it's noisy, replace the bearing/hub assembly with a new one. Wipe the bearing with a clean rag and inspect it for damage, wear and cracks. Don't immerse the bearing in solvent – it's sealed for life and to do so would ruin it. Also check the release lever for cracks and bends.

Installation

Refer to illustrations 4.5 and 4.6

5   Fill the inner groove of the release bearing with high-temperature grease. Also apply a light coat of the same grease to the transaxle input shaft splines and the front bearing retainer **(see illustration)**.
6   Lubricate the release fork ball socket, fork ends and release cylinder pushrod socket with high-temperature grease **(see illustration)**.
7   Attach the release bearing to the release fork.
8   Slide the release bearing onto the transaxle input shaft front bearing retainer while passing the end of the release fork through the opening in

the clutch housing. Push the clutch release fork onto the ball stud until it's firmly seated.
9   Apply a light coat of high-temperature grease to the face of the release bearing where it contacts the pressure plate diaphragm fingers.
10   The remainder of the installation is the reverse of the removal procedure, tightening all bolts to the specified torque.

---

5   Clutch master cylinder – removal, overhaul and installation

---

Note: *Before beginning this procedure, contact local parts stores and dealer service departments concerning the purchase of a rebuild kit or a new master cylinder. Availability and cost of the necessary parts may dictate whether the cylinder is rebuilt or replaced with a new one. If it's decided to rebuild the cylinder, inspect the bore as described in Step 12 before purchasing parts.*

Removal

Refer to illustration 5.2

1   Disconnect the negative cable from the battery.

5.2   To release the clutch pushrod from the clutch pedal, remove the clip and clevis pin

5.5   The reservoir is attached to the master cylinder with a large nut at the bottom

2   Under the dashboard, disconnect the pushrod from the top of the clutch pedal. It's held in place with a clevis pin **(see illustration)**.

3   Disconnect the hydraulic line at the clutch master cylinder. If available, use a flare-nut wrench on the fitting, which will prevent the fitting from being rounded off. Have rags handy as some fluid will be lost as the line is removed. **Caution:** *Don't allow brake fluid to come into contact with paint as it will damage the finish.*

4   From under the dash, remove the nut which secures the master cylinder to the engine firewall. Remove the master cylinder, again being careful

not to spill any of the fluid.

Overhaul

Refer to illustrations 5.5, 5.6a, 5.6b and 5.8

5   Remove the reservoir cap and drain all fluid from the master cylinder. Remove the hold-down bolt inside the reservoir, then pull off the reservoir **(see illustration)**.

6   Pull back the dust cover on the pushrod and remove the snap-ring **(see illustrations)**.

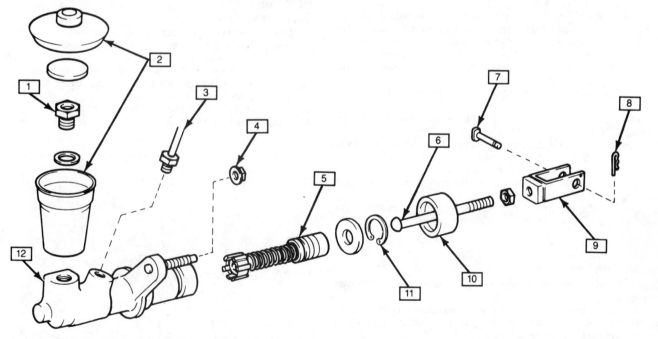

5.6a   Clutch master cylinder components – exploded view (Prizm shown, Nova similar)

1	Reservoir bolt	5	Piston
2	Reservoir	6	Pushrod
3	Clutch line	7	Clevis pin
4	Mounting nut	8	Clip

9	Clevis
10	Boot
11	Snap-ring
12	Master cylinder

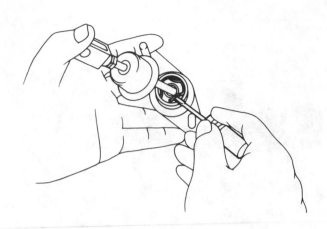

5.6b   Use a small screwdriver to pry the snap-ring out of the groove in the cylinder bore

5.8   Invert the cylinder and tap it against a block of wood to eject the piston

7   Remove the retaining washer and the pushrod from the cylinder.
8   Tap the master cylinder on a block of wood to eject the piston assembly from inside the bore **(see illustration)**. **Note:** *If the rebuild kit supplies a complete piston assembly, ignore the appropriate Steps.*
9   Separate the spring from the piston.
10   Remove the spring support, seal and shim from the pushrod.
11   Carefully remove the seal from the piston.
12   Inspect the bore of the master cylinder for deep scratches, score marks and ridges. The surface must be smooth to the touch. If the bore isn't perfectly smooth, the master cylinder must be replaced with a new or factory rebuilt unit.
13   If the cylinder will be rebuilt, use the new parts contained in the rebuild kit and follow any specific instructions which may have accompanied the rebuild kit. Wash all parts to be re-used with brake cleaner, denatured alcohol or clean brake fluid. DO NOT use petroleum-based solvents.
14   Attach the seal to the piston. The seal lips must face away from the pushrod end of the piston.
15   Assemble the shim, spring support and spring on the other end of the piston.
16   Lubricate the bore of the cylinder and the seals with plenty of fresh brake fluid (DOT 3).
17   Carefully guide the piston assembly into the bore, being careful not to damage the seals. Make sure the spring end is installed first, with the pushrod end of the piston closest to the opening.
18   Position the pushrod and retaining washer in the bore, compress the spring and install a new snap-ring.
19   Apply a liberal amount of Girling Rubber Grease or equivalent to the inside of the dust cover and attach it to the master cylinder.

Installation

20   Position the master cylinder on the firewall, installing the mounting nut finger-tight.
21   Connect the hydraulic line to the master cylinder, moving the cylinder slightly as necessary to thread the fitting properly into the bore. Don't cross-thread the fitting as it's installed.
22   Tighten the mounting nut to the specified torque, then tighten the hydraulic line fitting.
23   Inside the vehicle, connect the pushrod to the clutch pedal.
24   Fill the clutch master cylinder reservoir with brake fluid conforming to DOT 3 specifications and bleed the clutch system as outlined in Section 7.
25   Check the clutch pedal height and freeplay and adjust if necessary, following the procedure in Chapter 1.

6   Clutch release cylinder – removal, overhaul and installation

Note: *Before beginning this procedure, contact local parts stores and dealer service departments concerning the purchase of a rebuild kit or a new release cylinder. Availability and cost of the necessary parts may dictate whether the cylinder is rebuilt or replaced with a new one. If it's decided to rebuild the cylinder, inspect the bore as described in Step 8 before purchasing parts.*

Removal

Refer to illustration 6.3
1   Disconnect the negative cable from the battery.
2   Raise the vehicle and support it securely on jackstands.
3   Disconnect the hydraulic line at the release cylinder. If available, use a flare-nut wrench on the fitting, which will prevent the fitting from being rounded off **(see illustration)**. Have a small can and rags handy, as some fluid will be spilled as the line is removed.
4   Remove the release cylinder mounting bolts.
5   Remove the release cylinder.

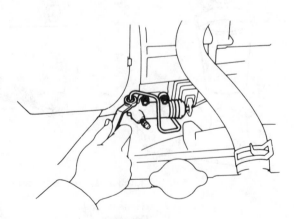

6.3   Use a flare-nut wrench when disconnecting the lines to prevent rounding off the corners of the fitting

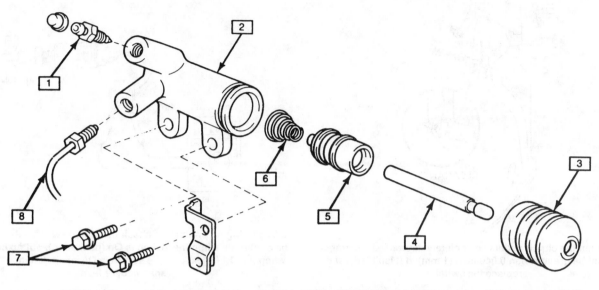

6.6   Clutch release cylinder components – exploded view

1	Bleeder valve	4	Pushrod	7	Mounting bolts
2	Release cylinder body	5	Piston/seal assembly	8	Hydraulic line
3	Boot	6	Spring		

Overhaul

Refer to illustration 6.6

6   Remove the pushrod and the boot **(see illustration)**.

7   Tap the cylinder on a block of wood to eject the piston and seal. Remove the spring from inside the cylinder.

8   Carefully inspect the bore of the cylinder. Check for deep scratches, score marks and ridges. The bore must be smooth to the touch. If any imperfections are found, the release cylinder must be replaced with a new one.

9   Using the new parts in the rebuild kit, assemble the components using plenty of fresh brake fluid for lubrication. Note the installed direction of the spring and the seal.

Installation

10   Install the release cylinder on the clutch housing. Make sure the pushrod is seated in the release fork pocket.

11   Connect the hydraulic line to the release cylinder. Tighten the connection.

12   Fill the clutch master cylinder with brake fluid (conforming to DOT 3 specifications).

13   Bleed the system as described in Section 7.

14   Lower the vehicle and connect the negative battery cable.

7   Clutch hydraulic system – bleeding

1   The hydraulic system should be bled of all air whenever any part of the system has been removed or if the fluid level has been allowed to fall so low that air has been drawn into the master cylinder. The procedure is very similar to bleeding a brake system.

2   Fill the master cylinder with new brake fluid conforming to DOT 3 specifications. **Caution:** *Do not re-use any of the fluid coming from the system during the bleeding operation or use fluid which has been inside an open container for an extended period of time.*

3   Raise the vehicle and place it securely on jackstands to gain access to the release cylinder, which is located on the left side of the clutch housing.

4   Remove the dust cap which fits over the bleeder valve and push a length of plastic hose over the valve. Place the other end of the hose into a clear container with about two inches of brake fluid. The hose end must be in the fluid at the bottom of the container.

5   Have an assistant depress the clutch pedal and hold it. Open the bleeder valve on the release cylinder, allowing fluid to flow through the hose. Close the bleeder valve when fluid stops flowing from the hose. Once closed, have your assistant release the pedal.

6   Continue this process until all air is evacuated from the system, indicated by a full, solid stream of fluid being ejected from the bleeder valve each time and no air bubbles in the hose or container. Keep a close watch on the fluid level inside the clutch master cylinder reservoir; if the level drops too low, air will be sucked back into the system and the process will have to be started all over again.

7   Install the dust cap and lower the vehicle. Check carefully for proper operation before placing the vehicle in normal service.

8   Clutch start switch – check and adjustment

Refer to illustrations 8.4, 8.5, 8.8a and 8.8b

1   Check the pedal height, pedal freeplay and pushrod play (refer to Chapter 1).

2   Verify that the engine will not start when the clutch pedal is released.

3   Verify that the engine will start when the clutch pedal is depressed all the way.

4   Measure clearance "A" **(see illustration)**. It must be as specified when the clutch pedal is depressed (see Step 8). If it isn't, adjust or replace the clutch start switch.

5   Verify that there is continuity between the clutch start switch terminals when the switch is On **(see illustration)**.

6   Verify that no continuity exists between the switch terminals when the switch is Off.

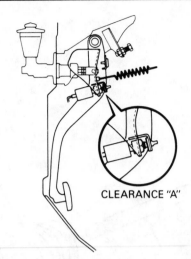

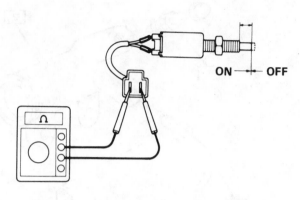

8.4   When the clutch pedal is completely depressed, clearance "A" must be greater than 0.040-inch (1 mm); if it isn't, adjust or replace the switch

8.5   Using an ohmmeter, check the clutch switch – there should be continuity when the switch is On (pushed in), but no continuity when it's Off (released) (the switch is On when distance "A" is as specified, or less)

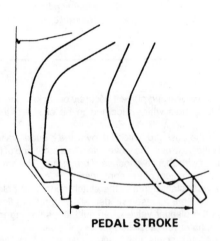

PEDAL STROKE

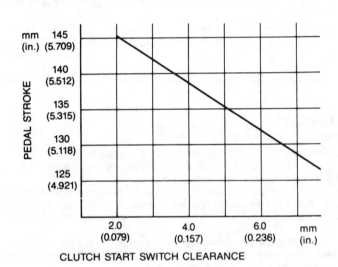

CLUTCH START SWITCH CLEARANCE

8.8a   Pedal stroke is the distance between the position of the pedal at rest (all the way up – released) and when it's depressed as far as possible

8.8b   Clearance "A" is inversely proportional to the pedal stroke – in other words, the longer the pedal stroke, the smaller clearance "A"

7   If the switch fails either of the tests, replace it. This is accomplished by removing the nut nearest the plunger end of the switch and sliding it off the bracket. Disconnect the wire harness. Installation is the reverse of removal.

8   To adjust the clutch start switch, measure the pedal stroke **(see illustration)** and calculate switch clearance "A" using the chart **(see illustration)**.

9   Change the switch position if necessary.

10   Verify again that the engine doesn't start when the clutch pedal is released.

9   Driveaxles – general information and inspection

Power is transmitted from the transaxle to the wheels through a pair of driveaxles. The inner end of each driveaxle is connected to the trans-

axle by a side gear shaft (flanged stub axle) splined to the differential. The side gear shafts can be driven out to replace the oil seals (see Chapter 7, Part A). The outer ends of the driveaxles are splined to the axle hubs and locked in place by a large nut.

The splined inner ends of the driveaxles are equipped with sliding tripod joints, which are capable of both angular and axial motion. Each inner joint assembly consists of a tripod bearing and a joint tulip (housing) in which the tripod is free to slide in-and-out as the driveaxle moves up-and-down with the wheel. The inner joints are rebuildable (see Section 12).

Each outer joint, which consists of ball bearings running between an inner race and an outer cage, is capable of angular but not axial movement. The outer joints are neither rebuildable nor removable. If one of them fails, a new driveaxle/outer joint assembly must be installed.

The boots should be inspected periodically for damage and leaking lubricant. Damaged CV joint boots must be replaced immediately or the joints can be damaged. Boot replacement involves removal of the driveaxle (see Section 10). **Note:** *Some auto parts stores carry "split" type replacement boots, which can be installed without removing the driveaxle*

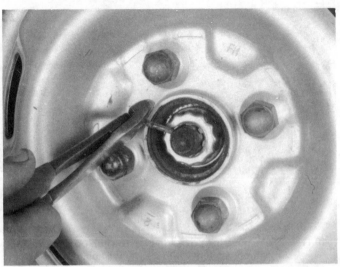

10.2   Remove the hubcap or cover, then pull out the cotter pin and nut lock cap

10.3   With the wheel on the ground, loosen the driveaxle nut with a long breaker bar and a socket

10.8   On some models, the inner CV joint is attached to the side gear shaft flange with six nuts

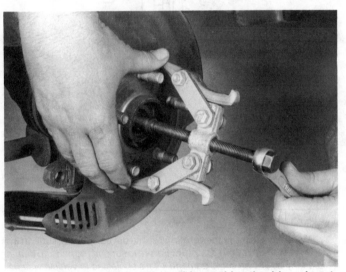

10.11   A two-jaw puller works well for pushing the driveaxle out of the hub

from the vehicle. This is a convenient alternative; however, the driveaxle should be removed and the CV joint disassembled and cleaned to ensure the joint is free from contaminants such as moisture and dirt which will accelerate CV joint wear. The most common symptom of worn or damaged CV joints, besides lubricant leaks, is a clicking noise in turns, a clunk when accelerating after coasting and vibration at highway speeds.

To check for wear in the CV joints and driveaxle shafts, grasp each axle (one at a time) and rotate it in both directions while holding the CV joint housings, feeling for play indicating worn splines or sloppy CV joints. Also check the driveaxle shafts for cracks, dents and distortion.

10   Driveaxle – removal and installation

Refer to illustrations 10.2 and 10.3

1   Disconnect the cable from the negative terminal of the battery.

2   Remove the cotter pin and bearing nut lock from the driveaxle nut **(see illustration)**.
3   Remove the driveaxle nut **(see illustration)**.
4   Loosen, but don't remove, the front wheel lug nuts.
5   Raise the vehicle and support it securely on jackstands.
6   Remove the wheel.
7   Drain the transaxle lubricant (see Chapter 1).

Nova models with 4A-GE engine

Refer to illustrations 10.8, 10.11 and 10.12

8   While an assistant depresses the brake pedal, remove the six nuts or bolts attaching the inner CV joint to the differential side gear shaft **(see illustration)** and detach the tripod joint from the side gear shaft.
9   Remove the disc brake caliper, bracket and disc (Chapter 9).
10   Remove the control arm-to-balljoint bolts and nuts and detach the arm from the balljoint (see Chapter 10).
11   Push the driveaxle out of the hub with a two-jaw puller **(see illustration)** and remove the driveaxle.

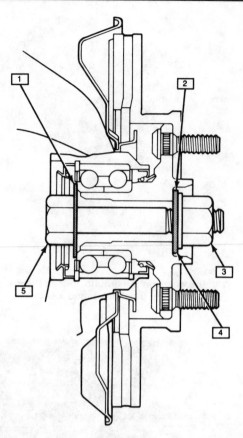

10.17a   To remove the driveaxle from the hub on most models, simply tap it out with a soft-face hammer

13   If you're replacing a differential oil seal, carefully tap the side gear shaft flange out with a hammer and punch and remove it.

14   Installation is the reverse of removal.

All other models

Refer to illustrations 10.17a, 10.17b and 10.18

15   Remove the lower control arm-to-balljoint nuts and bolts (Chapter 10).

16   Detach the tie-rod end from the knuckle (see Chapter 10).

17   Tap the end of the driveaxle with a soft-face hammer and knock it out of the hub and bearing assembly **(see illustration)**, then swing the entire assembly out of the way **(see illustration)**. If it won't slide out of the hub easily, use a puller as described in Step 11.

18   Pry the inner CV joint loose with a large screwdriver **(see illustration)** and remove the driveaxle assembly.

19   If you have to move the vehicle while the driveaxle is out, support the hub and bearings as shown in illustration 10.12.

20   Installation is the reverse of removal.

---

11   Driveaxle boot replacement and CV joint overhaul

Refer to illustrations 11.2, 11.3, 11.5a, 11.5b, 11.6, 11.7, 11.11, 11.12a, 11.12b and 11.14

Note: *If the CV joints must be overhauled (usually due to torn boots), ex-*

10.12   It's not a good idea to move the vehicle with a driveaxle removed, but if you must, first install a bolt and a pair of washers, as shown here, and tighten them securely

1	2-inch (O.D.) washer	4	Lock washer
2	1-3/4 inch (O.D.) washer	5	9/16-inch bolt
3	9/16-inch nut		

12   If you have to move the vehicle while the driveaxle is out, support it as shown **(see illustration)**. **Caution:** *Failure to support the hub and bearing assembly as shown could damage it if it's subjected to vehicle weight.*

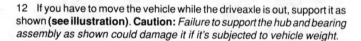

10.17b   Swing the steering knuckle out of the way . . .

10.18   . . . and pry the inner CV joint out of the transaxle with a large screwdriver or pry bar

11.2   Paint match marks (do not use a center punch) on the inner joint tulip and the driveaxle

11.3   The large boot clamps can be pried open with a small screwdriver

plore all options before beginning the job. Complete rebuilt driveaxles are available on an exchange basis, which eliminates much time and work. Whichever route you choose to take, check on the cost and availability of parts before disassembling the vehicle.

1   Remove the driveaxle (refer to Section 10).

2   Make a pair of match marks on the joint tulip and the driveaxle **(see illustration)**.

3   Pry the outer (larger) clamps loose with a small screwdriver **(see illustration)** and slide them off the ends of the driveaxle. Cut the inner (smaller) clamps and the damper clamp with a pair of diagonal cutters and discard them.

4   Separate the inner joint tulip from the tripod joint.

5   Remove the tripod joint snap-ring with a pair of snap-ring pliers **(see illustrations)**.

11.5a   Exploded view of the driveaxle assembly components

1	Outer CV joint race	11	Tripod joint spider
2	CV joint cage	12	Needle roller
3	CV joint inner race	13	Tripod joint ball
4	Shaft retaining ring	14	Ball and needle retainer
5	Ball bearings	15	Not used
6	Not used	16	Not used
7	CV joint seal	17	Right driveaxle
8	Seal retaining clamp	18	Not used
9	Left driveaxle	19	Race retaining ring
10	Tripod joint seal	20	Seal retaining clamp
		21	Not used
		22	Not used
		23	Joint retaining ring
		24	Tripod housing
		25	Not used
		26	Deflector ring
		27	Dust cover

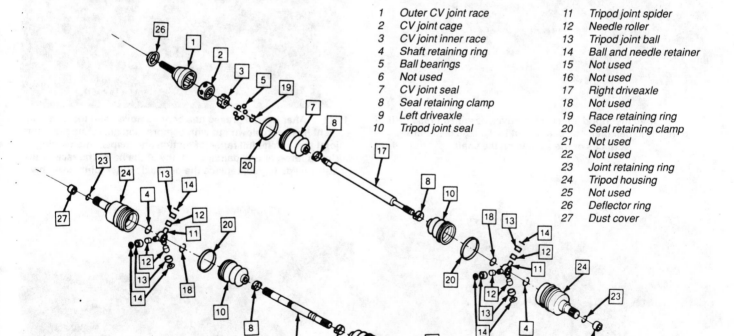

11.5b   Use snap-ring pliers to remove the snap-ring that retains the inner joint tripod

11.6   Use a center punch to make match marks (arrows) on the tripod and driveaxle to ensure they're reassembled properly

11.7   Drive the tripod joint off the driveaxle with a brass drift punch and hammer – be careful not to damage the bearing surfaces or the splines on the shaft

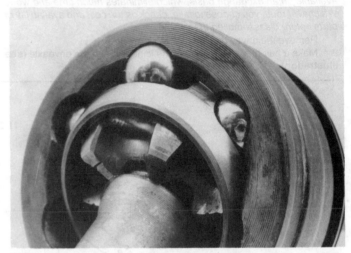

11.11   After the old grease has been removed and the cleaning solvent has been blown out with compressed air, rotate the outer joint through its full range of motion and inspect the bearing surfaces for wear and damage – if any of the balls, the race or the cage look damaged, replace the driveaxle/outer joint assembly

11.12a   To install the new clamps, bend the tang down . . .

11.12b   . . . and tap the tabs over to hold it in place

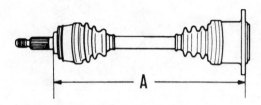

11.14   The driveaxle standard length (A) should be set to the dimension listed in this Chapter's Specifications

6   Make match marks on the tripod and driveaxle **(see illustration)**.
7   Using a hammer and brass punch, drive the tripod joint off the driveaxle **(see illustration)**.
8   Slide the inner joint boot and the outer joint boot off the driveaxle.
9   Clean the inner and outer CV joints with solvent and blow them dry with compressed air, if available. **Note:** *Since the outer joint can't be disas-*

sembled, it's difficult to wash away all the old grease and rid the bearing of solvent once it's clean. But it's imperative that the job be done thoroughly, so take your time and do it right.
10   Inspect the inner tripod joint for signs of wear and damage. If the tripod is obviously worn or damaged, replace it, along with the tulip, as an assembly.
11   Bend the outer CV joint housing at an angle to the driveaxle to expose the bearings, inner race and cage **(see illustration)**. Inspect the bearing surfaces for wear. If the bearings are damaged or worn, replace the driveaxle.
12   Slide the new outer boot onto the driveaxle. It's a good idea to wrap vinyl tape around the shaft splines to prevent damage to the boot. When the boot is in position, add the specified amount of grease (included in the boot replacement kit) to the outer joint and boot (pack the joint with as much grease as it will hold and put the rest in the boot). Slide the boot on the rest of the way and install the new clamps **(see illustrations)**.
13   Slide the inner boot onto the driveaxle. Align the match marks you made before removing the joint and, using a brass punch and hammer, tap the tripod onto the driveaxle. Install the snap-ring. Fill the inner joint tulip with grease and install it over the tripod joint. Slide the boot into place and equalize the pressure inside the boot by inserting a small screwdriver between the boot and joint.
14   Measure the driveaxle length and make sure the boot isn't stretched, contracted or distorted in any way **(see illustration)**. Tighten the boot clamps.
15   Install the driveaxle (see Section 10).

Chapter 9   Brakes

Contents

Specifications

General

Brake fluid type .... See Chapter 1
Brake pedal
  Height
    Nova .... 5.79 to 6.18 in (147 to 157 mm)
    Prizm .... 5.47 to 5.87 in (139 to 149 mm)
  Freeplay (all models) .... 0.12 to 0.24 in (3 to 6 mm)
  Reserve distance
    Nova .... More than 2.56 in (65 mm)
    Prizm .... More than 2.17 in (55 mm)
Power brake booster pushrod-to-master cylinder
  piston clearance .... 0.0 in (0.0 mm)

Disc brakes

Minimum brake pad thickness	See Chapter 1
Front brake disc	
Standard thickness	
Nova	0.531 in (13.5 mm)
Prizm	0.709 in (18.0 mm)
Minimum thickness*	
Nova	0.492 in (12.5 mm)
Prizm	0.669 in (17.0 mm)
Runout limit	
Nova	0.0059 in (0.15 mm)
Prizm	0.0035 in (0.09 mm)
Rear brake disc	
Standard thickness (all models)	0.354 in (9.0 mm)
Minimum thickness (all models)*	0.315 in (8.0 mm)
Runout limit (all models)	0.0039 in (0.10 mm)

Drum brakes

Drum inside diameter	
Standard (all models)	7.874 in (200.0 mm)
Maximum (all models)*	7.913 in (201.0 mm)

* Note: *If different specifications are cast into the disc or drum, they supercede information printed here.*

Torque specifications   **Ft-lbs (unless otherwise indicated)**

Disc brake caliper mounting bolts	
Front caliper	18
Rear caliper	14
Front caliper torque plate-to-steering knuckle bolts	65
Rear caliper torque plate-to-axle carrier bolts	34
Brake hose-to-caliper banjo fitting bolt	
Nova	17
Prizm	22
Wheel cylinder mounting bolts	84 in-lbs
Master cylinder-to-brake booster nuts	108 in-lbs
Power brake booster mounting nuts	108 in-lbs
Wheel lug nuts	See Chapter 1

1 General information

The vehicles covered by this manual are equipped with hydraulically operated front and rear brake systems. The front brakes are disc type and the rear brakes are either drum or disc type. Both the front and rear brakes are self adjusting. The disc brakes automatically compensate for pad wear, while the drum brakes incorporate an adjustment mechanism which is activated as the parking brake is applied.

Hydraulic system

The hydraulic system consists of two separate circuits. The master cylinder has separate reservoirs for the two circuits and in the event of a leak or failure in one hydraulic circuit, the other circuit will remain operative. A dual proportioning valve on the firewall provides brake balance between the front and rear brakes.

Power brake booster

The power brake booster, utilizing engine manifold vacuum and atmo-

spheric pressure to provide assistance to the hydraulically operated brakes, is mounted on the firewall in the engine compartment.

Parking brake

The parking brake operates the rear brakes only, through cable actuation. It's activated by a lever mounted in the center console.

Service

After completing any operation involving disassembly of any part of the brake system, always test drive the vehicle to check for proper braking performance before resuming normal driving. When testing the brakes, perform the tests on a clean, dry flat surface. Conditions other than these can lead to inaccurate test results.

Test the brakes at various speeds with both light and heavy pedal pressure. The vehicle should stop evenly without pulling to one side or the other. Avoid locking the brakes, because this slides the tires and diminishes braking efficiency and control of the vehicle.

Tires, vehicle load and front-end alignment are factors which also affect braking performance.

2.5   Using a large C-clamp, push the piston back into the caliper
bore – note that one end of the clamp is on the flat area near the
brake hose fitting and the other end (screw end) is pressing
against the outer brake pad

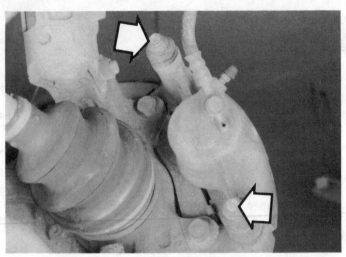

2.6a   Remove the two caliper mounting bolts (arrows) (front
brake shown, rear disc brake similar)

2.6b   Pull the caliper straight up and off the disc

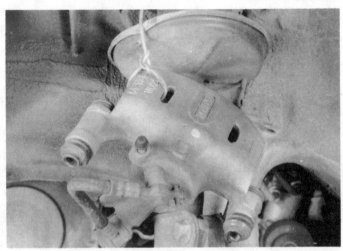

2.6c   Once the caliper is removed from the torque plate, hang it
from the coil spring with a piece of wire – DO NOT let it hang by
the brake hose!

2.6d   Remove the anti-squeal shims from the pads (note how
they're positioned – some models have only one shim per pad,
others utilize two on the inner pad and one on the outer pad)

2   Disc brake pads – replacement

Refer to illustrations 2.5 and 2.6a through 2.6h

Warning: *Disc brake pads must be replaced on both front or rear wheels
at the same time – never replace the pads on only one wheel. Also, the
dust created by the brake system may contain asbestos, which is harmful
to your health. Never blow it out with compressed air and don't inhale any
of it. An approved filtering mask should be worn when working on the
brakes. Do not, under any circumstances, use petroleum-based solvents
to clean brake parts. Use brake cleaner or denatured alcohol only! When
servicing the disc brakes, use only high-quality, nationally-recognized
brand-name pads.*

Note: *This procedure applies to both the front and rear disc brakes.*

1   Remove the cap from the brake fluid reservoir.

2   Loosen the wheel lug nuts, raise the front or rear of the vehicle and
support it securely on jackstands. Block the wheels at the opposite end.

3   Remove the wheels. Work on one brake assembly at a time, using the
assembled brake for reference if necessary.

4   Inspect the brake disc carefully as outlined in Section 4. If machining
is necessary, follow the information in that Section to remove the disc, at
which time the pads can be removed from the calipers as well.

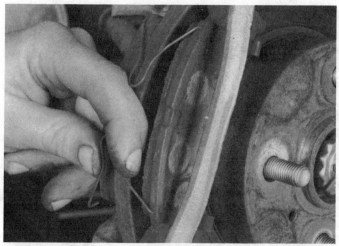

2.6e   Remove the anti-rattle springs from the brake pads

2.6f   To remove the pads, slide them to the side, then straight out of the torque plate

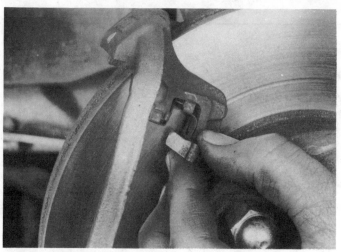

2.6g   Remove the pad support plates from the torque plate – they should be replaced with new ones if distorted in any way

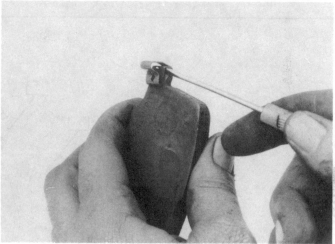

2.6h   Pry the wear indicators off the brake pads and transfer them to the new pads – if they're worn or bent, replace them (the remainder of the brake pad replacement procedure is the reverse of removal)

5   Push the piston back into its bore to provide room for the new brake pads. A C-clamp can be used to accomplish this **(see illustration)**. As the piston is depressed to the bottom of the caliper bore, the fluid in the master cylinder will rise. Make sure that it doesn't overflow. If necessary, siphon off some of the fluid.

6   Follow the accompanying photos, beginning with illustration 2.6a, for the actual pad replacement procedure. Be sure to stay in order and read the caption under each illustration.

7   When reinstalling the caliper, be sure to tighten the mounting bolts to the specified torque. After the job has been completed, firmly depress the brake pedal a few times to bring the pads into contact with the disc. Check the level of the brake fluid, adding some if necessary. Check the operation of the brakes carefully before placing the vehicle into normal service.

inhale any of it. An approved filtering mask should be worn when working on the brakes. Do not, under any circumstances, use petroleum-based solvents to clean brake parts. Use brake cleaner or denatured alcohol only!

Note: If an overhaul is indicated (usually because of fluid leakage) explore all options before beginning the job. New and factory rebuilt calipers are available on an exchange basis, which makes this job quite easy. If it's decided to rebuild the calipers, make sure a rebuild kit is available before proceeding. Always rebuild the calipers in pairs – never rebuild just one of them. Due to the relatively complex design of the rear brake caliper/parking brake actuator assembly, all service procedures requiring disassembly and reassembly should be left to a professional mechanic. The home mechanic can, however, remove the caliper and take it to a repair shop or dealer service department for repair, thereby saving the cost of removal and installation.

3   Disc brake caliper – removal, overhaul and installation

Refer to illustrations 3.1, 3.4a, 3.4b, 3.4c, 3.5, 3.7, 3.8a and 3.8b
Warning: Dust created by the brake system may contain asbestos, which is harmful to your health. Never blow it out with compressed air and don't

Removal

1   Disconnect the brake line from the caliper and plug it to keep contaminants out of the brake system and to prevent losing any more brake fluid than is necessary **(see illustration)**.

2   Refer to Section 2 for either front or rear caliper removal procedures (it's part of the brake pad replacement procedure).
3   If you're working on a rear caliper, disconnect the parking brake cable from the parking brake crank on the underside of the caliper.

Overhaul

4   To overhaul the caliper, remove the piston dust boot retaining ring and the piston dust boot **(see illustrations)**. Before you remove the piston, place a wood block between the piston and caliper to prevent damage as it is removed.
5   To remove the piston from the caliper, apply compressed air to the brake fluid hose connection on the caliper body **(see illustration)**. Use only enough pressure to ease the piston out of its bore. **Warning:** *Be careful not to place your fingers between the piston and the caliper as the piston may come out with some force.*
6   Inspect the mating surfaces of the piston and caliper bore wall. If there is any scoring, rust, pitting or bright areas, replace the complete caliper unit with a new one.

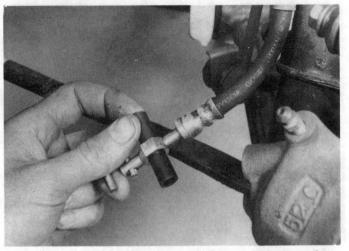

3.1   Use a piece of rubber hose of the appropriate size to plug the brake line

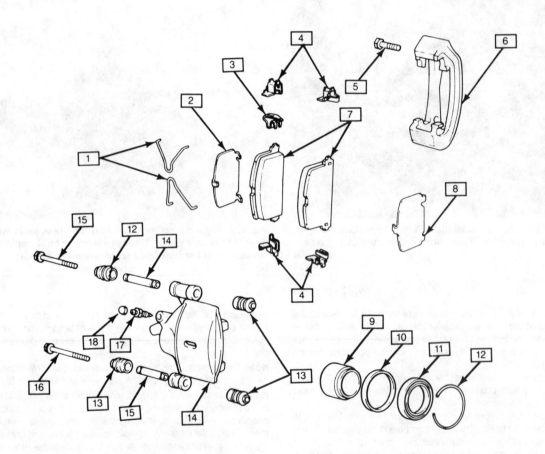

3.4a   Front brake caliper components – exploded view

1	Anti-squeal spring	7	Pads	13	Caliper slide bushing dust boots
2	Anti-squeal shim (inner)	8	Anti-squeal shim (outer)	14	Caliper housing
3	Pad wear indicator	9	Piston	15	Caliper slide bushings
4	Support plate	10	Piston seal	16	Caliper housing mounting bolt
5	Torque plate mounting bolts	11	Piston dust boot	17	Bleeder screw
6	Torque plate	12	Piston dust boot retaining ring	18	Cap

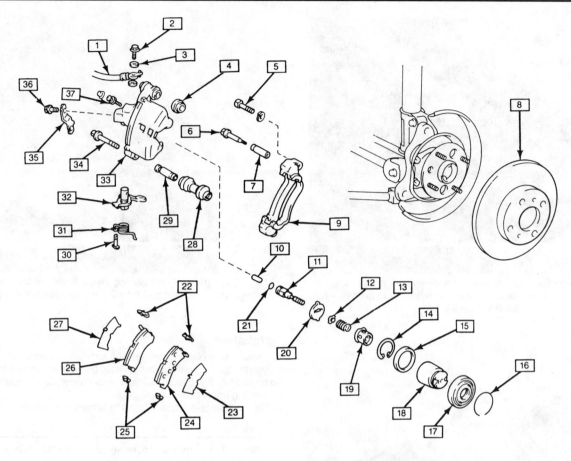

3.4b   Rear brake caliper components – exploded view

1 Brake hose	11 Adjusting bolt	20 Adjusting bolt stopper	29 Sliding bushing
2 Banjo fitting bolt	12 Adjusting bolt spring plate	21 O-ring	30 Stopper pin
3 Sealing washer	13 Spring	22 Anti-rattle spring	31 Parking brake spring
4 Main pin bolt	14 Snap-ring	23 Anti-squeal shim	32 Parking brake lever
5 Torque plate bolt	15 Piston seal	24 Outer brake pad	33 Brake caliper housing
6 Caliper bolt	16 Retaining ring	25 Pad guide plate	34 Caliper mounting bolt
7 Sliding bushing	17 Piston dust boot	26 Inner brake pad	35 Cable support bracket
8 Brake disc	18 Piston	27 Anti-squeal shim	36 Cable support bracket bolt
9 Torque plate	19 Adjusting bolt spring retainer	28 Dust boot	37 Bleeder screw
10 Parking brake strut			

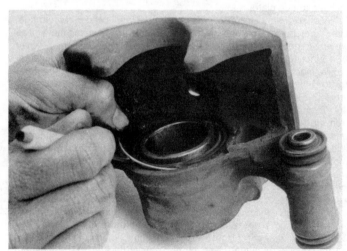

3.4c   Using a screwdriver, remove the piston dust boot retaining ring

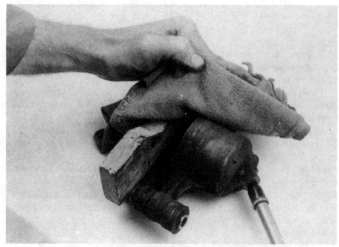

3.5   With the caliper padded to prevent damage, use compressed air to force the piston out of the bore – make sure your fingers aren't between the piston and caliper

3.7   The piston seal should be removed with a plastic or wooden tool to avoid damage to the bore and seal groove – a pencil will do the job

3.8a   Push the sliding bushing on each side of the caliper up through the boot and pull it free, then remove the dust boots

3.8b   Push the bushing sleeve out of the caliper

7   If these components are in good condition, remove the piston seal from the caliper bore using a wooden or plastic tool **(see illustration)**. Metal tools may damage the cylinder bore.

8   Push the sliding bushings out of the caliper ears **(see illustration)** and remove the dust boots from both ends. Slide the bushing sleeves out of the caliper ears **(see illustration)**.

9   Wash all the components in clean brake fluid or brake cleaner.

10   To reassemble the caliper, you should already have the correct rebuild kit for your vehicle. **Note:** *During reassembly apply silicone based grease (supplied with the rebuild kit) between the sliding bushing and the bushing sleeve.*

11   Submerge the new piston seal and the piston in brake fluid and install them into the caliper bore. Do not force the piston into the bore, but make sure that it is squarely in place, then apply firm (but not excessive) pressure to install it.

12   Install the new piston dust boot and retaining ring.

13   Lubricate the sliding bushings and sleeves with silicone-based grease (supplied in the kit) and push them into the caliper ears. Install the dust boots.

Installation

14   Install the caliper by reversing the removal procedure. Remember to replace the copper sealing washer on the brake line union bolt (comes with the rebuild kit). If you're installing the rear caliper, don't forget to reattach the parking brake cable.

15   Bleed the brake circuit according to the procedure in Section 9.

---

4   Brake disc – inspection, removal and installation

Note: *This procedure applies to both front and rear brake discs.*

Inspection

Refer to illustrations 4.2, 4.3, 4.4a, 4.4b, 4.5a and 4.5b

1   Loosen the wheel lug nuts, raise the vehicle and support it securely on jackstands. Remove the wheel and install two lug nuts to hold the disc in place. If the rear brake disc is being worked on, release the parking brake.

2   Remove the brake caliper as outlined in Section 3. It isn't necessary to disconnect the brake hose. After removing the caliper bolts, suspend the caliper out of the way with a piece of wire **(see illustration 2.6c)**. Remove the two torque plate-to-steering knuckle bolts **(see illustration)** and detach the torque plate.

3   Visually inspect the disc surface for score marks and other damage. Light scratches and shallow grooves are normal after use and may not always be detrimental to brake operation, but deep scoring – over 0.015-inch (0.38 mm) – requires disc removal and refinishing by an automotive machine shop. Be sure to check both sides of the disc **(see illustration)**. If pulsating has been noticed during application of the brakes, suspect disc runout.

4   To check disc runout, place a dial indicator at a point about 1/2-inch from the outer edge of the disc **(see illustration)**. Set the indicator to zero and turn the disc. The indicator reading should not exceed the specified allowable runout limit. If it does, the disc should be refinished by an automotive machine shop. **Note:** *The discs should be resurfaced regardless of the dial indicator reading, as this will impart a smooth finish and ensure a perfectly flat surface, eliminating any brake pedal pulsation or other undesirable symptoms related to questionable discs. At the very least, if you elect not to have the discs resurfaced, remove the glaze from the surface with emery cloth using a swirling motion* **(see illustration)**.

5   It's absolutely critical that the disc not be machined to a thickness under the specified minimum allowable disc refinish thickness. The minimum wear (or discard) thickness is cast into the inside of the disc **(see illustration)**. The disc thickness can be checked with a micrometer **(see illustration)**.

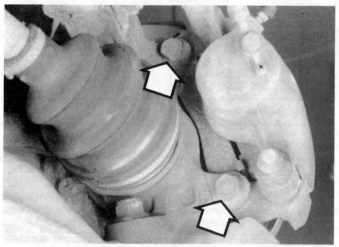

4.2　The caliper torque plate is secured to the steering knuckle with two bolts (arrows)

4.3　The brake pads on this vehicle were obviously neglected, as they wore down to the rivets and cut deep grooves in the disc – wear this severe will require replacement of the disc

4.4a　Use a dial indicator to check disc runout – if the reading exceeds the maximum allowable runout limit, the disc will have to be machined or replaced

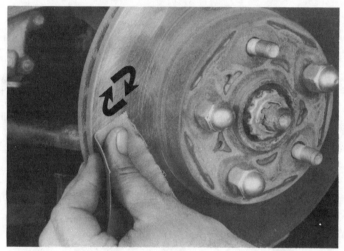

4.4b　Remove the glaze from the disc surface with emery cloth – use a swirling motion

4.5a　The minimum wear dimension is cast into the back side of the disc

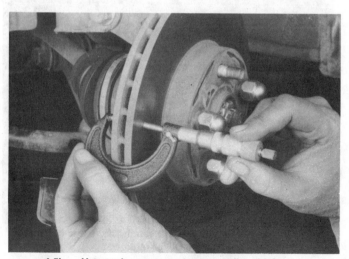

4.5b　Use a micrometer to measure disc thickness

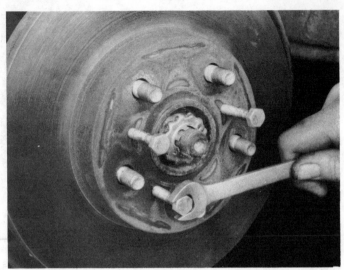

4.6   To remove the disc, thread bolts of the appropriate size into the holes provided – tighten the bolts in 1/4-turn increments until the disc is free

Removal

Refer to illustration 4.6

6   Remove the three lug nuts which were put on to hold the disc in place and remove the disc from the hub. If the disc is stuck to the hub and won't come off, thread bolts into the holes provided **(see illustration)** and tighten them. Alternate between the bolts, turning them 1/4-turn at a time, until the disc is free.

Installation

7   Place the disc in position over the threaded studs.

8   Install the torque plate and caliper assembly over the disc and position it on the steering knuckle. Tighten the torque plate bolts to the specified torque.

9   Install the wheel, then lower the vehicle to the ground. Depress the brake pedal a few times to bring the brake pads into contact with the disc. Bleeding won't be necessary unless the brake hose was disconnected from the caliper. Check the operation of the brakes carefully before driving the vehicle.

---

5   Drum brake shoes – replacement

Refer to illustrations 5.4a through 5.4x and 5.5

Warning: *Drum brake shoes must be replaced on both wheels at the same time – never replace the shoes on only one wheel. Also, the dust created by the brake system may contain asbestos, which is harmful to your health. Never blow it out with compressed air and don't inhale any of it. An approved filtering mask should be worn when working on the brakes. Do not, under any circumstances, use petroleum-based solvents to clean brake parts. Use brake cleaner or denatured alcohol only!*

Caution: *Whenever the brake shoes are replaced, the return and hold-down springs should also be replaced. Due to the continuous heating/cooling cycle the springs are subjected to, they lose tension over a period of time and may allow the shoes to drag on the drum and wear at a much faster rate than normal. When replacing the rear brake shoes, use only high-quality, nationally-recognized brand-name parts.*

1   Loosen the wheel lug nuts, raise the rear of the vehicle and support it securely on jackstands. Block the front wheels to keep the vehicle from rolling.

2   Release the parking brake.

3   Remove the wheel. **Note:** *All four rear brake shoes must be replaced at the same time, but to avoid mixing up parts, work on only one brake assembly at a time.*

4   Follow the accompanying illustrations (5.4a through 5.4x) for the brake shoe replacement procedure. Be sure to stay in order and read the caption under each illustration. **Note:** *If the brake drum cannot be easily pulled off the axle and shoe assembly, make sure the parking brake is completely released. If the drum still cannot be pulled off, the brake shoes will have to be retracted. This is done by first removing the plug from the backing plate. With the plug removed, push the lever off the adjusting star wheel with a narrow screwdriver while turning the adjusting wheel with another screwdriver, moving the shoes away from the drum* **(see illustration 5.4b)**. *The drum should now come off.*

5.4a   Mark the relationship between the drum and hub so the balance will be retained

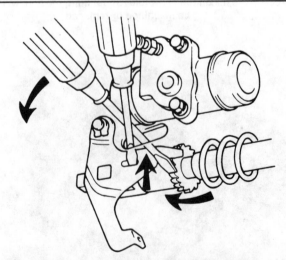

5.4b   If the brake shoes are hanging up on the drum (because of excessive wear), insert two screwdrivers through the hole in the backing plate to push the adjuster lever off the star wheel and turn the star wheel to retract the brake shoes

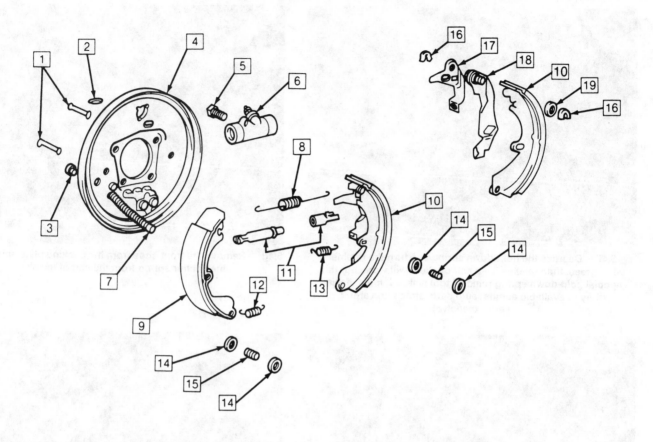

5.4c   Drum brake components – exploded view

1	Hold-down pin	8	Return spring	14	Retainer
2	Adjuster hole plug	9	Front shoe	15	Hold-down spring
3	Inspection hole plug	10	Rear shoe	16	C-washer
4	Backing plate	11	Strut	17	Automatic adjuster lever
5	Bolt	12	Anchor spring	18	Parking brake lever
6	Wheel cylinder	13	Adjuster lever spring	19	Shim
7	Parking brake cable				

5.4d   Before removing anything, clean the brake assembly with brake cleaner and allow it to dry – position a drain pan under the brake to catch the fluid and residue – DO NOT USE COMPRESSED AIR TO BLOW THE DUST OFF THE PARTS!

5.4e   Unhook the return spring from the front brake shoe – a pair of locking pliers can be used to stretch the spring and pull the end out of the hole in the shoe

5.4f   Depress the hold-down spring and turn the retainer 90-degrees, then release it – a pair of pliers will work, but this special hold-down spring removal tool makes it much easier (they're available at most auto parts stores and aren't very expensive)

5.4g   Remove the front shoe from the backing plate and unhook the anchor spring from the end of the shoe

5.4h   Remove the hold-down spring from the rear shoe

5.4i   Separate the rear shoe and adjuster assembly from the backing plate

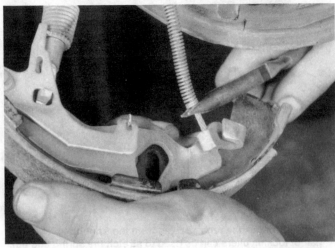

5.4j   Pull back the spring on the parking brake cable and detach the cable from the lever

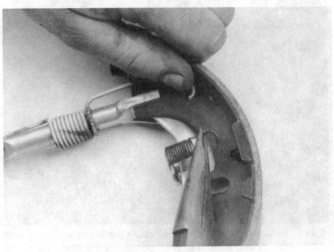

5.4k   Remove the adjuster lever spring

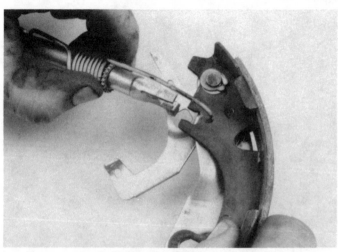

5.4l   Unhook the return spring from the shoe and slide the
adjuster and spring off

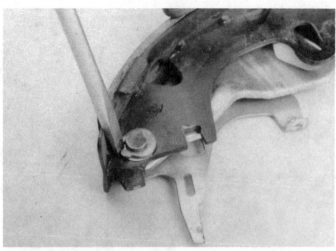

5.4m   Pry the C-washer apart and remove it to separate the
parking brake lever and adjuster lever from the rear shoe

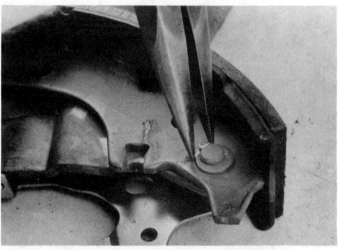

5.4n   Attach the parking brake lever and adjuster lever to the
new rear shoe and crimp the C-washer closed with a pair of pliers

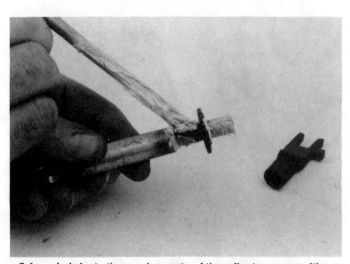

5.4o   Lubricate the moving parts of the adjuster screw with a
light coat of high-temperature grease

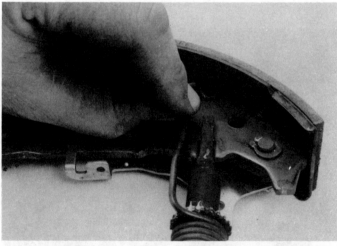

5.4p   Install the adjuster assembly on the rear shoe (make sure
the end fits properly into the slot in the shoe and hook the spring
into the opening in the shoe)

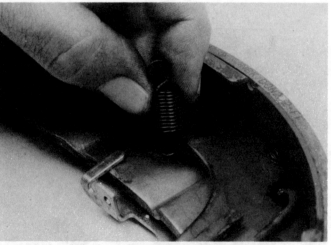

5.4q   Install the adjuster lever spring

5.4r   Lubricate the brake shoe contact areas on the backing
plate with high-temperature grease

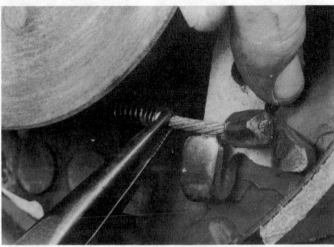

5.4s   Pull the parking brake cable spring back and hold it there
with a pair of pliers, then place the cable in the hooked end of the
parking brake lever

5.4t   Position the rear shoe assembly against the backing plate
and push the hold-down spring pin through the shoe – install the
retainers (one on each side of the spring) and lock the outer
retainer on the pin by turning it 90-degrees after the spring has
been compressed

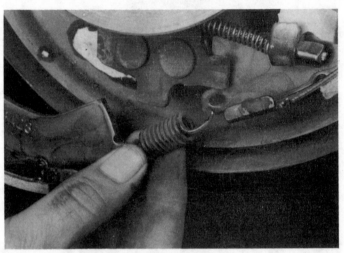

5.4u   Connect the anchor spring to the bottom of each shoe and
mount the front shoe on the backing plate – install the hold-down
spring and retainers

5.4v   Using a screwdriver, stretch the return spring into the hole
in the front shoe

5.4w   Pry the parking brake lever forward and check to make
sure the return spring didn't come unhooked from the rear shoe

5.4x   Wiggle the brake shoe assembly to make sure it's seated properly against the backing plate

5.5   The maximum diameter is cast into the inside of the rear drums

5   Before reinstalling the drum, it should be checked for cracks, score marks, deep scratches and hard spots, which will appear as small discolored areas. If the hard spots cannot be removed with fine emery cloth or if any of the other conditions listed above exist, the drum must be taken to an automotive machine shop to have it turned. **Note:** *Professionals recommend resurfacing the drums each time a brake job is done. Resurfacing will eliminate the possibility of out-of-round drums. If the drums are worn so much that they can't be resurfaced without exceeding the maximum allowable diameter (stamped into the drum), then new ones will be required* **(see illustration)**. At the very least, if you elect not to have the drums resurfaced, remove the glaze from the surface with emery cloth using a swirling motion.
6   Install the brake drum on the axle flange.
7   Mount the wheel, install the lug nuts, then lower the vehicle.
8   Make a number of forward and reverse stops and operate the parking brake to adjust the brakes until satisfactory pedal action is obtained.
9   Check the operation of the brakes carefully before driving the vehicle.

---

6   Wheel cylinder – removal, overhaul and installation

Note: *If an overhaul is indicated (usually because of fluid leaks or sticky operation) explore all options before beginning the job. New wheel cylin-* *ders are available, which makes this job quite easy. If it's decided to rebuild the wheel cylinder, make sure a rebuild kit is available before proceeding. Never overhaul only one wheel cylinder – always rebuild both of them at the same time.*

Removal
Refer to illustration 6.4

1   Raise the rear of the vehicle and support it securely on jackstands. Block the front wheels to keep the vehicle from rolling.
2   Remove the brake shoe assembly (see Section 5).
3   Remove all dirt and foreign material from around the wheel cylinder.
4   Disconnect the brake line with a flare-nut wrench, if available **(see illustration)**. Don't pull the brake line away from the wheel cylinder.
5   Remove the wheel cylinder mounting bolts.
6   Detach the wheel cylinder from the brake backing plate and place it on a clean workbench. Immediately plug the brake line to prevent fluid loss and contamination.

Overhaul
Refer to illustration 6.7

7   Remove the bleeder screw, cups, pistons, boots and spring assembly from the wheel cylinder body **(see illustration)**.

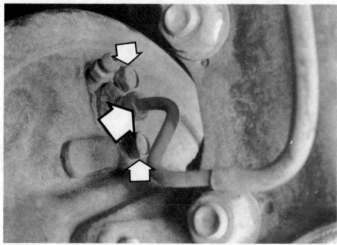

6.4   Disconnect the brake line fitting (arrow), then remove the two wheel cylinder bolts (arrows)

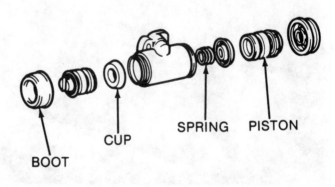

6.7   Wheel cylinder components – exploded view

8   Clean the wheel cylinder with brake fluid, denatured alcohol or brake system cleaner. **Warning:** *Do not, under any circumstances, use petroleum-based solvents to clean brake parts!*
9   Use compressed air to dry the wheel cylinder and blow out the passages.
10   Check the bore for corrosion and score marks. Crocus cloth can be used to remove light corrosion and stains, but the cylinder must be replaced with a new one if the defects cannot be removed easily, or if the bore is scored.
11   Lubricate the new cups with brake fluid.
12   Assemble the brake cylinder components **(see illustration 6.7)**. Make sure the cup lips face in.

Installation

13   Place the wheel cylinder in position and install the bolts. Don't tighten them completely until after the brake line fitting is tightened.
14   Connect the brake line and install the brake shoe assembly.
15   Bleed the brakes (see Section 9).
16   Check the operation of the brakes carefully before driving the vehicle.

---

7   Master cylinder – removal, overhaul and installation

Note: *Before deciding to overhaul the master cylinder, check on the availability and cost of a new or factory rebuilt unit and also the availability of a rebuild kit.*

Removal

Refer to illustration 7.4
1   The master cylinder is located in the engine compartment, mounted on the power brake booster.
2   Remove as much fluid as possible from the reservoir with a syringe.
3   Place rags under the fittings and prepare caps or plastic bags to cover the ends of the lines once they're disconnected. **Caution:** *Brake fluid will damage paint. Cover all body parts and be careful not to spill fluid during this procedure.*
4   Loosen the fittings at the ends of the brake lines where they enter the master cylinder **(see illustration)**. To prevent rounding off the flats, use a flare-nut wrench, which wraps around the fitting hex.
5   Pull the brake lines away from the master cylinder and plug the ends to prevent contamination.

7.4   Completely loosen the brake line fittings (arrows), unplug the electrical connector and remove the mounting nuts (arrows)

6   Disconnect the electrical connector at the master cylinder, then remove the nuts attaching the master cylinder to the power booster **(see illustration 7.4)**. Pull the master cylinder off the studs to remove it. Again, be careful not to spill the fluid as this is done.

Overhaul

Refer to illustrations 7.8a, 7.8b, 7.9, 7.10, 7.11a, 7.11b and 7.11c
7   Before attempting the overhaul of the master cylinder, obtain the proper rebuild kit, which will contain the necessary replacement parts and also any instructions which may be specific to your model.
8   Remove the reservoir retaining screw, pull off the reservoir and remove the grommets **(see illustrations)**.
9   Place the cylinder in a vise and use a punch or Phillips screwdriver to depress the pistons until they bottom against the other end of the master cylinder. Hold the pistons in this position and remove the stopper bolt from the master cylinder **(see illustration)**.
10   Carefully remove the snap-ring at the end of the master cylinder **(see illustration)**.
11   The internal components can now be removed from the bore **(see illustrations)**. Make a note of the proper order of the components so they

7.8a   On some models, the brake fluid reservoir is retained by a screw

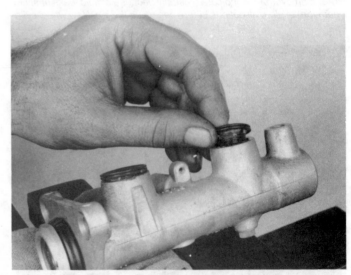

7.8b   After the reservoir has been removed, pull the grommets off (if they're hardened, damaged or appear to have been leaking, replace them)

7.9 Using a Phillips screwdriver, depress the pistons, then remove the stopper bolt – be sure to replace the copper washer on the stopper bolt before installation

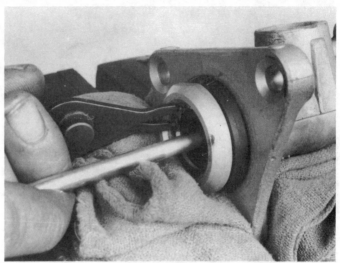

7.10 Depress the pistons again and remove the snap-ring with a snap-ring pliers

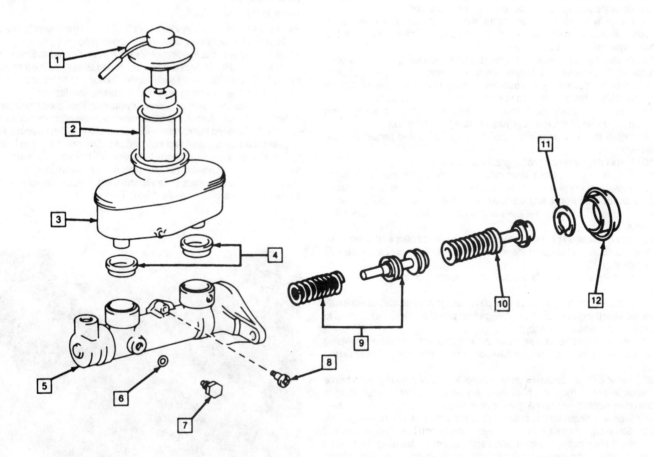

7.11a Typical master cylinder components – exploded view (Nova shown)

1	Cap*	6	Sealing washer	11	Snap-ring
2	Strainer*	7	Piston stopper bolt**	12	Boot
3	Reservoir*	8	Reservoir retaining screw		
4	Grommet	9	Secondary piston and spring	*	Prizm slightly different
5	Housing	10	Primary piston and spring	**	Under side of housing on Prizm

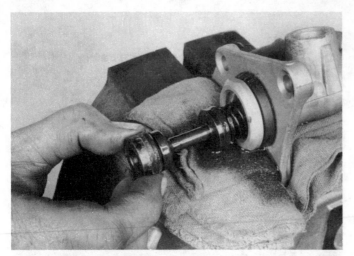

7.11b   After the snap-ring has been removed, the primary piston assembly can be withdrawn

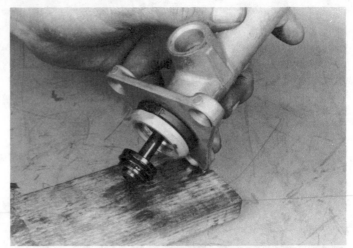

7.11c   Remove the master cylinder from the vise and tap it against a block of wood until the secondary piston is exposed – pull the piston assembly STRAIGHT OUT – if it gets even slightly cocked, the bore may be damaged

can be returned to their original locations. **Note:** *The two springs are different, so pay particular attention to their installed order.*

12   Carefully inspect the bore of the master cylinder. Any deep score marks or other damage will mean a new master cylinder is required. DO NOT attempt to hone the bore.

13   Replace all parts included in the rebuild kit, following any instructions in the kit. Clean all reused parts with new brake fluid, brake system cleaner or denatured alcohol. Do not use any petroleum-based solvents. During reassembly, lubricate all parts liberally with clean brake fluid.

14   Push the assembled components into the bore, bottoming them against the end of the master cylinder, then install the stopper bolt.

15   Install the new snap-ring, making sure it's seated properly in the groove.

16   Install the reservoir grommets, reservoir and screw.

17   Before installing the master cylinder, it should be bench bled. Since you'll have to apply pressure to the master cylinder piston and, at the same time, control flow from the brake line outlets, the master cylinder should be mounted in a vise, with the jaws of the vise clamping on the mounting flange.

18   Insert threaded plugs into the brake line outlet holes and snug them down so no air will leak past them, but not so tight that they can't be easily loosened.

19   Fill the reservoir with brake fluid of the recommended type (see Chapter 1).

20   Remove one plug and push the piston assembly into the bore to expel the air from the master cylinder. A large Phillips screwdriver can be used to push on the piston assembly.

21   To prevent air from being drawn back into the master cylinder, the plug must be replaced and snugged down before releasing the pressure on the piston.

22   Repeat the procedure until only brake fluid is expelled from the brake line outlet hole. When only brake fluid is expelled, repeat the procedure at the other outlet hole and plug. Be sure to keep the master cylinder reservoir filled with brake fluid to prevent the introduction of air into the system.

23   Since high pressure isn't involved in the bench bleeding procedure, an alternative to the removal and replacement of the plugs with each stroke of the piston assembly is available. Before pushing in on the piston assembly, remove the plug as described in Step 20. Before releasing the piston, however, instead of replacing the plug, simply put your finger tightly over the hole to keep air from being drawn back into the master cylinder. Wait several seconds for brake fluid to be drawn from the reservoir into the bore, then depress the piston again, removing your finger as brake fluid is expelled. Be sure to put your finger back over the hole each time before releasing the piston, and when the bleeding procedure is complete for that outlet, replace the plug and tighten it before going on to the other port.

Installation

Refer to illustration 7.27

24   Install the master cylinder over the studs on the power brake booster and tighten the nuts only finger-tight at this time.

25   Thread the brake line fittings into the master cylinder. Since the master cylinder is still a bit loose, it can be moved slightly so the fittings thread in easily. Don't strip the threads as the fittings are tightened.

26   Tighten the mounting nuts and the brake line fittings.

27   Fill the master cylinder reservoir with fluid, then bleed the master cylinder (only if hasn't been bench bled) and the brake system as described in Section 9. To bleed the master cylinder on the vehicle, have an assistant depress the brake pedal and hold it down. Loosen the fitting to allow air and fluid to escape. Tighten the fitting, then allow your assistant to return the pedal to its rest position. Repeat this procedure on both fittings until the fluid is free of air bubbles **(see illustration)**. Check the operation of the brake system carefully before driving the vehicle.

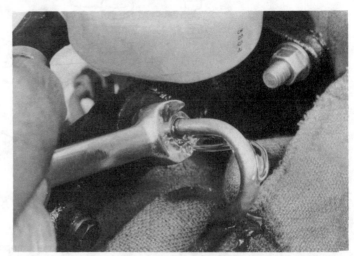

7.27   Have an assistant depress the brake pedal and hold it down, then loosen the fitting nut, allowing the air and fluid to escape – repeat this procedure on both fittings until the fluid is free of air bubbles

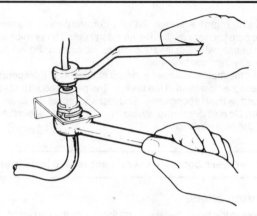

8.3   Hold the hose with a wrench, then loosen the fitting with a flare-nut wrench

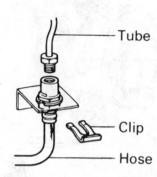

8.4   Once the fitting has been completely loosened, remove the hose clip with a pair of pliers

8   Brake hoses and lines – inspection and replacement

Inspection

1   About every six months, with the vehicle raised and supported securely on jackstands, the rubber hoses which connect the steel brake lines with the front and rear brake assemblies should be inspected for cracks, chafing of the outer cover, leaks, blisters and other damage. These are important and vulnerable parts of the brake system and inspection should be complete. A light and mirror will be helpful for a thorough check. If a hose exhibits any of the above conditions, replace it with a new one.

Replacement

Front brake hose
Refer to illustrations 8.3 and 8.4

2   Loosen the wheel lug nuts, raise the vehicle and support it securely on jackstands. Remove the wheel.
3   At the frame bracket, hold the hose fitting with an open-end wrench and unscrew the brake line fitting from the hose **(see illustration)**. Use a flare-nut wrench to prevent rounding off the corners.
4   Remove the U-clip from the female fitting at the bracket with a pair of pliers, then pass the hose through the bracket **(see illustration)**.
5   At the caliper end of the hose, remove the banjo fitting bolt, then separate the hose from the caliper. Note that there are two copper sealing washers on either side of the fitting – they should be replaced with new ones during installation.
6   Remove the U-clip from the strut bracket, then feed the hose through the bracket.
7   To install the hose, pass the caliper fitting end through the strut bracket, then connect the fitting to the caliper with the banjo bolt and copper washers. Make sure the locating lug on the fitting is engaged with the hole in the caliper, then tighten the bolt to the specified torque.
8   Push the metal support into the strut bracket and install the U-clip. Make sure the hose isn't twisted between the caliper and the strut bracket.
9   Route the hose into the frame bracket, again making sure it isn't twisted, then connect the brake line fitting, starting the threads by hand. Install the U-clip, then tighten the fitting securely.
10   Bleed the caliper as described in Section 9.
11   Install the wheel and lug nuts, lower the vehicle and tighten the lug nuts to the specified torque.

Rear brake hose
12   Perform Steps 2, 3 and 4 above, then repeat Steps 3 and 4 at the other end of the hose. Be sure to bleed the wheel cylinder (or caliper) as described in Section 9.

Metal brake lines
13   When replacing brake lines, be sure to use the correct parts. Don't use copper tubing for any brake system components. Purchase steel brake lines from a dealer or auto parts store.
14   Prefabricated brake line, with the tube ends already flared and fittings installed, is available at auto parts stores and dealers. These lines are also bent to the proper shapes.
15   When installing the new line, make sure it's securely supported in the brackets and has plenty of clearance between moving or hot components.
16   After installation, check the master cylinder fluid level and add fluid as necessary. Bleed the brake system as outlined in the next Section and test the brakes carefully before driving the vehicle in traffic.

9   Brake hydraulic system – bleeding

Refer to illustration 9.8

Warning: *Wear eye protection when bleeding the brake system. If the fluid comes in contact with your eyes, immediately rinse them with water and seek medical attention.*

Note: *Bleeding the hydraulic system is necessary to remove any air that manages to find its way into the system when it's been opened during removal and installation of a hose, line, caliper or master cylinder.*

1   You'll probably have to bleed the system at all four brakes if air has entered it due to low fluid level, or if the brake lines have been disconnected at the master cylinder.
2   If a brake line was disconnected only at a wheel, then only that caliper or wheel cylinder must be bled.
3   If a brake line is disconnected at a fitting located between the master cylinder and any of the brakes, that part of the system served by the disconnected line must be bled.
4   Remove any residual vacuum from the brake power booster by applying the brake several times with the engine off.
5   Remove the master cylinder reservoir cover and fill the reservoir with brake fluid. Reinstall the cover. **Note:** *Check the fluid level often during the bleeding operation and add fluid as necessary to prevent the fluid level from falling low enough to allow air bubbles into the master cylinder.*
6   Have an assistant on hand, as well as a supply of new brake fluid, a clear plastic container partially filled with clean brake fluid, a length of 3/16-inch plastic, rubber or vinyl tubing to fit over the bleeder valve and a wrench to open and close the bleeder valve.
7   Beginning at the right rear wheel, loosen the bleeder valve slightly, then tighten it to a point where it's snug but can still be loosened quickly and easily.

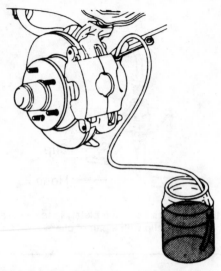

9.8   When bleeding the brakes, a piece of clear tubing is connected to the bleeder valve at the caliper or wheel cylinder and then submerged in brake fluid – air will be seen as bubbles in the tubing and container (all air must be expelled before moving to the next wheel)

wheel and the right front wheel, in that order, and perform the same procedure. Be sure to check the fluid in the master cylinder reservoir frequently.
12   Never use old brake fluid. It contains moisture which will deteriorate the brake system components.
13   Refill the master cylinder with fluid at the end of the operation.
14   Check the operation of the brakes. The pedal should feel solid when depressed, with no sponginess. If necessary, repeat the entire process. **Warning:** *Do not operate the vehicle if you're in doubt about the effectiveness of the brake system.*

---

10   Power brake booster – check, removal and installation

Operating check

1   Depress the brake pedal several times with the engine off and make sure there's no change in the pedal reserve distance.
2   Depress the pedal and start the engine. If the pedal goes down slightly, operation is normal.

Air tightness check

3   Start the engine and turn it off after one or two minutes. Depress the brake pedal slowly several times. If the pedal depresses less each time, the booster is airtight.
4   Depress the brake pedal while the engine is running, then stop the engine with the pedal depressed. If there's no change in the pedal reserve travel after holding the pedal for 30 seconds, the booster is airtight.

Removal

Refer to illustration 10.7

5   Power brake booster units shouldn't be disassembled. They require special tools not normally found in most automotive repair stations or shops. They're fairly complex and, because of their critical relationship to brake performance, should be replaced with a new or rebuilt one.
6   To remove the booster, first remove the brake master cylinder as described in Section 7.
7   Locate the pushrod clevis connecting the booster to the brake pedal **(see illustration)**. It's accessible from inside the vehicle, under the dash on the driver's side.

8   Place one end of the tubing over the bleeder valve and submerge the other end in brake fluid in the container **(see illustration)**.
9   Have the assistant pump the brakes slowly a few times to get pressure in the system, then hold the pedal down firmly.
10   While the pedal is held down, open the bleeder valve just enough to allow a flow of fluid to leave the valve. Watch for air bubbles to exit the submerged end of the tube. When the fluid flow slows after a couple of seconds, close the valve and have your assistant release the pedal.
11   Repeat Steps 9 and 10 until no more air is seen leaving the tube, then tighten the bleeder valve and proceed to the left front wheel, the left rear

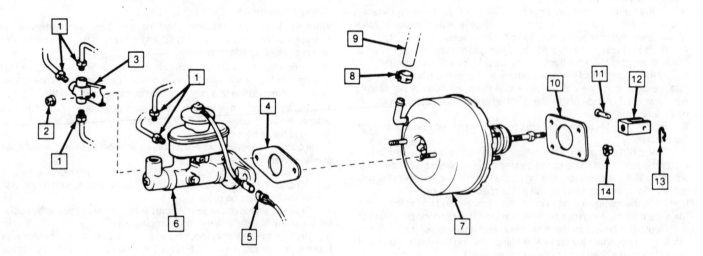

10.7   Power brake booster installation details (Nova model shown, Prizm similar)

1	Brake lines	6	Master cylinder	11	Clevis pin
2	Nut	7	Booster	12	Clevis
3	Three-way union	8	Clamp	13	Clip
4	Gasket	9	Hose	14	Nut
5	Connector	10	Gasket		

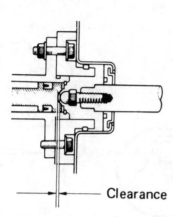

10.14b   To change the length of the booster pushrod, hold the serrated portion of the rod with a pair of pliers and turn the adjusting screw in or out, as necessary

10.14a   The booster pushrod-to-master cylinder pushrod clearance must be as specified – if there's interference between the two, the brakes may drag; if there's too much clearance, excessive brake pedal travel will result

8   Remove the clevis pin retaining clip with pliers and pull out the pin.
9   Holding the clevis with pliers, unscrew the locknut with a wrench. The clevis is now loose.
10   Disconnect the hose leading from the engine to the booster. Be careful not to damage the hose when removing it from the booster fitting.
11   Remove the four nuts and washers holding the brake booster to the firewall (you may need a light to see them).
12   Slide the booster straight out from the firewall until the studs clear the holes.

Installation

Refer to illustrations 10.14a and 10.14b

13   Installation procedures are basically the reverse of removal. Tighten the clevis locknut securely and the booster mounting nuts to the specified torque.
14   If the power booster unit is being replaced, the clearance between the master cylinder piston and the pushrod in the vacuum booster must be measured and, if necessary, adjusted. Using a depth micrometer or vernier calipers, measure the distance from the seat (recessed area) in the master cylinder to the master cylinder mounting flange. Next, measure the distance from the end of the vacuum booster pushrod to the mounting face of the booster (including gasket) where the master cylinder mounting flange seats. Subtract the two measurements to get the clearance **(see illustration)**. If the clearance is more or less than specified, turn the adjusting screw on the end of the power booster pushrod until the clearance is within the specified limit **(see illustration)**.
15   After the final installation of the master cylinder and brake hoses and lines, the brake pedal height and freeplay must be adjusted and the system must be bled. See the appropriate Sections of this Chapter for the procedures.

11   Parking brake – adjustment

Refer to illustration 11.3

1   The parking brake lever, when properly adjusted, should travel five to eight clicks when a moderate pulling force is applied. If it travels less than

11.3   Loosen the locknut, then turn the adjusting nut until the desired handle travel is obtained

five clicks, there's a chance the parking brake might not be releasing completely and might be dragging on the drum. If the lever can be pulled up more than eight clicks, the parking brake may not hold adequately on an incline, allowing the car to roll.
2   To gain access to the parking brake cable adjuster, remove the center console.
3   Loosen the locknut (the upper nut) while holding the adjusting nut (lower nut) with a wrench **(see illustration)**. Tighten the adjusting nut until the desired travel is attained. Tighten the locknut.
4   Install the console.

12   Parking brake cables – replacement

Equalizer-to-parking brake cable

Refer to illustrations 12.3, 12.4, 12.5, 12.6, 12.7 and 12.8

1   Loosen the rear wheel lug nuts, raise the rear of the vehicle and support it securely on jackstands. Block the front wheels. Remove the wheel.
2   Make sure the parking brake is completely released, then remove the brake drum (or disc).

12.3　The parking brake cable housing is bolted to the brake backing plate on drum brake models

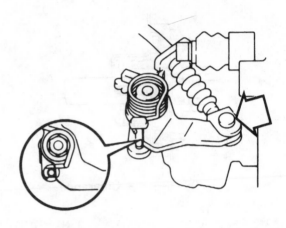

12.4　To detach the parking brake cable from the parking brake lever on rear disc brake models, remove the clevis pin (arrow)

12.5　Detach the cable bracket (arrow) from the frame at the forward end of the torque rod

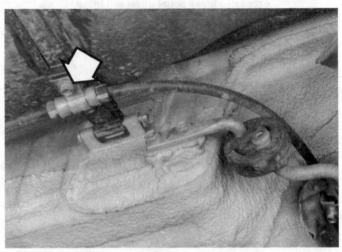

12.6　Detach the cable bracket (arrow) from the forward end of the fuel tank strap

12.7　Loosen the clamp bolt, then slide the cable out of the clamp

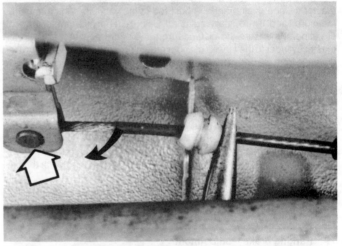

12.8　Pry the cable and grommet out of the guide with a pair of pliers, then rotate the cable end (arrow) clockwise about 90-degrees to align the cable with the slot in the upper half of the lever and detach the cable assembly

12.13   Detach the boot, grasp the cable firmly with a pair of pliers and pull it through the hole in the floorpan

3   If the vehicle has rear drum brakes, remove the brake shoes and disconnect the cable from the parking brake lever (see Section 5) and unbolt the cable housing from the backing plate **(see illustration)**.
4   If the vehicle has rear disc brakes, detach the cable from the parking brake levers on the under sides of the calipers **(see illustration)**.
5   Unbolt the cable bracket from the frame at the forward end of the strut rod **(see illustration)**.
6   Unbolt the cable bracket from the forward end of the fuel tank strap **(see illustration)**.
7   Follow the cable towards the front of the vehicle and locate the cable clamp **(see illustration)**. Loosen the clamp bolt and slide the cable housing out of the clamp.
8   Pry the cable and grommet out of the guide just to the rear of the equalizer **(see illustration)**.
9   Disconnect the cable end from the equalizer by aligning the cable with the slot in the top of the equalizer. Slide the cable end out of the hole.
10   To install the cable, reverse the removal procedure. Adjust the parking brake lever as outlined in the previous Section.

Equalizer-to-brake lever cable

Refer to illustration 12.13

11   Remove the center console.
12   With the lever in the down position, remove the locknut and the adjusting nut (see Section 11) and detach the cable from the lever.
13   Working under the vehicle, pull the cable to the rear, turn it 90-degrees and pass it through the center of the equalizer **(see illustration)**.
14   Installation is the reverse of the removal procedure. Apply a light coat of grease to the portion of the cable end that contacts the equalizer. Adjust the parking brake lever as outlined in the previous Section.

---

13   Brake pedal – removal, installation and adjustment

Refer to illustrations 13.6, 13.11 and 13.13

Removal and installation

1   Remove the left side under-dash panel.
2   Disconnect the return spring from the outer groove in the pushrod clevis pin.
3   Remove the clip and extract the clevis pin.
4   Unscrew the pivot bolt nut, withdraw the bolt and remove the pedal. Inspect the bushings for wear. Replace them if necessary.
5   Install the brake pedal in the reverse order of removal. Lubricate the pivot with grease.

Adjustment

6   The pedal height is measured from the floor to the top of the pedal. Compare your measurement to the Specifications **(see illustration)**.
7   To adjust the pedal height, block the wheels and release the parking brake lever.
8   Loosen the locknut on the brake light switch and unscrew the switch until it no longer contacts the brake pedal shaft.
9   Depress the pedal a few times to remove any vacuum in the system.
10   Loosen the pushrod locknut and turn the rod in the desired direction to set the pedal.
11   Check the brake pedal freeplay **(see illustration)**. Press on the pedal with your fingers until initial resistance is felt. Compare the measurement to the Specifications.

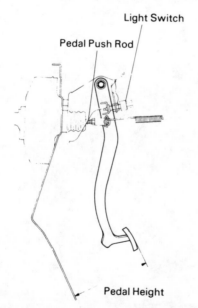

13.6   Measure the distance from the floor to the front of the pedal pad and compare it to the Specifications

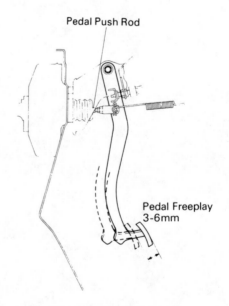

13.11   The pedal freeplay is the distance the pedal moves before the pushrod contacts the booster air valve

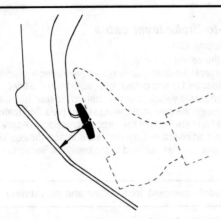

13.13   Measure the pedal reserve distance from the floor to the top of the pedal while the pedal is held down

12   If the freeplay is incorrect, recheck the pedal height and adjust accordingly.
13   Check brake pedal reserve travel **(see illustration)**. Start the engine, depress the brake pedal a few times, then press down hard and hold it.
14   Pedal reserve travel is measured from the floor to the top of the pedal while it's being depressed. Compare the measurement to the Specifications.
15   If the pedal reserve is less than specified, have the brakes adjusted by a dealer service department or a repair shop.
16   Readjust the brake light switch so it's actuated when the pedal is up (not depressed) (refer to Section 14).

14   Brake light switch – removal, installation and adjustment

Refer to illustration 14.1

Removal and installation

1   The brake light switch is located on a bracket at the top of the brake

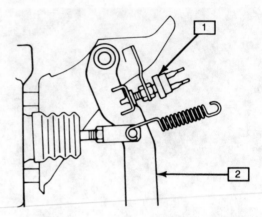

14.1 Brake light switch installation details

    1   Brake light switch
    2   Brake pedal

pedal **(see illustration)**. The switch activates the brake lights at the rear of the vehicle when the pedal is depressed.
2   Disconnect the negative battery cable from the battery.
3   Disconnect the wiring harness at the brake light switch.
4   Loosen the locknut and unscrew the switch from the pedal bracket.
5   Installation is the reverse of removal.

Adjustment

6   Loosen the locknut, adjust the switch so the threaded portion lightly contacts the pedal stop, then tighten the locknut.
7   Connect the wires at the switch and the battery. Make sure the rear brake lights are functioning properly.

Chapter 10
Suspension and steering systems

Contents

Specifications

Torque specifications	Ft-lbs
Front suspension	
Balljoint-to-control arm nuts/bolts	47
Balljoint-to-steering knuckle nut	
Nova	82
Prizm	94
Lower control arm bracket bolts	
Nova	64
Prizm	30
Lower control arm through-bolt	105
Strut-to-knuckle nuts	
Nova	105
Prizm	194
Upper strut-to-body nuts	
4A-GE engine	29
4A-LC engine	23
Strut damper shaft nut	34
Stabilizer bar link bolt(s)	
Nova	13
Prizm	26
Stabilizer bar bracket nuts and bolts	14

Rear suspension

Steering

1   General information

Refer to illustrations 1.1 and 1.2

The front suspension is a Macpherson strut design. The upper end of each strut is attached to the vehicle's body strut support. The lower end of the strut is connected to the upper end of the steering knuckle. The steering knuckle is attached to a balljoint mounted on the outer end of the suspension control arm. On Nova models with a 4A-GE engine and Prism GSi models, the front control arms are connected by a stabilizer bar, which also controls fore-and-aft movement of the control arms **(see illustration)**.

The rear suspension also utilizes Macpherson struts. The upper end of each strut is attached to the vehicle body by a strut support. The lower end of the strut is attached to a knuckle. The knuckle is located by a pair of suspension arms on each side, and a longitudinally mounted strut rod between the body and each knuckle **(see illustration)**.

The rack-and-pinion steering gear is located behind the engine/transaxle assembly on the firewall and actuates the tie-rods, which are attached to the steering knuckles. Most vehicles are equipped with power steering. The steering column is designed to collapse in the event of an accident.

Frequently, when working on the suspension or steering system components, you may come across fasteners which seem impossible to loosen. These fasteners on the underside of the vehicle are continually subjected to water, road grime, mud, etc., and can become rusted or "frozen," making them extremely difficult to remove. In order to unscrew these stubborn fasteners without damaging them (or other components), be sure to use lots of penetrating oil and allow it to soak in for a while. Using a wire brush to clean exposed threads will also ease removal of the nut or bolt and prevent damage to the threads. Sometimes a sharp blow with a hammer and punch will break the bond between a nut and bolt threads, but care must be taken to prevent the punch from slipping off the fastener and ruining the threads. Heating the stuck fastener and surrounding area with a torch sometimes helps too, but isn't recommended because of the obvious dangers associated with fire. Long breaker bars and extension, or "cheater," pipes will increase leverage, but never use an extension pipe on a ratchet – the ratcheting mechanism could be damaged. Sometimes tightening the nut or bolt first will help to break it loose. Fasteners that require drastic measures to remove should always be replaced with new ones.

Since most of the procedures dealt with in this Chapter involve jacking up the vehicle and working underneath it, a good pair of jackstands will be needed. A hydraulic floor jack is the preferred type of jack to lift the vehicle, and it can also be used to support certain components during various operations. **Warning:** *Never, under any circumstances, rely on a jack to support the vehicle while working on it. Whenever any of the suspension or steering fasteners are loosened or removed they must be inspected and, if necessary, replaced with new ones of the same part number or of original equipment quality and design. Torque specifications must be followed for proper reassembly and component retention. Never attempt to heat or straighten any suspension or steering components. Instead, replace any bent or damaged part with a new one.*

2   Stabilizer bar (front) – removal and installation

Refer to illustrations 2.2a and 2.2b
Warning: *Whenever any of the suspension or steering fasteners are loosened or removed they must be inspected and, if necessary, replaced with new ones of the same part number or original equipment quality and design. Torque specifications must be followed for proper reassembly and component retention.*

1   Raise the front of the vehicle and support it securely on jackstands. Apply the parking brake and block the rear wheels to keep the vehicle from rolling off the stands.
2   Detach the stabilizer bar retainer (Nova) or link (Prizm) from the control arms **(see illustrations)**.
3   Detach both stabilizer bar brackets from the vehicle floor pan.
4   Disconnect the exhaust pipe from the exhaust manifold (Chapter 4).
5   Remove the stabilizer bar.
6   While the stabilizer bar is off the vehicle, slide the bracket bushings off and inspect them. If they're cracked, worn or deteriorated, replace them.
7   Clean the bushing area of the stabilizer bar with a stiff wire brush to remove any rust or dirt.
8   Lubricate the inside and outside of the new bushing with vegetable oil (used in cooking) to simplify reassembly. **Caution:** *Don't use petroleum or mineral-based lubricants or brake fluid – they will lead to deterioration of the bushing*
9   Installation is the reverse of removal. Be sure to tighten the exhaust pipe-to-exhaust manifold nuts, the stabilizer bar bracket bolts and the stabilizer bar-to-control arm retainer nuts (Nova) or the stabilizer link nuts (Prizm) to the specified torque.

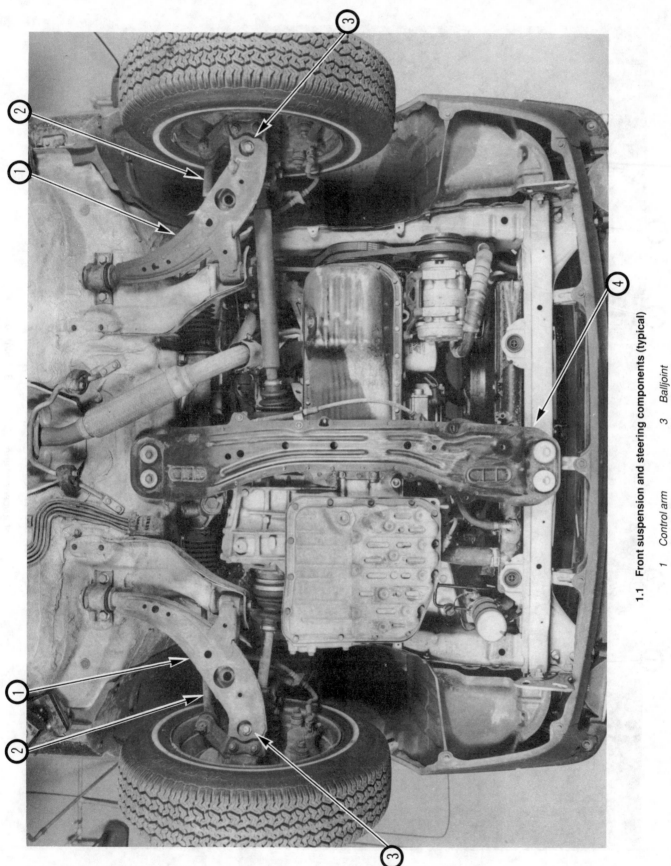

1.1   Front suspension and steering components (typical)

1   Control arm   3   Balljoint
2   Tie-rod   4   Center beam

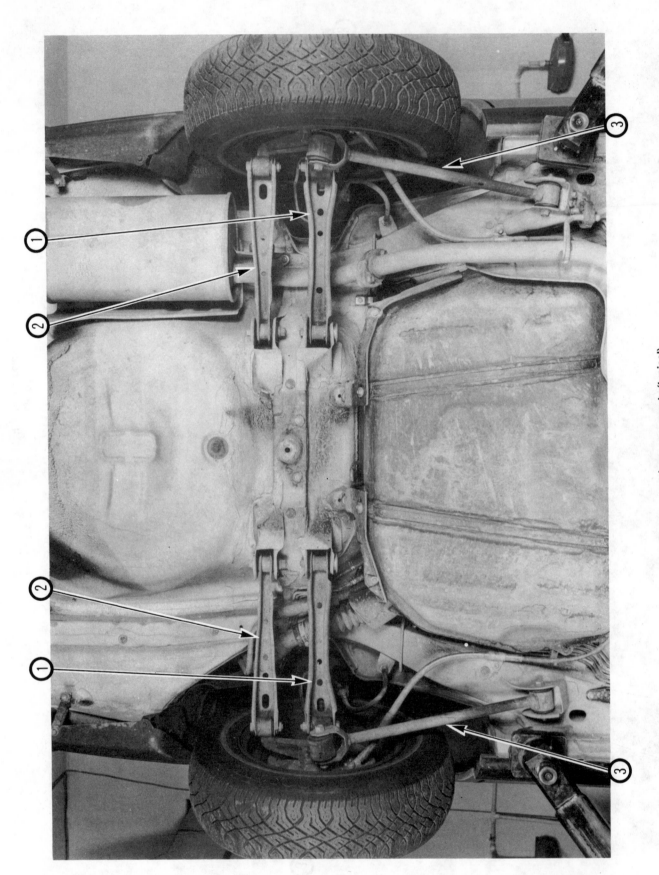

1.2 Rear suspension components (typical)

1 Front suspension arm   3 Strut rod
2 Rear suspension arm

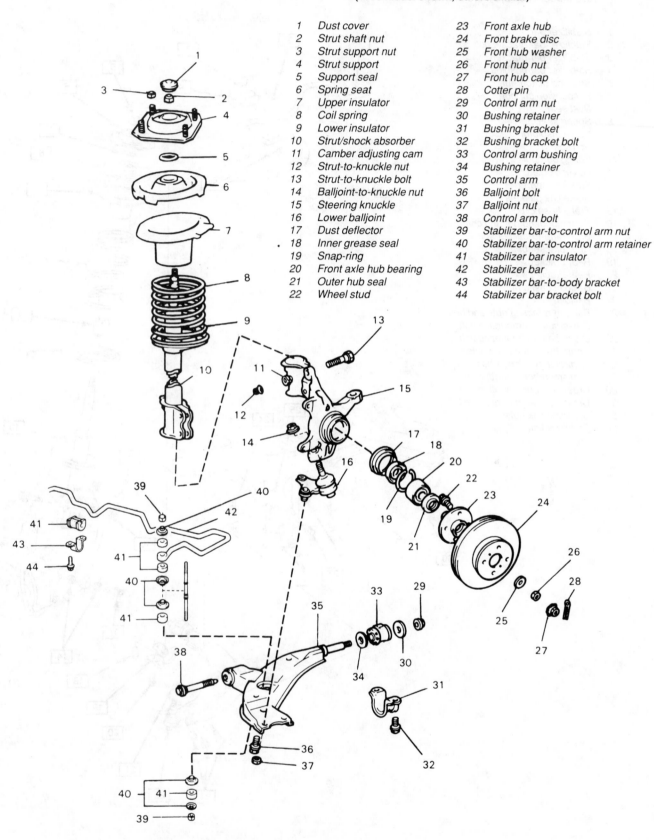

2.2a   Typical Nova front suspension components
(1988 model shown, others similar)

1	Dust cover	23	Front axle hub
2	Strut shaft nut	24	Front brake disc
3	Strut support nut	25	Front hub washer
4	Strut support	26	Front hub nut
5	Support seal	27	Front hub cap
6	Spring seat	28	Cotter pin
7	Upper insulator	29	Control arm nut
8	Coil spring	30	Bushing retainer
9	Lower insulator	31	Bushing bracket
10	Strut/shock absorber	32	Bushing bracket bolt
11	Camber adjusting cam	33	Control arm bushing
12	Strut-to-knuckle nut	34	Bushing retainer
13	Strut-to-knuckle bolt	35	Control arm
14	Balljoint-to-knuckle nut	36	Balljoint bolt
15	Steering knuckle	37	Balljoint nut
16	Lower balljoint	38	Control arm bolt
17	Dust deflector	39	Stabilizer bar-to-control arm nut
18	Inner grease seal	40	Stabilizer bar-to-control arm retainer
19	Snap-ring	41	Stabilizer bar insulator
20	Front axle hub bearing	42	Stabilizer bar
21	Outer hub seal	43	Stabilizer bar-to-body bracket
22	Wheel stud	44	Stabilizer bar bracket bolt

**2.2b   Typical Prizm front suspension components
(1990 model shown, others similar)**

1   Stabilizer bar
2   Stabilizer bar bracket bolt
3   Stabilizer bar bracket
4   Stabilizer bar bushing
5   Strut rod piston nut
6   Suspension support
7   Dust seal
8   Spring seat
9   Upper insulator
10 Coil spring
11 Spring bumper
12 Lower insulator
13 Shock absorber
14 Brake line gaskets
15 Brake hose clip
16 Strut mounting nut and bolt
17 Brake line-to-caliper bolt
18 Rear bracket bolt
19 Rear bracket
20 Rear bracket bolt
21 Balljoint castle nut
22 Balljoint
23 Balljoint retaining nuts and bolt
24 Crossmember mounting bolt
25 Crossmember mounting bolt
26 Control arm mounting nuts
27 Control arm through-bolt
28 Crossmember mounting bolt
29 Crossmember mounting bolt
30 Crossmember mounting bolt
31 Stabilizer link nuts
32 Stabilizer link

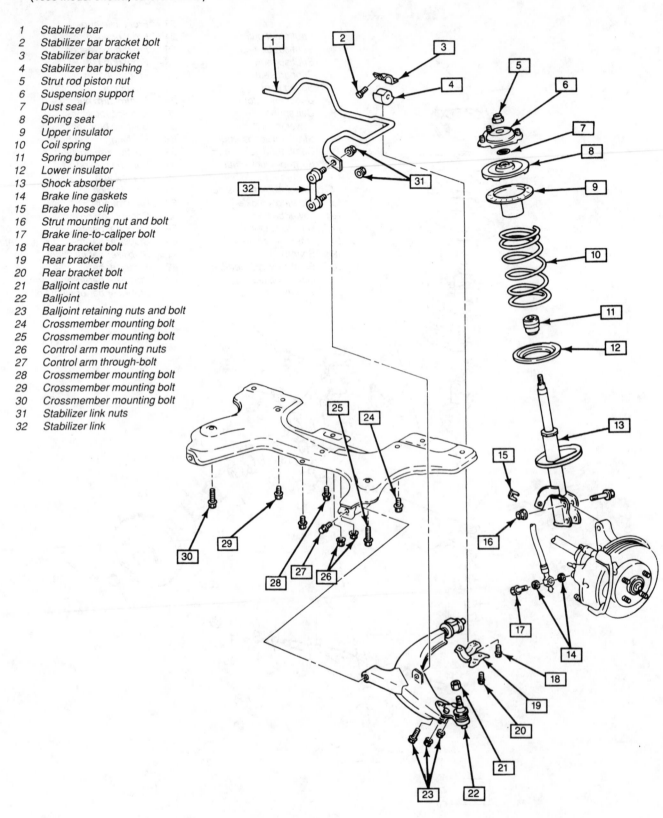

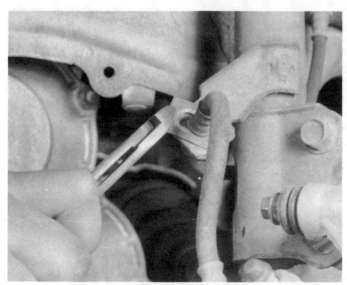

3.3   Pull the brake hose-to-strut bracket clip off with a pair of pliers

3.5   Using white paint, mark the relationship of the strut, camber adjusting cam and steering knuckle

3   Strut assembly (front) – removal, inspection and installation

Refer to illustrations 3.3, 3.5, 3.6, 3.7a, 3.7b and 3.8

Removal

1   Loosen the wheel lug nuts, raise the vehicle and support it securely on jackstands.
2   Remove the wheel.
3   Detach the brake hose banjo fitting from the caliper (see Chapter 9). Have some rags and a container handy to catch the brake fluid. Detach the brake hose clip from the strut bracket **(see illustration)**. Pull the brake hose through the opening in the strut bracket. Tape or cap the brake hose and caliper to keep out dirt.
4   Remove the brake caliper (see Chapter 9). Hang it from the strut spring with a piece of wire – not with the brake hose. Don't disconnect the hose from the caliper.

5   Using white paint or a scribe, make a mark from the strut to the camber adjusting cam and steering knuckle **(see illustration)**.
6   Remove the strut-to-knuckle nuts and knock the bolts out with a hammer and punch **(see illustration)**. Don't misplace the nuts or the camber adjusting cam.
7   Separate the strut from the steering knuckle **(see illustrations)**. Be careful not to damage the outer CV joint boot during strut removal. And don't over-extend the inner CV joint (one way to prevent this from happening is to wire the top of the steering knuckle to the body).
8   Mark the relationship of the upper strut nuts to the body and remove them, then detach the strut from the vehicle **(see illustration)**.

Inspection

9   Check the strut body for leaking fluid, dents, cracks and other obvious damage which would warrant repair or replacement. Check the coil spring for chips and cracks in the spring coating (this will cause premature spring failure due to corrosion).

3.6   Remove the nuts from the steering knuckle-to-strut bolts and drive the bolts out with a hammer and punch

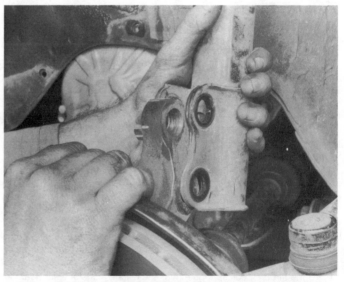

3.7a   Pull the steering knuckle out of the strut bracket – be careful not to pull it out too far or the driveaxle inner CV joint will be over-extended

3.7b   **The camber adjuster slides into the upper hole in the steering knuckle – don't forget to install it**

3.8   **The upper end of the strut assembly is fastened to the shock tower with three or four nuts**

10   Inspect the spring seat for damage, hardness and general deterioration.

11   If any undesirable conditions exist, proceed to Section 4 for the strut disassembly procedure.

Installation

12   Guide the strut assembly up into the fender well and insert the three upper mounting studs through the holes in the shock tower. Once the three studs protrude from the shock tower, install the nuts so the strut won't fall back through. This is most easily accomplished with the help of an assistant, as the strut is quite heavy and awkward.

13   Insert the camber adjuster into the upper hole in the steering knuckle, if it fell out. Slide the steering knuckle into the strut flange and insert the two bolts. Install the nuts, align the marks and tighten the nuts to the specified torque.

14   Install the brake caliper. Reinstall the brake hose (Chapter 9).

15   Install the wheel, lower the vehicle and tighten the lug nuts to the torque specified in Chapter 1.

16   Tighten the three upper mounting nuts to the specified torque.

17   Drive the vehicle to an alignment shop to have the front end alignment checked and, if necessary, adjusted.

---

4   Strut/spring assembly (front) – replacement

Refer to illustrations 4.4, 4.5, 4.6, 4.7, 4.8, 4.13, 4.14a and 4.14b

Warning: *Whenever any of the suspension or steering fasteners are loosened or removed they must be inspected and, if necessary, replaced with new ones of the same part number or original equipment quality and design. Torque specifications must be followed for proper reassembly and component retention.*

Note: *You'll need a spring compressor for this procedure. Spring compressors are available on a daily rental basis at most auto parts stores or equipment yards.*

1   If the struts or coil springs exhibit the telltale signs of wear (leaking fluid, loss of damping capability, chipped, sagging or cracked coil springs) explore all options before beginning any work. The strut/shock absorber assemblies are not serviceable and must be replaced if a problem devel-

ops. However, strut assemblies complete with springs may be available on an exchange basis, which eliminates much time and work. Whichever route you choose to take, check on the cost and availability of parts before disassembling your vehicle. **Warning:** *Disassembling a strut assembly is a potentially dangerous undertaking and utmost attention must be directed to the job at hand, or serious bodily injury may result. Use only a high quality spring compressor and carefully follow the manufacturer's instructions furnished with the tool. After removing the coil spring from the strut assembly, set it aside in a safe, isolated area (a steel cabinet is preferred).*

2   Remove the strut and spring assembly (see Section 3).

3   Mount the strut assembly in a vise. Line the vise jaws with wood or rags to prevent damage to the unit and don't tighten the vise excessively.

4   Install the spring compressor in accordance with the manufacturer's instructions **(see illustration)**. Compress the spring until you can wiggle the strut (suspension) support.

5   Loosen the damper shaft nut with a socket wrench **(see illustration)**. To prevent the suspension support and damper shaft from turning, wedge a screwdriver or pry bar between one of the upper mounting studs and the socket.

6   Remove the nut and suspension support **(see illustration)**. Inspect the bearing in the suspension support for smooth operation. If it doesn't turn smoothly, replace the suspension support. Check the rubber portion of the suspension support for cracking and general deterioration. If there is any separation of the rubber, replace it.

7   Lift the spring seat and upper insulator from the damper shaft **(see illustration)**. Check the rubber spring seat for cracking and hardness, replacing it if necessary.

8   Carefully lift the compressed spring from the assembly **(see illustration)** and set it in a safe place, such as a steel cabinet. **Warning:** *Never place your head near the end of the spring!*

9   Slide the rubber bumper and dust boot off the damper shaft.

10   Check the lower insulator for wear, cracking and hardness and replace it if necessary.

11   Assemble the strut beginning with the dust boot and rubber bumper – extend the damper rod as far as it will go and slide the boot and bumper down to the strut body.

12   If the lower insulator is being replaced, set it into position with the dropped portion seated in the lowest part of the seat.

13   Carefully place the coil spring onto the lower insulator, with the end of the spring resting in the lowest part of the insulator **(see illustration)**.

4.4   Install the spring compressor according to the tool manufacturer's instructions and compress the spring until all pressure is relieved from the upper spring seat

4.5   Remove the damper shaft nut

4.6   Lift the suspension support off the damper shaft

4.7   Remove the spring seat from the damper shaft

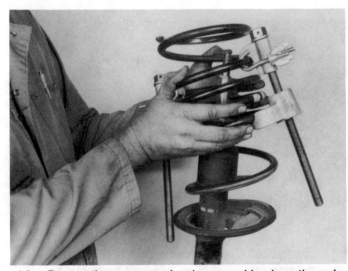

4.8   Remove the compressed spring assembly – keep the ends of the spring pointing away from your body!

4.13   When installing the spring, make sure the end fits into the recessed portion of the lower seat (arrow)

4.14a   The flats on the damper shaft (arrow) must match up with the flats in the spring seat

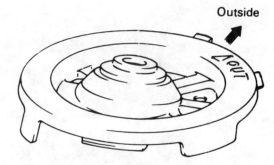

4.14b   The OUT mark on the spring seat must face the strut bracket opening

14   Install the upper insulator and spring seat, making sure that the flats in the hole in the seat match up with the flats on the damper shaft **(see illustration)**. Also make sure that the "out" marking on the spring seat faces toward the lower bracket, where the steering knuckle fits **(see illustration)**.
15   Install the dust seal and suspension support to the damper shaft.
16   Install the nut and tighten it to the specified torque.
17   Install the strut/shock absorber and coil spring assembly (see Section 3).

---

5   Control arm (front) – removal, inspection and installation

---

Refer to illustrations 5.3, 5.4a and 5.4b
Warning: *Whenever any of the suspension or steering fasteners are loosened or removed they must be inspected and, if necessary, replaced with new ones of the same part number or of original equipment quality and design. Torque specifications must be followed for proper reassembly and component retention.*

Removal

1   Loosen the wheel lug nuts, raise the front of the vehicle, support it securely on jackstands and remove the wheel.

2   Detach the stabilizer bar, if equipped, from the control arm (see Section 2).
3   Remove the balljoint-to-control arm bolt and nuts **(see illustration)**.
4   Remove the front and rear control arm mounting bolts **(see illustrations)**.
5   Remove the control arm from the vehicle.

Inspection

6   Check the control arm for distortion and the bushings for wear, damage and deterioration. Replace a damaged or bent control arm with a new one. If the inner pivot bushing or stabilizer bar bushings are worn, take the control arm assembly to a dealer service department or a repair shop, as special tools are required to replace them.

Installation

7   Installation is the reverse of removal.
8   Have the front wheel alignment checked and adjusted when you're done.

---

6   Balljoint (front) – replacement

Warning: *Whenever any of the suspension or steering fasteners are loosened or removed, they must be inspected and, if necessary, replaced with new ones of the same part number or of original equipment quality and design. Torque specifications must be followed for proper reassembly and component retention.*

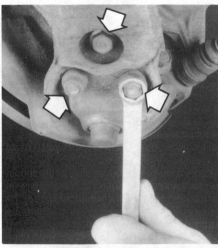

5.3   Remove the balljoint-to-control arm bolts and nuts (arrows)

5.4a   Remove the front control arm nut and through-bolt

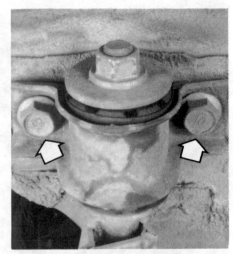

5.4b   Remove the bracket bolts (arrows) at the rear control arm pivot

1   Loosen the wheel lug nuts, raise the vehicle and support it securely on jackstands. Remove the wheel.

2   Separate the control arm from the knuckle (see Section 5).

3   Separate the outer driveaxle CV joint from the steering knuckle (see Chapter 8).

4   Remove the cotter pin and castellated nut from the balljoint stud.

5   Using a pickle fork or a puller, separate the balljoint stud from the knuckle.

6   Installation is the reverse of removal. Be sure to tighten the castellated nut to the specified torque.

7   Steering knuckle and hub – removal and installation

Refer to illustration 7.11

Warning: *Whenever any of the suspension or steering fasteners are loosened or removed they must be inspected and, if necessary replaced with new ones of the same part number or of original equipment quality and design. Torque specifications must be followed for proper reassembly and component retention. Dust created by the brake system may contain as-* bestos, *which is harmful to your health. Never blow it out with compressed air and don't inhale any of it. Do not, under any circumstances, use petroleum-based solvents to clean brake parts. Use brake cleaner or denatured alcohol only.*

1   Loosen the wheel lug nuts, raise the vehicle and support it securely on jackstands. Remove the wheel.

2   Remove the brake caliper and support it with a piece of wire. Separate the brake disc from the hub (see Chapter 9).

3   Loosen the hub nut (see Chapter 8).

4   Mark the relationship of the strut to the steering knuckle and camber adjuster (see Section 3).

5   Separate the tie-rod from the steering knuckle arm (see Section 20).

6   Remove the balljoint-to-control arm bolt and nuts (see Section 6).

7   Remove the strut-to-knuckle bolts (see Section 3).

8   Push the driveaxle from the hub (see Chapter 8). Support the end of the driveaxle with a piece of wire.

9   Carefully separate the steering knuckle from the strut and balljoint.

10 Separate the balljoint from the steering knuckle and hub assembly (see Section 6).

11 Installation is the reverse of removal **(see illustration)**. Be sure to tighten all critical fasteners to the specified torque.

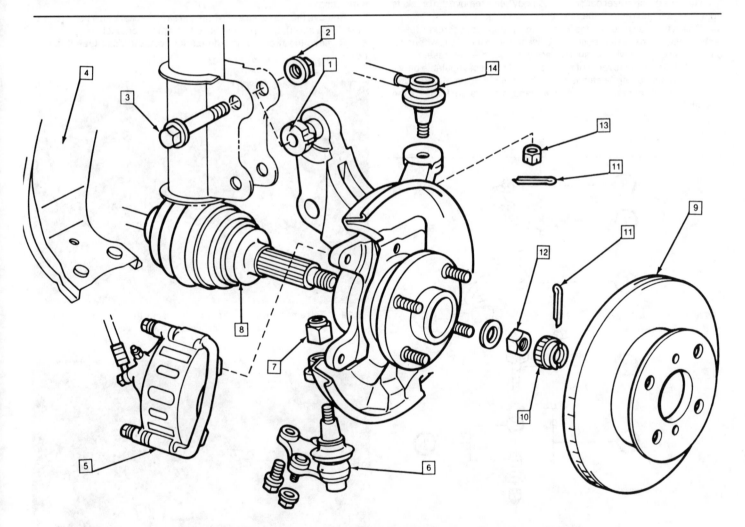

7.11   Typical steering knuckle and hub assembly (Nova shown, Prizm similar)

1	Camber adjusting cam	6	Lower balljoint	11	Cotter pin
2	Strut-to-knuckle nut	7	Balljoint nut	12	Driveaxle nut
3	Strut-to-knuckle bolt	8	Front driveaxle	13	Tie-rod end nut
4	Control arm	9	Disc brake rotor	14	Tie-rod end
5	Brake caliper	10	Locknut cap		

8   Hub and bearing assembly (front) – removal and installation

Due to the special tools and expertise required to press the hub and bearing from the steering knuckle, this job should be left to a professional mechanic. However, the steering knuckle and hub may be removed and the assembly taken to a local dealer service department or repair shop. Refer to Section 7 for steering knuckle and hub removal.

9   Stabilizer bar (rear) – removal and installation

Refer to illustration 9.2

1   Raise the vehicle and support it securely on jackstands.
2   Disconnect the stabilizer bar link from the suspension control arm **(see illustration)**. Note the order in which the bushings and spacers are arranged.
3   Remove the stabilizer bar bracket-to-body bolts, remove the brackets from the body and remove the bar from the vehicle.
4   Check the bracket bushings for cracking, hardness or general deterioration. Also check the link bushings for wear. Clean the areas where the bushings ride with a wire brush. Replace worn parts as necessary.
5   Installation is the reverse of removal. A light coat of vegetable oil will ease installation of the bushings and U-brackets (don't use petroleum-based lubricants or brake fluid – they will lead to premature failure of the bushing).

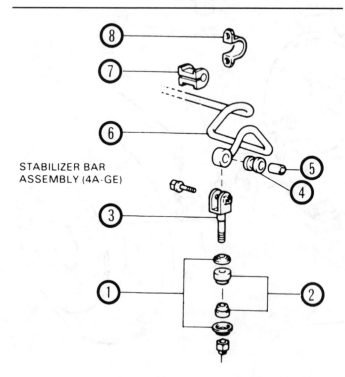

STABILIZER BAR
ASSEMBLY (4A-GE)

9.2   Typical stabilizer bar components – exploded view

1	Retainers	5	Collar
2	Cushions	6	Stabilizer bar
3	Stabilizer link	7	Bushing
4	Bushing	8	Bracket

10   Strut assembly (rear) – removal, inspection and installation

Warning: *Whenever any of the suspension or steering fasteners are loosened or removed they must be inspected and, if necessary, replaced with ones of the same part number or of original equipment quality and design. Torque specifications must be followed for proper reassembly and component retention.*

Removal

Refer to illustrations 10.1a, 10.1b, 10.5, 10.6a, 10.6b, 10.6c and 10.7

1   Remove the plastic molding from the rear shock tower **(see illustrations)**.
2   Loosen the wheel lug nuts, raise the rear of the vehicle and support it securely on jackstands. Remove the wheel.
3   Unscrew the brake line from the wheel cylinder (or caliper). Use a flare-nut wrench to avoid rounding off the corners of the nut.
4   Disconnect the fitting between the brake line and the flexible hose. Again, use a flare-nut wrench. Plug the hose end or wrap a plastic bag tightly around the end of the hose to prevent excessive leakage and contamination.
5   Remove the brake hose clip from the strut bracket with a pair of pliers **(see illustration)**, then pull the hose through the bracket.
6   Remove the two strut-to-axle carrier nuts and bolts **(see illustrations)**.

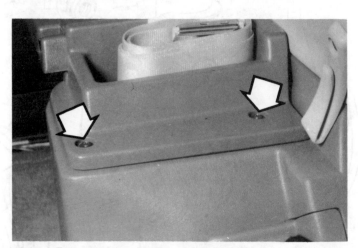

10.1a   To remove the plastic molding from the rear shock tower, remove the screws (arrows), . . .

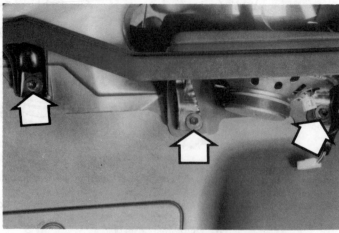

10.1b   . . . then remove the three nuts underneath (arrows) (Nova shown, Prizm similar)

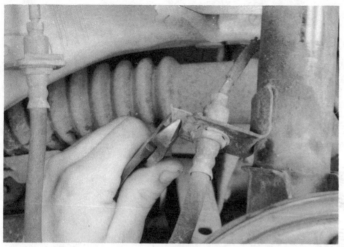

10.5   Use a pair of pliers to remove the retaining clip from the brake hose bracket on the strut, then pull the hose through the bracket

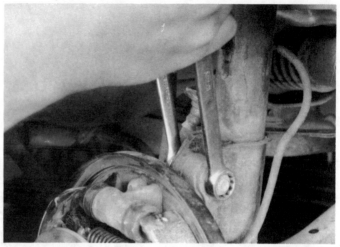

10.6a   Remove the strut-to-axle carrier bolts and nuts

10.6b   **Typical Nova rear suspension components – exploded view**

1	Dust cover	11	Flexible brake hose	21	Bolt
2	Strut piston rod nut	12	Nut	22	Bushing
3	Suspension support	13	Bolt	23	Toe-in adjusting cam nut
4	Upper insulator	14	Carrier, hub and drum assembly	24	Toe-in indicator
5	Coil spring	15	Strut rod	25	Bolt
6	Bumper	16	Bolts	26	Body suspension arm mounts
7	Lower insulator	17	Nut		
8	Strut assembly	18	Rear suspension arm		
9	Brake line	19	Front suspension arm		
10	Retaining clip	20	Nut		

VIEW **A**

FWD

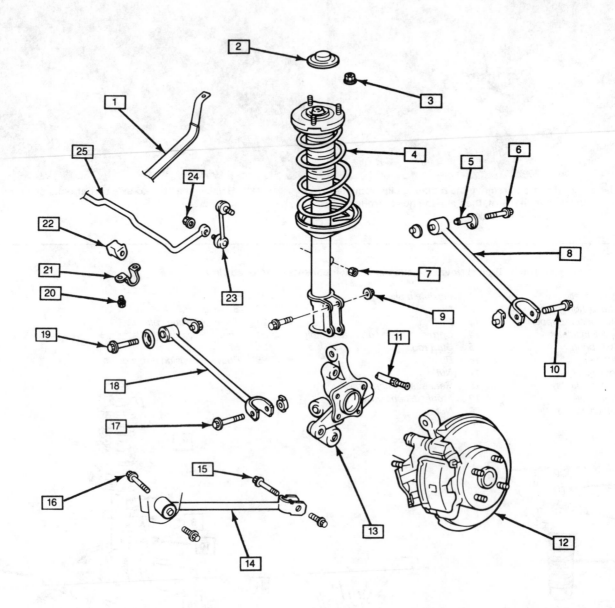

10.6c   Typical Prizm rear suspension components – exploded view

1	Fuel tank band	10	No. 2 suspension arm-to-knuckle bolt	19	No. 1 suspension arm-to-body bolt
2	Strut tower cover	11	Brake line	20	Stabilizer bracket bolt
3	Strut rod piston nut	12	Rear disc brake assembly	21	Stabilizer bar bracket
4	Strut assembly	13	Rear suspension knuckle	22	Bushing
5	Rear toe adjustment bolt	14	Strut rod	23	Stabilizer bar link
6	No. 2 suspension arm-to-body bolt	15	Strut rod-to-knuckle bolt	24	Stabilizer bar link nut
7	Stabilizer bar link-to-strut assembly nut	16	Strut rod-to-body bolt	25	Stabilizer bar
8	No. 2 suspension arm	17	No. 1 suspension arm-to-knuckle bolt		
9	Strut assembly-to-knuckle nut	18	No. 1 suspension arm		

7   Unscrew the three strut upper mounting nuts **(see illustration)** while an assistant supports the strut so it doesn't fall.
8   Remove the strut.

Inspection

9   Follow the inspection procedures described in Section 3. If it is determined that the strut assembly must be disassembled for replacement of the strut or the coil spring, refer to Section 4.
10   When reassembling the strut, make sure the suspension support is aligned with the lower bracket (where the axle carrier fits).

Installation

11   Installation is the reveres of removal. Tighten all critical fasteners to the specified torque.
12   Bleed the brake system (see Chapter 9).

---

11   Suspension arms (rear) – removal and installation

Refer to illustrations 11.2, 11.3, and 11.4

Warning: *Whenever any of the suspension or steering fasteners are loosened or removed they must be inspected and, if necessary replaced with new ones – discard the originals and don't reuse them. They must be replaced with new ones of the same part number or of original equipment quality and design. Torque specifications must be followed for proper reassembly and component retention.*

1   Raise the rear of the vehicle and support it securely on jackstands. Block the front wheels.
2   Remove the suspension arm-to-spindle bolt and nut **(see illustration)**.
3   If one of the rear suspension arms is being removed, mark the relationship of the toe adjuster wheel to the suspension arm inner mounting bracket **(see illustration)**. This will ensure that the toe adjustment will be returned to the same setting.
4   Remove the suspension arm-to-body mounting bolt and nut while supporting the suspension arm **(see illustration)**.
5   Remove the control arm from the vehicle.
6   Installation is the reverse of removal. Tighten all critical fasteners to the specified torque.
7   Have the rear wheel alignment checked by a dealer service department or an alignment shop.

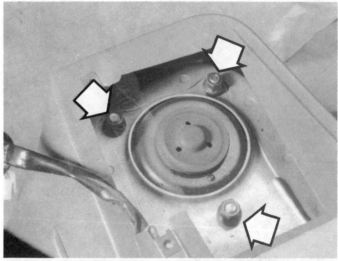

10.7   Support the strut, remove the nuts (arrows) and lower the strut from the vehicle

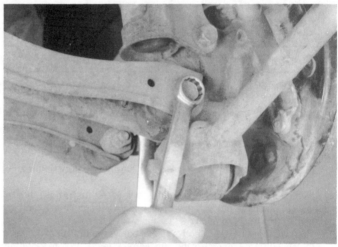

11.2   Remove the control arm-to-spindle bolt – use a back-up wrench on the nut

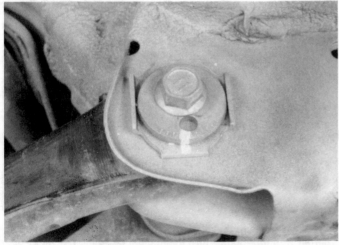

11.3   Mark the relationship of the toe adjuster to the body on the inner end of the rear suspension arm

11.4   Remove the suspension arm-to-body bolt and nut

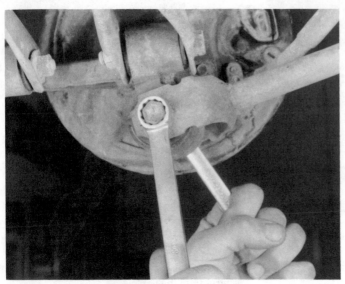

12.2　To remove the strut rod, remove the strut rod-to-axle carrier bolt and nut, . . .

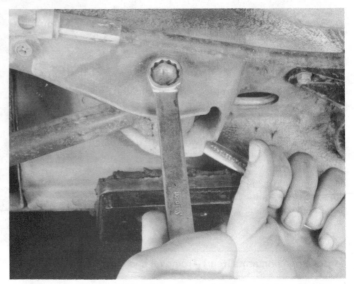

12.3　. . . then remove the strut rod-to-frame bolt and nut

12　Strut rod – removal and installation

Refer to illustrations 12.2 and 12.3

Warning: *Whenever any of the suspension or steering fasteners are loosened or removed they should be inspected, and if necessary, replaced with ones of the same part number or of original equipment quality and design. Torque specifications must be followed for proper reassembly and component retention.*

1　Loosen the wheel lug nuts, raise the vehicle and support it securely on jackstands. Remove the wheel.

2　Remove the strut rod-to-axle carrier bolt **(see illustration)**. It isn't necessary to hold the nut with a wrench, because the nut has a tang attached to it to prevent rotation.

3　Remove the strut rod-to-body bracket bolt **(see illustration)**.

4　Installation is the reverse of the removal procedure. Be sure to tighten the bolts to the specified torque.

13　Hub and bearing assembly (rear) – removal and installation

Refer to illustrations 13.3 and 13.5

Warning: *Whenever any of the suspension or steering fasteners are loosened or removed they must be inspected, and if necessary replaced with new ones of the same part number or of original equipment quality and design. Torque specifications must be followed for proper reassembly and component retention. Dust created by the brake system contains asbestos, which is harmful to your health. Never blow it out with compressed air and don't inhale any of it. Do not, under any circumstances, use petroleum-based solvents to clean brake parts. Use brake cleaner or denatured alcohol only.*

Note: *Due to the special tools required to replace the bearing, the hub and bearing assembly should not be disassembled by the home mechanic. The assembly can be removed, however, and taken to a dealer service department or repair shop to have the bearing replaced.*

Removal

1　Loosen the wheel lug nuts, raise the vehicle and support it securely on jackstands. Remove the wheel.

2　Pull the brake drum (or disc) from the hub (see Chapter 9).

3　Remove the four hub-to-axle carrier bolts, accessible by turning the hub flange so that the large circular cutout exposes each bolt **(see illustration)**.

4　Remove the hub and bearing assembly from its seat, maneuvering it out through the brake assembly.

Installation

5　Remove the old O-ring from the hub seat and install a new one **(see illustration)**.

6　Position the hub and bearing assembly on the axle carrier and align the holes in the backing plate. Install the bolts. A magnet is useful in guiding the bolts through the hub flange and into position. After all four bolts have been installed, tighten them to the specified torque.

7　Install the brake drum or disc and wheel. Lower the vehicle and tighten the wheel lug nuts to the specified torque.

13.3　The rear hub and bearing assembly is held to the axle carrier with four bolts – turn the hub flange so the hole lines up with each bolt, then remove the bolt with a socket and extension (brake shoes removed for clarity)

13.5   Be sure to replace this O-ring on the hub seat

14   Axle carrier (rear) – removal and installation

Refer to illustrations 14.4 and 14.6

Warning: *Whenever any of the suspension or steering fasteners are loosened or removed they must be inspected and, if necessary replaced with new ones of the same part number or of original equipment quality and design. Torque specifications must be followed for proper reassembly and component retention. Dust created by the brake system contains asbestos, which is harmful to your health. Never blow it out with compressed air and don't inhale any of it. Do not, under any circumstances, use petroleum-based solvents to clean brake parts. Use brake cleaner or denatured alcohol only.*

14.4   Once the hub and bearing assembly has been removed, slide the brake backing plate (with the brake shoes still attached) off the axle carrier and hang it from the coil spring with a piece of wire (vehicles with rear drum brakes only)

Removal

1   Loosen the wheel lug nuts, raise the vehicle and support it on jackstands. Block the front wheels and remove the rear wheel.
2   Remove the rear brake drum (or disc) (see Chapter 9).
3   On drum brake-equipped models, disconnect the brake line from the wheel cylinder, using a flare nut wrench to prevent rounding off the tube nut corners.
4   Remove the rear hub and bearing assembly (see Section 13). Detach the backing plate and rear brake assembly from the axle carrier and suspend it with a piece of wire from the suspension spring (drum brake models only). It isn't necessary to remove the parking brake cable from the backing plate **(see illustration)**.
5   Loosen, but don't remove the strut-to-axle carrier bolts **(see illustration 10.6a)**.
6   Remove the suspension arm-to-axle carrier bolts, nuts and washers **(see illustration)**.
7   Remove the rear strut-rod bolt **(see illustration 12.2)**.
8   Remove the previously loosened strut-to-axle carrier bolts while supporting the spindle so it doesn't fall.
9   Detach the axle carrier from the strut bracket.

Installation

10   Inspect the carrier bushing for cracks, deformation and signs of wear. If it is worn out, take the carrier to a dealer service department or repair shop to have the old one pressed out and a new one pressed in.
11   Push the axle carrier into the strut bracket, aligning the two bolt holes. Insert the two strut-to-carrier bolts and tighten them finger tight.
12   Install the suspension arm-to-spindle bolt, washers and nut from the front. Tighten the nut by hand.
13   Place a jack under the carrier and raise it to simulate normal ride height.
14   Tighten the strut-to-carrier bolts to the specified torque.
15   Connect the strut rod and tighten the bolt to the specified torque.
16   Tighten the suspension arm bolt/nut to the specified torque.
17   Attach the brake backing plate to the spindle, install the hub and tighten the four bolts securely.
18   Connect the brake tube to the wheel cylinder. Be careful not to damage the line when bending it back into place.
19   Install the rear brake drum (or disc) (see Chapter 9).
20   Install the wheel and lug nuts.
21   Lower the vehicle and tighten the lug nuts to the torque specified in Chapter 1.

15   Steering system – general information

All models are equipped with rack-and-pinion steering. Some are power assisted. The rack-and-pinion assembly is bolted to the firewall and operates the steering arms via tie-rods. The inner ends of the tie-rods are protected by rubber boots which should be inspected periodically for secure attachment, tears and leaking lubricant.

The power assist system consists of a belt-driven pump and associated lines and hoses. The power steering pump reservoir fluid level should be checked periodically (see Chapter 1).

The steering wheel operates the steering shaft, which actuates the steering gear through universal joints. Looseness in the steering can be caused by wear in the steering shaft universal joints, the steering gear, the tie-rod ends and loose retaining bolts.

16   Steering wheel – removal and installation

Refer to illustrations 16.2, 16.3 and 16.4
1   Disconnect the cable from the negative terminal of the battery.

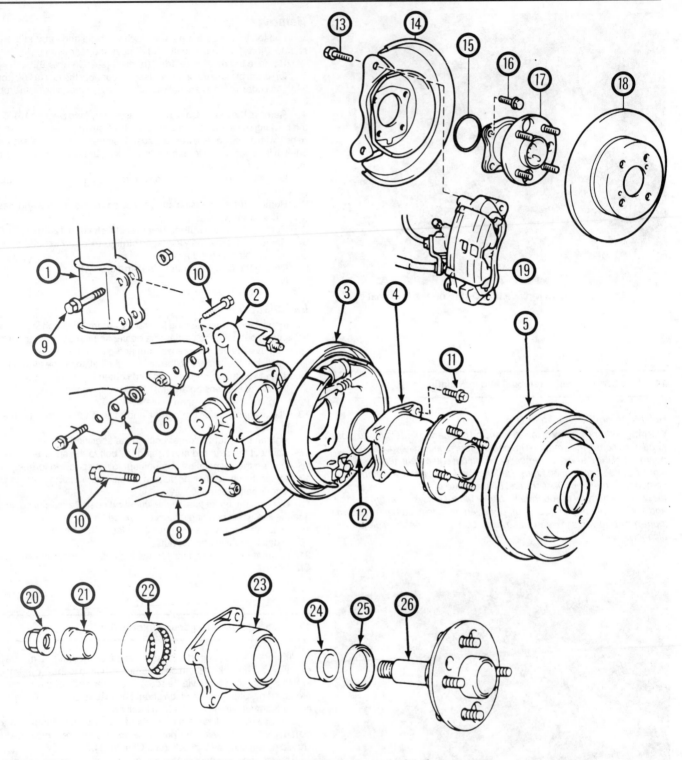

14.6   Exploded view of the rear axle carrier and related components

1 Strut	10 Suspension arm-to-body through-bolt	19 Disc brake caliper
2 Axle carrier assembly	11 Hub-to-axle carrier bolt	20 Nut
3 Rear brake backing plate assembly	12 O-ring	21 Inner bearing race
4 Rear axle hub assembly	13 Disc brake mounting bracket bolt	22 Bearing outer race with
5 Brake drum	14 Disc brake dust cover	bearings installed
6 Rear suspension arm	15 Disc brake O-ring	23 Bearing case assembly
7 Front suspension arm	16 Disc brake hub-to-axle carrier bolt	24 Outer bearing inner race
8 Strut rod	17 Disc brake rear axle hub assembly	25 Seal
9 Strut-to-axle carrier bolt	18 Disc brake rotor	26 Axle hub

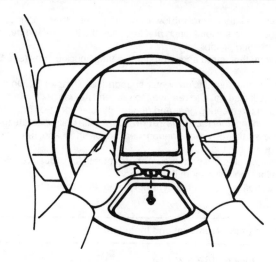

16.2   To detach the horn pad, remove the screw from the bottom of the pad, then pull the pad straight off the steering wheel

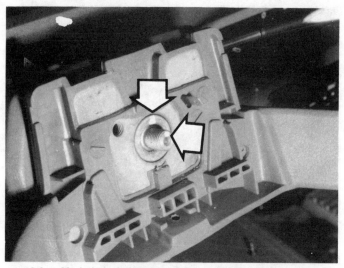

16.3   Mark the relationship of the steering wheel hub and steering shaft (arrows)

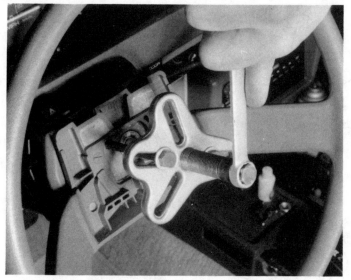

16.4   Use a steering wheel puller to separate the steering wheel from the shaft – DON'T attempt to remove the wheel with a hammer!

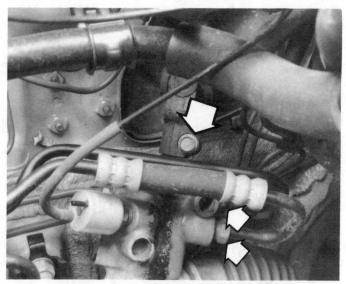

17.2   Detach the power steering lines (if equipped) (arrows), mark the relationship of the steering shaft universal joint and the steering pinion, then loosen the pinch bolt (arrow) and detach the universal joint from the steering pinion

2   Remove the screws from the bottom of the horn pad and pull the pad from the steering wheel **(see illustration)**. Disconnect the wire to the horn switch.

3   Remove the steering wheel retaining nut, then mark the relationship of the steering shaft to the hub (if marks don't already exist or don't line up) to simplify installation and ensure steering wheel alignment **(see illustration)**.

4   Use a puller to disconnect the steering wheel from the shaft **(see illustration)**.

5   To install the wheel, align the mark on the steering wheel hub with the mark on the shaft and slip the wheel onto the shaft. Install the hub nut and tighten it to the specified torque.

6   Connect the horn wire and install the horn pad.

7   Connect the negative battery cable.

17   Steering gear – removal and installation

Refer to illustrations 17.2, 17.6 and 17.8

Note: *This procedure applies to both power and manual steering gear assemblies. When working on a vehicle equipped with a manual steering gear, ignore any references made to the power steering system.*

1   Loosen the front wheel lug nuts, raise the front of the vehicle and support it securely on jackstands. Apply the parking brake and remove the wheels. Remove the engine undercovers on models so equipped.

2   If the vehicle has power steering, place a drain pan under the steering gear. Detach the power steering pressure and return lines **(see illustration)** and cap the ends to prevent excessive fluid loss and contamination.

17.6   Remove the steering gear mounting nuts (arrows)

3   Mark the relationship of the lower universal joint to the steering pinion. Loosen the universal joint pinch bolt and slide the joint up and detach it from the steering pinion.
4   Separate the tie-rod ends from the steering knuckle arms (see Section 18).
5   Remove the suspension center support (see Chapter 7). On some models, you'll also have to remove the rear engine/transaxle mount.
6   Support the steering gear and remove the steering gear bracket-to-firewall mounting nuts **(see illustration)**. Lower the unit, separate the intermediate shaft from the steering gear input shaft and remove the steering gear from the vehicle.
7   Check the steering gear mounting grommets for excessive wear or deterioration, replacing them if necessary.
8   Installation is the reverse of removal **(see illustration)**.

18   Tie-rod ends – removal and installation

Refer to illustrations 18.2 and 18.4

Removal
1   Loosen the wheel lug nuts. Raise the front of the vehicle, support it

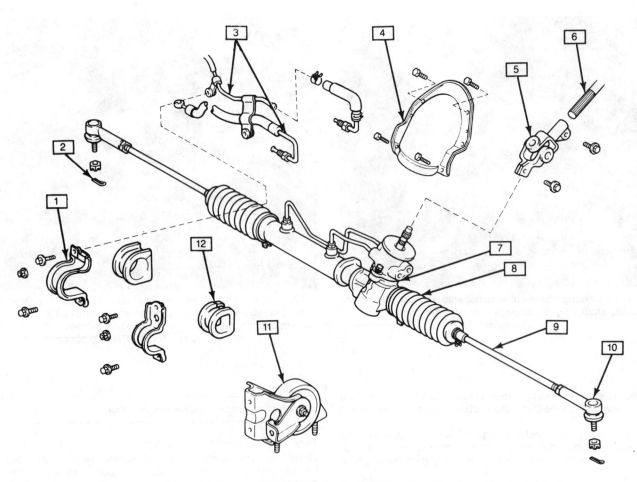

17.8   Typical steering gear mounting details

1	Mounting bracket	5	Universal joint	9	Tie-rod
2	Cotter pin	6	Intermediate shaft	10	Tie-rod end
3	Pressure and return lines	7	Gear housing assembly	11	Engine mount
4	Column hole cover	8	Rubber boot	12	Grommet

securely, block the rear wheels and set the parking brake. Remove the front wheel.

2   Loosen the jam nut enough to mark the position of the tie-rod end in relation to the threads **(see illustration)**.

3   Remove the cotter pin and loosen the nut on the tie-rod end stud.

4   Disconnect the tie-rod from the steering knuckle arm with a puller **(see illustration)**. Remove the nut and separate the tie-rod.

5   Unscrew the tie-rod end from the tie-rod.

Installation

6   Thread the tie-rod end on to the marked position and insert the tie-rod stud into the steering knuckle arm. Tighten the jam nut securely.

7   Install the castellated nut on the stud and tighten it to the specified torque. Install a new cotter pin.

18.2   Loosen the jam nut and mark the relationship of the tie-rod end to the tie-rod with white paint

8   Install the wheel and lug nuts. Lower the vehicle and tighten the lug nuts to the torque specified in Chapter 1.

9   Have the alignment checked by a dealer service department or an alignment shop.

19   Steering gear boots – replacement

1   Loosen the lug nuts, raise the vehicle and support it securely on jack-stands. Remove the wheel.

2   Remove the tie-rod end and jam nut (see Section 18).

3   Remove the steering gear boot clamps and slide the boot off.

4   Before installing the new boot, wrap the threads and serrations on the end of the steering rod with a layer of tape so the small end of the new boot isn't damaged.

5   Slide the new boot into position on the steering gear until it seats in the groove in the steering rod and install new clamps.

6   Remove the tape and install the tie-rod end (See Section 18).

7   Install the wheel and lug nuts. Lower the vehicle and tighten the lug nuts to the torque specified in Chapter 1.

20   Power steering pump – removal and installation

Refer to illustration 20.4, 20.5, 20.8 and 20.9

Warning: *Whenever any of the suspension or steering system components are loosened or removed, they must be inspected and if, necessary, replaced with ones with the same part number or of original equipment quality and design.*

1   Disconnect the cable from the negative battery terminal.

2   On Nova models, remove the air cleaner assembly (see Chapter 4).

3   Using a large syringe or suction gun, suck as much fluid out of the power steering fluid reservoir as possible. Place a drain pan under the vehicle to catch any fluid that spills out when the hoses are disconnected.

4   Loosen the clamp and disconnect the fluid return hose from the pump **(see illustration)**.

20.4   Detach the power steering pump return line (arrow)

18.4   A two-jaw puller works well for separating the tie-rod end from the steering knuckle arm – note that the nut hasn't been removed (it will prevent the two components from separating violently)

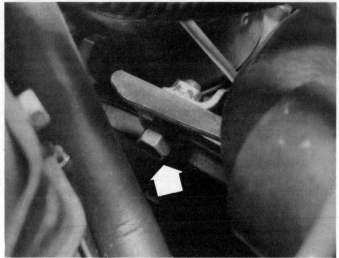

20.5   Remove the power steering pump adjuster bolt (arrow)

20.8   Remove the power steering pump banjo bolt (arrow)

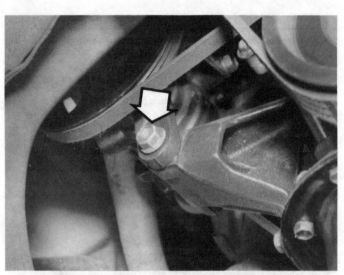

20.9   Remove the power steering pump through-bolt (arrow)

5   Remove the adjuster bolt **(see illustration)**.

6   Loosen the right front wheel lug nuts, raise the vehicle and support it securely on jackstands. Remove the right front wheel.

7   On Prizm models, remove the bolt from the right engine mount (see Chapter 2), place a jack (with the jack head padded) below the engine and raise the engine about two inches to gain access to the lower power steering pump through-bolt. **Warning:** *Don't place any part of your body under the engine when it's supported only by a jack!*

8   Remove the pressure line-to-pump banjo bolt **(see illustration)** and separate the line from the pump. Discard the copper crush washers on each side of the banjo fitting and replace them.

9   Remove the through-bolt **(see illustration)** and remove the pump.

10   Installation is the reverse of removal.

11   Adjust the drivebelt tension (see Chapter 1).

12   Top up the fluid level in the reservoir and bleed the system (see Section 21).

---

21   Power steering system – bleeding

---

1   Following any operation in which the power steering fluid lines have

been disconnected, the power steering system must be bled to remove all air and obtain proper steering performance.

2   With the front wheels in the straight ahead position, check the power steering fluid level and, if low, add fluid until it reaches the Cold mark on the dipstick.

3   Start the engine and allow it to run at fast idle. Recheck the fluid level and add more if necessary to reach the Cold mark on the dipstick.

4   Bleed the system by turning the wheels from side to side, without hitting the stops. This will work the air out of the system. Keep the reservoir full of fluid as this is done.

5   When the air is worked out of the system, return the wheels to the straight ahead position and leave the vehicle running for several more minutes before shutting it off.

6   Road test the vehicle to be sure the steering system is functioning normally and noise free.

7   Recheck the fluid level to be sure it is up to the Hot mark on the dipstick while the engine is at normal operating temperature. Add fluid if necessary (see Chapter 1).

---

22   Wheels and tires – general information

Refer to illustration 22.1

All vehicles covered by this manual are equipped with metric-sized fiberglass or steel belted radial tires **(see illustration)**. Use of other size or type of tires may affect the ride and handling of the vehicle. Don't mix different types of tires, such as radials and bias belted, on the same vehicle as handling may be seriously affected. It's recommended that tires be replaced in pairs on the same axle, but if only one tire is being replaced, be sure it's the same size, structure and tread design as the other.

Because tire pressure has a substantial effect on handling and wear, the pressure on all tires should be checked at least once a month or before any extended trips (see Chapter 1).

Wheels must be replaced if they are bent, dented, leak air, have elongated bolt holes, are heavily rusted, out of vertical symmetry or if the lug nuts won't stay tight. Wheel repairs that use welding or peening are not recommended.

Tire and wheel balance is important in the overall handling, braking and performance of the vehicle. Unbalanced wheels can adversely affect handling and ride characteristics as well as tire life. Whenever a tire is installed on a wheel, the tire and wheel should be balanced by a shop with the proper equipment.

METRIC TIRE SIZES

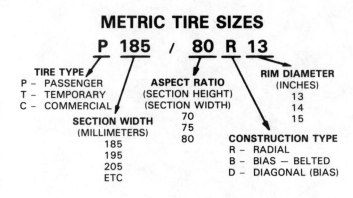

P 185 / 80 R 13

TIRE TYPE
P – PASSENGER
T – TEMPORARY
C – COMMERCIAL

SECTION WIDTH
(MILLIMETERS)
185
195
205
ETC

ASPECT RATIO
(SECTION HEIGHT)
(SECTION WIDTH)
70
75
80

CONSTRUCTION TYPE
R – RADIAL
B – BIAS – BELTED
D – DIAGONAL (BIAS)

RIM DIAMETER
(INCHES)
13
14
15

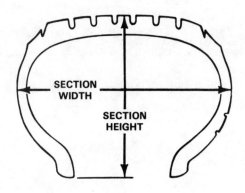

SECTION WIDTH

SECTION HEIGHT

22.1   Metric tire size code

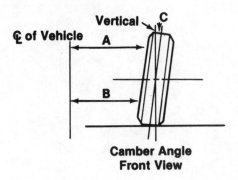

Camber Angle Front View

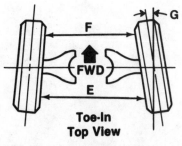

Toe-In Top View

23.1   Front end alignment details – camber (top) and toe-in (bottom) – the actual adjustment of these angles is beyond the scope of the home mechanic and must be performed by an alignment shop or service station

A minus B = C (degrees camber)
E minus F = toe-in (measured in inches)
G = toe-in (expressed in degrees)

23   Front end alignment – general information

Refer to illustration 23.1

A front end alignment refers to the adjustments made to the front wheels so they are in proper angular relationship to the suspension and the ground. Front wheels that are out of proper alignment not only affect steering control, but also increase tire wear. The front end adjustments normally required are camber, caster and toe-in **(see illustration)**.

Getting the proper front wheel alignment is a very exacting process, one in which complicated and expensive machines are necessary to perform the job properly. Because of this, you should have a technician with the proper equipment perform these tasks. We will, however, use this space to give you a basic idea of what is involved with front end alignment so you can better understand the process and deal intelligently with the shop that does the work.

Toe-in is the turning in of the front wheels. The purpose of a toe specifi-cation is to ensure parallel rolling of the front wheels. In a vehicle with zero toe-in, the distance between the front edges of the wheels will be the same as the distance between the rear edges of the wheels. The actual amount of toe-in is normally only a fraction of an inch. Toe-in adjustment is controlled by the tie-rod end position on the inner tierod. Incorrect toe-in will cause the tires to wear improperly by making them scrub against the road surface.

Camber is the tilting of the front wheels from the vertical when viewed from the front of the vehicle. When the wheels tilt out at the top, the camber is said to be positive (+). When the wheels tilt in at the top the camber is negative (-). The amount of tilt is measured in degrees from the vertical and this measurement is called the camber angle. This angle affects the amount of tire tread which contacts the road and compensates for changes in the suspension geometry when the vehicle is cornering or travelling over an undulating surface.

Caster is the tilting of the front steering axis from the vertical. A tilt toward the rear is positive caster and a tilt toward the front is negative caster. Caster is not adjustable on the vehicles covered by this manual.

Chapter 11   Body

Contents

1   General information

These models feature a "unibody" layout, using a floor pan with front and rear frame side rails which support the body components, front and rear suspension systems and other mechanical components.

Certain components are particularly vulnerable to accident damage and can be unbolted and repaired or replaced. Among these parts are the body moldings, bumpers, hood and trunk lids and all glass.

Only general body maintenance practices and body panel repair procedures within the scope of the do-it-yourselfer are included in this Chapter.

2   Body – maintenance

1   The condition of your vehicle's body is very important, because the resale value depends a great deal on it. It's much more difficult to repair a neglected or damaged body than it is to repair mechanical components. The hidden areas of the body, such as the wheel wells, the frame and the engine compartment, are equally important, although they don't require as frequent attention as the rest of the body.

2   Once a year, or every 12,000 miles, it's a good idea to have the underside of the body steam cleaned. All traces of dirt and oil will be removed and the area can then be inspected carefully for rust, damaged brake lines, frayed electrical wires, damaged cables and other problems. The

front suspension components should be greased after completion of this job.

3   At the same time, clean the engine and the engine compartment with a steam cleaner or water soluble degreaser.

4   The wheel wells should be given close attention, since undercoating can peel away and stones and dirt thrown up by the tires can cause the paint to chip and flake, allowing rust to set in. If rust is found, clean down to the bare metal and apply an anti-rust paint.

5   The body should be washed about once a week. Wet the vehicle thoroughly to soften the dirt, then wash it down with a soft sponge and plenty of clean soapy water. If the surplus dirt is not washed off very carefully, it can wear down the paint.

6   Spots of tar or asphalt thrown up from the road should be removed with a cloth soaked in solvent.

7   Once every six months, wax the body and chrome trim. If a chrome cleaner is used to remove rust from any of the vehicle's plated parts, remember that the cleaner also removes part of the chrome, so use it sparingly.

3   Vinyl trim – maintenance

Don't clean vinyl trim with detergents, caustic soap or petroleum-based cleaners. Plain soap and water works just fine, with a soft brush to clean dirt that may be ingrained. Wash the vinyl as frequently as the rest of the vehicle.

After cleaning, application of a high quality rubber and vinyl protectant will help prevent oxidation and cracks. The protectant can also be applied to weatherstripping, vacuum lines and rubber hoses, which often fail as a result of chemical degradation, and to the tires.

4   Upholstery and carpets – maintenance

1   Every three months remove the carpets or mats and clean the interior of the vehicle (more frequently if necessary). Vacuum the upholstery and carpets to remove loose dirt and dust.

2   Leather upholstery requires special care. Stains should be removed with warm water and a very mild soap solution. Use a clean, damp cloth to remove the soap, then wipe again with a dry cloth. Never use alcohol, gasoline, nail polish remover or thinner to clean leather upholstery.

3   After cleaning, regularly treat leather upholstery with a leather wax. Never use car wax on leather upholstery.

4   In areas where the interior of the vehicle is subject to bright sunlight, cover leather seats with a sheet if the vehicle is to be left out for any length of time.

5   Body repair – minor damage

See color photo sequence

Repair of minor scratches

1   If the scratch is superficial and does not penetrate to the metal of the body, repair is very simple. Lightly rub the scratched area with a fine rubbing compound to remove loose paint and built-up wax. Rinse the area with clean water.

2   Apply touch-up paint to the scratch, using a small brush. Continue to apply thin layers of paint until the surface of the paint in the scratch is level with the surrounding paint. Allow the new paint at least two weeks to harden, then blend it into the surrounding paint by rubbing with a very fine rubbing compound. Finally, apply a coat of wax to the scratch area.

3   If the scratch has penetrated the paint and exposed the metal of the body, causing the metal to rust, a different repair technique is required. Remove all loose rust from the bottom of the scratch with a pocket knife, then apply rust inhibiting paint to prevent the formation of rust in the future. Us-

ing a rubber or nylon applicator, coat the scratched area with glaze-type filler. If required, the filler can be mixed with thinner to provide a very thin paste, which is ideal for filling narrow scratches. Before the glaze filler in the scratch hardens, wrap a piece of smooth cotton cloth around the tip of a finger. Dip the cloth in thinner and then quickly wipe it along the surface of the scratch. This will ensure that the surface of the filler is slightly hollow. The scratch can now be painted over as described earlier in this section.

Repair of dents

4   When repairing dents, the first job is to pull the dent out until the affected area is as close as possible to its original shape. There is no point in trying to restore the original shape completely as the metal in the damaged area will have stretched on impact and cannot be restored to its original contours. It is better to bring the level of the dent up to a point which is about 1/8-inch below the level of the surrounding metal. In cases where the dent is very shallow, it is not worth trying to pull it out at all.

5   If the back side of the dent is accessible, it can be hammered out gently from behind using a soft-face hammer. While doing this, hold a block of wood firmly against the opposite side of the metal to absorb the hammer blows and prevent the metal from being stretched.

6   If the dent is in a section of the body which has double layers, or some other factor makes it inaccessible from behind, a different technique is required. Drill several small holes through the metal inside the damaged area, particularly in the deeper sections. Screw long, selftapping screws into the holes just enough for them to get a good grip in the metal. Now the dent can be pulled out by pulling on the protruding heads of the screws with locking pliers.

7   The next stage of repair is the removal of paint from the damaged area and from an inch or so of the surrounding metal. This is done with a wire brush or sanding disk in a drill motor, although it can be done just as effectively by hand with sandpaper. To complete the preparation for filling, score the surface of the bare metal with a screwdriver or the tang of a file, or drill small holes in the affected area. This will provide a good grip for the filler material. To complete the repair, see the subsection on filling and painting later in this Section.

Repair of rust holes or gashes

8   Remove all paint from the affected area and from an inch or so of the surrounding metal using a sanding disk or wire brush mounted in a drill motor. If these are not available, a few sheets of sandpaper will do the job just as effectively.

9   With the paint removed, you will be able to determine the severity of the corrosion and decide whether to replace the whole panel, if possible, or repair the affected area. New body panels are not as expensive as most people think and it is often quicker to install a new panel than to repair large areas of rust.

10   Remove all trim pieces from the affected area except those which will act as a guide to the original shape of the damaged body, such as headlight shells, etc. Using metal snips or a hacksaw blade, remove all loose metal and any other metal that is badly affected by rust. Hammer the edges of the hole inward to create a slight depression for the filler material.

11   Wire brush the affected area to remove the powdery rust from the surface of the metal. If the back of the rusted area is accessible, treat it with rust inhibiting paint.

12   Before filling is done, block the hole in some way. This can be done with sheet metal riveted or screwed into place, or by stuffing the hole with wire mesh.

13   Once the hole is blocked off, the affected area can be filled and painted. See the following subsection on filling and painting.

Filling and painting

14   Many types of body fillers are available, but generally speaking, body repair kits which contain filler paste and a tube of resin hardener are best for this type of repair work. A wide, flexible plastic or nylon applicator will be necessary for imparting a smooth and contoured finish to the surface of the filler material. Mix up a small amount of filler on a clean piece of wood or

cardboard (use the hardener sparingly). Follow the manufacturer's instructions on the package, otherwise the filler will set incorrectly.

15   Using the applicator, apply the filler paste to the prepared area. Draw the applicator across the surface of the filler to achieve the desired contour and to level the filler surface. As soon as a contour that approximates the original one is achieved, stop working the paste. If you continue, the paste will begin to stick to the applicator. Continue to add thin layers of paste at 20-minute intervals until the level of the filler is just above the surrounding metal.

16   Once the filler has hardened, the excess can be removed with a body file. From then on, progressively finer grades of sandpaper should be used, starting with a 180-grit paper and finishing with 600-grit wet or-dry paper. Always wrap the sandpaper around a flat rubber or wooden block, otherwise the surface of the filler will not be completely flat. During the sanding of the filler surface, the wet-or-dry paper should be periodically rinsed in water. This will ensure that a very smooth finish is produced in the final stage.

17   At this point, the repair area should be surrounded by a ring of bare metal, which in turn should be encircled by the finely feathered edge of good paint. Rinse the repair area with clean water until all of the dust produced by the sanding operation is gone.

18   Spray the entire area with a light coat of primer. This will reveal any imperfections in the surface of the filler. Repair the imperfections with fresh filler paste or glaze filler and once more smooth the surface with sandpaper. Repeat this spray-and-repair procedure until you are satisfied that the surface of the filler and the feathered edge of the paint are perfect. Rinse the area with clean water and allow it to dry completely.

19   The repair area is now ready for painting. Spray painting must be carried out in a warm, dry, windless and dust free atmosphere. These conditions can be created if you have access to a large indoor work area, but if you are forced to work in the open, you will have to pick the day very carefully. If you are working indoors, dousing the floor in the work area with water will help settle the dust which would otherwise be in the air. If the repair area is confined to one body panel, mask off the surrounding panels. This will help minimize the effects of a slight mismatch in paint color. Trim pieces such as chrome strips, door handles, etc., will also need to be masked off or removed. Use masking tape and several thicknesses of newspaper for the masking operations.

20   Before spraying, shake the paint can thoroughly, then spray a test area until the spray painting technique is mastered. Cover the repair area with a thick coat of primer. The thickness should be built up using several thin layers of primer rather than one thick one. Using 600-grit wet-or-dry sandpaper, rub down the surface of the primer until it is very smooth. While doing this, the work area should be thoroughly rinsed with water and the wet-or-dry sandpaper periodically rinsed as well. Allow the primer to dry before spraying additional coats.

21   Spray on the top coat, again building up the thickness by using several thin layers of paint. Begin spraying in the center of the repair area and then, using a circular motion, work out until the whole repair area and about two inches of the surrounding original paint is covered. Remove all masking material 10 to 15 minutes after spraying on the final coat of paint. Allow the new paint at least two weeks to harden, then use a very fine rubbing compound to blend the edges of the new paint into the existing paint. Finally, apply a coat of wax.

6   Body repair – major damage

1   Major damage must be repaired by an auto body shop specifically equipped to perform unibody repairs. These shops have the specialized equipment required to do the job properly.

2   If the damage is extensive, the body must be checked for proper alignment or the vehicle's handling characteristics may be adversely affected and other components may wear at an accelerated rate.

3   Due to the fact that all of the major body components (hood, fenders, etc.) are separate and replaceable units, any seriously damaged compo-

nents should be replaced rather than repaired. Sometimes the components can be found in a wrecking yard that specializes in used vehicle components, often at considerable savings over the cost of new parts.

7   Hinges and locks – maintenance

Once every 3000 miles, or every three months, the hinges and latch assemblies on the doors, hood and trunk should be given a few drops of light oil or lock lubricant. The door latch strikers should also be lubricated with a thin coat of grease to reduce wear and ensure free movement. Lubricate the door and trunk locks with spray-on graphite lubricant.

8   Windshield and fixed glass – replacement

Replacement of the windshield and fixed glass requires the use of special fast-setting adhesive/caulk materials and some specialized tools. It is recommended that these operations be left to a dealer or a shop specializing in glass work.

9   Hood – removal, installation and adjustment

Refer to illustrations 9.2, 9.10 and 9.11
Note: *The hood is heavy and somewhat awkward to remove and install – at least two people should perform this procedure.*

Removal and installation

1   Use blankets or pads to cover the cowl area of the body and fenders. This will protect the body and paint as the hood is lifted off.

2   Make marks around the bolt heads to ensure proper alignment during installation (**see illustration**).

3   Disconnect any cables or wires that will interfere with removal.

4   Have an assistant support the hood. Remove the hinge-to-hood screws or bolts.

5   Lift off the hood.

6   Installation is the reverse of removal.

9.2   Use a permanent felt-tip pen or a scribe to mark the hood bolt locations – note the rags protecting the windshield and body from damage if the hood swings back

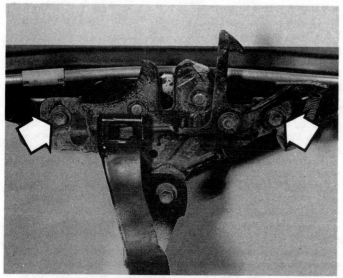

**9.10   To adjust the hood latch, loosen the bolts (arrows),
reposition the latch and retighten the bolts before checking the
hood alignment**

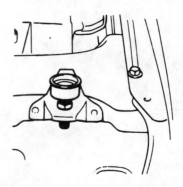

**9.11   Turn the bumpers with a screwdriver to adjust the hood so
it's flush with the fenders when closed**

Adjustment

7   Fore-and-aft and side-to-side adjustment of the hood is done by moving the hinge plate slot after loosening the bolts or nuts.

8   Scribe a line around the entire hinge plate so you can judge the amount of movement **(see illustration 9.2)**

9   Loosen the bolts or nuts and move the hood into correct alignment. Move it only a little at a time. Tighten the hinge bolts or nuts and carefully lower the hood to check the position.

10   If necessary after installation, the entire hood latch assembly can be adjusted up-and-down as well as from side-to-side on the radiator support so the hood closes securely, flush with the fenders. To make the adjustment, scribe a line around the hood latch mounting bolts to provide a reference point, then loosen them and reposition the latch assembly, as necessary **(see illustration)**. Following adjustment, retighten the mounting bolts.

11   Finally, adjust the hood bumpers on the radiator support so the hood, when closed, is flush with the fenders **(see illustration)**.

12   The hood latch assembly, as well as the hinges, should be periodically lubricated with white, lithium-base grease to prevent binding and wear.

10   Door trim panel – removal and installation

Refer to illustrations 10.2a, 10.2b, 10.3a, 10.3b, 10.3c, 10.4 and 10.6

1   Disconnect the negative cable from the battery.

2   Remove the outside mirror trim panel (see Section 17), the door handle bezel and the door pull/armrest assembly **(see illustrations)**.

**10.2a   Pull out the door handle for access to the screw (arrow)
that secures the handle bezel**

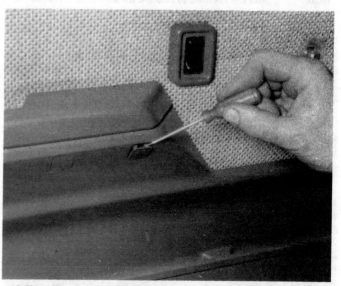

**10.2b   The armrest retaining screws are hidden under covers
which can be pried off with a small screwdriver**

10.3a   Work a cloth up behind the regulator handle and move it back-and-forth . . .

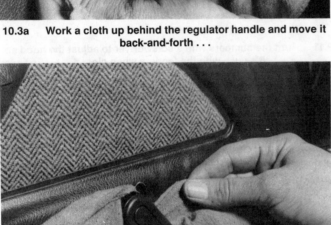

10.3b   . . . until the retainer is pushed up so you can remove it

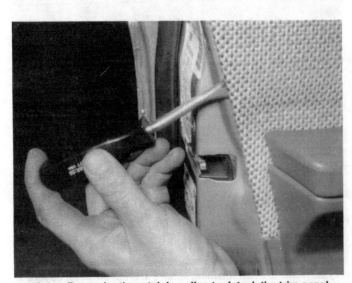

10.4   Pry under the retaining clips to detach the trim panel

3   On manual window regulator equipped models, remove the window crank by working a cloth back-and-forth behind the handle to dislodge the retainer **(see illustrations)**. A special tool is available for this purpose **(see illustration)** but it's not essential. With the retainer removed, pull off the handle.

4   Insert a wide putty knife or a thin pry bar between the trim panel and door to disengage the retaining clips. Work around the outer edge until the panel is free **(see illustration)**.

5   Once all of the clips are disengaged, detach the trim panel, unplug any electrical connectors and remove the trim panel from the vehicle.

6   For access to the inner door, peel back the plastic water deflector, taking care not to tear it **(see illustration)**. To install the trim panel, first press the water deflector into place.

7   Prior to installation of the door panel, be sure to reinstall any clips in the panel which may have come out during the removal procedure and stayed in the door.

8   Plug in any electrical connectors and place the panel in position. Press it into place until the clips are seated and install any retaining screws and armrest/door pulls. Install the manual regulator window crank or power switch assembly.

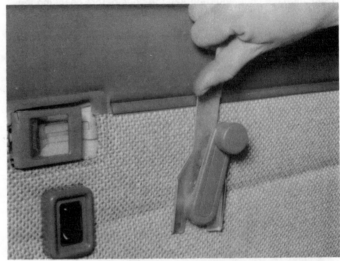

10.3c   If you have access to a special tool like this one, use it to disengage the retainer

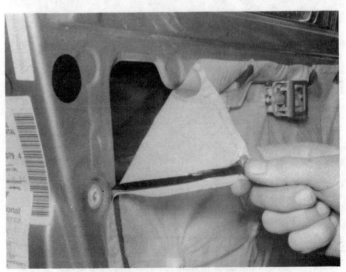

10.6   Be very careful when pulling the plastic water deflector off – don't tear or distort it

11   Trunk lid/rear hatch – removal, installation and adjustment

Refer to illustrations 11.3a, 11.3b, 11.4, 11.8a and 11.8b

1   Open the trunk lid and cover the edges of the trunk compartment with pads or cloths to protect the painted surfaces when the lid is removed.

2   Disconnect any cables or wire harness connectors attached to the trunk lid that would interfere with removal.

3   Make alignment marks around the hinge bolt mounting flanges **(see illustrations)**.

4   On hatchback models, have an assistant support the hatch and detach the support struts **(see illustration)**.

5   While an assistant supports the lid or hatch, remove the lid-to-hinge bolts on both sides and lift it off.

6   Installation is the reverse of removal. **Note:** *When reinstalling the trunk lid or hatch, align the lid-to-hinge bolts with the marks made during removal.*

7   After installation, close the lid and make sure it's in proper alignment with the surrounding panels. Fore-and-aft and side-to-side adjustments of the lid are controlled by the position of the hinge bolts in the slots. To make an adjustment, loosen the hinge bolts, reposition the lid and retighten the bolts.

8   The height of the lid in relation to the surrounding body panels when closed can be changed by loosening the lock and/or striker bolts, repositioning the striker and tightening the bolts **(see illustrations)**.

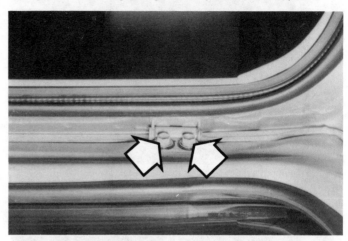

11.3a   Mark around the hinge bolts (arrows) so you can return the rear hatch to the same position when you install it

11.4   Use an open-end wrench to detach the support strut end from the rear hatch

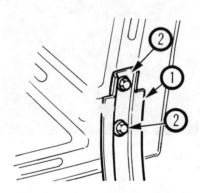

11.3b   Mark around the hinge bolt mounting flange (1) so you can reinstall the trunk lid in its original location – unscrew or loosen the trunk lid-to-hinge bolts (2) to remove or adjust it

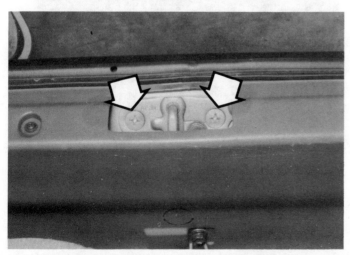

11.8a   The position of the trunk lid/rear hatch striker can be changed after loosening the retaining screws (arrows)

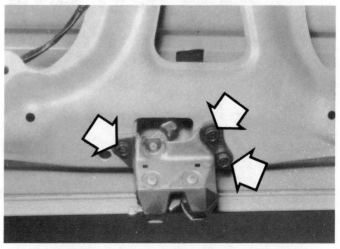

11.8b   To change the engagement of the trunk lid/rear hatch, loosen the three latch mounting screws (arrows)

This photo sequence illustrates the repair of a dent and damaged paintwork. The procedure for the repair of a hole is similar. Refer to the text for more complete instructions

After removing any adjacent body trim, hammer the dent out. The damaged area should then be made slightly concave

Use coarse sandpaper or a sanding disc on a drill motor to remove all paint from the damaged area. Feather the sanded area into the edges of the surrounding paint, using progressively finer grades of sandpaper

The damaged area should be treated with rust remover prior to application of the body filler. In the case of a rust hole, all rusted sheet metal should be cut away

Carefully follow manufacturer's instructions when mixing the body filler so as to have the longest possible working time during application. Rust holes should be covered with fiberglass screen held in place with dabs of body filler prior to repair

Apply the filler with a flexible applicator in thin layers at 20 minute intervals. Use an applicator such as a wood spatula for confined areas. The filler should protrude slightly above the surrounding area

Shape the filler with a surform-type plane. Then, use water and progressively finer grades of sandpaper and a sanding block to wet-sand the area until it is smooth. Feather the edges of the repair area into the surrounding paint.

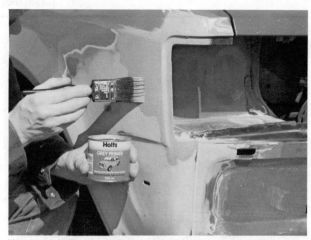

Use spray or brush applied primer to cover the entire repair area so that slight imperfections in the surface will be filled in. Prime at least one inch into the area surrounding the repair. Be careful of over-spray when using spray-type primer

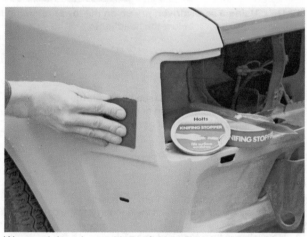

Wet-sand the primer with fine (approximately 400 grade) sandpaper until the area is smooth to the touch and blended into the surrounding paint. Use filler paste on minor imperfections

After the filler paste has dried, use rubbing compound to ensure that the surface of the primer is smooth. Prior to painting, the surface should be wiped down with a tack rag or lint-free cloth soaked in lacquer thinner

Choose a dry, warm, breeze-free area in which to paint and make sure that adjacent areas are protected from over-spray. Shake the spray paint can thoroughly and apply the top coat to the repair area, building it up by applying several coats, working from the center

After allowing at least two weeks for the paint to harden, use fine rubbing compound to blend the area into the original paint. Wax can now be applied

12.1a   Using a pair of needle-nose pliers, squeeze each of the four retaining clips and pull out on the grille assembly

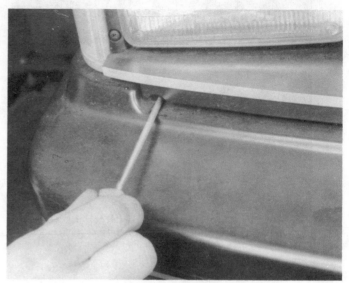

12.1b   Using a screwdriver, pry up on the lower retaining tabs below the headlights

12   Radiator grille – removal and installation

Refer to illustrations 12.1a and 12.1b

1   Disengage the grille retaining clips with a pair of needle-nose pliers **(see illustrations)**. On some models, the center of the grille may be retained by two screws instead of clips.

2   Once all of the retaining clips are disengaged, pull the grille out and remove it.

3   To install the grille, press it into place until the clips lock in position.

13   Door latch, lock cylinder and handle – removal and installation

1   Remove the door trim panel and water deflector (Section 10).

Door latch

Refer to illustrations 13.2a and 13.2b

2   Reach in through the door service hole and disconnect the control links from the latch **(see illustrations)**.

3   Remove the three door lock retaining screws from the end of the door. Detach the door lock and (if equipped) solenoid.

4   Installation is the reverse of removal.

Lock cylinder

Refer to illustration 13.6

5   Disconnect the control link and electrical connector (if equipped) from the lock cylinder.

6   Use pliers to slide the retaining clip off and remove the lock cylinder from the door **(see illustration)**.

7   Installation is the reverse of removal.

Inside handle

Refer to illustration 13.8

8   Remove the retaining bolts **(see illustration)**.

9   Rotate the handle away and detach it from the door.

10   Installation is the reverse of removal.

Outside handle

Refer to illustration 13.12

11   Disconnect the control link from the handle.

12   Remove the nuts and detach the handle from the door **(see illustration)**.

13   Installation is the reverse of removal.

14   Door – removal, installation and adjustment

Refer to illustrations 14.2, 14.3, 14.5a and 14.5b

1   Remove the door trim panel. Disconnect any electrical connectors and push them through the door opening so they won't interfere with removal.

2   Position a jack or jackstand under the door or have an assistant on hand to support it when the hinge bolts are removed **(see illustration)**. **Note:** *If a jack or stand is used, place a rag between it and the door to protect the door's paint.*

3   Scribe around the door bolts **(see illustration)**.

4   Remove the hinge-to-door bolts and carefully detach the door. Installation is the reverse of removal.

5   Following installation, make sure it's aligned properly. Adjust it if necessary as follows:

   a)   Up-and-down and forward-and-backward adjustments are made by loosening the hinge-to-body bolts and moving the door, as necessary. A special offset tool may be required to reach some of the bolts **(see illustration)**.

   b)   The door lock striker can also be adjusted both up-and-down and sideways to provide a positive engagement with the locking mechanism. This is done by loosening the screws and moving the striker, as necessary **(see illustration)**.

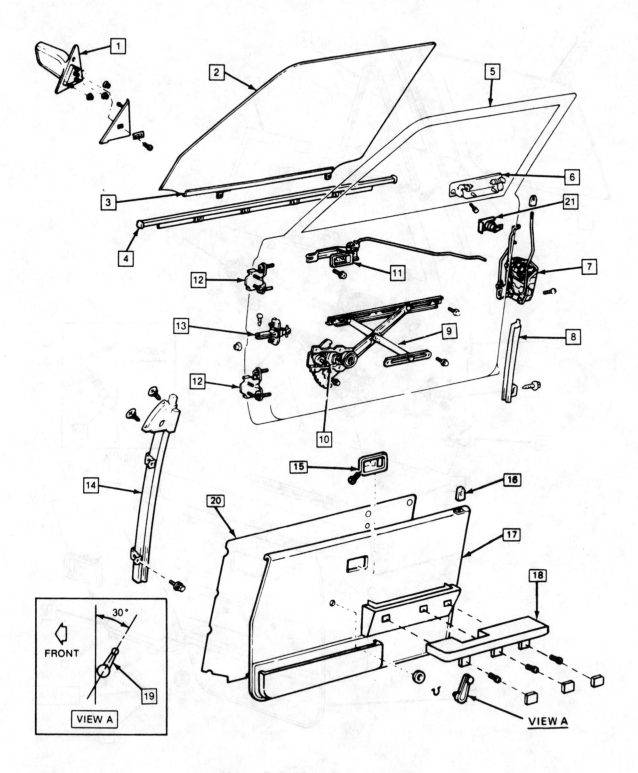

13.2a   Typical front door components

1	Mirror assembly	8	Run channel guide (rear)	15	Inside handle bezel
2	Window	9	Equalizer arm	16	Door lock knob
3	Sash channel	10	Window regulator	17	Door trim panel
4	Door belt molding	11	Window regulator	18	Armrest
5	Door	12	Door hinge	19	Window regulator handle
6	Outside mirror	13	Door check assembly	20	Water deflector
7	Door lock assembly	14	Run channel guide (front)		

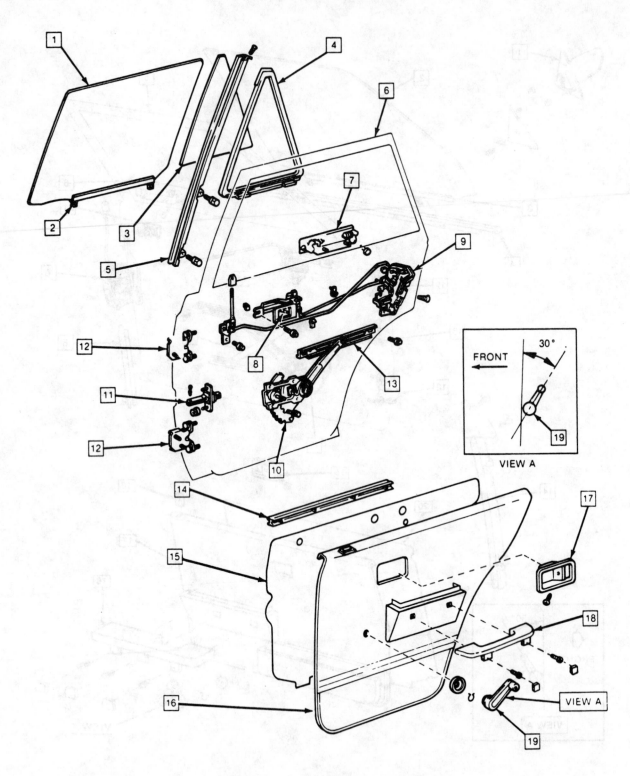

13.2b   Typical rear door components

1	Window	8	Inside handle	15	Water deflector
2	Sash channel	9	Door lock assembly	16	Door trim panel
3	Stationary window	10	Window regulator	17	Inside handle bezel
4	Stationary window weather strip	11	Door check assembly	18	Armrest
5	Run channel guide	12	Door hinge assembly	19	Window regulator handle
6	Door assembly	13	Lift arm bracket		
7	Outside handle	14	Door belt molding		

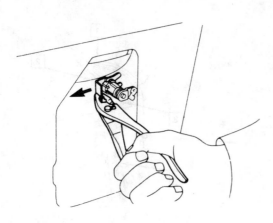

13.6   Use pliers to pull off the lock cylinder retaining clip

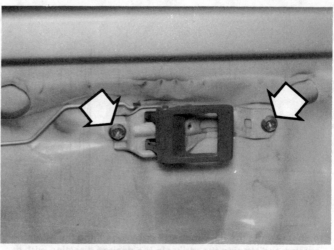

13.8   Use a screwdriver or nut driver to remove the inside door handle bolts (arrows)

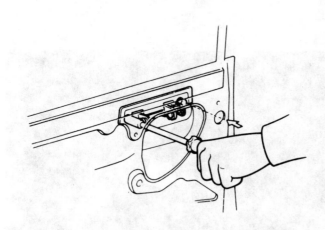

13.12   Remove the outside door handle retaining nuts from inside the door, using a socket and extension or a nut driver

14.2   Use two jackstands padded with rags (to protect the paint) to support the door during the removal and installation procedures

14.3   Before loosening or removing them, mark the door bolt locations

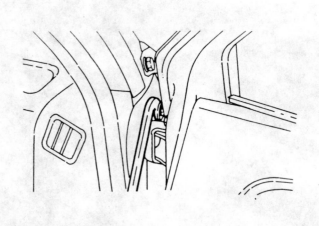

14.5a   An offset wrench like this one is required to reach the hinge-to-body bolts when adjusting the doors

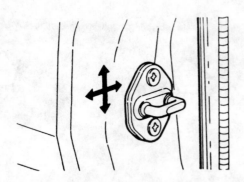

14.5b   Adjust the door lock striker by loosening the retaining screws and tapping the striker in the desired direction with a soft-face hammer

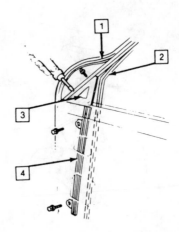

15.3a   Typical front door run channel details

1	Weatherstrip	3	Filler panel
2	Run channel	4	Run channel guide

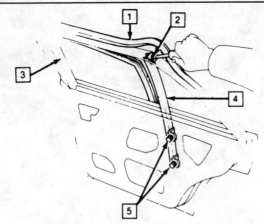

15.3b   Typical rear door run channel details

1	Weatherstrip	4	Run channel guide
2	Guide screw	5	Guide bolts
3	Door assembly		

17.1a   Remove the screw and the adjusting lever (arrow)

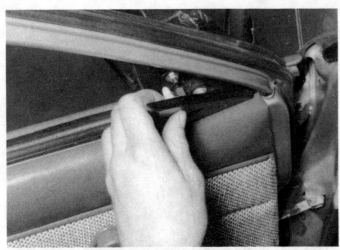

17.1b   Remove the trim panel

17.2   The mirror is retained by three nuts (arrows)

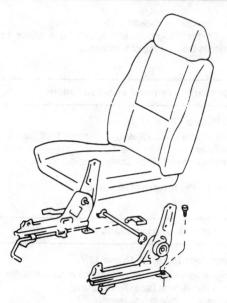

18.1a   Typical front seat installation details

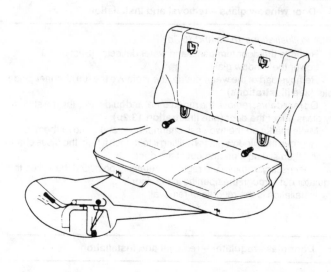

18.1b   Typical rear seat installation details (sedan models)

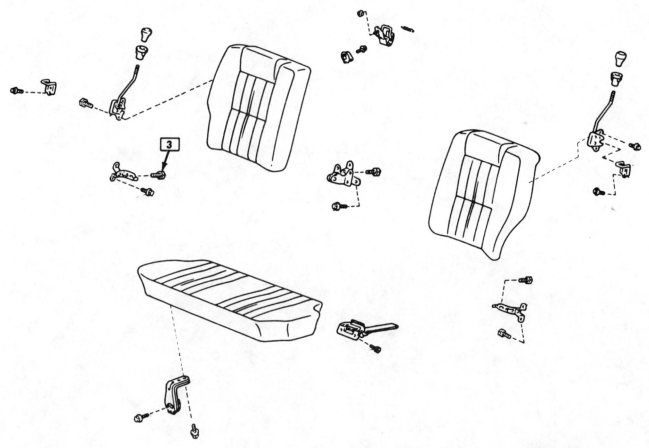

**18.1c   Typical rear seat installation details
(hatchback models)**

15   Door window glass – removal and installation

Refer to illustrations 15.3a and 15.3b
1   Remove the door trim panel and water deflector (Section 10).
2   Lower the window glass.
3   Remove part of the weatherstrip, then remove the run channel/guide bolts **(see illustrations)**.
4   On rear doors, remove the run channel and guide. Pull the the stationary glass out of the door **(see illustration 13.2b).**
5   Make marks on the two sash channel bolts and remove them .
6   Remove the window glass by tilting it to detach it from the glass channel and then sliding it up and out of the door.
7   If necessary, remove the regulator retaining bolts and then slide the regulator out through the opening in the door.
8   Installation is the reverse of removal.

16   Door glass regulator – removal and installation

1   Remove the door trim panel and water deflector (see Section 10).

2   Remove the window assembly (see Section 15).
3   Remove the mounting bolts and detach the regulator from the door.
4   Installation is the reverse of removal.

17   Outside mirror – removal and installation

Refer to illustrations 17.1a, 17.1b and 17.2
1   Remove the screw and adjusting lever and lift off the mirror trim cover **(see illustrations)**.
2   Remove the three retaining screws and detach the mirror **(see illustration)**.
3   Installation is the reverse of removal.

18   Seats – removal and installation

Refer to illustrations 18.1a, 18.1b and 18.1c
1   Remove the retaining bolts, unplug any electrical connectors and lift the seats from the vehicle **(see illustrations)**.
2   Installation is the reverse of removal.

Chapter 12   Chassis electrical system

Contents

1   General information

The electrical system is a 12-volt, negative ground type. Power for the lights and all electrical accessories is supplied by a lead/acid-type battery which is charged by the alternator.

This Chapter covers repair and service procedures for the various electrical components not associated with the engine. Information on the battery, alternator, distributor and starter motor can be found in Chapter 5.

It should be noted that when portions of the electrical system are serviced, the cable should be disconnected from the negative battery terminal to prevent electrical shorts and/or fires.

2   Electrical troubleshooting – general information

A typical electrical circuit consists of an electrical component, any switches, relays, motors, fuses, fusible links or circuit breakers related to that component and the wiring and connectors that link the component to both the battery and the chassis. To help you pinpoint an electrical circuit problem, wiring diagrams are included at the end of this book.

Before tackling any troublesome electrical circuit, first study the appropriate wiring diagrams to get a complete understanding of what makes up that individual circuit. Trouble spots, for instance, can often be narrowed down by noting if other components related to the circuit are operating properly. If several components or circuits fail at one time, chances are the problem is in a fuse or ground connection, because several circuits are often routed through the same fuse and ground connections.

Electrical problems usually stem from simple causes, such as loose or corroded connections, a blown fuse, a melted fusible link or a bad relay. Visually inspect the condition of all fuses, wires and connections in a problem circuit before troubleshooting it.

If testing instruments are going to be utilized, use the diagrams to plan ahead of time where you will make the necessary connections in order to accurately pinpoint the trouble spot.

The basic tools needed for electrical troubleshooting include a circuit tester or voltmeter (a 12-volt bulb with a set of test leads can also be used), a continuity tester, which includes a bulb, battery and set of test leads, and a jumper wire, preferably with a circuit breaker incorporated, which can be used to bypass electrical components. Before attempting to locate a problem with test instruments, use the wiring diagram(s) to decide where to make the connections.

Voltage checks

Voltage checks should be performed if a circuit is not functioning properly. Connect one lead of a circuit tester to either the negative battery terminal or a known good ground. Connect the other lead to a connector in the circuit being tested, preferably nearest to the battery or fuse. If the bulb of the tester lights, voltage is present, which means that the part of the circuit between the connector and the battery is problem free. Continue checking the rest of the circuit in the same fashion. When you reach a point at which no voltage is present, the problem lies between that point and the last test point with voltage. Most of the time the problem can be traced to a loose connection. **Note:** *Keep in mind that some circuits receive voltage only when the ignition key is in the Accessory or Run position.*

Finding a short

One method of finding shorts in a circuit is to remove the fuse and connect a test light or voltmeter in its place to the fuse terminals. There should be no voltage present in the circuit. Move the wiring harness from side to side while watching the test light. If the bulb goes on, there is a short to ground somewhere in that area, probably where the insulation has rubbed through. The same test can be performed on each component in the circuit, even a switch.

Ground check

Perform a ground test to check whether a component is properly grounded. Disconnect the battery and connect one lead of a selfpowered

test light, known as a continuity tester, to a known good ground. Connect the other lead to the wire or ground connection being tested. If the bulb goes on, the ground is good. If the bulb does not go on, the ground is not good.

Continuity check

A continuity check is done to determine if there are any breaks in a circuit – if it is passing electricity properly. With the circuit off (no power in the circuit), a self-powered continuity tester can be used to check the circuit. Connect the test leads to both ends of the circuit (or to the "power" end and a good ground), and if the test light comes on the circuit is passing current properly. If the light doesn't come on, there is a break somewhere in the circuit. The same procedure can be used to test a switch, by connecting the continuity tester to the power in and power out sides of the switch. With the switch turned On, the test light should come on.

Finding an open circuit

When diagnosing for possible open circuits, it is often difficult to locate them by sight because oxidation or terminal misalignment are hidden by the connectors. Merely wiggling a connector on a sensor or in the wiring harness may correct the open circuit condition. Remember this when an open circuit is indicated when troubleshooting a circuit. Intermittent problems may also be caused by oxidized or loose connections.

Electrical troubleshooting is simple if you keep in mind that all electrical circuits are basically electricity running from the battery, through the wires, switches, relays, fuses and fusible links to each electrical component (light bulb, motor, etc.) and to ground, from which it is passed back to the battery. Any electrical problem is an interruption in the flow of electricity to and from the battery.

---

3   Fuses – general information

Refer to illustrations 3.1a, 3.1b and 3.3

The electrical circuits of the vehicle are protected by a combination of fuses, circuit breakers and fusible links. The fuse blocks are located under the instrument panel on the left side of the dashboard and next to the battery in the engine compartment **(see illustrations)**.

Each of the fuses is designed to protect a specific circuit, and the various circuits are identified on the fuse panel itself.

3.1a   This fuse block is located in the left kick panel

3.1b   The engine compartment fuse block is located next to the battery, under a cover

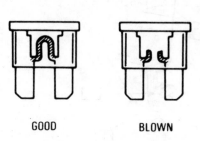

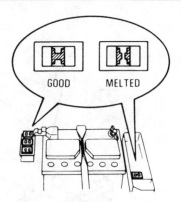

3.3   The fuses used on these models can be checked visually to determine if they're blown

4.2   Fusible links can be checked visually to determine if they're melted

Miniaturized fuses are employed in the fuse block. These compact fuses, with blade terminal design, allow fingertip removal and replacement. If an electrical component fails, always check the fuse first. A blown fuse is easily identified through the clear plastic body. Visually inspect the element for evidence of damage **(see illustration)**. If a continuity check is called for, the blade terminal tips are exposed in the fuse body.

Be sure to replace blown fuses with the correct type. Fuses of different ratings are physically interchangeable, but only fuses of the proper rating should be used. Replacing a fuse with one of a higher or lower value than specified is not recommended. Each electrical circuit needs a specific amount of protection. The amperage value of each fuse is molded into the fuse body.

If the replacement fuse immediately fails, don't replace it again until the cause of the problem is isolated and corrected. In most cases, this will be a short circuit in the wiring caused by a broken or deteriorated wire.

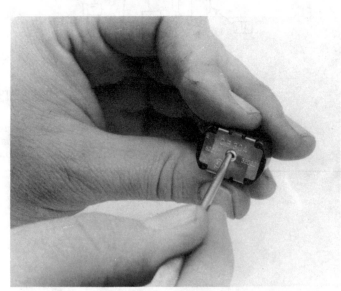

5.3   Insert a pin or paper clip into the circuit breaker reset hole and push in to reset it

4   Fusible links – general information

Refer to illustration 4.2

Some circuits are protected by fusible links. The links are used in circuits which are not ordinarily fused, such as the ignition circuit.

The fusible links on these models are similar to fuses in that they can be visually checked to determine if they are melted **(see illustration)**.

To replace a fusible link, first disconnect the negative cable from the battery. Unplug the burned out link and replace it with a new one (available from your dealer). Always determine the cause for the overload which melted the fusible link before installing a new one.

5   Circuit breakers – general information

Refer to illustration 5.3

Circuit breakers protect components such as power windows, power door locks and headlights. Some circuit breakers are located in the fuse box.

Because on some models the circuit breaker resets itself automatically, an electrical overload in a circuit breaker protected system will cause the circuit to fail momentarily, then come back on. If the circuit does not come back on, check it immediately. Note, however, that some circuit breakers must be reset manually. Once the condition is corrected, the circuit breaker will resume its normal function.

To reset a manual circuit breaker, first disconnect the cable from the negative battery terminal. Remove the circuit breaker, insert a pin into the reset hole and push in **(see illustration)**. Reinstall the circuit breaker.

6   Relays – general information

Refer to illustrations 6.2a, 6.2b and 6.2c

Several electrical accessories in the vehicle use relays to transmit the electrical signal to the component. If the relay is defective, that component will not operate properly.

The various relays are located in several locations throughout the vehicle **(see illustrations)**.

If a faulty relay is suspected, it can be removed and tested by a dealer or other qualified shop. Defective relays must be replaced as a unit.

7   Turn signal/hazard flashers – check and replacement

1   The turn signal/hazard flasher, a small canister shaped unit located behind the left kick panel (Nova models) or under the dash (Prizm models) **(see illustrations 6.2a and 6.2b)**, flashes the turn signals.

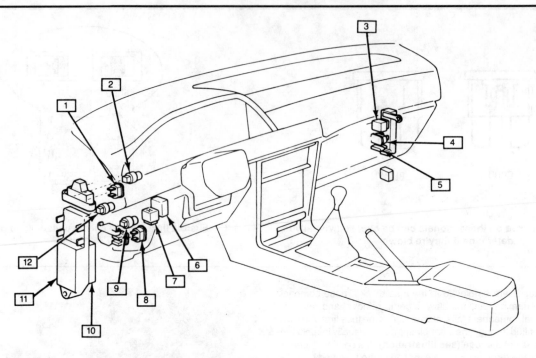

6.2a   Typical dashboard relay locations (Prizm)

1	Defogger circuit breaker	5	A/C fuse	9	Power window main relay
2	Rear window defogger	6	Door lock control relay	10	No. 1 fuse and relay block
3	Heater main relay	7	Turn signal flasher	11	Integration relay
4	Heater circuit breaker	8	Power window circuit breaker	12	Taillight control relay

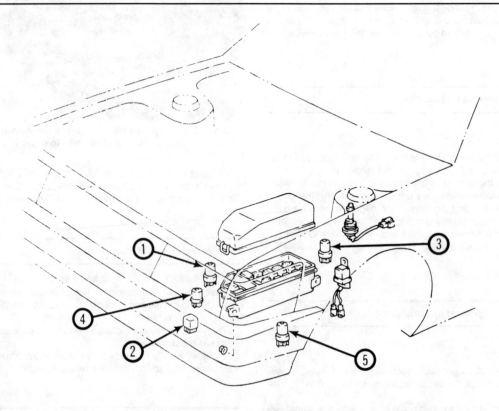

6.2b   Typical engine compartment relay block (Nova shown, Prizm similar)

1	Main relay (through 1986 models)	4	A/C relay
2	A/C relay	5	Fan relay
3	Headlight relay		

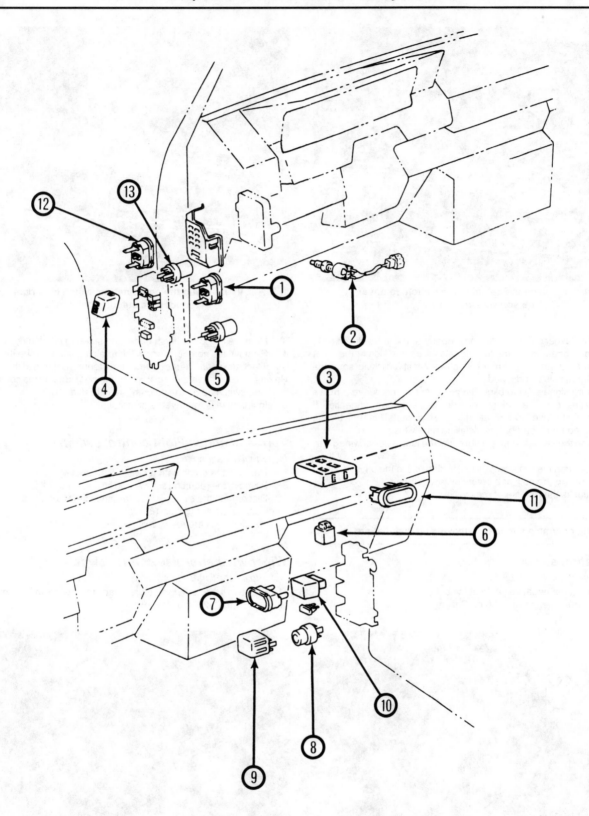

6.2c Typical dashboard relay locations (Nova)

1	Circuit breaker		6	Charge light relay		11	Circuit breaker (for door lock)	
2	Clutch switch (manual transaxle)		7	Circuit breaker (for heater)		12	Circuit breaker	
3	Seatbelt relay		8	Defogger relay			(for power window)	
4	Flasher		9	Heater relay		13	Power window relay	
5	Taillight relay		10	Clutch start relay				

8.4   To detach the combination switch, remove the screws (arrows), . . .

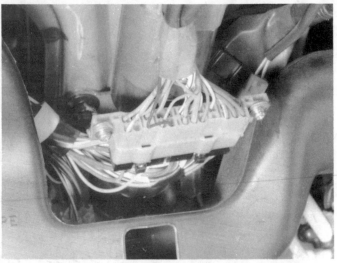

8.5   . . . then unplug the combination switch electrical connector under the steering column

2   When the flasher unit is functioning properly, and audible click can be heard during its operation. If the turn signals fail on one side or the other and the flasher unit does not make its characteristic clicking sound, a faulty turn signal bulb is indicated.

3   If both turn signals fail to blink, the problem may be due to a blown fuse, a faulty flasher unit, a broken switch or a loose or open connection. If a quick check of the fuse box indicates that the turn signal fuse has blown, check the wiring for a short before installing a new fuse.

4   To replace the flasher, simply pull it out of the fuse block or wiring harness.

5   Make sure that the replacement unit is identical to the original. Compare the old one to the new one before installing it.

6   Installation is the reverse of removal.

8   Steering column switches – removal and installation

Combination switch

Refer to illustrations 8.4 and 8.5

1   Disconnect the negative cable at the battery.

2   Remove the steering wheel (see Chapter 10).

3   Remove the lower finish panel and steering column cover.

4   Remove the combination switch retaining screws **(see illustration)**.

5   Trace the wiring harness down the steering column to the connector. Release the wiring retainer clamp (if equipped), unplug the connector and slide the switch up off the column **(see illustration)**.

6   Installation is the reverse of removal.

Turn signal/headlight control switch

Refer to illustration 8.8

7   Remove the combination switch (see above).

8   Remove the retaining screws and lift the switch off **(see illustration)**.

9   Disconnect the switch wiring terminals from the combination switch electrical connector (Steps 18 through 22).

10   Installation is the reverse of removal.

Wiper/washer/cruise control switch

Refer to illustration 8.11

11   Remove the retaining screws, detach the switch and lift it off the combination switch **(see illustration)**.

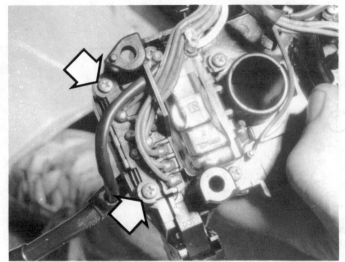

8.8   To detach the turn signal/headlight dimmer switch, remove the screws and slide the switch up and off the column

8.11   To detach the windshield wiper/washer switch, remove the screws (arrows)

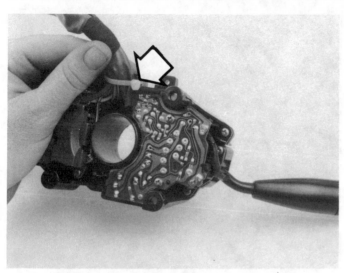

8.18   Cut or disconnect all wire ties (arrow) or straps to allow switch removal

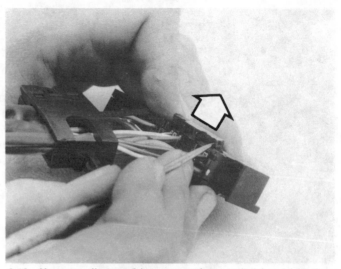

8.19   Use a small screwdriver or punch to push the combination switch connector up (arrow) for access to the terminals

12   Disconnect the switch wiring terminals from the combination switch electrical connector (Steps 18 through 22).
13   Installation is the reverse of removal.

Hazard warning flasher switch

14   Remove the turn signal/headlight control switch.
15   Remove the retaining screws, detach the switch and lift it off the combination switch **(see illustration 8.8)**.
16   Disconnect the switch wiring terminals from the combination switch electrical connector (Steps 18 through 22).
17   Installation is the reverse of removal.

Electrical connectors

Refer to illustrations 8.18, 8.19, 8.20a, 8.20b and 8.21

18   Trace the wiring harness from the switch be disconnected to the combination switch connector. It may be necessary to detach or cut some of the wiring ties or straps to separate the wires of a particular switch from the harness **(see illustration)**. Mark the wires and combination switch terminals with pieces of tape so that only the wires involved with a specific switch are disconnected.

19   Use a small screwdriver or punch to pry the combination switch cover up for access to the terminals **(see illustration)**.
20   Insert a small screwdriver or punch into the connector and pry the locking lug down, disconnect the terminal and then pull it out to remove it **(see illustrations)**.
21   To connect the terminal, insert it into the connector and push in with a small screwdriver until the locking lug snaps into place **(see illustration)**.
22   Snap the connector cover shut to lock the terminals.

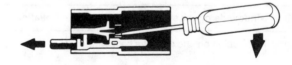

8.20b   . . . and pry the locking lug down so the terminal can be disconnected

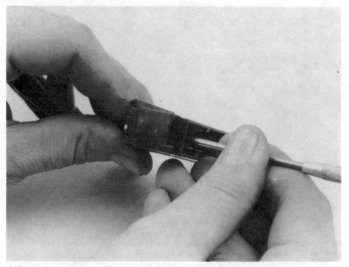

8.20a   Insert a small screwdriver or punch into the connector . . .

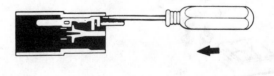

8.21   Push in on the connector collar until the connector snaps into place

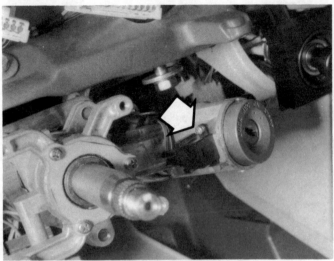

9.5   Remove the key lock warning buzzer switch screw (arrow), then detach the switch

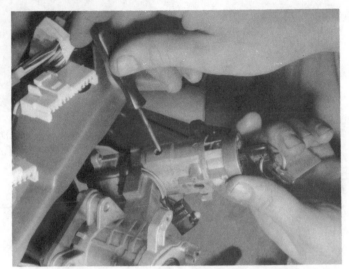

9.6   Insert a pin or paper clip into the casting hole and, with the key in the Accessory position, pull the lock cylinder out

9   Ignition switch key lock cylinder – removal and installation

Refer to illustrations 9.5 and 9.6

1   Disconnect the negative cable at the battery.
2   Remove the steering wheel (see Chapter 10).
3   Remove the lower finish panel and the steering column cover.
4   Remove the combination switch and windshield wiper switch (see Section 8).
5   Unscrew and detach the key warning buzzer switch **(see illustration)**.
6   With the key in the Accessory position, insert a pin in the hole in the casting, pull the lock cylinder straight out and remove it from the steering column **(see illustration)**.
7   Installation is the reverse of removal.

10   Rear window defogger switch – removal and installation

1   Detach the cable from the negative battery terminal.

2   Remove the steering wheel (see Chapter 10).
3   Remove five screws from the instrument cluster trim panel and remove the trim panel.
4   Unplug the electrical connector from the rear window defogger switch.
5   Pop the switch from the instrument cluster trim panel.
6   Installation is the reverse of removal.

11   Radio, speakers and antenna – removal and installation

1   Disconnect the negative cable at the battery.

Radio

Refer to illustrations 11.3a, 11.3b, 11.3c and 11.4

2   Remove the steering column covers.
3   Remove the trim bezel **(see illustrations)**.

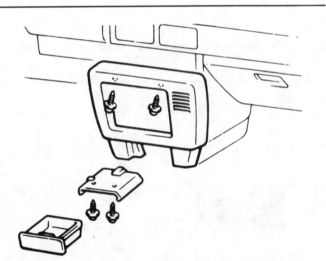

11.3a   To get at the radio mounting screws on Nova models, remove the two mounting screws and detach the ashtray assembly, . . .

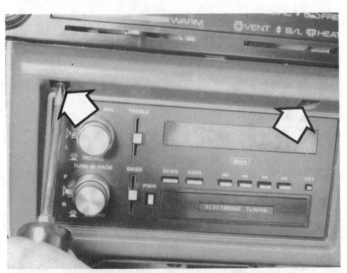

11.3b   . . . then remove the two radio trim panel screws (arrows) and detach the trim panel

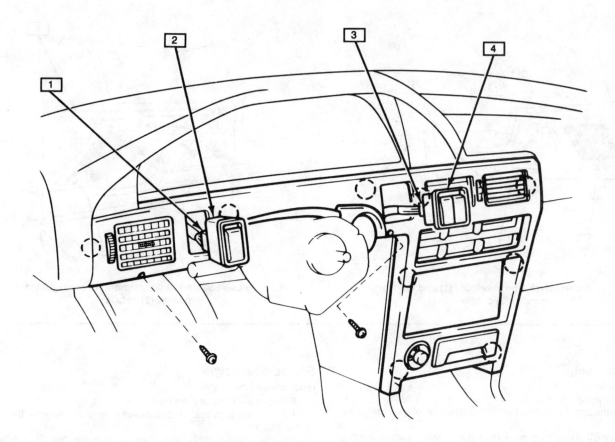

11.3c   To get at the radio mounting screws on Prizm models, you'll have to remove the entire dash trim bezel assembly: Pop out the rear wiper/washer switch (2) and unplug it (1), pop out the cruise control/defogger switch (4) and unplug it (3), remove the screws and pull off the bezel

4   Remove the radio mounting screws or bolts **(see illustration)**.
5   Pull the radio out, reach behind it, unplug the electrical connector and the antenna lead and lift the radio from the instrument panel.
6   Installation is the reverse of removal.

Speakers

Nova (front)

7   Remove the speaker cover screw and pry off the cover.
8   Remove the speaker retaining screws, pull the speaker out of the dash, unplug the connector and remove the speaker.
9   Installation is the reverse of removal.

Nova (rear)

10   Pry off the speaker cover from the plastic molding covering the rear shock tower.
11   Remove the speaker retaining screws, lift the speaker out of the molding, unplug the connector and remove the speaker.
12   Installation is the reverse of removal.

Prizm (left front)

Refer to illustration 11.14

13   Remove the attaching screws from the hood release lever and remove the lever.
14   Remove the four attaching screws from the left lower dash trim panel **(see illustration)** and remove the panel.
15   Unplug the electrical connector, remove the three attaching screws and remove the speaker.
16   Installation is the reverse of removal.

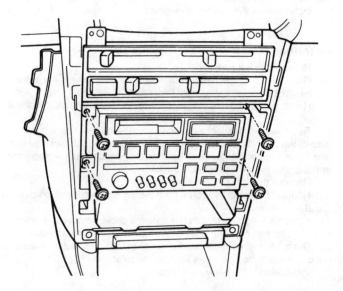

11.4   Typical radio installation

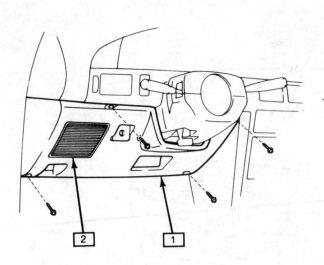

11.14   Left lower dash trim assembly (1) and left front speaker (2) details

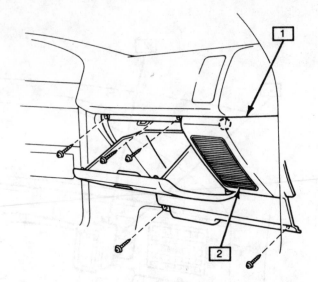

11.19   Glove box and trim assembly (1) and right front speaker (2) details

Prizm (right front)
Refer to illustration 11.19

17   Remove the right scuff plate.
18   Remove the attaching screw from the right kick panel and remove the panel.
19   Remove the five attaching screws from the glove box and trim assembly **(see illustration)** and pull out the assembly.
20   Unplug the electrical connector, remove the three attaching screws and remove the speaker.
21   Installation is the reverse of removal.

Prizm (rear)

22   Remove the rear window shelf.
23   Unplug the electrical connector, remove the three attaching screws and remove the speaker.
24   Installation is the reverse of removal.

Antenna

25   Remove the left side panel.
26   Reach into the side panel access hole and disconnect the antenna cable from the cable coming from the radio.
27   Remove the hood release lever attaching screws and remove the lever.
28   Remove the four attaching screws from the left lower dash trim panel **(see illustration 11.14),** pull out the panel, unplug the speaker connector and the connectors for the rear wiper/washer switch and the cruise control/defogger switch and remove the panel.
29   Remove the left scuff plate.
30   Remove the attaching screw from the left kick panel and remove the panel.
31   Fasten a length of wire to the antenna cable, remove the antenna mounting screws from the pillar and remove the antenna and cable.
32   Detach the wire from the old antenna cable and attach it to the new cable, then pull the new cable through the pillar.
33   Installation is the revere of removal.

12   Headlights – removal and installation

1   Disconnect the negative cable from the battery.

Sealed-beam type
Refer to illustration 12.4

2   Remove the radiator grille (see Chapter 11).
3   Remove the park and front sidemarker lens and remove the side-marker assembly.
4   Remove the headlight trim, then remove the headlight retainer screws **(see illustration)**. Don't disturb the adjustment screws.
5   Pull the headlight out, unplug the connector and remove the headlight assembly.
6   Installation is the reverse of removal.

Bulb type
Refer to illustration 12.9

7   Remove the headlight bulb (see Section 14).
8   Remove the front parking/side marker light housing.
9   Remove the headlight fasteners **(see illustration)** and detach the headlight assembly.
10   Installation is the reverse of removal.

13   Headlights – adjustment

Refer to illustrations 13.6a and 13.6b

Note: *It is important that the headlights be aimed correctly. If adjusted incorrectly they could blind the driver of an oncoming vehicle and cause a serious accident or seriously reduce your ability to see the road. The headlights should be checked for proper aim every 12 months and any time a new headlight is installed or front end body work is performed. It should be emphasized that the following procedure is only an interim step which will provide temporary adjustment until the headlights can be adjusted by a properly equipped shop.*

1   Headlights have two adjusting screws, one on the top controlling up and down movement and one on the side controlling left and right movement.
2   There are several methods of adjusting the headlights. The simplest method requires a blank wall 25 feet in front of the vehicle and a level floor.
3   Position masking tape vertically on the wall in reference to the vehicle centerline and the centerlines of both headlights.

12.4   Headlight mounting screws (arrows) (Nova)

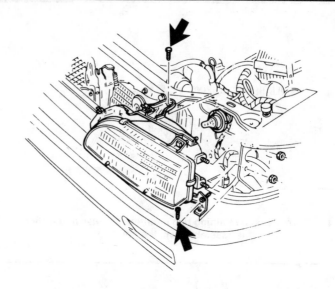

12.9   Headlight mounting screws (arrows) (Prizm)

4   Position a horizontal tape line in reference to the centerline of all the headlights. **Note:** *It may be easier to position the tape on the wall with the vehicle parked only a few inches away.*
5   Adjustment should be made with the vehicle sitting level, the gas tank half-full and no unusually heavy load in the vehicle.
6   Starting with the low beam adjustment, position the high intensity zone so it is two inches below the horizontal line and two inches to the right of the headlight vertical line. Adjustment on sealed beam equipped models is made by turning the top adjusting screw clockwise to raise the beam and counterclockwise to lower the beam **(see illustration)**. The adjusting screw on the side should be used in the same manner to move the beam left or right. On bulb-type headlights, the top adjusting screw moves the headlight assembly right or left and the lower one moves it up and down **(see illustration)**.
7   With the high beams on, the high intensity zone should be vertically

centered with the exact center just below the horizontal line. **Note:** *It may not be possible to position the headlight aim exactly for both high and low beams. If a compromise must be made, keep in mind that the low beams are the most used and have the greatest effect on driver safety.*
8   Have the headlights adjusted by a dealer service department at the earliest opportunity.

14   Bulb replacement

Headlight bulb (Prizm models)

Refer to illustrations 14.2 and 14.4
Warning: *The halogen gas filled bulbs used on these models are under pressure and may shatter if the surface is scratched or the bulb is dropped.*

13.6a   Sealed beam headlight adjusting screw locations

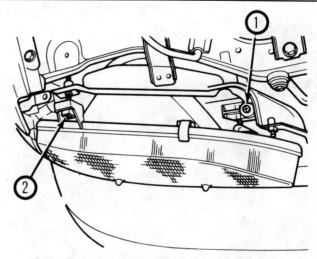

13.6b   Bulb-type headlight adjusting screw locations

1   *Horizontal adjustment screw*   2   *Vertical adjustment screw*

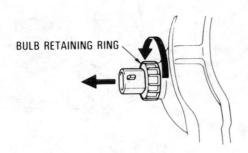

14.2   Turn the bulb retaining ring counterclockwise and withdraw the assembly from the housing

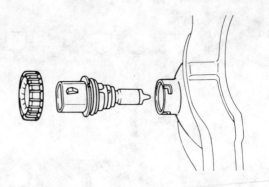

14.4   Bulb housing installation details – align the tab with the slot in the headlight housing, push in and turn the housing clockwise to lock it

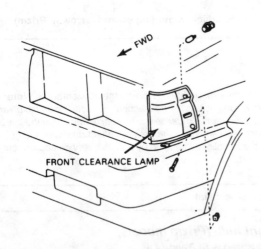

14.6a   To replace a park or front side marker light bulb on Nova models, unscrew the lens and housing assembly and pull it off, turn the bulb housing counterclockwise, remove the holder from the housing and pull the bulb straight out

14.6b   Prizm side marker light mounting details

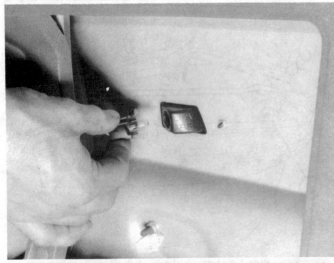

14.8   To replace a rear side marker light bulb, simply remove the small access door near the rear corner of the luggage compartment, turn the bulb holder counterclockwise and pull the bulb straight out

Wear eye protection and handle the bulbs carefully, grasping only the base whenever possible. Do not touch the surface of the bulb with your fingers because the oil from your skin could cause it to overheat and fail prematurely. If you do touch the bulb surface, clean it with rubbing alcohol.

1   Unplug the electrical connector.
2   Reach behind the headlight assembly, grasp the bulb holder and turn it counterclockwise to remove it **(see illustration)**. Lift the holder assembly out for access to the bulb.
3   Push in and rotate the bulb counterclockwise to remove it.
4   Insert the new bulb into the holder and turn it clockwise to seat it in the holder **(see illustration)**.
5   Install the bulb holder in the headlight assembly.

Miscellaneous bulbs

Refer to illustrations 14.6a, 14.6b, 14.8, 14.9a, 14.9b and 14.11

6   The lenses of many lights are held in place by screws. To gain access to the bulbs in these assemblies, simply remove the lenses **(see illustrations)**.

14.9a   To replace one of the rear lights, open the small access door, turn the locking bulb holder counterclockwise, pull it out and pull the bulb straight out of the holder

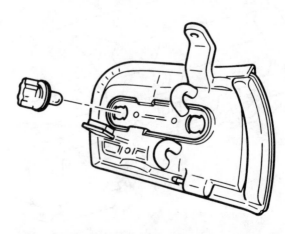

14.9b   Here's a closeup view of the back side of a Prizm front park and side marker light housing – to change a bulb, simply turn the bulb holder counterclockwise, pull it out and pull the bulb out of the holder

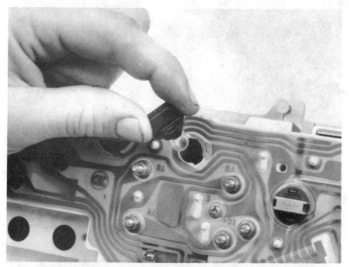

14.11   Instrument cluster bulbs have locking holders – to replace a bulb, simply turn the holder counterclockwise, pull it out, pull the bulb straight out of the holder, push in a new bulb, insert the holder into the back of the cluster and turn it clockwise to lock it in place

15.4   The wiper motor is attached to the firewall with three bolts

7   The lenses of some light assemblies are held in place by clips. You can remove them by unsnapping them or by prying them off with a small screwdriver.

8   Some bulbs can be removed simply by pushing them in and turning them counterclockwise (see illustration).

9   Other bulbs are installed in bulb holders. To release a bulb holder, push it in, turn it counterclockwise and pull it out (see illustrations).

10   Other holders can be unclipped from the terminals or pulled straight out of the socket.

11   To gain access to the instrument cluster illumination lights (see illustration), the instrument cluster will have to be removed as described in Section 16.

15   Windshield wiper motor – removal and installation

Refer to illustration 15.4

1   Disconnect the cable from the negative terminal of the battery.

2   Following the procedure in Chapter 3, remove the heater core housing.

3   Disconnect the linkage from the wiper motor arm.

4   From inside the engine compartment, unplug the electrical connector and remove the mounting bolts (see illustration). Lift the motor up and tilt it to allow the wiper motor arm to pass through the firewall.

5   Installation is the reverse of removal.

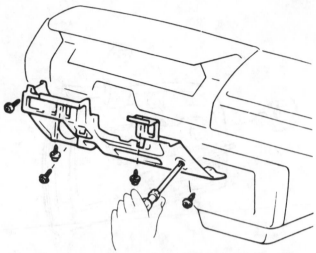

16.3   Steering column lower trim cover details (Nova)

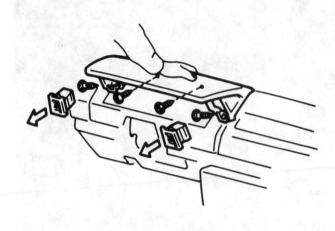

16.4   Details of the meter hood assembly (Nova)

16.5   Instrument cluster mounting screws (arrows) (Nova)

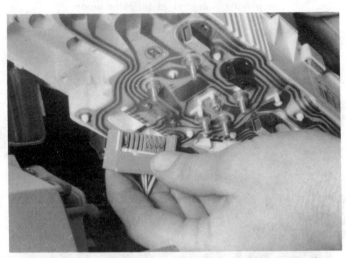

16.6a   After you've removed the instrument cluster mounting
screws and pulled the cluster out as far as possible, unplug the
wire harness connectors from the back side (Nova shown,
Prizm similar)

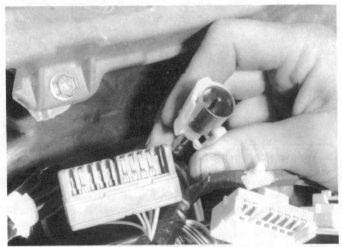

16.6b   To disconnect the speedometer cable from the back side
of the instrument cluster, pinch the two tabs together and pull
(Nova shown, Prizm similar)

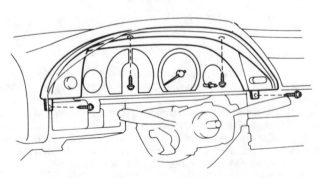

16.15   Instrument cluster bezel screws (Prizm)

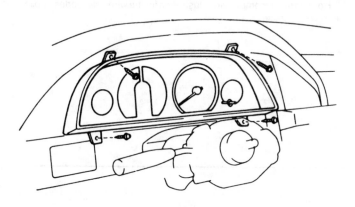

16.16   Instrument cluster mounting screws (Prizm)

16   Instrument cluster – removal and installation

Nova

Refer to illustrations 16.3, 16.4, 16.5, 16.6a and 16.6b

1   Detach the cable from the negative battery terminal.
2   Remove the steering wheel (see Chapter 10).
3   Remove the steering column lower trim cover **(see illustration)**.
4   Remove the meter hood **(see illustration)**.
5   Remove the instrument cluster screws **(see illustration)**.
6   Pull the cluster out from the dash, unplug the electrical connectors **(see illustration)** and detach the speedometer cable **(see illustration)**.
7   Installation is the reverse of removal.

Prizm

Refer to illustrations 16.15 and 16.16

8   Detach the cable from the negative battery cable.
9   Remove the two attaching screws from the hood release lever and remove the hood release lever.
10   Remove the four attaching screws from the left lower dash trim **(see illustration 16.3)** and pull off the trim.
11   Unplug the electrical connector from the left front speaker.
12   If the vehicle is equipped with A/C, remove the A/C duct from the lower A/C register.
13   Remove the screws from the steering column covers and remove the covers.
14   Remove the two attaching screws from the trim bezel **(see illustration 11.3c)**, pull out the trim bezel, unplug the electrical connectors from the cigarette lighter and the cruise control/defogger switch and/or the rear wiper-washer switch (if equipped) and remove the bezel.
15   Remove the four attaching screws from the cluster bezel **(see illustration)**, pull out the bezel, unplug the electrical connectors from the hazard flasher and dimmer switches and remove the bezel.

16   Remove the four attaching screws from the instrument cluster **(see illustration)**, pull the cluster out of the dash, unplug the electrical connectors, detach the speedometer cable and remove the cluster.
17   Installation is the reverse of removal.

17   Cruise control system – description and check

The cruise control system maintains vehicle speed by means of a vacuum actuated servo motor located in the engine compartment which is connected to the throttle linkage by a cable. The system consists of the servo motor, clutch switch, stoplight switch, control switches, a relay and associated vacuum hoses.

Because of the complexity of the cruise control system and the special tools and techniques required for diagnosis and repair, this should be left to a dealer or properly equipped shop. However, it is possible for the home mechanic to make simple checks of the wiring and vacuum connections for minor faults which can be easily repaired. These include:

a) Inspecting the cruise control actuating switches and wiring for broken wires or loose connections.
b) Checking the cruise control fuse.
c) Checking the hoses in the engine compartment for tight connections, cracked hoses and obvious vacuum leaks. The cruise control system is operated by a vacuum so it is critical that all vacuum switches, hoses and connections be secure.

18   Power door lock system – description and check

The power door lock system operates the door lock actuators mounted in each door. The system consists of the switches, actuators and associated wiring. Special tools and techniques are required to fully diagnose this system, and this should be left to a dealer or properly equipped shop. However, it is possible for the home mechanic to make simple checks of the wiring connections and actuators for minor faults which can be easily repaired. These include:

a) Checking the system fuse and/or circuit breaker.
b) Checking the switch wiring for damage or loose connections.
c) Checking the switches for continuity.
d) Removing the door panel(s) and checking the actuator wiring connections for looseness or damage. Inspect the actuator rods (if equipped) to make sure they are not bent, damaged or binding. The actuator can be checked by applying battery power momentarily. A solid click indicates the solenoid is operating properly.

19   Power window system – description and check

The power window system operates the electric motors mounted in the doors which lower and raise the windows. The system consists of the control switches, the motors (regulators), glass mechanisms and associated wiring.

Because of the complexity of the power window system and the special tools and techniques required for diagnosis and repair, this should be left to a dealer or properly equipped shop. However, it is possible for the home mechanic to make simple checks of the wiring connections and motors for minor faults which can be easily repaired. These include:

a) Inspecting the power window actuating switches and wiring for broken wires or loose connections.
b) Checking the power window fuse and/or circuit breaker.
c) Removing the door panel(s) and checking the power window motor wiring connections for looseness and damage, and inspecting the glass mechanisms for damage which could cause binding.

20   Wiring diagrams – general information

Since it isn't possible to include all wiring diagrams for every year covered by this manual, the following diagrams are those that are typical and most commonly needed.

Prior to troubleshooting any circuits, check the fuse and circuit break-ers (if equipped) to make sure they are in good condition. Make sure the battery is properly charged and has clean, tight cable connections (see Chapter 1).

When checking the wiring system, make sure that all connectors are clean, with no broken or loose pins. When unplugging a connector, do not pull on the wires, only on the connector housings themselves.

Refer to the accompanying illustration for the wire color codes applicable to your vehicle.

B	=	Black	L	=	Light Blue	R	=	Red
BR	=	Brown	LG	=	Light Green	V	=	Violet
G	=	Green	O	=	Orange	W	=	White
GR	=	Gray	P	=	Pink	Y	=	Yellow

**The first letter indicates the basic wire color
second letter indicates the color of the stripe.**

Wiring diagram color codes

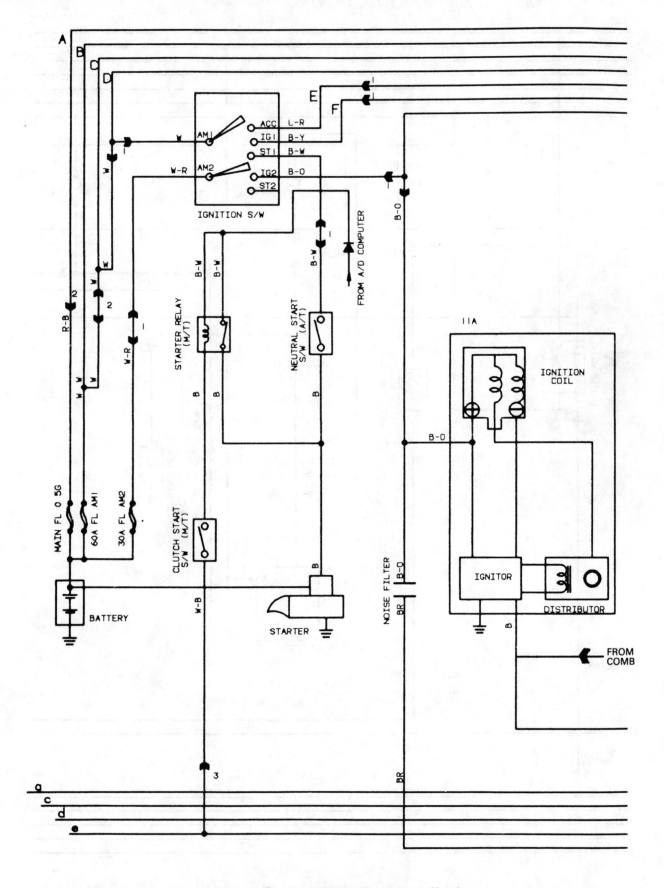

Power source, starting and ignition systems (Nova)

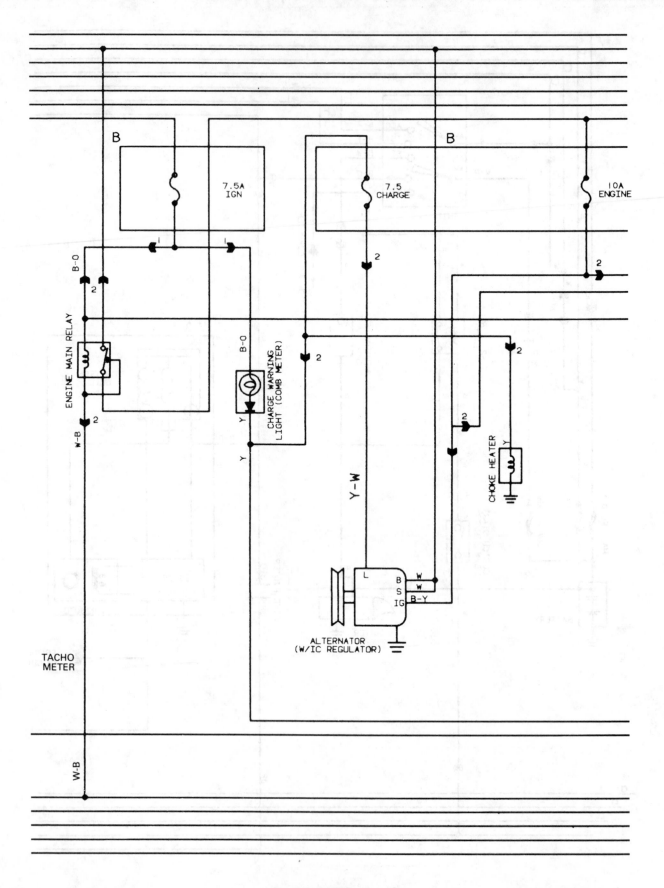

Charging system (Nova)

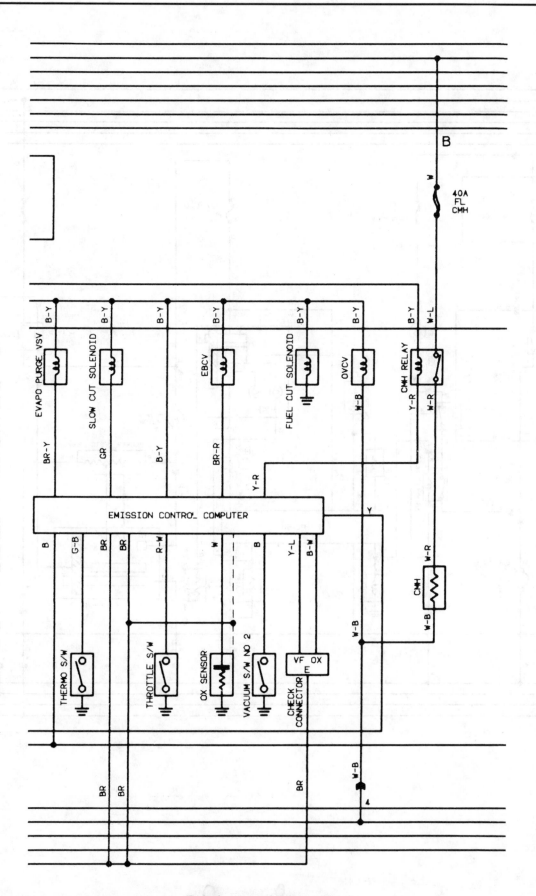

Emission control systems (Nova)

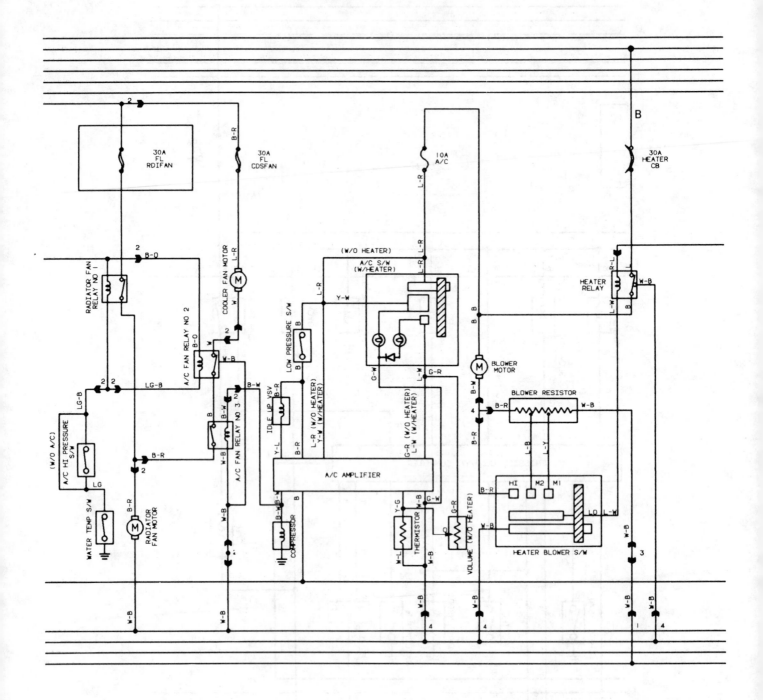

Engine cooling fan, air conditioner and heater (Nova)

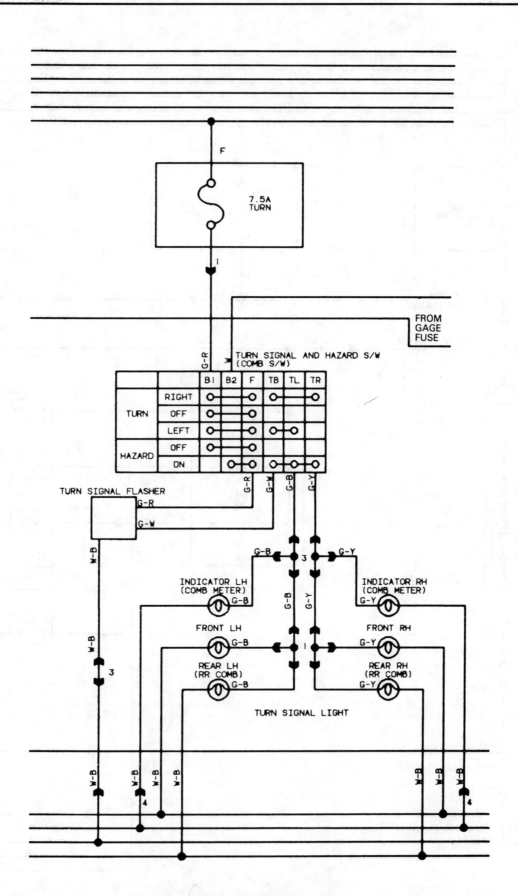

Turn signal and hazard systems (Nova)

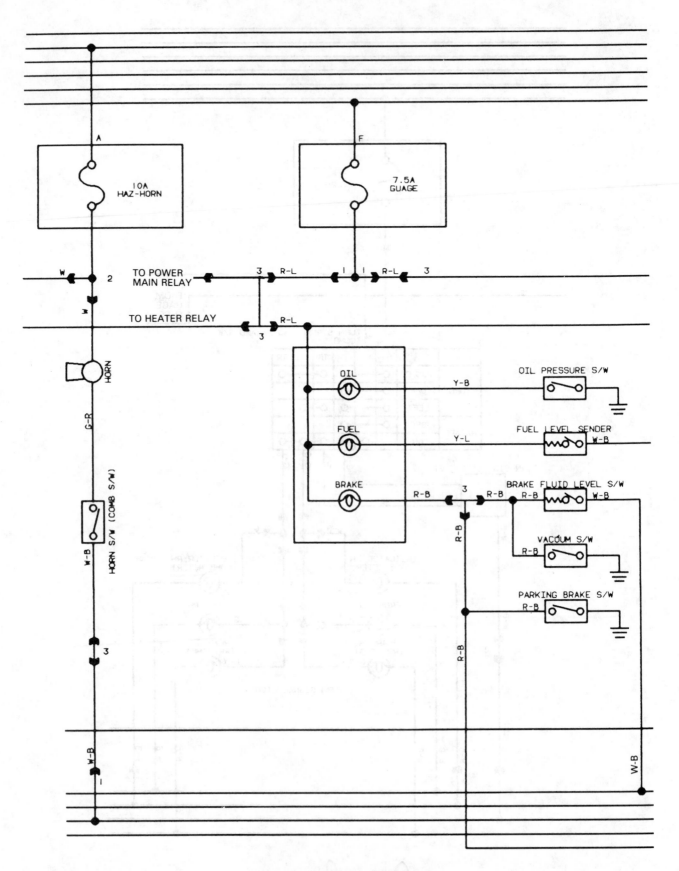

Horn and combination meter (Nova)

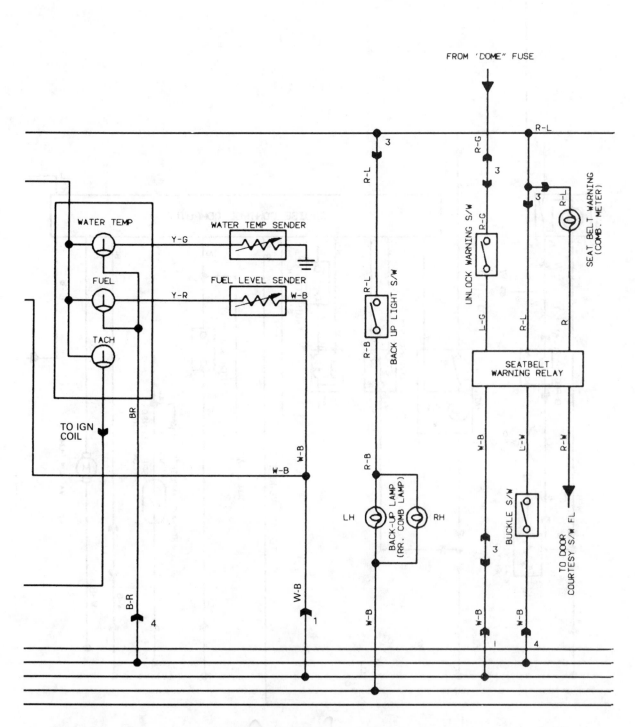

Back-up lights and seatbelt (Nova)

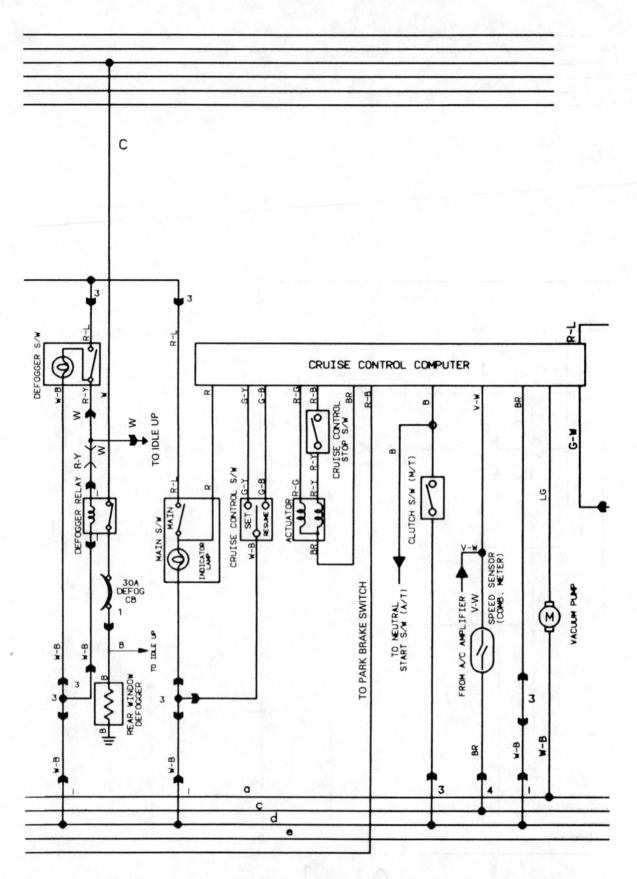

Defogger and cruise control (Nova)

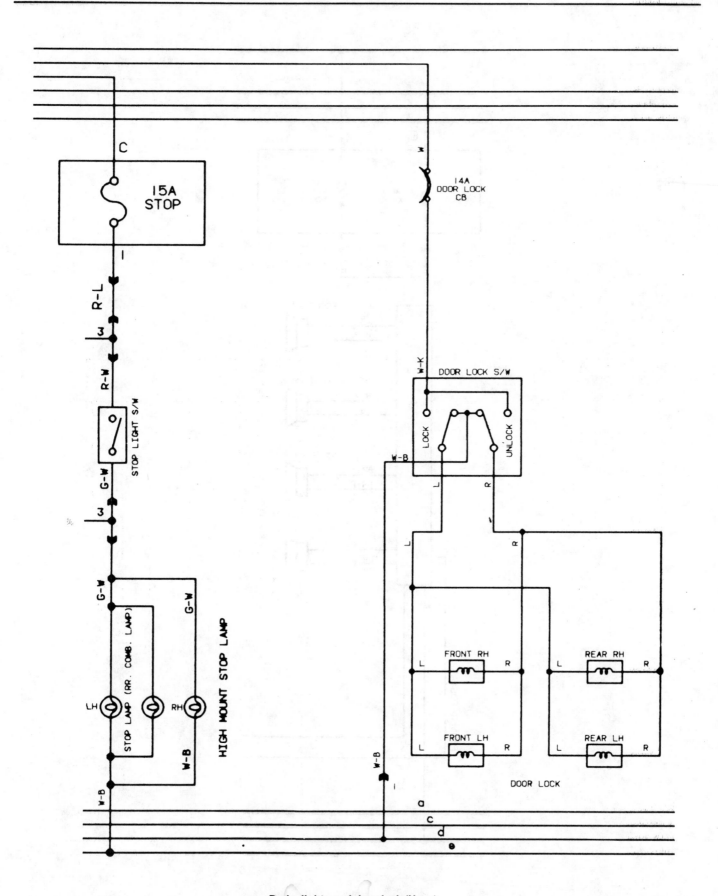

Brake lights and door lock (Nova)

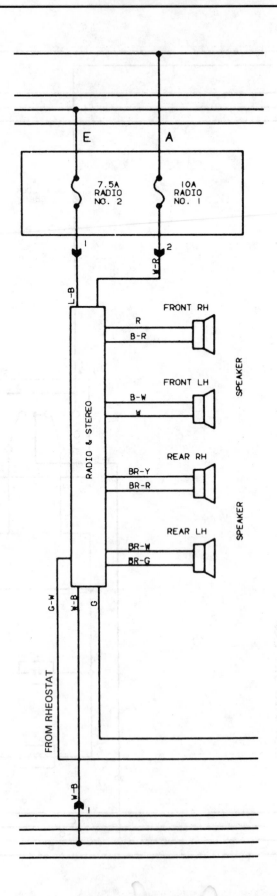

Radio and stereo (Nova)

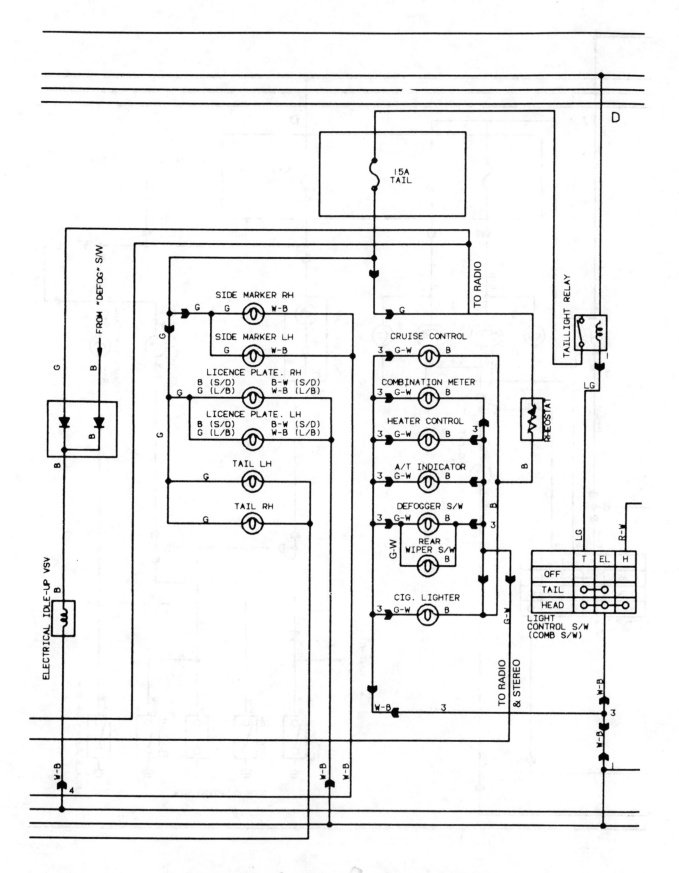

Idle-up system and taillight and illumination circuits (Nova)

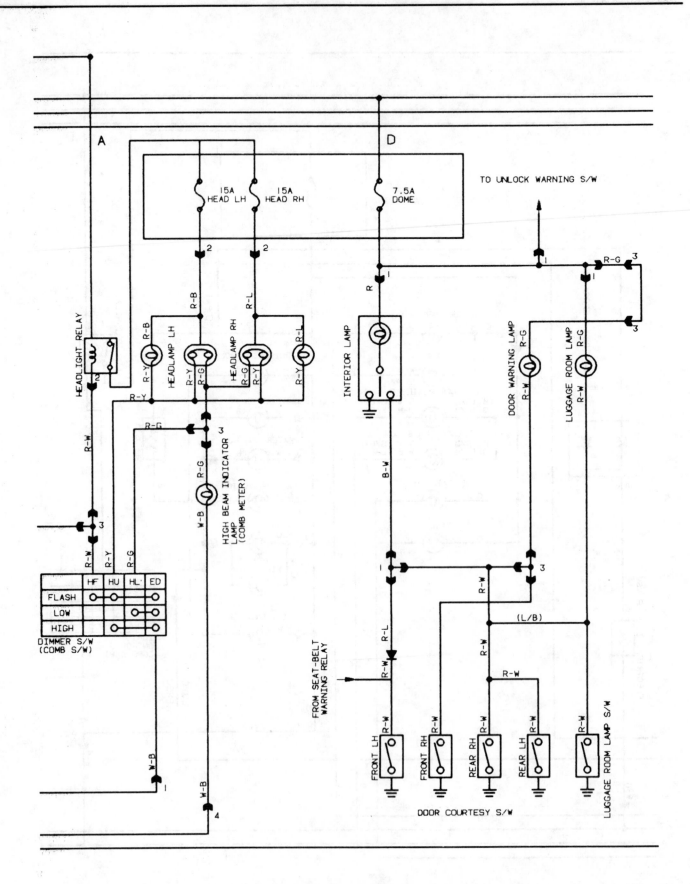

Headlights and interior lights (Nova)

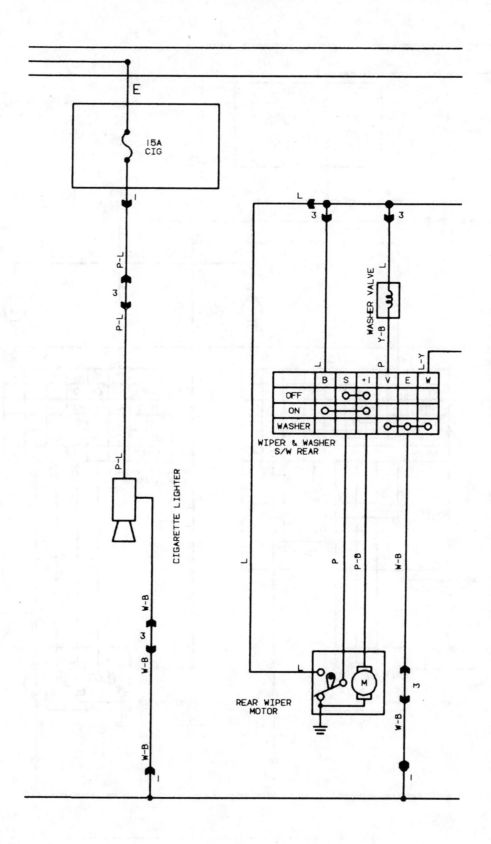

Cigarette lighter (Nova)

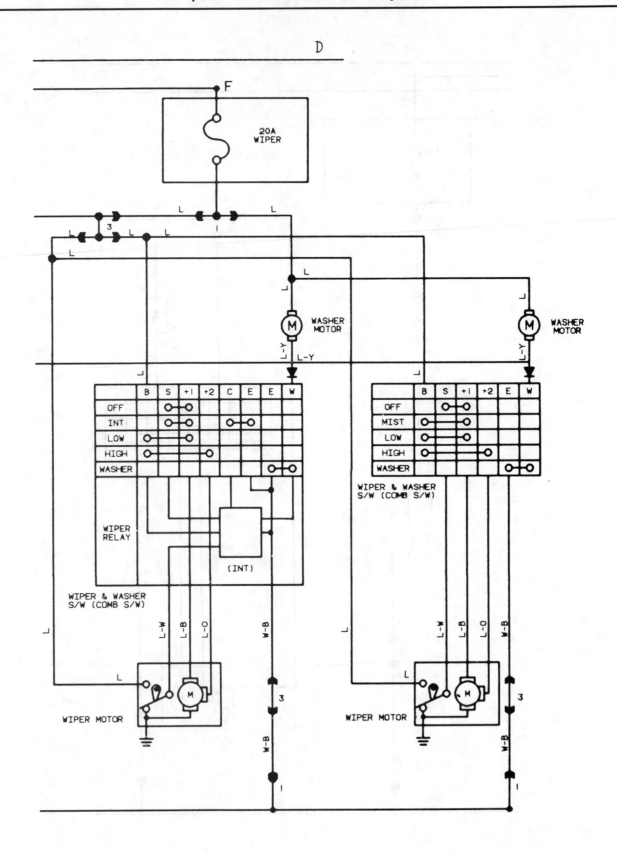

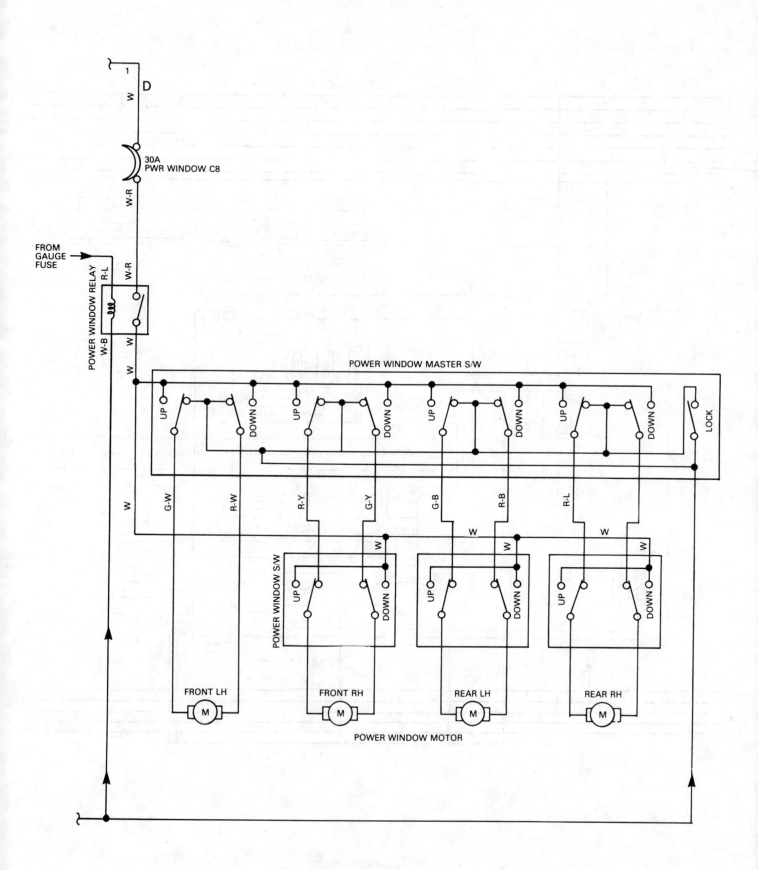

Power windows (Nova)

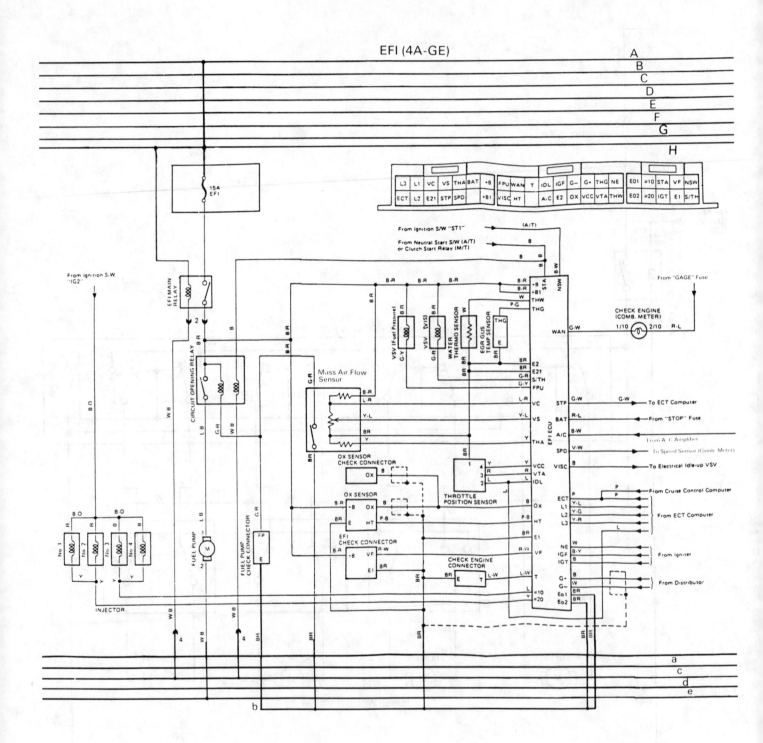

Fuel injection system (Nova with 4A-GE engine)

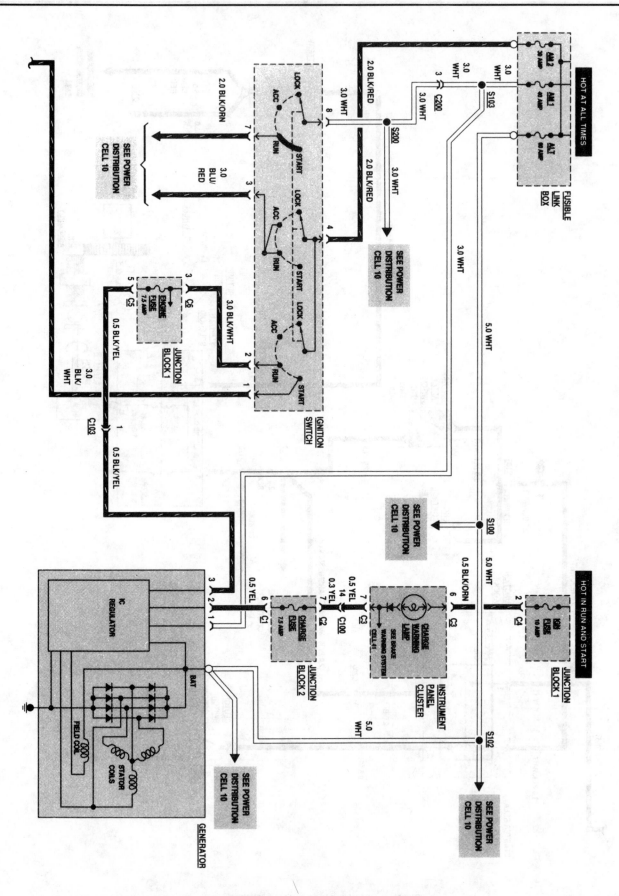

Starting and charging systems (Prizm)

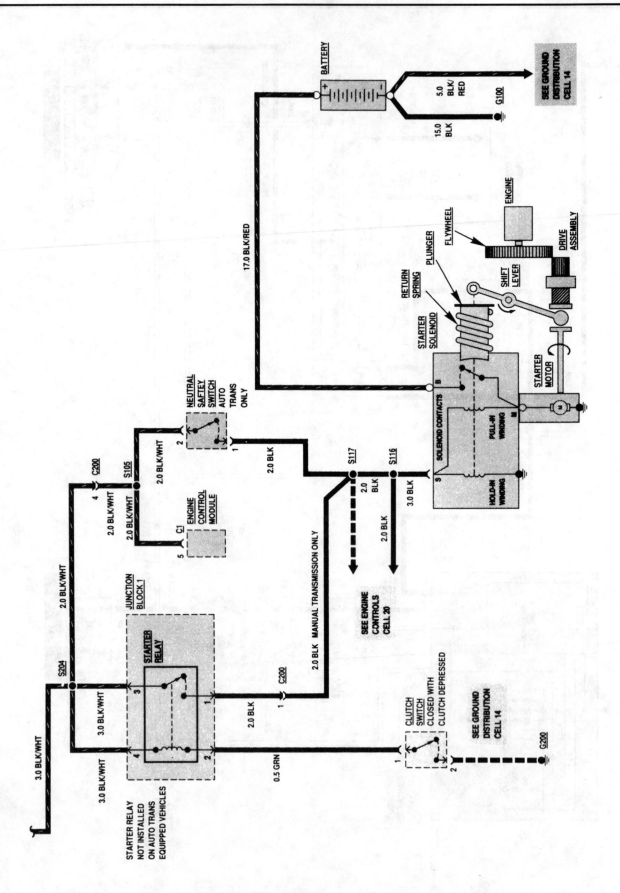

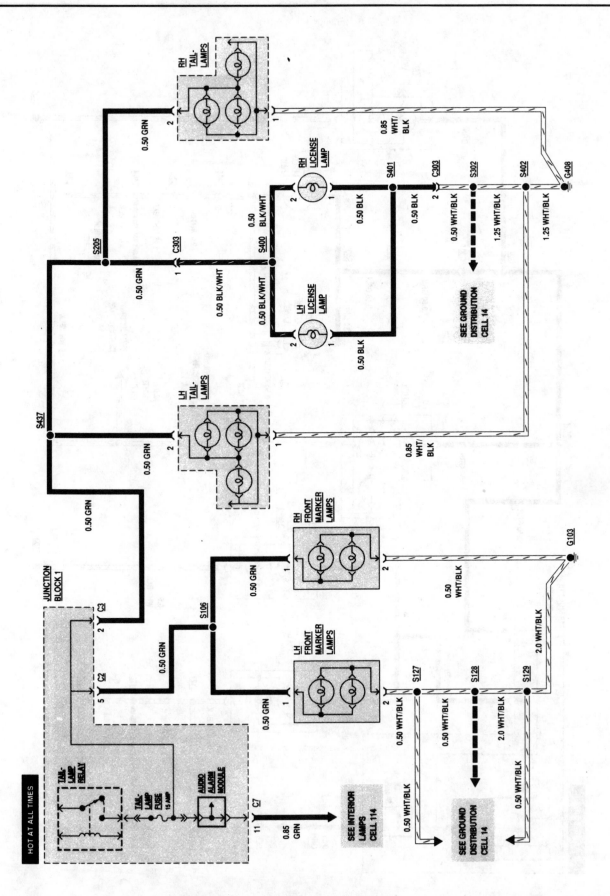

Exterior lights: Park/front side marker/tail/rear marker/license (Prizm)

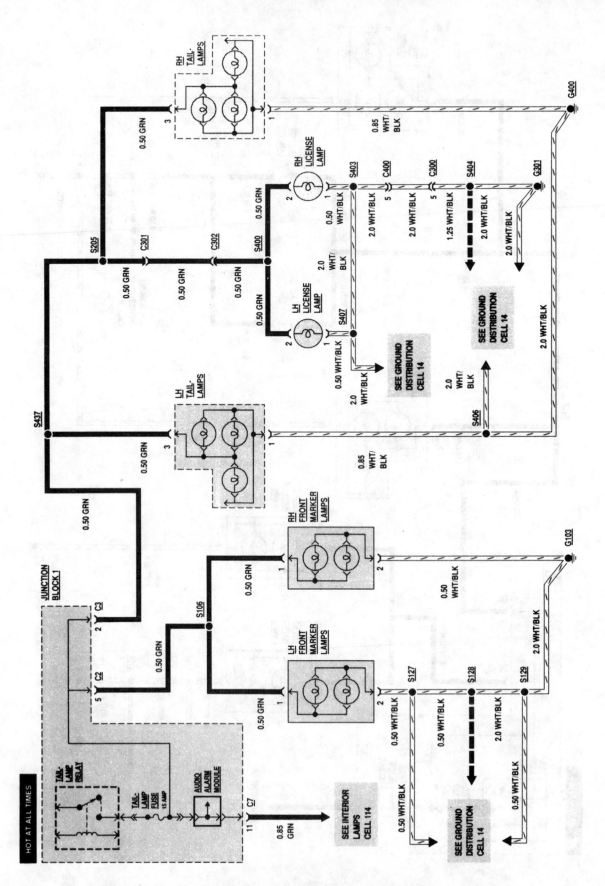

Exterior lights: Park/front side marker/tail/rear marker/license – continued (Prizm)

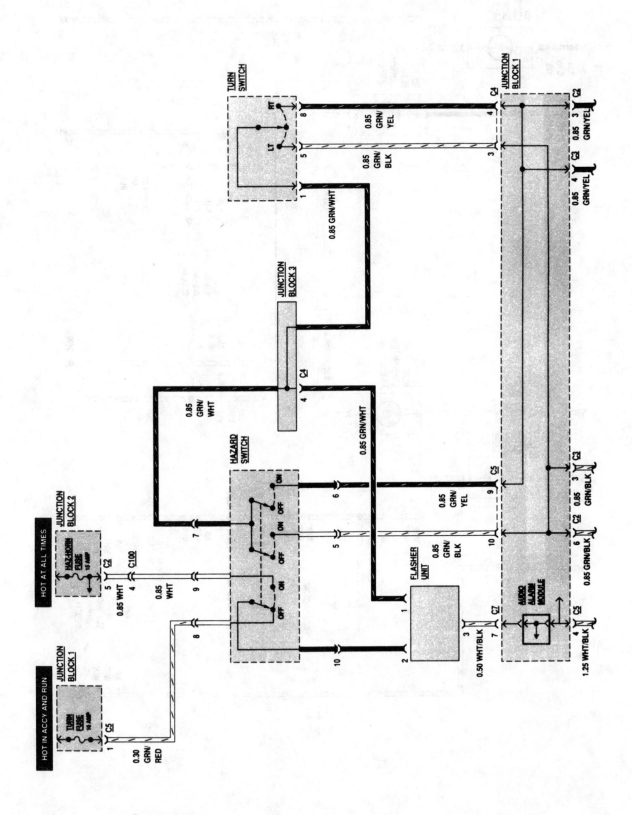

Exterior lights: Turn signal/hazard (Prizm)

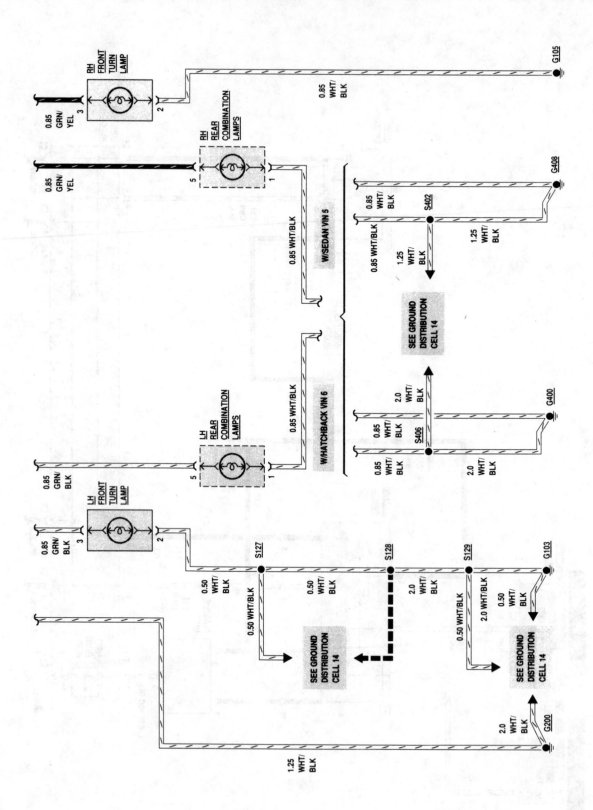

Exterior lights: Turn signal/hazard – continued (Prizm)

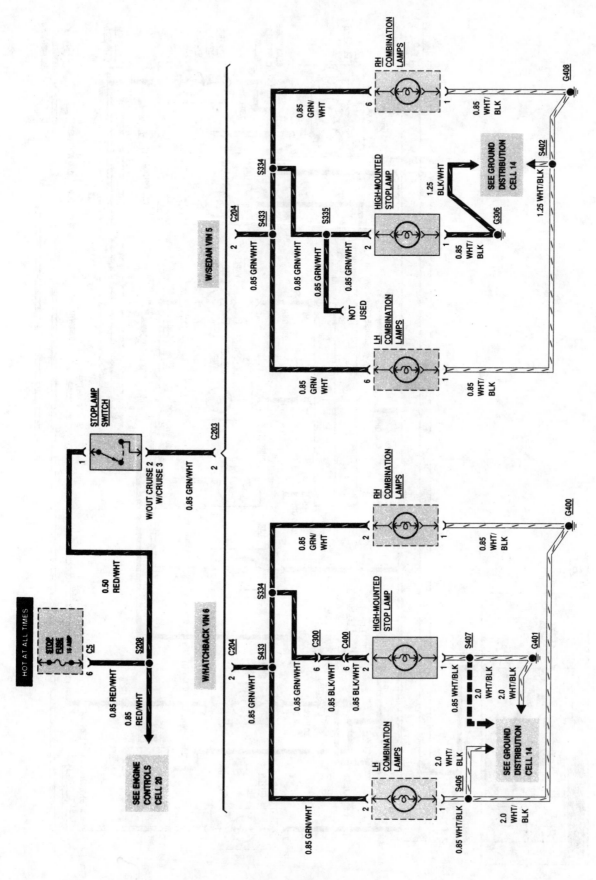

Brake lights (Prizm)

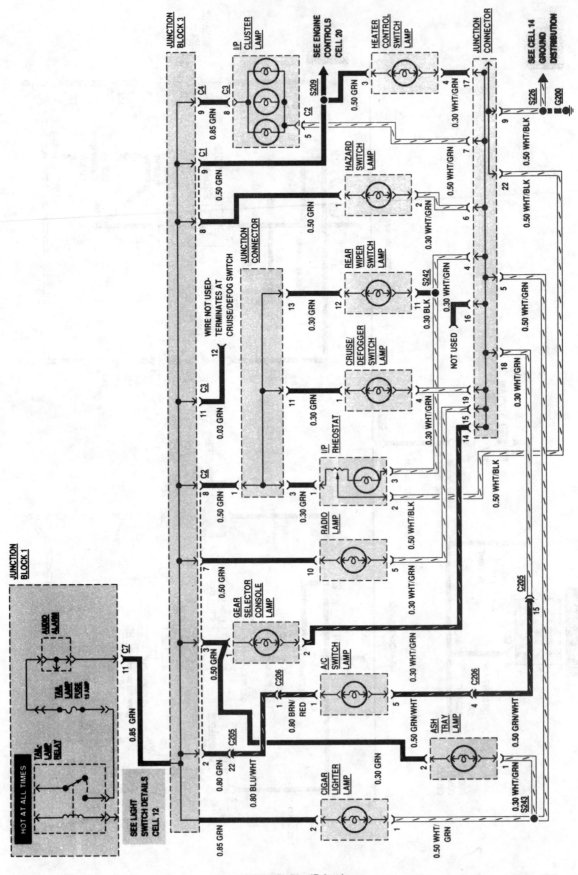

Interior lights (Prizm)

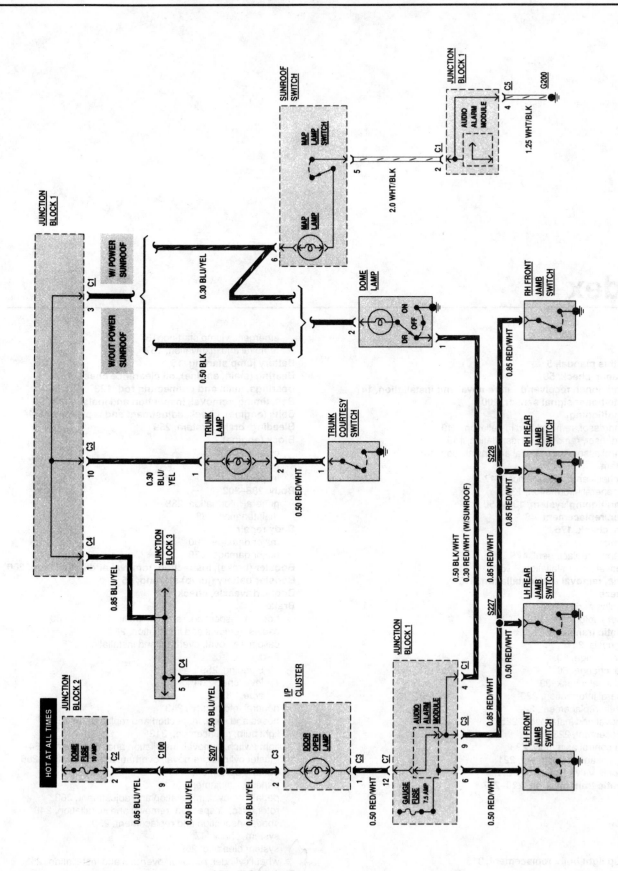

Interior lights – continued (Prizm)

Index